The Black Regulars

The Black Regulars, 1866–1898

BY WILLIAM A. DOBAK
AND THOMAS D. PHILLIPS

UNIVERSITY OF OKLAHOMA PRESS : NORMAN

ALSO BY WILLIAM A. DOBAK

Fort Riley and Its Neighbors: Military Money and Economic Growth, 1853–1895
(Norman, 1998)

Library of Congress Cataloging-in-Publication Data

Dobak, William A., 1943–
    The Black regulars, 1866–1898 / by William A. Dobak and Thomas
D. Phillips.
        p.   cm.
    Includes bibliographical references and index.
    ISBN 0–8061–3340–6 (alk. paper)
    1. United States. Army—African Americans—History—19th
century.   I. Phillips, Thomas D.   II. Title.

UB418.A47 D63 2001
355'.008996'073—dc21

2001027139

1   2   3   4   5   6   7   8   9   10

To the memory of
SARA DUNLAP JACKSON

Contents

Illustrations

FIGURES

MAPS

"Equally Entitled to Participate"

This book tells the story of the black enlisted men—fewer than twenty thousand of them—who served as regulars in the United States Army from the aftermath of the Civil War to the Spanish-American War. It is not a campaign history, nor does it discuss black West Point graduates or regimental chaplains except in their dealings with enlisted men. Its topic is the everyday lives of the first generation of black men to serve in America's peacetime army from enlistment to discharge and after: their daily routine and discipline; religious services and education; and their pastimes, licit and illicit. In order to tell their story, it is necessary to devote several chapters to the administrative and political aspects of organizing and maintaining the all-black regiments in which they served.[1]

It is also necessary, for the most part, to use the words of white observers, military and civilian. Except for occasional letters to a few black newspapers in the East, black regulars did not write much during their service. In the early years the great majority of them were illiterate. Those who had learned to write left nothing at all like the record of the black volunteers in the U.S. Colored Troops (USCT) who wrote during the Civil War to the *Christian Recorder*, the weekly newspaper of the African Methodist Episcopal Church.[2]

America's newspapers, black or white, paid little attention to peacetime soldiers. As the *Recorder*'s volunteer correspondents left the Union army, military affairs disappeared from its pages. Even the *New Orleans Tribune*, a black newspaper in the city where two of the black regular regiments began organizing in the fall of 1866, only acknowledged their existence with a few lines that directed readers' attention to a recruiter's advertisement in another column.[3]

The black press was a middle-class institution interested in black cadets at West Point and the 1884 enlistment of William H. Greene, a black college graduate, in the Signal Corps. Black newspapers paid little attention to the military service of the farmhands, laborers, barbers, musicians, cooks, and waiters who filled the ranks of the black regiments. Not until the nationwide surge of patriotism that accompanied the Spanish-American War did the press devote much space to black enlisted men.[4]

The black regulars' own words survive, for the most part, in court-martial testimony and pension affidavits. These documents deal largely with misbehavior and misery, often casting a bleak light on military life. Nevertheless, they provide a valuable lens through which to examine black soldiers' years in the army and their lives both before and afterward. Pension applications in particular afford a view of black Americans' marriage practices, kinship, and other social relations from the 1850s until well into the twentieth century. They give a voice to a group of people who have remained mostly mute throughout history.

For readers to understand why these men were in the army, some background explanation is necessary. Although black Americans had served in the Revolution, the War of 1812, and the Civil War, the regular army had never attempted to recruit them during peacetime. A look at the military situation after the Civil War explains why the War Department broke with tradition and enlisted black soldiers beginning in 1866. The army's responsibilities extended throughout most of the United States: to keep the peace along the lower Rio Grande while Mexicans south of the river fought to eject a French army of occupation; to suppress or forestall actual or threatened Indian hostilities in the West from Arizona to Oregon, Montana to Texas; and to occupy the former Confederacy.[5]

Regiments of the USCT performed all three of these duties. Soon after the Confederate surrender in Virginia, the Union Twenty-fifth Army Corps, made up entirely of U.S. Colored Troops, sailed to Texas and took posts along the Rio Grande. The 125th U.S. Colored Infantry marched overland from Kansas to Santa Fe and scattered its companies among the forts of New Mexico. Meanwhile, dozens of regiments of USCT remained on duty throughout the South. As the Union army's volunteer regiments mustered out and the year 1865 drew to a close, Congress pondered the question of enlarging the regular force.[6]

In January 1866 Senator Henry M. Wilson of Massachusetts introduced a draft of a bill to reorganize and expand the army. It provided for seventy-seven regiments: seven artillery, ten cavalry, and sixty infantry. Black enlisted men, Wilson proposed, would make up one of the artillery regiments, two of the cavalry, and ten of the infantry. Former officers of the USCT would lead them.[7]

Lieutenant General Ulysses S. Grant was uncertain about black soldiers. In the fall of 1865 he had told Major General William T. Sherman that four USCT regiments that were then headed west would "do very well on the Plains, much better than dissatisfied [white] Volunteers." But Grant saw black soldiers principally as a source of labor and protested Wilson's proposal to include them in an expanded regular army. Their presence, he thought, would impair the army's efficiency, particularly that of the artillery. At best these men might constitute a separate corps, with their officers' promotion confined entirely within the corps.[8]

The Senate pondered Wilson's bill for the rest of the winter. In debate the Radical Republican Benjamin F. Wade argued for the inclusion of black regiments, pointing out the high desertion rate among white troops in the West, while "there is scarcely anything of the kind among the colored troops." Wilson seized on the issue of efficiency, calling it "a great matter of economy to put some of these colored regiments into the field in . . . sections of the country where white men desert largely and go to the mines." Black troops, Wilson said, were "far less likely" to desert.[9]

The *Army and Navy Journal*, a privately owned professional weekly, commented favorably on the Senate's passing a bill that would allow black soldiers in the regular army and grant regular commissions to former volunteer officers whether they were USCT veterans or not, promoting them on the same basis as officers serving with white regiments. As Congress debated whether black soldiers should be enlisted for the cavalry or restricted to the infantry, the *Journal*'s editor allowed that "two first-class regiments of colored cavalry could be raised, so far as horsemanship goes; and, doubtless, as far as all soldierly deportment and character go." As for the matter of race, there was "no distinction whatever" to be made between white and black. During the war, there had been "as wide difference between the free negroes of the North and the slaves, as between the Germans, the Irish and the native-born" whites in the Union army. Then, black soldiers had "manifested no special vice or virtue, no special adaptability or character or style in fighting" while performing "very good, and, upon the whole, very creditable service." The editor pointed out that USCT regiments still in service contained "good and trustworthy material" and hoped that black soldiers would serve in the enlarged peacetime army.[10]

As winter turned to spring, both houses of Congress debated their respective bills for the army's expansion. Representative James A. Garfield, a wartime major general and future president, decried suggestions that the proposed black regiments be further segregated within the army by continuing to designate them as "colored troops"; "nothing can be worse for the efficiency and success of our Army" than to create a corps of second-class soldiers, he warned. The *Army and Navy Journal* reported Congressional debate about army reorganization, but its editor seemed to regard the presence of black soldiers in an enlarged army as a foregone conclusion.[11]

In the Senate, Benjamin F. Wade urged raising four black cavalry regiments instead of two. "In time of peace," he argued, "it is exceedingly difficult . . . to keep your white soldiers from leaving the Army. They are, unfortunately, more apt to desert, . . . as the experience of the Army after the war was over shows." Wade thought it best to recruit troops who "can be kept there best in time of peace, . . . can be the most easily raised, and . . . remain the most permanently at their post." Black soldiers, he insisted, met these criteria, and he suggested that it would make sense to have them make up at least one-third of the army.[12]

Wade's speech shows that, in mandating the enlistment of black soldiers, Congressional Radicals sought an economical and practical way to expand the regular army. Wade did not suggest that blacks would benefit from military service; rather, he declared that the army would benefit from the addition of black regiments. This view differed markedly from the one he and other Senate Radicals had voiced during heated debates of the Civil Rights and Freedmen's Bureau Bills. In contrast to his remarks about the pressing need to secure and protect the rights of black people, Wade's arguments in favor of army reorganization lacked the idealistic rhetoric he had used so effectively to help defeat presidential vetoes of Reconstruction laws.

On July 28, 1866, after months of debate and compromise, Congress passed the army reorganization bill, which provided for six all-black regiments, two of cavalry and four of infantry, in a sixty-regiment army. The only difference in the composition of the black and white units was that each black regiment was assigned a chaplain to provide instruction in "the common English branches of education" as well as to offer spiritual guidance. Otherwise, the black regiments' organization was the same as that of their new white counterparts. Although they were among the junior organizations in their branches, they did not constitute a separate corps. More junior still were the four white infantry regiments of the Veteran Reserve Corps—comprising wounded Civil War veterans— that furnished garrisons for Washington, D.C.; Nashville, Tennessee; and posts along the Great Lakes. The new black regiments were intended for active service, and the men's uniforms, weapons, and pay were the same as those of white soldiers.[13]

Although the reorganization act of 1866 brought black soldiers into the regular army for the first time, it was not part of the Radical program of legislation designed to secure and protect the rights and liberties of black Americans. While the provision of regimental chaplains to promote literacy recognized that "colored troops have necessities which do not exist in the case of . . . white troops," as one Congressman put it, debaters' arguments clearly showed that they favored enlisting black soldiers in order to provide a body of men who would not desert after the government had gone to the expense of bringing them to the West, a land of scarce labor and high wages. The army needed soldiers in 1866, and Congress heeded reports that black men were willing to enlist and serve faithfully. Expedience and economy led to the recruitment of black soldiers. During the years that followed, the same practical considerations dictated that the army feed, clothe, house, mount, and arm its black troops as it did whites. Not until the twentieth century, with an industrialized economy supporting vastly expanded armed forces, did a two-tier army evolve, with black soldiers mostly confined to segregated labor battalions. Until then, black regulars soldiered from the Rio Grande to the Canadian border, in the Plains and the Rockies, and as far west as Arizona.[14]

Historians and journalists have drawn two conflicting inferences from the black regulars' historical record, both of which are false. The first is that the army's staff bureaus—commissary, ordnance, and quartermaster—systematically discriminated against the black regiments; that the 9th and 10th Cavalry, as William H. Leckie writes, received "second-rate equipment and the worst horseflesh in the army." Leckie cites a letter in which Colonel Benjamin H. Grierson told his wife about inspecting some horses that a civilian was trying to sell to the Quartermaster Department. "Many were wind-blown cripples of the Civil War," Leckie writes, "and others were more than a dozen years old." What Grierson actually wrote was: "Have inspected (50) fifty Horses to-day and did not accept even *one*. . . . Of course the contractor does not like my inspection—but I did not come here to please him." Grierson did not mention the horses' ages, or whether they had belonged to the army before. He inspected them in St. Louis, on the other side of the state of Missouri from Fort Leavenworth, Kansas, where he was organizing the 10th Cavalry. The horses that Grierson rejected never reached his regiment. (Chapter 5 of this book describes more fully the allocation of equipment and horses.)[15]

This is not to say that black regulars did not suffer, individually and collectively, from officers' personal prejudices and spite. At the most immediate level, there were company commanders like Captain Ambrose E. Hooker, who tried to impress on his 9th Cavalrymen "the great difference between soldiers in the United States Army and cornfield niggers." Far above Hooker in the military hierarchy was Brigadier General John M. Schofield, commander of the Department of the Missouri, who the 10th Cavalry's Captain Louis H. Carpenter suspected of malice. Carpenter complained that the other cavalry regiment serving in the department had better equipment and its pick of horses. When Schofield rose to higher command, Carpenter remarked that his successor was "said to be a radical [Republican] so I conclude that we can obtain justice from Dept HdQrs." Whether Schofield's chief quartermaster really favored the other regiment or whether it merely had the advantage of being stationed at posts on the Kansas Pacific Railroad, thus having convenient communications to department headquarters, while the 10th Cavalry was in Indian Territory hundreds of miles from a railroad, is impossible to determine. Nevertheless, Carpenter's complaint was typical of those that came from officers who felt themselves abused by assignment to a black regiment.[16]

The other false inference, based largely on the black regulars' high reenlistment rate, is that the black regiments "had become elite units of the army" by 1890, that they were "the most professional, experienced and effective troops in the service." Succeeding chapters will show that the army's recruiting procedures, including its physical examinations, and the high rate of illiteracy among black soldiers, the result of slavery in the South and inadequate education in the North, made the adjective "elite" inapplicable. There were some statistical differences in behavior between black soldiers and white, but on the whole neither group was much better, or much worse, than the other.[17]

For this reason, the authors have decided to refer to nineteenth-century black enlisted men as "black regulars" and to avoid the term "buffalo soldiers," which the men themselves seem never to have used. The latter term does not appear in their letters to newspapers, their court-martial testimony, or their pension applications. In 1873 a journalist at Fort Sill, Indian Territory, noticed that Comanche Indians there called 10th Cavalry troopers "buffalo soldiers," and by the 1890s white newspapermen used that phrase to refer to any black soldier. To the men, though, "buffalo" was an insult, as when one soldier remarked that an officer "had the men out on drill the other day, and he cursed one of the men, and they stood it like black buffalo sons of bitches." Another private called a sergeant a "God damned black, cowardly, buffalo son of a bitch." Language like this was the stuff of court-martial offenses, and trial transcripts recorded the men's words. Although many black regulars had great racial as well as professional pride, they did not express it by a nickname.[18]

Theirs was not a life of high adventure during the years between 1866 and 1898, with each day bringing fresh Indians and outlaws to chase. Their task—the entire army's task—was to preserve order, which they did in the 1870s by trying to ensure that Indians left their reservations only to hunt, in the 1880s by keeping white intruders out of those same reservations, and in the 1890s by guarding property during labor strikes.

They escorted railroad surveyors and tracklayers, built roads, and strung miles of telegraph and telephone wire themselves.[19]

While bearing their share of the army's responsibilities, black regulars carried on a tradition begun during the Civil War. After the turn of the century, as the number of Civil War veterans dwindled and the public treated the peacetime army with characteristic inattention, the black soldiers' story slipped from the mainstream of American history. Ignorance became so prevalent that one popular white author was able to write in 1928: "The American negroes are the only people in the history of the world, so far as I know, that ever became free without any effort of their own. . . . They twanged banjos around the railroad stations, sang melodious spirituals, and believed that some Yankee would soon come along and give each of them forty acres of land and a mule." Only in the last generation or so, since the appearance of *The Sable Arm* (1956) and *The Buffalo Soldiers* (1967), has there been a revival of interest in the history of black Americans' military service.[20]

This book concentrates on enlisted men, for it was on their efforts that the black regulars' reputation rested. Some attention to their officers is necessary, but it was the enlisted men who embodied the idea that one congressman expressed during the debates of 1866: "It is . . . either a burden or a privilege to serve in the Army, and . . . the colored people are equally entitled to bear the burden or equally entitled to participate in the privilege." During the decades after the Civil War, service in the regular army kept open to black Americans one means of participating in the civic life of the United States. This is the black regulars' enduring legacy.[21]

The Black Regulars

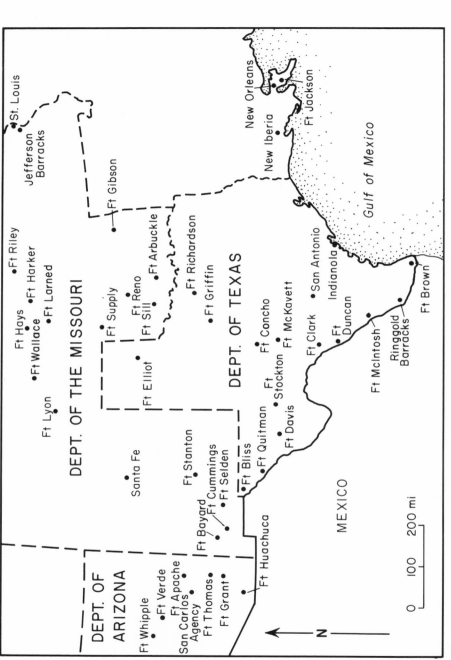

Military departments of the Southwest in which black regulars served. The boundaries stayed pretty much the same from 1870, when the Reconstruction-era Fifth Military District reverted to its prewar name, the Department of Texas, until 1893, when Arizona, Colorado, New Mexico, and Utah became the Department of the Colorado. *Map by Sarah Moore Illustration Services, Pullman, Washington*

CHAPTER ONE

"I Much Wrother Souldier Then to Be Any Thing Else"

In the summer of 1866, a year after the Civil War ended and more than six months after the Thirteenth Amendment finally banned slavery throughout the country, the United States needed the largest peacetime army in its history for several tasks: to occupy the recalcitrant South, to patrol the Mexican border, to protect construction of transcontinental railroads, and to guard wagon roads to the Colorado and Montana goldfields. The expanded force would include some black soldiers, both because the U.S. Colored Troops (USCT) had proved their worth during the Civil War and because emancipation had made available several hundred thousand potential recruits. The army reorganization act provided, among other innovations, for two new regiments of cavalry and four of infantry "composed of colored men."[1]

Within a week, Lieutenant General Ulysses S. Grant urged the Secretary of War to begin raising the new regiments at once. Grant wanted their ranks filled before winter and suggested that enough men could be found among the thirteen thousand Civil War veterans in the USCT regiments still in service. To speed enlistments, USCT officers would act as recruiters, serving temporarily with the new organizations until the War Department awarded them commissions in the regular army.[2]

Orders went the next day to Major Generals William T. Sherman and Philip H. Sheridan for each to raise one black regiment of infantry and one of cavalry. In Sherman's command, the 38th Infantry would organize at St. Louis and the 10th Cavalry at Fort Leavenworth, Kansas, while Sheridan's Department of the Gulf would furnish the 39th Infantry and the 9th Cavalry. At the same time, Major General Nelson A. Miles would raise the 40th Infantry from U.S. Colored Troops still serving in Virginia and the Carolinas. Major General George H. Thomas, commanding the Department of the Tennessee, was responsible for recruiting the 41st Infantry.[3]

If enough veterans could be enrolled, the new regiments would not have to go through much training before being ordered into the field, and Grant gave instructions not to enlist civilians until the USCT no longer yielded recruits. Nor were army officers "to disturb labor con-tracts" (the infamous annual contracts by which Southern planters sought to substitute a year-long obligation for outright chattel slavery) in order to find men. The regular regiments would establish headquar-ters close to the USCT regiments from which their recruits came so that, as the new organizations grew in strength, they could take over the duties of military occupation.[4]

While recruitment of the black regulars began, army boards reviewed the qualifications of applicants for commissions in the new regiments. The work of these boards did not keep pace with enlistments, and the regiments often ran short of officers. In August, Colonel Joseph A. Mower of the 39th Infantry began recruiting around New Orleans, although only ten out of the regiment's authorized strength of thirty-six officers had reported for duty. Nevertheless, Mower succeeded in enlisting more than three hundred men by the end of September. The 9th Cavalry's Colonel Edward Hatch also took advantage of the heavy concentration of U.S. Colored Troops in southern Louisiana and man-aged to enroll nearly seven hundred men by November. Disregarding the shortage of officers, Sheridan predicted that both regiments would be ready for service before Christmas.

The two regiments raised farther north took shape much more slowly. There were fewer U.S. Colored Troops in Sherman's command than in Sheridan's, and many of them were scattered by companies at isolated posts in New Mexico, where recruiters found it hard to reach them. By the end of October, Colonel Benjamin H. Grierson of the 10th Cavalry could report the enlistment of fewer than forty men. The 38th Infantry's

Colonel William B. Hazen obtained equally bleak results: nearly a month's effort yielded only twenty-seven men.

Officers often had to seek out men in the countryside and small towns far from the army's usual urban recruiting stations. In October 1866 Captain James S. Brisbin of the 9th Cavalry reported the recent discharge of two regiments of U.S. Colored Cavalry that had been raised in Kentucky. He urged prompt action because "most of the men have returned to their homes in the Blue Grass region of that state. It would be greatly to the interest of the service if some of them could be re-enlisted as they are natural horsemen, and physically the finest black men in the country." The 9th Cavalry's chief recruiting officer asked Adjutant General Lorenzo Thomas for permission to recruit in Kentucky, hoping to find "at least five hundred able bodied colored men who have seen two years service as volunteer cavalry . . . within sixty days"; Thomas approved the request.[5]

Former USCT officers and agents of the Freedmen's Bureau helped enlist men for the new regular regiments, telling recruiters where they might find prospective soldiers. In a chatty unofficial letter, the Bureau's assistant commissioner for Alabama remarked to Colonel Hazen that "there is nothing doing in this State to recruit colored troops though there are a good many discharged soldiers who would make good material," and he suggested that the Bureau agent at Selma "might attend to that matter in addition to his present duties. . . . [H]e can come up [to Montgomery] occasionally, and I think we might secure him valuable cooperation at Mobile and perhaps elsewhere." Hazen wrote at once to army headquarters, Grant approved the request, and the project went forward within weeks.[6]

Black soldiers also helped recruit others for their new regiments. A recruiting party usually consisted of an officer, two noncommissioned officers, and several privates. They rarely stayed in one place for long and moved on when the supply of applicants ran out. The shortage of officers, though, sometimes led commanding officers to use newly enlisted men to recruit others. Colonel Hazen reported in February 1867 that he could only use his own soldiers to recruit in St. Louis, near the 38th Infantry's headquarters, because "as yet they cannot be trusted to send away" to the offices that he wanted to open in Chicago and

Memphis. Hazen had only been with his new regiment for a couple of months and had never before commanded black troops. He complained several times that "none of the Colored recruits received in the South and West can read or write . . . well enough to perform any clerical duty." In a few more weeks, though, the Colonel had become better acquainted with his men. Urging his recruiting officer at Memphis to open stations in outlying towns, Hazen told him to "place the best men you have in charge of the branches."[7]

The same difficulties dogged the 40th Infantry. In March 1867 Colonel Nelson A. Miles (acting in his regular army rank) complained that few of his men could "write a hand sufficiently neat and intelligible to allow them to be detailed upon clerical duty." By November, though, he was able to select a group of three men—Sergeant John Stanley and Privates James R. Cook, a company clerk, and John H. Hedgeman, an orderly at regimental headquarters—to accompany an officer to New York City to set up a regimental recruiting station. Stanley was a native New Yorker who had enlisted there; in the spring of 1868, he returned from recruiting duty to become the regiment's commissary sergeant. Private Frank Smith, who had served as an orderly at regimental headquarters, took Stanley's place in New York. In all of the new regiments, men like these showed ability, attracted the attention of officers, and assumed responsible positions. The men who helped recruit their regiments were the forerunners of those who later commanded the guards at isolated stagecoach stations and railroad water tanks and who carried the mail in the West.[8]

The War Department furnished recruiting parties with funds and required each officer to report expenses. Losses due to carelessness or faulty bookkeeping were deducted from the officer's pay. Most of a recruiter's money went for office rent, enlistment bounties, and advertising, whether in local newspapers or by posters and handbills. Asked to explain his large printing bill, the 41st Infantry's Captain John C. Conner fumed: "I was sent to Shreveport to recruit, without instructions, without a Recruiting Party, without a *flag*, without any means whatever of advertising, and I deemed as an officer that the interests of the Service demanded that I should have the printing [of handbills] done that was done."[9]

Government funds also paid for housing and feeding recruits. A commissary officer at Nashville supplied the 38th Infantry's Lieutenant

William F. Spurgin with rations for his men but no cooking utensils. Spurgin had to hire a civilian cook to prepare the rations, he explained to the Adjutant General. Concern for the "health and comfort of the men" prompted Lieutenant H. Baxter Quimby of the 39th Infantry, recruiting in Boston, to ask permission to spend twenty dollars on repairs to his building because of "the rapid approach of cold weather in this latitude." It was late September of 1867 when Quimby wrote, and an outbreak of yellow fever in New Orleans kept him from sending recruits south. Rather than spend money to repair rented premises, the army shipped Quimby's recruits to David's Island in New York Harbor, where they waited out the epidemic.[10]

Scarcity of medical officers also hindered recruitment. Army regulations specified that each applicant had to pass a thorough physical examination before enlisting. When the War Department proposed that regimental recruiting officers make the necessary examinations if no doctor was available, the 38th Infantry's Lieutenant Charles G. Penney protested from his station in Cincinnati that only a trained physician could diagnose "organic and incipient diseases, which . . . if not discovered before enlistment, would probably cause the rejection of a recruit after he had been forwarded to the regiment. In this case the expenses of enlistment, transportation &c. would be an entire loss to the government." A few weeks later, after the surgeon at regimental headquarters rejected two of his recruits, Penney told how he had examined them. "I caused them to be entirely divested of their clothing, and then examined them as closely as was possible. . . . I caused [them] to walk, run, and hop on either foot, twice across the room. These movements, requiring the free and unimpeded action of all the limbs, were made naturally, easily, and without evidence of discomfort." The Adjutant General finally authorized recruiters to hire civilian doctors at the rate of fifty cents per examination, warning that if no cheap doctor could be found, officers would have to examine applicants "to the best of [their] ability."[11]

As might have been expected, this system admitted men with all sorts of disabilities. Examiners accepted Leonard Scott, although he had had trouble with his legs while serving with the 110th U.S. Colored Infantry (USCI) during the Civil War. "I got stiff some times and the veins on my leg began to puff up some but I could get around as well as any of them," he declared in a pension deposition thirty years afterward. Other recruits convinced the examiners to overlook their ailments. When Lorenzo George stripped "plum naked," the surgeon "said I had the piles," George told a pension examiner years later, "but I told him I wanted to go and he passed me." Lafayette Mundy ruptured his testicles while serving with the 4th U.S. Colored Cavalry in 1865, but examiners accepted him for the 40th Infantry the following year. William Henry did not mention his history of epileptic fits during the Civil War when he enlisted at Philadelphia in December 1866. The results of inept medical examinations would plague the new black regiments for years, and the Bureau of Pensions for decades.[12]

Despite the disadvantages imposed by shortages of funds and doctors, recruiting for most of the new regiments proceeded steadily during the early months of 1867. Colonel Grierson, though, believed that "the quality is more important than the number" and continually reminded 10th Cavalry recruiters to enlist only the most capable men. Colonel Ranald S. Mackenzie also wanted "the best black men in the country" for the 41st Infantry. As a result, the 10th had enrolled only 392 men by the end of May, and the 41st sailed for Texas in June with only eight of its ten companies organized.[13]

The black regiments especially needed men who could read and write. Before the Civil War, state laws across the South had forbidden slave literacy. A few whites had taught their slaves to read out of a paradoxical sense of Christian duty to the souls of those whom they held in bondage; others did so from a contrary notion that it was not the state's business to dictate how they treated their property. Free black people too had sometimes risked punishment to teach slaves the rudiments of literacy. Yet everywhere in the South, the vast majority of the black population remained illiterate, and it was hard for recruiters to find men well enough educated to serve as clerks and noncommissioned officers. Daily reports, bimonthly muster rolls, requisitions for supplies, and a host of other documents required attention. Colonel Mower complained that in the 39th Infantry, "officers are compelled to perform the clerical duties . . . which usually devolve upon a noncommissioned officer." All the commanders of the black regiments reported this difficulty.[14]

Several colonels asked to hire civilian clerks, but the Adjutant General disapproved these requests, although he sometimes assigned white enlisted men to assist officers in the black regiments. Unsatisfied by such stopgap measures, officers pleaded for permission to enlist white recruits to serve as clerks and noncommissioned officers. One company commander recommended the transfer of ten sergeants "from some of the old [i.e., white] Infantry Regts" to serve as company first sergeants in the 40th Infantry. The 9th Cavalry's Captain George A. Purington asked that "nine intelligent white men . . . from the recruits of the Cavalry Service" be sent to him to "assist in bringing the company to a proper state of discipline." But the War Department could not consider these suggestions and reminded officers that, under the law, white men could not be assigned to the black regiments.[15]

Barred by law from enrolling whites, officers pondered the question of educating the men themselves. Colonel Miles believed that 40th Infantry recruits, properly trained, could fill the need for clerks. "During their leisure time the men should be required to study and practice in penmanship," he told company officers. If blank copybooks were not available "from some of the benevolent societies that have heretofore supplied many of the colored soldiers," Miles wrote, "the sutler at your post should be required to keep them on hand for sale." Despite these efforts, the post schools could not quickly transform illiterate recruits into qualified clerks and noncommissioned officers.[16]

By late 1866 most recruiting officers admitted the futility of trying to enlist literate men in the South. Colonel Hatch reported in November that no 9th Cavalry recruits had "the necessary education for company clerks and sergeants." Officers from several of the black regiments had succeeded in enlisting literate men in some northern cities, and regimental commanders began increasingly to send their recruiters there. By the spring of 1867 all of the black regiments had established offices in the North.[17]

Recruiting officers had explicit instructions to find literate men. Major George W. Schofield of the 41st Infantry told one of his recruiters that if "good, sound, active and intelligent men cannot be found in one section of the country, we must seek them in another. There is abundance of material from which to select men for the Colored Regiments of the Army; and though it may take a long time to complete a regiment from the *best* class of men, it will be better and cheaper in the end to accept no others." Men "who . . . though uneducated are naturally intelligent" and "honorably discharged N.C. officers or good mechanics" might be enlisted even if they were illiterate.[18]

Northern cities turned out to be a good source of manpower, and recruiters began to enlist literate black applicants as soon as they opened their offices. Captain Brisbin, recruiting for the 9th Cavalry in Ohio, found "seventeen very intelligent colored men"; ten of them could read and write, and "with a little training will make good clerks." From Philadelphia the 39th Infantry's Lieutenant Charles L. Cooper reported that twelve of his eighteen recruits were literate and that the rest were USCT veterans. A two-thirds literacy rate was far better than what recruiters could hope to find anywhere in the South.[19]

War Department officials cooperated with recruiters wherever possible, even to the extent of ignoring some army regulations. Despite an official ban on the enlistment of married men, Captain James F. Randlett pleaded for the retention of Sergeant Pierre A. Leduc because he was "a reliable soldier, and a very intelligent man . . . and it will be difficult (if he is discharged) to fill his position well, from the material of which his Company is made up." The army waived the height requirement of five feet, four inches for recruit Thomas Boyd, "a smart intelligent man, [who] can read and write, and would benefit the service," and allowed Captain William J. Broatch to enlist short men "who were excellent penmen" for the 40th Infantry.[20]

As recruiters fanned out across the northern states, the pattern of enlistments in the black regiments began to change. When they began recruiting, officers tried to capitalize on the heavy concentration of U.S. Colored Troops in the South and limited their efforts to that section. During 1866 nearly six times as many men enlisted in the South as did in the North. By the end of 1867, though, the North was providing more than half of the total. Officers went north primarily to find literate recruits, but although instructions were explicit to enroll only educated men, nearly one-third of those signed up were illiterate.

The cavalry in particular needed men with the skills of blacksmiths, farriers, and saddlers. In February 1867 Colonel Hatch announced that, although the 9th Cavalry was nearly full, "there is only one Blacksmith attached to the command and no Clerks or Saddlers." Adjutant General Thomas directed officers of the Mounted Recruiting Service to find craftsmen for the regiment.[21]

Recruiters were also on the lookout for musicians. For many officers and men, especially for Colonel Grierson of the 10th Cavalry, who had been a music teacher before the Civil War, the band was a vital part of the regiment. When he heard from an officer in Columbus, Ohio, that an all-black band there might join *en masse*, Grierson replied that he was "highly pleased" and urged "every possible effort" to recruit them. The musicians had second thoughts, though, and decided not to enlist. The 41st Infantry needed musicians so badly that Colonel Mackenzie asked recruiters to enlist any willing bandsmen, even if they were illiterate.[22]

When they had enrolled enough men, recruiters sent them to regimental headquarters under the supervision of an officer or noncommissioned officer. Men enlisted in Philadelphia for the 39th Infantry went by train to New York, where they boarded an ocean-going steamship for New Orleans. Travel by sea could be hazardous. The steamer *Flambeau*, carrying men of the 40th Infantry, struck a sandbar near Wilmington, North Carolina, and sank. "While everyone was hurrying to escape from the sinking vessel, I fell or was knocked downstairs," Noah Spiller recalled more than twenty years afterward, when he based part of a pension claim on injuries sustained during the shipwreck. No one died, but the men's extra clothing, weapons, and equipment went down with the ship. In the wreck, Joseph Luckadoe lost his discharge papers from the 4th USCI, which would complicate his pension application in later years.[23]

Several officers complained that railroad and steamship companies had overcharged them for transporting soldiers. Usually, they received fair treatment on public carriers, but in 1869 Lieutenant Colonel Edward W. Hinks denounced the Quartermaster Department for sending the 40th Infantry from Raleigh, North Carolina, to New Orleans "in live stock cars and box freight cars without seats." Hinks alleged that white troops rode in "first class passenger cars" and declared that there was "no just cause for the discrimination made against my command." Adjutant General Thomas demanded an explanation from the Quartermaster General, who relayed an alibi from the Chief Quartermaster of the Department of the South: responsibility for accepting the inferior transportation lay with Hinks, who had been in command at Goldsboro.[24]

The War Department did demand an explanation, though, when a military guard had to board the steamboat *David White* to arrest a party of 9th Cavalry recruits on their way to New Orleans. The soldiers had gotten hold of some whiskey to celebrate their leaving Kentucky and became "so disorderly, and riotous, during the voyage, as to render it necessary, for the safety of the passengers and vessel, to obtain armed guards at Memphis and Vicksburg." The Adjutant General warned Captain Brisbin to avoid a repetition of such "disgraceful conduct" by his recruits. Colonel Grierson, on the other hand, preferred recruits to travel by rail and did not "consider it at all necessary that an officer accompany the men." One party of fourteen recruits for the 10th Cavalry had an uneventful trip from Philadelphia to Fort Leavenworth in the care of Lance Sergeant James Speakes, a veteran of the 25th USCI.[25]

When they reached regimental headquarters, recruits were assigned to companies and began to receive instruction, usually from noncommissioned officers. "The sergeant did not take out the old soldiers from the volunteer service to drill" while companies of the 39th Infantry were organizing, veteran Price L. Mitchell recalled nearly thirty years later, "but he took out the new recruits twice every day." Colonel Miles realized that the dispersal of the 40th Infantry's companies at several posts and the inexperience of some of the officers impeded recruit training. In order to establish "a uniform system of instruction," Miles wanted all recruits sent to the regimental depot in Virginia, where they could be "properly organized and prepared for any duty." He ordered recruiters to forward new men there for training and picked his most competent officers to act as instructors. None of the other regiments adopted such a centralized program, and most recruits continued to receive their initial military instruction after assignment to their companies.[26]

Lieutenant Richard H. Pratt found that most of the Civil War veterans in his company of the 10th Cavalry had served in the infantry and knew little about horses. To his surprise, though, the former foot soldiers quickly mastered mounted drill. "Our negro troopers grew in [the officers'] estimate by their ready obedience and faithful performance of duty," Pratt recalled. At Fort Leavenworth, Lieutenant Samuel L. Woodward compared the 10th Cavalry's recruits with those of white regiments and told Colonel Grierson, "I fear that the white troops have been organized from such scallywags that it will be hard to make them very effective and I believe in time the colored troops will become the most efficient in the service." Woodward also remarked that Major

General Winfield S. Hancock, commanding the Department of the Missouri, was favorably impressed with the 10th Cavalry and that "it only requires the right kind of training from the start to make them good soldiers."[27]

Often, though, recruits did not receive much instruction. Sickness hampered the organization of most of the new regiments at one time or another. In July 1867 eight men deserted from the 10th Cavalry at Fort Harker, Kansas, during a cholera outbreak there. Before the epidemic ran its course, the disease killed at least ninety-four men of the 10th Cavalry and 38th Infantry. That September, Colonel Mower of the 39th Infantry ordered recruiters not to send any more men to regimental headquarters in New Orleans because of a yellow fever epidemic. Seven enlisted men of that regiment died of the fever during the next few weeks.[28]

During the months of organization, many Civil War veterans became noncommissioned officers. At least thirty-six of the 40th Infantry's sergeants and corporals had served in the USCT regiments raised in Baltimore and Washington. The 39th Infantry's Sergeant Major Rodolphe Baqui seems to have been a natural leader. A free man before the Civil War, Baqui had worked as a bricklayer—a skilled trade in which he faced competition from white laborers. During the war, he became sergeant major of the 99th USCI; nine officers of that regiment recommended him for a commission.[29]

A shortage of officers in all of the new regiments constituted the greatest obstacle to training. For the first few months, USCT officers held temporary command in some of the black regular regiments, but the War Department ordered them mustered out without providing regular commissioned officers as replacements. The departure of these volunteers sometimes left the new black regiments with hundreds of recruits and few officers to command them. In December 1866 Lieutenant Colonel Frank Wheaton complained that there were only six company officers to command 472 enlisted men of the 39th Infantry in camp at Greenville, Louisiana. Officers continued to arrive, but slowly, during the first half of 1867. As late as February, Major Schofield continued to command the 41st Infantry in the absence of its two senior officers. Colonel Mackenzie, who arrived in May, managed to organize eight companies of the regiment and ship them to Texas even though only a dozen company officers had reported for duty.[30]

The slow process of commissioning officers hampered recruit train-ing, as did the army's practice of detaching officers from their regiments. In late 1866 and throughout most of 1867, regimental officers, includ-ing colonels, served in a variety of jobs that kept them from their men. In February 1867, with Colonel Mower commanding the District of Louisiana in his wartime brevet rank of major general and Lieutenant Colonel Wheaton on leave, responsibility for organizing the 39th Infantry devolved on Captain Dennis T. Kirby. The War Department also detached many junior officers to serve as Freedmen's Bureau agents and as aides on the staffs of departmental and divisional commanders.[31]

As the enlisted strength of the new regiments neared authorized numbers, colonels began to order recruiters and detached officers to rejoin their companies. In the 9th Cavalry, Lieutenant Colonel Wesley Merritt asked for the release of several company officers from staff duty. Without officers "in a new regiment . . . , the Company soon loses all mil-itary knowledge and discipline which it may have had. This demoraliza-tion takes place much sooner among colored troops," Merritt wrote, "than with any it has ever been my fortune to serve with before joining the 9th Cavalry." Colonel Hazen's irritation erupted when he asked the Adjutant General to release four 38th Infantry officers from detached service with the Freedmen's Bureau: "The absence of these officers at the time of organizing the Regiment Especially as in Colored regiments but few men can act as clerks, or as yet, as efficient non c[ommissioned] officers is very materially felt, and is greatly more detrimental . . . [than] were it an old or a white regiment." Both officers chafed at the extra effort needed to surmount the disadvantages that had been imposed on generations of black Americans, slave or free.[32]

The possibility of field service also encouraged commanders to recall their officers. When Hazen learned that his regiment was to march over-land to New Mexico in May 1867, eleven company officers were absent on detached service, and he asked the War Department to order them to rejoin immediately. Two months later Colonel Mackenzie com-plained that none of the 41st Infantry's companies had all its officers. Field service along the Rio Grande required maximum strength, he explained, adding that "there can be certainly no place in the country where officers are more needed at present than with this regiment." It was a plea that any colonel in the West could have made.[33]

Even with a shortage of officers, the regiments gradually reached their authorized minimum strength. By the end of 1867 nearly all regimental recruiters had closed their stations. A War Department order eased the strain somewhat by reducing the number of enlisted men in infantry companies from 64 to 50 (a decrease of 140 men in each regiment), the first of many attempts to reduce the army's strength.[34]

Soon, the army assumed a shape that would endure until after the Spanish-American War. The appropriation act of 1869 did not mention the artillery or cavalry but stipulated that there would be no new commissions, no promotions, and no enlistments in the infantry "until the total number of infantry regiments is reduced to twenty-five." The Secretary of War was to effect this reduction by consolidating the forty-five existing infantry regiments "as rapidly as the requirements of the public service . . . permit." Unlike the army reorganization act three years earlier, the 1869 appropriation act did not mention race. It was one of the last measures passed by the Fortieth Congress.[35]

President Grant's inauguration was the next day. John A. Rawlins, the President's wartime aide and new Secretary of War, and General Sherman, who had taken Grant's place at the head of the army, had a plan for consolidating the infantry regiments ready within two weeks. Although Congress had left the reorganization entirely to their discretion, Rawlins and Sherman decided to keep two all-black regiments in the reduced force. Benjamin Butler, James Garfield, Henry Wilson, and others who had passed the 1866 act that created the black regiments were still in Congress, and it would have been impolitic to mar their work by eliminating the black infantry.[36]

After 1869, black soldiers would make up slightly less than 10 percent of the army's entire strength. In the West, where the cavalry served, black regiments would constitute one-fifth of the mounted force. The black infantry regiments had quietly survived a possible threat to their existence, and although a later generation of congressmen would refuse to increase black representation in the peacetime army, a place for black soldiers was assured.[37]

To effect this reduction in the infantry, the War Department ordered the consolidation of the 38th and 41st Regiments to form the new 24th Infantry and the 39th and 40th Regiments to form the new 25th Infantry. Colonel Mower of the 39th would command the 25th, and since his headquarters were at New Orleans, the 40th Infantry traveled there by rail from North Carolina. Meanwhile, companies of the 38th Infantry marched overland to Texas from their posts in Kansas and New Mexico to consolidate with the 41st Infantry. The 41st's Colonel Mackenzie commanded the new 24th Regiment. Natural attrition by expiration of infantrymen's three-year enlistments during 1869–70 would help the reduction, and the army briefly suspended recruiting, although veterans could reenlist in the two infantry regiments.[38]

The War Department's plans failed to take into account the wishes of the soldiers themselves, though. Lieutenant Colonel Edward W. Hinks, now of the 25th Infantry, outlined some of the problems in a report the Adjutant General. Most of his men would take their discharges by January 1870, and "many of the best . . . were adverse to re-enlistment." Moreover, "colored men who are fit to enlist" would not sign up as long as they could "find employment, and foster habits more congenial to their tastes, out of the service." Colonel Mower agreed, adding that civilian economic opportunities attracted the more intelligent enlisted men and kept the best prospective recruits from considering the army at all.[39]

By February 1870 Hinks reported great difficulty in getting veterans to reenlist. Few black civilians wanted to join the army either. By this time Hinks had asked each company commander in the 25th Infantry for his opinions on recruiting problems, and he forwarded their letters to the Adjutant General along with his own. Together, they constitute the only systematic attempt during these decades to investigate the minds and motives of the army's black enlisted men.[40]

Nearly all of the 25th's captains agreed that comparatively high wages offered by civilian employers kept many civilians from enlisting and persuaded veterans to leave the army. Frank M. Coxe thought that "able bodied colored men of respectability and intelligence can command greater inducements from the planter, than the army offers." Another captain offered Corporal John R. Jones, a Civil War veteran, a promotion to company quartermaster sergeant if he reenlisted, but Jones declined, explaining "he could do better in civil life." Several officers reported that unskilled and even stupid ex-soldiers could find good jobs as civilians.

Officers' comments suggest that most soldiers saw military service only as a stopgap until better opportunities opened up in civilian life. Hard times in Louisiana during the fall of 1866 had helped fill the ranks of the 39th Infantry three years earlier. Now, officers noted, most discharged soldiers found jobs and seemed to be doing well. Coxe said that a few of his former soldiers, "after squandering their final pay, have become vagrants," but "some are industriously engaged in planting; . . . several are working on river steamers; and others have returned to their former avocations and homes in the Eastern and Northern States." John McKennon, Coxe's former first sergeant, left the 25th Infantry to become a policeman in New Orleans, as did at least four other veterans. Private Luzienne Duprie, a Civil War veteran, saved his pay and used it to buy a farm after he was discharged.[41]

The 25th's captains also suggested that extending infantry enlistments from three to five years, as mandated by the act of 1869, kept men from enlisting or reenlisting. Questioned about their motives for leaving the army, some soldiers objected to the hard labor and strict discipline of military life. They complained that Forts Jackson and St. Philip, on the Mississippi River below New Orleans, were poorly constructed and unhealthy and that the isolation of the regiment's stations prevented social contact with civilians. Many who had enlisted in the North left the service in order to visit friends and family.

Besides giving reasons why men declined to reenlist, several company commanders took the opportunity to offer their views on the general fitness of black men as soldiers. Coxe announced that he had enlisted only three out of fifteen applicants since his company moved to New Orleans and "nearly all" of the men rejected had "the disqualifications common to the lower order of the African race." This was not a bigoted judgment; Coxe was one of the officers who reported how well the former soldiers of the 25th Infantry were doing in civilian life. He served with black troops for more than eleven years during and after the Civil War and found that many of them possessed "the highest traits of intelligence, honor and ambition," but he also claimed that recruiters had failed to enlist enough of these men. Coxe blamed the presence of poor soldiers in his company on inept or apathetic recruiters, who he believed accepted men "without any proper regard for their competency to become soldiers."

Hinks also asked his officers to name those of their men whom they considered best qualified to remain in the army. Captain John W. French

forwarded brief remarks on ten "intelligent and reliable" soldiers, of
whom only three had reenlisted. Captain Gaines Lawson, a Tennessean
who had fought for the Union, voiced a common opinion when he told
Hinks that all the men in his company worth reenlisting were "mulattoes, born of free parents. . . . [A]s a general rule, men of this class are
better soldiers than those recruited around Southern cities." Four of the
soldiers Lawson named in his report were from Philadelphia and Boston,
and he found them "much better adapted to perform the duties of a soldier, than the majority of colored men, enlisted from plantations in the
Southern states." Captain David Schooley, on the other hand, found that
previous military service mattered more than color or previous condition of servitude in predicting a man's ability as a soldier. Four of the
seven men named in his report were former slaves; six of the seven were
USCT veterans.[42]

Some officers also included suggestions for future recruiting. Captain
Wyllys Lyman proposed that the black regiments send their own officers
to find men and that the northern and border states were the best places
to look. Coxe, too, thought that this method would assure that "the standard of the colored regiments could be maintained second to none in
the service."

Hinks summarized his own observations and those of his officers and
went on to discuss the army's color line and how it affected the black
regiments. He thought that segregation hurt the army. Many whites, he
wrote, enlisted in hopes of obtaining a commission, "and by the infu-
sion of this element the character of the whole organization is improved,
and its efficiency advanced." In the black regiments, though, the "want
of equal incentives" kept many potential recruits from enlisting. There
was no legal provision for awarding commissions to black soldiers, and
most officers interpreted the law as excluding the possibility altogether.
Hinks disagreed and suggested that the army open enlistment in all regiments and in all positions without regard to color. He proposed complete integration of the army.

While Hinks mentioned in passing the incongruity of segregated regiments and the principles of the Fourteenth Amendment, he did not base
his proposal on constitutional grounds. As a practical soldier, he argued
that elimination of the color line would open enlistment in all regiments
to the most qualified men. In an integrated army, he predicted, educated

and skilled men "would be found in abundance in all the regiments."
Urging action, Hinks reminded the War Department that by the summer
of 1870 nearly half of the men in the 25th Infantry would be discharged
and that recruits, regardless of their color, were needed urgently. He did
not address the question of whether the army would continue to enlist
blacks at all if it were not forced to do so by specific legislation. This problem would later plague proponents of a completely integrated army.[43]

Hinks realized, though, that the War Department would turn down
any plan for integrating the army. In order to keep his segregated regiment filled with good men, Hinks asked that only regimental officers be
used as recruiters. Enough officers could be found who were "competent by experience to determine the fitness of colored recruits for the
service," he believed.

Like Hinks, Colonel Mackenzie of the 24th Infantry favored regimental recruiters and proposed that even after the ranks were filled, several officers should remain detailed for recruiting. In December 1869
Mackenzie reminded the Adjutant General that within six months all
but two hundred of his men would leave the regiment. "Very few of these
men will at once re-enlist," he predicted, although many would probably "drift back into the service" eventually. In the meantime, Mackenzie needed four hundred recruits, "pains being taken to secure the most
intelligent." The Adjutant General told him that since the 25th Infantry's
strength was almost four hundred men below that of the 24th, he would
have to wait until the 25th was filled.[44]

Mackenzie continued to push the War Department for permission
to use unassigned officers, regimental officers, and officers of the General Recruiting Service to find men for his regiment. Like Colonel Grierson of the 10th Cavalry, Mackenzie persistently emphasized the need
for high standards. The Adjutant General was reluctant to detach regimental officers for recruiting duty, but in the spring of 1870 he agreed
to allow the 24th Infantry to recruit, using officers who had been left
unassigned by the previous year's consolidation. Hinks received the same
authority and called on former officers of the 39th and 40th Infantry
who were awaiting orders.[45]

Recruiters from the "unassigned list" managed to raise 125 men for
the black infantry regiments in a few months. Lieutenant Samuel K.
Schwenk, a former officer of the 41st who was waiting for an assignment

after the army's reorganization, wrote from Nashville that he had accepted nine of twenty-seven applicants in one day, had a total of forty-four recruits on hand for the 24th Infantry, and that "it would be difficult to select that number of better looking soldiers out of any full company in the army." Men were coming in from as far away as Chattanooga and Columbia, and with a little assistance, he predicted, he could enroll three hundred more in a few months. When Mackenzie read this, he asked the Adjutant General for permission to send regimental officers to Nashville. "If my regiment is to be kept black, which seems to be the desire of those in authority, . . . it is much to its interest, that the officers who are detailed to recruit . . . are those who take interest in its efficiency," Mackenzie explained. "My experience thus far," he added, "has been that the best class of negroes make very good soldiers, while the poor are worse than useless."[46]

While army records contain an abundance of material about the recruitment of black regulars, there is only sketchy information about the soldiers themselves. This scarcity makes it hard to determine why black men decided to serve in the regular army. Mackenzie thought that peacetime soldiering attracted "as a rule only . . . the poorest classes of whites in this country," but that it was "probably the best position that is offered to a black man, and . . . the United States can probably receive the services of the best." His observation was close to the truth.[47]

Military life, however authoritarian and unattractive, was more appealing than what awaited many men outside the army. The racial violence that prevailed everywhere in the former slave states may have prompted many enlistments. Thirty-four black men died in a police riot at New Orleans in July 1866, a few weeks before the army began accepting black recruits. Near Louisville earlier that month, a gang of unidentified white men beat "Sam Buky a Colored Man that came here to see his wife after being sold down the river and Serving in the Union army that was not the first nor will not be the last mean unlawful deed they have perpetrated on innocent Men for being in the Union Army." From Queen Anne's County, Maryland, USCT veteran Charles A. Watkins wrote to the Freedmen's Bureau: "the returned collard Solgers are in many cases beten, and their guns taken from them, we darcent walk out of an evening, if we do and we are met by some of these roudies that were in the rebbel army they beat us badly and sum time shoot us." Daily turmoil like this must have made military routine seem like a tranquil haven.[48]

Unemployment forced some men to join up. Edward Smith had been born a slave in Staunton County, Virginia. "[A]fter emancipation I went to Cincinnati, Ohio," he recalled years later. "[F]inding nothing better to do I enlisted." Floods along the lower Mississippi River in the spring of 1866 followed by an infestation of army worms that destroyed that year's cotton crop must have impelled many of the more than one hundred men who enlisted at Natchez, Vicksburg, and small towns in Louisiana. Planters began "to discharge the Freedmen under contract on the ground that they have no further use for them as the cotton is about to be eaten up by Worms," a Freedmen's Bureau inspector at Lake Providence reported at the end of August. When a 9th Cavalry recruiter visited there a month later, thirty-one men enlisted in three days. A disastrous drought in Georgia that caused the near "utter failure" of the corn crop probably assisted recruiting efforts for the 38th Infantry.[49]

Natural disasters made farm work scarce, and jobseekers who moved to town were apt to find living conditions wretched. During the war, former slaves fled to cities, where they sheltered near Union army garrisons, and shantytowns sprang up from Washington, D.C., to Memphis. The black population of Xenia, Ohio, where Captain Brisbin sought literate recruits for the 9th Cavalry at nearby Wilberforce University, doubled during the 1860s, and the newcomers crowded, sometimes five or more to a room, into shacks where a health inspector might record, as one did in 1867, "privy vault full[,] house filthy[,] children dirty and alone." Life in the army could hardly be worse than this.[50]

Some recruits, too young to have served in the Civil War, enlisted as soon as they could to find out what they had missed. One young man, Madison Bruin, had watched Union and Confederate troops move through Fayette County, Kentucky. "What did I think when I seed all dem sojers?" he asked an interviewer, seventy-five years afterward. "I wants to be one, too. I didn't care what side, I jis' wants a gun and a hoss and be a sojer." A generation after Bruin joined, "a very great desire for adventure and to see the Wild West" prompted young Horace W. Bivins to enlist in the 10th Cavalry. Bivins served with the regiment in Arizona, Montana, Cuba, and the Philippines, retiring from the army in 1913.[51]

Company E, 4th U.S. Colored Infantry, at the close of the Civil War. Within a few years, Pvt. Daniel Lincoln would enlist in the 40th Infantry and Pvt. Silas Howard in the 9th Cavalry, two of more than 3,000 veterans of the U.S. Colored Troops who joined the regular army's new black regiments. *Courtesy U.S. Army Military History Institute.*

Officers persuaded more than five hundred men to transfer directly to the regular army from the last USCT regiments in service in the fall of 1866. "The captain of my old company asked me if I wanted to reenlist," Hector Preston later told a pension examiner, "and I told him yes after I had rested awhile." Some black Civil War veterans joined the regulars simply because they had grown accustomed to the army. When Jerry Jenkins wanted to return to the 24th Infantry after a few months of civilian life, he wrote to Lieutenant John L. Bullis, "I much Wrother Souldier then to be Any thing else."[52]

Although regulations forbade the enlistment of married men, recruiters apparently offered military service as an asylum to some men with marital difficulties. At least twice, the War Department had to tell the irate wives of black soldiers that their husbands could not be released from the service. Youths under twenty-one years of age were not allowed to enlist without their parents' consent, but this rule was impossible to enforce in the black regiments. Slavery had separated many children from their parents, particularly during the decades just before the Civil War, when tens of thousands of slaves were sold from the Border States and the Atlantic Seaboard to cotton and sugar plantations farther south and west. During the war, Confederate slaveholders had moved their people long distances to avoid the liberating Union armies, while those in the Border States had sent slaves to Kentucky, where slavery survived until the adoption of the Thirteenth Amendment more than six months after all fighting had stopped. These massive population movements particularly affected Kentucky, Louisiana, and Missouri, three of the states that furnished the largest number of recruits for the regular army's new black regiments. Besides, wartime USCT recruiters, eager to sign up men to fill state draft quotas, had often enlisted youths in their middle teens, and many veterans with one or two years' war service had barely turned eighteen when they applied to regular army recruiters. During the first year of recruiting, a large number of minors found their way into the black regiments.[53]

Descriptive rolls of recruits suggest that a typical black regular of the 1860s stood about five feet, six inches tall; claimed to be in his early twenties; listed his civilian occupation as farmer or laborer (although most who had served in the war described themselves as "soldier"); and could not sign his name. Nearly all of those born in the South had been slaves.

Recruits from the North had more varied experiences. In 1867 the 40th Infantry's Company K included two former bakers, two carpenters, a tinsmith, a painter, and a brickmason. When Daniel Johnson enlisted in New York City, he noted his trade as "orator." Johnson put his ability to good use and became one of Company K's sergeants in a few months.[54]

About half of the black men who joined the regular army in the late 1860s had served during the Civil War. Of these, at least 533 transferred directly from USCT regiments that were mustering out in the fall of 1866. They received a credit for continuous service that would entitle them to one dollar a month reenlistment pay when their time in the volunteers and the regular army totaled five years. About 2,500 other USCT veterans joined the regulars more than thirty days after their discharge from the volunteers and so were not eligible for this credit, although many of them listed their occupation as "soldier" when they signed on again. The presence of these veterans in the black regiments helped offset a shortage of educated soldiers and furnished experienced comrades for recruits fresh from civilian life.[55]

Scanty information about the black regulars' personal histories, though, limits any conclusions about their motives for enlisting to a few educated guesses. The postwar South was a dangerous place for black people, and for Union army veterans in particular. Unskilled labor was plentiful in the cities to which many black people had moved, places where the army recruited. While the usual reasons that prompted whites to enlist—including unemployment and sheer restlessness—drew black men to the army too, the tumultuous and uncertain social, economic, and psychological situation of black Americans after the upheaval of the war years also helped fill the ranks of the new black regiments.

CHAPTER TWO

"How Would You Like to Command a Colored Regiment?"

The black regulars' success would depend a great deal on the abilities of the officers who led them. Even the most optimistic forecasters agreed that it would take a special effort to turn illiterate field hands and unskilled laborers into proficient soldiers. The performance of the U.S. Colored Troops (USCT) during the Civil War and of the all-black Twenty-fifth Army Corps along the Rio Grande for a year after the war had convinced many officers that black Americans, properly trained and properly led, could be a valuable addition to the regular army. Few military planners claimed that they would be the equals of white soldiers, but even some of the most persistent critics conceded the possibility of molding them into an effective force. Members of the Thirty-ninth Congress, which passed the army reorganization act of 1866, recognized this and discussed at length who would receive commissions in the new regiments.

Some politicians who favored enlisting blacks believed that creation of all-black regiments would allow Congress to reward former USCT officers. During the debates, legislators praised the courage of the men who had led the Union army's least-favored regiments. USCT officers had often been socially ostracized by those of white units and were the target of jibes and bigoted remarks. Members of Congress tactfully neglected to mention that many had taken USCT commissions in order to gain promotion. True, others had viewed service with blacks as a chance to aid and train former slaves, but the command of black soldiers during the

war had offered a chance for advancement that often attracted oppor-
tunists. Such a commission meant a jump of several grades in rank: lieutenants from white regiments became majors and colonels while former
sergeants commanded companies.[1]

Despite attempts to screen applicants, a number of undesirables had
gained commissions. For two years after the fighting stopped—as long
as USCT regiments remained in service—complaints arose of payroll
fraud and of officers borrowing money from enlisted men. As late as
November 1866, one regimental adjutant warned an officer that his resignation could not take effect until he had furnished a list of the men
in his company to whom he owed money. More than 137 soldiers from
this regiment, the 10th U.S. Colored Heavy Artillery, joined the regular
army directly in the fall of 1866 and brought with them the lessons about
officer conduct that they had learned in the volunteer service. Clearly,
applicants for commissions in the new regular regiments would require
close scrutiny.[2]

Nevertheless, USCT officers, whatever their motives and performance and regardless of the disadvantages they encountered, had experience commanding black soldiers. If the new regiments required special leadership, some legislators asked, did it not make sense to officer
the new regiments with men who had such experience? This was the
rationale of Henry Wilson's proposal that all officers commissioned in
the black regular regiments must have served at least two years with the
USCT. Senators who thought that commissions should be open to all
criticized the idea, and Charles Sumner and Benjamin F. Wade finally
persuaded Wilson to modify the proposal. Wade and Sumner, unlike
Wilson and his allies, were less intent on rewarding Civil War service than
on providing black regulars with the best available officers.[3]

In the end, officers for the black regiments were chosen in the same
way as were those of white regiments. All lieutenancies in the cavalry
would be filled by former officers and enlisted men from volunteer regiments, whether state or USCT. Two-thirds of the captains and field officers would also come from the volunteers while regular army cavalry
officers would make up the remainder. Candidates must "have served
two years in the field during the war, and have been distinguished for
capacity and good conduct." In the new infantry regiments, officers and
men from the volunteers would fill the lieutenants' positions and half

of the other vacancies, the rest going to officers who had held regular-army commissions during the war.[4]

Congress clearly intended to tap all of the Union army's manpower resources. By opening the regular army to volunteer officers and, in the junior grades, to enlisted men from the volunteers, legislators appeased veterans who demanded that the government reward citizen-soldiers who had proven themselves in battle. Regular officers in senior grades would provide the new regiments with a degree of professionalism that the volunteer forces had lacked. Another important provision of the appropriation act was the approval of all officer candidates by examining boards. Candidates for cavalry or infantry would appear before a board composed of officers of that branch to be questioned about their war records, general education, and other qualifications for a commission in the regular army.

Applicants began to flood the War Department and the Adjutant General's Office with petitions and recommendations months before the passage of the reorganization act. Secretary of War Edwin M. Stanton established examining boards in several northern cities soon after President Andrew Johnson approved the legislation. While Stanton allowed the boards to make selections for company and some field-grade officers, he and Lieutenant General Ulysses S. Grant took special interest in the men who would command the new regiments. Grant knew many able officers and Stanton frequently relied on his judgment. Other generals like Philip H. Sheridan submitted their own lists of candidates. Stanton referred most of these recommendations to Grant, who indicated his preference subject to the Secretary's final approval.[5]

An exchange of letters between Sheridan, Grant, and Stanton shows how this worked. In April 1866 Sheridan recommended several officers for promotion in the expanded army. He suggested George A. Custer, who had led a division in Sheridan's cavalry corps, as colonel of one of the new cavalry regiments. Similar suggestions poured in from other generals as well as federal, state, and local officials until the War Department had a long list of candidates. In a letter to Stanton, Grant indicated which officers on the list he wished to command the new black regiments. Grant did not think that Custer deserved regimental command and suggested a commission as lieutenant colonel of one of the black cavalry regiments instead. Custer declined but accepted the same rank in the new, white 7th Cavalry. Thomas C. Devin and Wesley Merritt, two of Sheridan's other division commanders, became lieutenant colonels of the white 8th Cavalry and the black 9th Cavalry.[6]

Generals who submitted recommendations rarely specified the regiments to which they wished their candidates assigned. Some officers, though, must certainly have been startled when they were offered a commission in a black regiment. Thomas W. Higginson, one of the first men to command black troops during the Civil War, had been astounded by his appointment: "Had an invitation reached me to take command of a regiment of Kalmuck Tartars, it could hardly have been more unexpected." Wartime generals like Nelson A. Miles, Joseph A. Mower, and William B. Hazen may have reacted similarly when they received identically worded letters from Stanton asking, "How would you like to command a colored regiment?"[7]

By early August, Grant and Stanton had chosen the new regiments' colonels. None of these men had commanded black soldiers before, but all had impressive war records. The 9th and 10th Cavalry regiments went to Edward Hatch and Benjamin H. Grierson. Although neither man had any military experience before the war, both had attained the brevet rank of major general, U.S. Volunteers. Hatch had begun the war as a captain in the 2d Iowa Cavalry but rose quickly to command the regiment. Grierson had started as a major in the 6th Illinois Cavalry in 1861 and became its colonel the next year. In early 1863 he established his reputation by leading a mounted brigade, of which Hatch's regiment was part, on a raid through Mississippi intended to draw Confederate forces away from Grant's campaign against Vicksburg. The raid earned Grant's admiration and his later support for Grierson and Hatch as colonels in the regular army. The lieutenant colonels of the 9th and 10th Cavalry, Wesley Merritt and John W. Davidson, were both West Point graduates who had commanded cavalry divisions during the war.[8]

William B. Hazen, one of the two West Pointers to command black regiments, accepted command of the 38th Infantry. After graduating from the U.S. Military Academy in 1855, Hazen served in the West until the Civil War. Like the other three colonels of the black infantry regiments, he ended the war as a brevet major general, U.S. Volunteers. The 39th Infantry went to Joseph A. Mower, who had served as an enlisted man in the Mexican War before obtaining a commission in 1855. Nelson

A. Miles, who had joined a Massachusetts infantry regiment at the beginning of the Civil War and served throughout with the Army of the Potomac, received command of the 40th Infantry. Ranald S. Mackenzie had graduated at the head of his class at West Point and two years later led an infantry brigade in the Shenandoah Valley; he became colonel of the 41st Infantry. The lieutenant colonels of the new infantry regiments— Cuvier Grover, Frank Wheaton, Edward W. Hinks, and William R. Shafter—all held brevets as brigadier or major general. Shafter, who had been colonel of the 17th U.S. Colored Infantry (USCI), was the only one among them who had served with black soldiers at the regimental level; Hinks had commanded an all-black division in Virginia late in the war.

The colonels of the new black regiments were among the best officers in the army. Hazen, Mackenzie, and Mower were regulars; Grierson, Hatch, and Miles had been volunteer officers during the Civil War. Grierson had led a cavalry corps during the conflict; Hazen and Mower had only gained corps command in the spring of 1865. All six men were experienced division commanders; even Mackenzie, the twice-wounded 1862 West Point graduate, had led a cavalry division in the Appomattox campaign.

In contrast to active young men like these, the colonels of the older regiments were a lackluster crowd who commanded solely by reason of seniority. Three of the cavalry colonels in 1866 had held no active command since 1862. Their brevets were for "faithful and meritorious service"; one colonel had earned no brevets at all during the war. The roster of infantry colonels in 1866 shows a similar difference, with younger and more energetic men leading the newer regiments. Some of the army's best leaders went to the black organizations.[9]

While they were commanding large formations as general officers of volunteers, Hazen, Mackenzie, and Mower were acquiring brevet rank in the regular army for their bravery in battle. All three men received simultaneous brevets as brigadier and major general, U.S. Army, in March 1865. Grierson, Hatch, and Miles held general's rank in the volunteers but were not eligible for regular brevets until their regular army appointments as colonel in July 1866. All three also received simultaneous brevets as brigadier and major general, U.S. Army, in March 1867, which brought them into line with other regular army colonels. Officers in the black regiments clearly did not suffer in awards of honor.

If these men had any doubts about service with black soldiers, they did not express them; all accepted their commissions without demur. Some of them, particularly the lieutenant colonels, were neither Grant's nor Stanton's first choices and received appointments only after others had declined to serve in a black regiment. Custer's refusal was but one. Frederick W. Benteen accepted a captain's commission in the 7th Cavalry rather than serve as major in the 9th Cavalry. Stanton and Grant did not object to refusals and accepted them without comment or opposition.[10]

Stanton preferred to let the examining boards select the junior officers, but he and Grant still had to sift through hundreds of applications in order to determine which men would face the examiners. Well before passage of the reorganization act, candidates had begun to marshal all the support they could from both elected officials and their former commanders. Members of the Illinois congressional delegation signed a petition recommending Grierson for a colonel's commission in the expanded army. Even applicants for the junior grades often came recommended by prominent military and political figures. Frank M. Coxe's application received support from fellow-Pennsylvanians George G. Meade, former commander of the Army of the Potomac and victor of Gettysburg; the Radical Republican Congressional leader Thaddeus Stevens; Governor Andrew G. Curtin; and the mayor of Philadelphia.[11]

It is hard to tell whether Stanton and Grant paid more attention to recommendations from politicians or to those from army officers when deciding which applicants would go before the boards. Officers were certainly in a better position to evaluate the candidates' military abilities. Grant carefully considered letters he received from other generals, for while he was well acquainted with the records of men like Grierson and Hatch, he knew little about most of those suggested for junior grades. He was shrewd enough, though, to realize that the wishes of Congressional delegations, governors, legislators, and occasionally the President himself could not be ignored.

Once appointed, the colonels of the new regiments often sent their own lists of prospective officers to the War Department. Nearly all of the colonels sent letters recommending officers they had served with during the war. Letters came too for USCT officers who were helping to enlist black soldiers in the regular army. The War Department knew the value of these volunteer officers, and in August 1866 the Adjutant

General told Sheridan and Major General William T. Sherman, who commanded the departments where both cavalry regiments and two of the infantry regiments were organizing, that he would welcome information as to "whether [the USCT officers] are fitted for permanent appointment in the regular army."[12]

Most of the men who sought commissions in the regular army expressed no preference as to regiment; a few, though, made clear their aversion to service with black soldiers. Henry L. Stone, a former captain in the 103d USCI, wanted a commission in one of the "old"—that is, white—infantry regiments. Louis H. Carpenter, wartime colonel of the 5th U.S. Colored Cavalry and a regular officer with a lieutenant's commission in the 6th Cavalry, wrote to the War Department in August 1866 asking for a captain's commission "in one of the regiments of White cavalry." Neither officer got his wish: Stone received a lieutenant's commission in the 41st Infantry and Carpenter's promotion to captain was in the 10th Cavalry.[13]

A few candidates did request assignment to the new black regiments. Henry C. Corbin, former colonel of the 14th USCI, wrote to Stanton in July 1866, "soliciting a field position [that is, at least a major's commission] in one of the Colored regiments of Infantry." James Pratt assured the Adjutant General that "having three years experience in a colored regiment, I should prefer that branch of the service." Louis E. Granger claimed that he could obtain "nearly forty recruits" for the regular army among the men in his company of the 80th USCI.[14]

In staffing the new regiments, Stanton and Grant did not emphasize USCT service. Of 106 former USCT officers who obtained regular commissions, only 51 wound up in the new black regiments, while the rest were scattered among the white regiments. That 44 of the 51 found places in the new black infantry regiments, and only 7 in the cavalry, reflects the composition of the Union army's black contingent: 7 regiments of cavalry and about 150 of infantry and artillery.[15]

Nearly 15 percent of the volunteer officers who entered the regular army during its postwar expansion had served with the USCT, a proportion well above their numbers in the Union army as a whole. Men who had been willing to leave the familiar surroundings of a locally recruited company in a state regiment in order to advance a few grades, and then to continue serving after the war while white volunteers were returning to civilian life, may have been more likely than other volunteer officers to consider the peacetime army as a career. Moreover, the screening process through which candidates for USCT commissions passed may have assured a better-qualified group of applicants for regular-army commissions. The two reasons were complementary, and officers who had once complained of discrimination now found their service with the black volunteers an advantage.[16]

After approval by Stanton and Grant, applicants still had to face the examining boards. Elementary questions about history, geography, and arithmetic determined whether candidates had "a fair knowledge" of these subjects. The most intricate of the arithmetic questions was: "How many pounds of beef, flour, and coffee will you require for a command of 10,000 men for 60 days, the ration of beef being 1 1/4 lbs, flour 1 1/4, coffee 1/16 to each man." Candidates had to name the principal rivers of the United States that empty into the Atlantic, locate the Straits of Gibraltar, and name "some of the principal events" in American history. Those who failed any part of the examination would be allowed to retake it. Few of the questions had to do with military topics. The boards seemed to rely on candidates' service records to determine their military ability and asked questions only to test their "general intelligence."[17]

Some applicants did fail. Theodore A. Boice listed Borneo, Sumatra, and Java as the principal islands of the West Indies, but the president of the board, citing his war record, agreed to another examination in three months. This time Boice passed and became a first lieutenant in the 9th Cavalry. After Edwin A. Rigg failed, he managed to obtain the signatures of several politicians, including a U.S. senator, on his petition for another examination. Rigg received a commission in the 38th Infantry.[18]

Nearly half of the officers of the four original black infantry regiments left the army in 1869, crowded out of the reduced officer corps, when that year's appropriations act reduced the number of infantry regiments from forty-five to twenty-five. Some who were unassigned temporarily sought transfers to white regiments. First Lieutenant Charles L. Cooper of the 39th Infantry told the War Department that he would even accept reduced rank if there were a vacancy in the 3d or 8th Cavalry. On December 31, 1870, Cooper was instead assigned to the 10th Cavalry, in which he served until 1898. Captain David Schooley of the 40th Infantry, who had been an artillery officer during the war, tried to transfer from the new 25th Infantry to a regular artillery regiment. After this attempt failed, Schooley stayed with the 25th for nineteen more years until he retired.[19]

Some infantry officers who did not mind service with black soldiers, but were tired of walking, sought transfers to the 9th and 10th Cavalry. Captain Orville Burke of the 40th Infantry managed such a move, as did Gustave H. Radetzki, from the white 28th Infantry to the 9th Cavalry. Another officer from a white infantry regiment, Captain Charles D. Viele, accepted a transfer to the 10th Cavalry rather than be left on the unassigned list.[20]

The three years that followed consolidation saw a rapid turnover in command of the new 24th and 25th Infantry Regiments. Between 1869 and 1873, each had a succession of three colonels. These men used the black units only as career way-stations while they awaited reassignment or retirement. Ranald Mackenzie left the 24th Infantry in December 1870 to command the 4th Cavalry and was succeeded by Abner Doubleday, who stayed with the regiment until his retirement three years later. Joseph H. Potter followed him as colonel and commanded the 24th Infantry until his retirement in 1886.

Zenas R. Bliss became colonel of the 24th when Potter left the army. A graduate of West Point, Bliss had served five years in the West before the Civil War. He had been appointed major of the 39th Infantry in 1866 and held the same rank in the 25th after the consolidation of 1869. Promoted to lieutenant colonel of the 19th Infantry in 1879, Bliss stayed there for seven years until Potter's retirement brought him to the 24th. Like all promotions through the grade of colonel, Bliss's was due to seniority alone, but his long experience with black troops made him the best-qualified officer to replace Potter. Bliss commanded the 24th Infantry until his retirement in 1895.

Colonel Mower's sudden death in January 1870 brought Joseph J. Reynolds to command the 25th Infantry. Reynolds had commanded the army in Texas in the late 1860s, when the 9th Cavalry and 41st Infantry had served there, but he took little interest in his new regiment and accepted command of the 3d Cavalry that December. The next colonel, John D. Stevenson, commanded the 25th for only seventeen days before being "discharged at his own request" on December 31, 1870. His successor, George L. Andrews, stayed with the regiment from

January 1871 until his retirement in 1892. Andrews had received a regular commission during the Civil War and had been lieutenant colonel of the 13th Infantry since 1864. When the consolidation of infantry regiments left him unassigned, he raised no objection to commanding black troops.

Unlike the black infantry regiments, the 9th and 10th Cavalry enjoyed a continuity of command that was unique in the post–Civil War era. Of all the colonels in the army, Hatch and Grierson had the longest continuous service with their regiments. Hatch led the 9th from its formation until his death in 1889. Grierson commanded the 10th until 1890, when he was promoted to brigadier general.

The colonels who succeeded Andrews, Grierson, Hatch, and Potter came to the black regiments solely on the basis of seniority. Besides Bliss, only two of them had commanded black soldiers before and none had at the company level. Guy V. Henry had been a major in the 9th Cavalry from 1881 to 1892 and became colonel of the 10th Cavalry in 1897. David Perry had been lieutenant colonel of the 10th for five years before taking command of the 9th Cavalry in 1896. Like others of their rank throughout the army, the field officers of the black regiments—majors and lieutenant colonels as well as colonels—were Civil War veterans heading toward mandatory retirement at age sixty-four.[21]

The army's system of promotion depended entirely on seniority up to and including the grade of colonel. Through the rank of captain, officers advanced within their regiment. Once he became senior captain in the regiment, an officer usually transferred to another regiment on his promotion to major. When the senior captain left, the regiment's senior first lieutenant became a captain and took over his company. The senior second lieutenant then moved to fill the resulting vacancy, and his position would be taken, typically, by a member of West Point's next graduating class, who became the regiment's junior second lieutenant. A few lieutenants received direct appointments from civilian life or promotions from the ranks of the regular army. By the 1890s two-thirds of cavalry officers and more than half of those in the infantry had joined since the Civil War.[22]

Promotion of field-grade officers was lineal (within the branch: artillery, cavalry, or infantry) rather than regimental. Advancement throughout the entire army was painfully slow. In 1882 a medical officer published a table that showed the average age at which officers attained certain grades and how long they remained in that position before promotion. According to the table, an officer who entered the army as a second lieutenant at the age of twenty-four might become a colonel just before his seventy-sixth birthday. In 1884 the *Army and Navy Register* listed the names of 173 first lieutenants with more than fourteen years' service (including the Civil War, 88 had served for more than twenty years; two for more than thirty). Charles E. Nordstrom of the 10th Cavalry was a lieutenant for twenty-two years before becoming a captain. It was an era when, as one officer recalled in his memoirs, "few died and none retired."[23]

At the beginning of the postwar period, only the more optimistic regimental officers entertained the idea that black recruits could be turned into good soldiers. Many whites both in and out of the army considered black men to be ignorant, lazy draft animals and doubted their fitness for military service. Some officers must have been disappointed and discouraged when they met the soldiers they would command. Zenas Bliss, whose previous service had been entirely with white troops, recalled years later that 39th Infantry recruits "were of a very low level of intelligence." Raised in the sugar parishes of Louisiana, the 39th Infantry and 9th Cavalry probably had more men who had grown up in the insular world of the large plantation than did any of the other black regiments. Captain George A. Purington remarked that some of his 9th Cavalry recruits spoke only French. Colonel Hatch asked that "a limited number of colored men may be recruited in the north who have the necessary education for company clerks and sergeants" since he could find none among the 9th Cavalry's six hundred Louisianians in the fall of 1866.[24]

The high rate of illiteracy—the heritage of slavery—and the consequent absence of trained clerks and noncommissioned officers forced white officers to take on many tasks that usually fell to enlisted men. Many loathed the extra paperwork, but a white veteran who had seen black regulars in Texas thought that it had advantages. Harry H. McConnell's company of the 6th Cavalry served at Fort Richardson with companies of the 38th Infantry in 1869. "The intimate and practical knowledge of the requirements of the men . . . , in addition to the greater responsibility thus placed on their shoulders, accounts for the marked efficiency" that McConnell attributed to the 38th's officers.

Most of them seemed to be "a very superior set of men," he recalled twenty years afterward.[25]

But good opinions could not lessen officers' workloads, nor could they dispel a growing belief in the minds of many that the black regiments manned some of the army's least desirable posts. The War Department would not grant transfers to dissatisfied officers, but some took advantage of a policy that permitted exchange between regiments by officers of equal rank. Those who wanted to switch often advertised in the *Army and Navy Journal*. A typical offer, perhaps from an officer in the 38th Infantry, read, "A Captain in a regiment, now stationed in New Mexico, is desirous of an exchange into a white regiment stationed in the 'States.'" Whether the captain objected to black soldiers or to New Mexico is uncertain; he may have disliked both. Another officer wrote: "A First Lieutenant of Artillery desires to transfer with a First Lieutenant of Cavalry. The regiment must be white." The frequency with which advertisements explicitly stated a preference for white regiments clearly showed many officers' reluctance to serve with black troops.[26]

Gradually, during the decades that followed the army reduction of 1869, officers' attitudes about the abilities of black soldiers, and about service with them, began to change. At no time did racist sentiment vanish from the officer corps, nor were these officers able to judge the performance of their men without resorting to a vocabulary that grew out of their racial preconceptions. There still were complaints about the ignorance of black troops or their particular dependence on their officers, but each year more reports by regimental officers and other military observers declared that black regulars had proven themselves to be capable soldiers. These compliments showed a slow but steady improvement in the reputation of the black regiments. Several factors contributed to this shift in thinking, and the quality of officers was one of them.

After 1869 the great majority of new regular officers were graduates of the U.S. Military Academy. Although former volunteer officers often disagreed, many West Pointers considered themselves the elite of the military establishment. From constituting less than one-fourth of the officer corps in 1867, West Pointers came to hold 42 percent of the regular commissions in 1882, and by the 1890s well over half of all officers on active duty were graduates.[27]

Before graduation, each cadet wrote to the Adjutant General naming the regiment or regiments in which he desired an appointment. Assignments depended entirely on class rank—a combination of a cadet's academic standing and military record. Throughout the late nineteenth century, a clear hierarchy of assignments existed, and the placement of graduates reflected this order. Cadets highest in their class took commissions in the Corps of Engineers. Those somewhat lower on the list accepted posts in the artillery, while new second lieutenants of cavalry and infantry stood lower still. The 9th and 10th Cavalry usually received officers who graduated in the lower half of their class and, almost without exception, cadets posted to the 24th and 25th Infantry were the lowest ranking.

Infantry service held the least status for regular-army officers. Sixty percent or more of all West Pointers assigned to infantry regiments between 1871 and 1889 graduated in the lower half of their class, and the number rose to 80 percent in the 24th and 25th Infantry. This high proportion of low-ranking cadets in all infantry regiments, white or black, indicates the units' low status; by the time the higher-ranking cadets had received assignments, the only vacancies left were in the infantry. To be black, as well as infantry, made the 24th and 25th the least-regarded regiments in the eyes of graduating cadets.

An important change, though, occurred in the 9th and 10th Cavalry over the years. Cavalry assignments had traditionally ranked below artillery, but during the post–Civil War era West Point graduates came to prefer cavalry regiments to artillery. Cavalry saw more active service than artillery or infantry and wore out more senior officers (medical retiring boards caused more vacancies than did battle casualties). Moreover, a ten-company infantry regiment had ten captains and one major, while a twelve-company cavalry regiment had twelve captains and three majors, a much lower ratio that favored promotion in the mounted branch. Hugh L. Scott "was glad to be admitted to any cavalry regiment" when he graduated near the bottom of his class in 1876.[28]

But the increased attractiveness of cavalry service did nothing to eliminate racial prejudice among cadets or officers' complaints that black regiments manned the worst posts. These factors also kept some able cadets from requesting service in the black infantry units. The fear of undesirable stations was "one reason that cadets have such a dread of being assigned to one of these regiments," a 24th Infantry captain explained in a letter to the *Army and Navy Journal*.[29]

As opportunities for promotion made cavalry service more attractive, a larger number of high-ranking graduates put aside their misgivings and requested service in the 9th and 10th Regiments. The change, though, was not appreciable until late in the 1880s. By 1889, for instance, one-fourth of the West Pointers serving with the 10th Cavalry had graduated in the upper half of their class, as had 21 percent of the graduates serving in the 9th Cavalry. These figures contrast sharply with those of 1878, when only one out of twenty-one West Pointers in the two regiments had graduated in the upper half of his class.

During the late 1870s and on into the 1880s, the black regulars amassed an admirable record of action. Reports from the 9th Cavalry in New Mexico and the 10th west of the Pecos River in Texas appeared regularly in the *Army and Navy Journal* and, after 1878, in the *Army and Navy Register*. Small bodies of troops, often led by junior officers, operated independently, staying in the field for weeks at a time. These operations received less notice in the daily newspapers than larger campaigns in the northern plains, where colonels and even generals led expeditions, but reports from the Southwest in the service weeklies must have captured the attention of many West Pointers. In 1880 alone, eight lieutenants of the 9th and 10th Cavalry received mention for leading companies—normally a captain's command—in New Mexico. Cadets eager for field service and the chance of (comparatively) rapid promotion could not overlook these regiments. After joining the 9th Cavalry, Lieutenant Edmund S. Wright told some of his classmates that "I like my post and my regiment, and feel very well contented with army life." The presence of high-ranked graduates in the 9th and 10th Regiments of course does not indicate an absence of racial prejudice among West Pointers, but their choice of assignment suggests that some cadets believed that the opportunity for active service overrode all other considerations.[30]

A young officer's practical education shows in letters home written by West Point graduate Powhatan H. Clarke, who noticed that "during my time at the Academy, some of the best men in the upper classes took" the 10th Cavalry. Soon after joining the 10th in 1884, Clarke, a Louisianian, wrote to his mother, "The nigs are very military and take a

Lieutenants Valois and Burnett, of the Ninth Cavalry Distinguish Themselves.

[New York Herald.]

CANADA, ALAMOSA,
NEAR BLACK RANGE, N. M., August 16,
VIA SAN MARCIAL, N. M., August 17, 1881.

About 2 o'clock this afternoon a Mexican arrived in Canada with the intelligence that about sixty warriors had attacked ranches five miles below, and that a fight was then going on between the Mexican ranchers and the Indians. Lieutenant G. Valois, who arrived here yesterday from Fort Sprague, and who had been making a thorough scout of the mountains southwest and northwest, immediately ordered his company of twenty-two men to horse. Lieutenant Burnett, with ten men, were despatched at full speed to the scene of action. Lieutenant Valois immediately collected the remainder of his small force, and started on the trail of Lieutenant Burnett, who, in the meantime, had arrived in the canyon, and discovered the Indians in large numbers climbing the steep hills on the south side, so as to get the high ground for a fight.

Headlines like this one in the *Army and Navy Journal* advertised the fact that lieutenants in the black regiments often commanded men in battle with no senior officers present. News of these opportunities may have led West Point graduates with higher class ranking to begin serving with the black regiments in the 1880s and later.

great deal of pride in being a soldier." After a week spent escorting a party of Comanches through the Big Bend region of Texas in search of peyote cactus, Clarke "was delighted with the conduct of my men they never complained always volunteer[e]d to do anything they could for me, when they got into camp after a hard march they sit around their fires laughing and singing. The old sergeant with his fifteen years experience proved invaluable to me being an excellent guide tough as leather and very responsible. [The interpreter] asked him if he did not have a good deal to do he said no not much. It was the lieutenant's first trip and he felt responsible for se[e]ing that none of the property was lost as the lieutenant would have to pay for so that not a tent peg was missing." In 1884 Sergeant Phillip Jones was serving his fourth enlistment in the 10th Cavalry. He first joined the army in Boston in 1867, and the record of his reenlistments reads like a regimental history: 1872, Fort Sill, Indian Territory; 1877, Fort Clark, Texas; 1882, Fort Davis, Texas; 1887, San Carlos, Arizona; 1892, Fort Keogh, Montana. A man like Jones was a wise choice to send along with a twenty-two-year-old second lieutenant.[31]

A few months later, the 10th Cavalry changed stations from Texas to Arizona, and in the spring of 1886, Clarke wrote to his father that his company had "followed an awful trail 27 miles in mountains yesterday broke camp at 6 a.m. struck remains of a large camp. Walked all day over the worse trail I ever want to see. Spotted Indians in a saddle of very high mountains . . . drove them off the saddle but caught flank fire from inaccessible rocks on our left at 200 yds while the Indians from the same place let our horses have it and stampeded the whole of them. One man was killed and a Corporal shot through both legs." Clarke dragged Corporal Edward Scott to cover, an action that earned him the Medal of Honor. "I had some close calls while I was trying to pull the corporal from under fire and succeeded in getting him behind a bush and you can be sure it was a very new sensation to hear the bullets whiz and strike within six inches of me and not be able to see anything."[32]

A week later, Clarke wrote to his mother: "[T]here is not a troop in the U.S. Army that I would trust my life to as quickly as this K troop of ours. . . . [N]o men could have been more determined and cooler than these same darkies were and as for their officers they like them and will risk themselves for them. The wounded Corporal has had to have his leg cut off the ball that shattered it lodging in the other instep. . . . [T]his man rode seven miles without a groan remarking to the Captain that he had seen forty men in one fight in a worse fix than he was. . . . Such have I found the colored soldier." Corporal Scott had served his first enlistment in the 9th Cavalry's Company D and was with them in 1879 when they rode seventy miles in twenty hours to relieve besieged troops at Milk Creek, Colorado; quickly lost all their horses to enemy fire; and had to wait for rescue themselves. Clarke did not receive his Medal of Honor until after his promotion to first lieutenant five years later, but word of his exploit must have spread quickly among the men of the 10th Cavalry and earned him their respect.[33]

The black regiments had more than their share of unfit officers. In 1874, when examiners found 24th Infantry Lieutenant Robert Neely's accounts short more than three thousand dollars in cash and supplies, Neely evaded his guard and disappeared—one of the few army officers listed as a deserter. Three years after Lieutenant Thomas J. Spencer left the 10th Cavalry in 1875, Colonel Grierson called him "absolutely worthless" and protested his reinstatement. (Spencer was dismissed again, finally, in 1881.) In 1887 Captain Cyrus N. Gray was dismissed from the 25th Infantry for drunkenness on duty. During a twenty-year period, of ninety-nine cavalry and infantry officers removed by general courtsmartial, twenty-six were from the black regiments.[34]

Racially prejudiced officers were always present in the black regiments, and if transfers had been easier to obtain, more of them might have tried to move to white regiments. Since these reassignments rarely involved a change in rank but could result in a loss of seniority in the new regiment, racial prejudice probably motivated many of these moves from black regiments. After attending West Point for four years, Joseph B. Batchelor Jr. failed to graduate in 1880 but secured a direct appointment in the 24th Infantry later that year. As one who stood at the "foot of the list of 2d Lieutenants in a colored regiment," he had no seniority to swap but sought an exchange anyway. "As a general rule these transfers are disturbing and injurious to the service," General Sherman observed, adding that Batchelor "doubtless wants to get into a white regiment." The transfer was not approved, and Batchelor stayed with the 24th until 1902.[35]

Dissatisfaction with life in the West caused other officers to transfer. John Conline wrote to his father in 1872 about the possibility of a move from the 9th Cavalry to the artillery: "I am thoroughly disgusted with life on the frontier." After years of service, some officers managed to transfer to one of the staff departments. Francis S. Dodge led the 9th Cavalry's Company D through twelve years of campaigning in Texas, New Mexico, and Colorado before he became a major in the Pay Department. John W. Clous spent nineteen years as a captain in the 38th and 24th Infantry, during which time he studied law and became a member of the Texas bar, before his transfer to the Judge Advocate General's Department.[36]

After the consolidation of 1869, the *Army and Navy Journal* still advertised offers to exchange, some of them from officers in the black regiments who wanted to get out. An infantry officer, aware that he was not in a good bargaining position, offered "liberal inducements" in 1871 in order to transfer to a white regiment. That same year, an officer in a white regiment stationed "at a very desirable post in the Department of the South" indicated his understanding of the disadvantages of service with black troops when he announced that he would transfer "on equal terms if in a white regiment" but insisted on "a reasonable bonus" if he went to a black regiment. By the late 1870s, though, and concurrent with the gradual increase in the reputation of the black regiments, fewer of the exchange offers stated a racial preference. Some officers even declared they would accept transfers to either a white or black regiment: "A Second Lieutenant of Infantry ranking from '79, wishes to transfer into the cavalry, either white or colored." The next year an artillery officer seeking to transfer into the cavalry specified, "No objection to a colored regiment."[37]

In early 1886 the *Army and Navy Journal* carried a report that Captain James Spaulding, the senior captain of the 2d Cavalry, had declined a promotion to major in the 9th because he did not wish to serve with black troops. Spaulding denied the report, claiming to have had no knowledge of the transfer and declaring that if he had known about it he would "not have opposed it because it sent me to a colored regiment." In the end, Spaulding's promotion was into the 4th Cavalry, but another officer wrote to the *Journal* that Spaulding's declaration had the "ring of a man and a soldier." Spaulding's remarks and the letter of approval indicate slowly changing attitudes within the officer corps toward service with black soldiers.[38]

In assigning officers, the War Department treated the black regiments no differently than it did the rest of the army. The Adjutant General might have kept in mind the special needs of black troops and assigned only especially qualified men to them. On the other hand, he might have sent only the worst officers to what many considered the least desirable regiments in the service. Stingy budgets prevented the former course; the need to maintain an adequate fighting force prevented the latter. Racial prejudice worked to keep some good officers from accepting posts in black regiments. It is hard to blame the army for not assigning specially chosen officers to the black regiments in an era before psychological screening, when examining boards asked officer candidates only the most elementary general-knowledge questions. In not following such a plan, though, the army did not load the dice against the black regiments. While most of the men who commanded black troops had no particular qualifications when they were first commissioned, many of them proved their abilities during long years of service in the West.

CHAPTER THREE

"To the Colored Man the Service Offers a Career"

Careful selection of recruits, Colonels Benjamin Grierson and Ranald Mackenzie thought, would be the key to their new regiments' success. In the years after 1869, recruiting for the regular army required a bureaucracy headed by the Adjutant General, a senior officer who reported directly to the Secretary of War. To handle enlistments, the War Department established the Mounted Recruiting Service, which furnished recruits for the cavalry, and the General Recruiting Service, which supplied the other branches. Captains and lieutenants, detailed from their regiments on two-year assignments, served as recruiters. After the army's convulsive expansion and contraction in the late 1860s, the system remained essentially unaltered for the next twenty-five years. Securing enough black recruits to maintain segregated regiments, though, posed problems that would never be entirely solved.

The army's post–Civil War expansion severely taxed recruiters' abilities. After the reorganization of 1869, the colonels of the black regiments complained frequently that General and Mounted Recruiting Services could not supply them with enough men. These were years when the regiments' strength plummeted as the three-year enlistments of infantrymen expired in 1869–70 and the cavalry's five-year terms ran out in 1871–72. In order to keep the regiments filled, the War Department authorized their colonels to send out recruiting parties. Officers of the General and Mounted Recruiting Services continued to enroll black applicants, but until 1874, when the army finally shrank to a statutory limit of about twenty-five thousand men, the black regiments' officers carried on most of their own recruiting.

Between 1870 and 1874, each colonel usually assigned no more than two of his junior officers as recruiters. While a few tried their luck north of the Ohio River, most operated in Kentucky and Tennessee. At one time or another, officers from each of the four regiments opened stations in Lexington, Memphis, and Nashville. Sometimes officers set up temporary stations in small towns nearby or moved their offices altogether. The Adjutant General usually approved these relocations if the budget allowed and if they seemed likely to bring in more men. In August 1871, though, he explained to a 24th Infantry recruiter that Nashville was "a much better station for colored recruits than Cincinnati" and refused permission to move.[1]

A shrewd recruiter opened his office close to a black neighborhood or workplace, timing his stay to obtain the best results. Seasonal unemployment sometimes worked in his favor. Lieutenant Robert G. Smither wrote from Lexington, Kentucky, in the fall of 1872 that he was "picking up about Twenty recruits per month and . . . will soon commence to enlist them faster. Most of the colored men in this section of the country are now engaged in cutting corn, and they are also having county fairs, after which I think they will come in." Another 10th Cavalry officer asked for a detail of enlisted men from the regiment to help run his St. Louis office, believing that black recruiters would be more likely to draw black recruits.[2]

A much smaller source of men, but one that could not be ignored, was a captain's authority to enlist men for his own company, if it was under strength, without permission from regimental or higher headquarters. This meant not only fresh recruits but in later years reenlistments as well. Dozens of veterans stayed near military posts after receiving their discharges and worked either for army quartermasters or neighboring civilians. When one of the government's budgetary spasms made the quartermaster cut his civilian employees, or if other jobs did not turn out well, some veterans returned to the army.[3]

In 1874, Congress reduced the army's size from 30,000 to 25,000 enlisted men, which remained the authorized strength until the Spanish-American War. Despite the reduction, the army never was able to recruit up to its statutory limit, and rarely did a year pass when most line regiments were not short of men. Deaths, discharges, and desertions continually sapped the strength of the army. The general unattractiveness of military life kept many from enlisting, and few persons of ability were willing to exchange the economic opportunities of civilian life for the minimal pay offered by the military. Nor did black men flock to the recruiting offices in large numbers, despite the low pay and indignities that they suffered as civilians. Like the rest of the army, the black regiments remained greatly understrength through most of the post–Civil War era.

Men who wanted to enlist had first to travel to the nearest recruiting station. Throughout the late nineteenth century, the army maintained offices in a dozen or so cities, though seldom south of the Ohio and Potomac Rivers. This failure to tap the largest source of black manpower partly explains why colonels sometimes found their regiments at three-quarters or even half of authorized strength.[4] During 1866 and 1867, though, officers had recruited in towns across the South, and their experience with unskilled, illiterate recruits had convinced them that better-educated recruits could be found north of the Cotton Belt.

Most black soldiers enlisted in Maryland, Kentucky, Tennessee, and the District of Columbia. Year after year, officers of the General and Mounted Recruiting Services reported success in signing up black men in Baltimore and Washington, with St. Louis and Cincinnati close behind. Prospective soldiers who lived in the country often had to travel a great distance to the nearest recruiting station at their own expense. Infrequently, when a little expenditure seemed to promise a number of enlistments, the War Department would dispatch an officer to enlist men who did not live near a recruiting office. In 1872 a former officer of the 39th Infantry who lived in Jonesboro, Tennessee, told the Adjutant General that a number of black men in his neighborhood wished to join the army but had no money for transportation; the Superintendent of the Mounted Recruiting Service sent an officer to Jonesboro to sign them up.[5]

For more than half a century between the Civil War and the First World War, all of the army's recruits were volunteers. This does not imply, though, that a soldier's life attracted all of them; misfortune, certainly, drove many to enlist. What sort of men might join became obvious as early as 1867, when police in Boston raided the 39th Infantry's office and arrested four recruits for larceny. There is no record of Zachariah Pope's motive for joining the 10th Cavalry in 1867, but when he came home to East Carondelet, Illinois, after his discharge ten years later, he knifed a man, crossed the river to St. Louis, and enlisted again. Twenty years afterward, Pope retired from the 25th Infantry as a first sergeant.[6]

Most soldiers, of course, did not flee to the army because of legal difficulties. Samuel Harris, a resident of Washington, D.C., thought that an honorable discharge with a good character reference would be useful in getting a federal job. Some men joined in order to take advantage of the army's schools. "The white folks learned my father how to read and write," 9th Cavalry trooper George Conrad Jr. recalled, "but I didn't learn how . . . till I enlisted in the U.S. Army in 1883." Perhaps the most extraordinary reason for enlisting was Joshua Johnson's. He had developed hemorrhoids during his Civil War service but could not afford medical treatment afterward; he got it by joining the regular army. "I was not examined very much," Johnson recalled in his pension application years later. After joining the 10th Cavalry, he "was laid up at Fort Sill Indian Territory eight or ten months" but managed to finish his five-year enlistment. More usual reasons for enlisting, of course, were the boredom, restlessness, and unemployment that drove hundreds of men each year toward the army's recruiting offices.[7]

When a prospective recruit appeared, the officer in charge questioned him and an army surgeon or a civilian doctor under contract conducted a physical examination. Sober, unmarried adult males who met weight and height requirements and passed the medical examination were allowed to sign enlistment papers. In most years, examining surgeons rejected more than one-third of the men who applied for enlistment. About the same proportion of black recruits failed to pass the initial medical examination as did whites. Causes for medical rejection, though, varied widely between the two groups. Syphilis kept a greater percentage of black men from enlisting, but relatively few were barred for alcoholism. In 1886 the Surgeon General reported that the rate of rejection because of alcoholism was almost four times higher among white applicants than among blacks.[8]

In their desire to sign up men, both recruiting officers and doctors sometimes conducted perfunctory examinations and approved the enlistment of men who turned out to be unfit. Medical officers at the depots managed to detect some disabled or unfit recruits who had passed at the recruiting stations, but enough slipped through to prompt Colonel Mackenzie's plea that no more men with malformed feet be sent to the 24th Infantry. In 1884 Colonel Edward Hatch asked for the immediate discharge of Norman F. Carter, who had served previously in the 24th Infantry and in Hatch's own 9th Cavalry but had been discharged both times for medical disability. This time, Hatch wanted Carter discharged for fraudulent enlistment.[9]

Most soldiers, black or white, enlisted for the first time when they were between the ages of eighteen and twenty-five. The average age of white recruits in 1881 was twenty-six, while that of blacks was twenty-three. After Samuel L. Woodward became a captain in 1887, he told the 10th Cavalry's Colonel Benjamin H. Grierson that his new company contained "nearly three fourths recruits and three fourths of them are boys. Of course it is good material to work on, but it takes lots of work to discipline and make soldiers out of a lot of boys." Woodward was a Civil War veteran whose regular army commission dated from 1867, and who had been in the army since before most of his young recruits were born.[10]

During the late nineteenth century, the army maintained three recruit depots: one for cavalry at St. Louis Barracks (later at nearby Jefferson Barracks) and two for other branches, one of them in New York Harbor (first on Governor's Island and later David's Island) and the other at Newport Barracks, Kentucky (later at Columbus Barracks, Ohio). The depots served mostly as holding pens and, by the 1890s, as initial training camps for the recruits until an order came from the Adjutant General's Office to dispatch a draft, which might number from a few dozen men to more than a hundred, to a regimental headquarters, where the men would be assigned to companies. When the time came to send some men to one of the black regiments, the Adjutant General's daily special orders usually instructed the Superintendent of the General or Mounted Recruiting Service to "forward all disposable colored recruits," thus effectively cleaning out the depot. Another draft would not be possible until a sufficient number of black recruits had arrived.[11]

At the depots, black soldiers first encountered the military form of segregation, which they would endure throughout their service in the regular army. Placed in separate recruit companies, usually under the supervision of white noncommissioned officers, the new men received instruction in the duties and responsibilities of soldiers. A few black noncommissioned officers helped train recruits, but not at all the depots and especially not during the early years. Black recruits usually lived and drilled in separate companies, although a civilian visitor observed in 1890 that black and white recruits at the David's Island depot "occupy the same dormitories, march and drill together, and mess together." The commanding officer told him that close interracial contact had caused little friction.[12]

A recruit's stay at the depot varied, depending on the season of the year, on regiments' need for replacements, and on military exigencies in the West. By enlisting at an office of the Mounted or General Recruiting Service, soldiers indicated the branch in which they wished to serve, but the army did not allow them to pick a regiment. After a few weeks at the depot, a man would be assigned to a draft and leave, usually for a post in the West. Except for those who lingered at the depots for several months, most recruits were untrained when they joined their regiments. At the depots, they may have learned their right feet from their left and the rudiments of drill, but they remained ignorant of the knowledge that would turn them into soldiers.

When a recruit arrived at regimental headquarters, he was assigned to a company—which often meant another journey, sometimes of several hundred miles—in which he usually spent the balance of his enlistment. Companies fielded baseball teams, subscribed to magazines and newspapers, and took up collections for charitable causes. Many of the affidavits supporting a veteran's pension application came from members of his old company; residential segregation assured that many black veterans lived near each other. The members of a company constituted a soldier's most immediate circle of friends and comrades.

Some men eased their introduction to military life by enlisting along with relatives. When three 10th Cavalry recruits named Pumphrey arrived at Fort Stockton in 1882, their company commander told Colonel Grierson that they "must have been descendents [*sic*] of some large footed family . . . , and will be very useful in wearing out all the large sized boots at this post." Still, the Captain quipped, what his company needed was "a little more recruit and not so much foot." Two of the Pumphreys liked the army and served three enlistments, going home to Baltimore each time before signing on again. There were at least two pairs of relatives in other companies of the 10th Cavalry in that year, and the Kellums of Accomac County, Virginia, had three representatives in the 9th.[13]

In the black regiments, the men's backgrounds made for even closer relations than were common in the rest of the army. Many of the men came from the rural South, perhaps with a brief interval of city life just before enlistment. Most often they had worked as farmhands or unskilled laborers. More than two thousand veterans of the U.S. Colored Troops joined the new regiments at the outset, and sergeants with more than twenty years' service continued to make their influence felt well into the 1890s. A common past and the veterans' presence must have eased many men's transition from civilian to soldier. When a new man arrived in a black company he was, in a very real sense, not a complete stranger to the others with whom he would serve.

Limited by education, training, and the social and economic barriers raised by American society, few black men in the nineteenth century had advanced much beyond the status of unskilled laborers. The new regiments' need for artisans often became desperate. Officers, particularly in the cavalry, continually complained that their regiments and companies could not function without skilled workers. Enlistment of trained men was clearly necessary if the army expected black soldiers to perform the same tasks as whites. Throughout these decades, requests for skilled recruits poured into the War Department from the black regiments (as, indeed, they did from white regiments), but the army achieved only limited success in providing them.[14]

Preparation of the accounts, lists, reports, and rolls that made possible the army's day-to-day operations often threw the officers of black regiments into fits of despair. The work had to be done, but few enlisted men had the education to do it. In 1877 Colonel Grierson had to ask for extra candles for his 10th Cavalry clerks at Fort Concho because there was not "sufficient clerical labor to perform the duties required by day light and frequently the adjutant and clerks are required to work late at night." When regimental headquarters and four companies of the 25th Infantry served at Fort Snelling during the 1880s, the commanding officer complained that he could not find enough clerks to handle all the paperwork and began to employ a few convicts from the military prison there. By 1895, though, company muster rolls showed that nearly every company in the four regiments had a company clerk, and several had men detailed as regimental clerks and post librarians besides. Thirty years after Emancipation, the effects of a generation of schooling were becoming apparent in the army.[15]

Beside clerks, the black regiments needed literate, experienced noncommissioned officers. The duties of sergeants and corporals demanded an ability to understand orders, give clear commands, and prepare reports. The Adjutant General frowned on requests for skilled recruits and warned recruiting officers against promising prospective soldiers a sergeant's or corporal's chevrons (selection of noncommissioned officers was a company commander's prerogative). At times, though, the special needs of the black regiments demanded attention. In 1874 Adjutant General Edward D. Townsend responded favorably to Captain Francis S. Dodge's request for selected recruits (four potential noncommissioned officers in addition to a blacksmith, a clerk, a shoemaker, a tailor, and a trumpeter) for his company of the 9th Cavalry, remarking that "exceptions have to be made for colored regiments." Townsend's remark was not a statement of policy, but the War Department sometimes bent the rules to help officers in the black regiments secure good noncommissioned officers.[16]

Construction and maintenance work at military posts suffered continually because of the black regiments' shortage of artisans. The lack of a glazier prompted the 25th Infantry's Colonel George L. Andrews to transfer Private Henry Johnson from Company G at Fort Hale, Dakota Territory, to Company I at Fort Snelling, Minnesota. Johnson's services were "absolutely necessary," Andrews wrote, "and as there is no enlisted man here, competent to do the work, nor civilian obtainable, even if there were money with which to pay him," Johnson spent the last nine months of his enlistment at Fort Snelling.[17]

Tending horses demanded special skills too. In the 9th and 10th Cavalry, lack of blacksmiths, farriers, and saddlers often meant poor care for horses and tack. In 1875 Lieutenant Byron Dawson complained that his 9th Cavalry company had been without a blacksmith for nearly two years, and as late as 1886 Captain Patrick Cusack's company of the same regiment had been unable to get a qualified blacksmith for more than six months. Lieutenant Colonel John W. Davidson responded to recruiters' inability to supply the necessary craftsmen by ordering one noncommissioned officer from the 10th Cavalry companies at Forts Richardson, Griffin, and Concho in Texas to report to regimental headquarters at Fort Sill, Indian Territory, for instruction as farriers by the regiment's veterinary surgeon.[18]

The army needed trained men for other important tasks as well. Food preparation required cooks and bakers. Bread—along with beans, coffee, and meat—was a staple of the military diet. In 1881 at Fort Supply, Indian Territory, a white soldier of the 4th Cavalry had to be detailed when officers could find no men there among the companies of the 24th Infantry who were able to bake bread. The next year, the commanding officer at Fort Hale complained that the absence of a competent baker in the 25th Infantry garrison deprived the men of good, edible bread.[19]

Playing music was one of the few occupations open to black men that required abilities beyond brute strength, and enough musicians usually enlisted to supply the regiments with bandsmen. When a shortage did occur, though, officers made special efforts to find them. The army needed printers and telegraph operators too, especially at regimental headquarters. Since few black men, and virtually no black recruits, had these technical skills, officers had to train men in these jobs after enlistment. In 1877, 10th Cavalry bandsman Edward H. Harris was the only man at Fort Concho with "any knowledge whatever of printing," Colonel Grierson complained, "and the only work that can be done by him has to be superintended by an officer." Private James Richards of the 24th Infantry tried to transfer in 1890 from his company in Arizona to the Presidio of San Francisco for a Signal Corps course in telegraphy, but he received orders instead to report to regimental headquarters at Fort Bayard, New Mexico, where he would find plenty of opportunity to practice.[20]

Since army uniforms came in only four sizes, they often needed alterations, and every company was supposed to include a man who had been a tailor in civilian life. Few tailors, though, could be found in the black regiments. In 1878 the Superintendent of the Mounted Recruiting Service told a company commander that only one black tailor had enlisted during the previous eight years. Black soldiers often had little better luck at finding civilian tailors. In 1889 Company E of the 9th Cavalry went so far as to advertise for a tailor in the *Army and Navy Journal.* Racial prejudice kept some civilians for working for black soldiers. A white tailor who worked for Company D of the 25th Infantry quit in 1890 because of repeated remarks by his friends that he was "working for niggers—eating with niggers—and sleeping with niggers." In white regiments, "skilled labor and tradesmen can be found competent to be detailed as Tailors . . . , while in the colored troops this is impossible," as Captain Owen J. Sweet reminded Colonel Andrews when he reported the incident.[21]

Lack of opportunity in civilian life meant that few black men came to the army with occupational skills. Army generals ignored this fact, though, and expected regiments made up mostly of farmhands and unskilled laborers to accomplish the same tasks as regiments that drew on all the trades that were open to white men in nineteenth-century America. Special training programs would have helped, and the army might have made extra effort to induce skilled black workers to enlist, but the overpowering dictates of the annual budget prevented specialized recruiting. That the army did not adopt these plans does not mean that military leaders purposely discriminated against the black regiments and cared little whether they included intelligent, trained men. Throughout these decades, white regiments needed more skilled men too, and the Adjutant General's Recruiting Division files contain hundreds of requests for soldiers with specific talents. While the army's policy was clearly shortsighted, the pressures of tradition, tight budgets, and the very real shortage of black skilled workers throughout the country all prevented recruiters from supplying the black regiments with craftsmen.

Many officers, given a choice, might have preferred to bar blacks from the army, or at least to integrate the regiments, rather than continually face the problem of maintaining four all-black regiments. The army had difficulty in attracting enough fit white recruits to keep the regular force near authorized strength without having to worry about four regiments with racial requirements. But just as whites did not rush to enlist as long as civilian jobs were available, neither did blacks. Few regular regiments recruited up to, or maintained, full strength for very long. In many years, the flow of recruits failed even to match the normal loss from death, desertion, and discharges. Moreover, the army's inability to keep a substantial number of men beyond the first enlistment compounded its failure to attract enough recruits in the first place.

Even diligent recruiting officers could scarcely be expected to disguise the hardships of military service. Certain types of men—youths in search of adventure, the unemployed, those wanted by the law, and paupers— had always been easy marks for recruiters, but except during nationwide economic depressions, widespread knowledge of the army's drawbacks kept many from enlisting. A great number of black men, though, lived in constant financial and social insecurity. Limited job opportunities in civil life should have driven many of them into the army; yet, while the four black regiments represented about 9 percent of the army's author- ized strength, in most years black men made up only about 5 percent of the total number of recruits.[22]

The black regiments' strength varied from year to year. By March 1872 the 24th and 25th Infantry had reached authorized strength. Within three years, though, both regiments had lost half their men. All recruit- ing was suspended throughout most of 1874 after a rush of unemployed men driven by a nationwide economic depression brought the army sud- denly to its maximum authorized strength. Early in 1875 the colonels of both regiments warned that more discharges would further reduce the size of their commands, Andrews noting that in six months the 25th Infantry would be reduced to fewer than 300 men. Colonel Joseph H. Potter told Adjutant General Townsend that by fall more than 250 men in the 24th Infantry would be eligible for discharge. Both colonels hoped that at least one-fourth of the men would reenlist but urged Townsend to send sufficient replacements for, as Andrews observed, rigorous serv- ice in Texas severely taxed the slender resources of his command.[23]

In 1875 the army alleviated the manpower shortage in an inverted way by reducing the strength of infantry regiments to five hundred men, but that August both the 24th and 25th Infantry were still more than fifty men under strength. Brigadier General Edward O. C. Ord, command- ing the Department of Texas, joined the chorus for more men, report- ing Colonel Potter's claim that the 24th Regiment would average thir- teen men to a company by the end of September. The Adjutant General could only remark that "colored recruits . . . enlist very slowly."[24]

Throughout most of 1876, the black infantry regiments remained about one hundred men below strength. The bitter political battle that erupted the following year, when Democrats gained control of the House of Representatives for the first time since before the Civil War, resulted in failure to pass a military appropriations bill, and lack of funds forced the army to suspend all recruiting for most of 1877. That November, after the politicians had agreed on a compromise measure, Assistant Adjutant General Thomas M. Vincent told the superintendents of the General and Mounted Recruiting Services to recruit diligently for the black regiments.[25]

In late 1878 the colonels of the 24th and 25th Infantry once again reported that their regiments were dangerously understrength. Colonel Andrews noted that some of his companies mustered fewer than 10 men fit for duty and that the largest had only 21 men. He asked that "measures may be taken at an early day to fill the regiment to at least 375 men, and if possible to fifty men per company," which would have increased the 25th Infantry to maximum strength. Andrews reminded Adjutant General Townsend that officers of the 24th and 25th Infantry had enlisted 434 men in Memphis, Nashville, and Paducah between July 1870 and May 1871. These figures must have impressed Townsend, for he recommended to General William T. Sherman that the regimental system of recruiting be tried again. Sherman agreed to "any practicable method for securing enough recruits," and in early December Andrews and Potter received orders to open offices in Memphis and Nashville. Regimental recruiting went on for most of 1879 until an outbreak of yellow fever shut down the 24th Infantry's operation and a shortage of funds ended efforts by the 25th Infantry. While the two stations were open, though, regimental officers managed to enlist 195 men in less than a year.[26]

Responsibility for enlistments in both regiments reverted to the General Recruiting Service in late 1879. For the next three years, the 24th and 25th Regiments remained near full strength. In November 1880 officers of the General Recruiting Service received orders "that no more enlistments should be made for colored infantry, . . . both regiments being up to their organized strength." Recruiters could waive this restriction "only in the cases of exceptionally good men." Richard C. Drum, Townsend's successor as adjutant general, halted recruiting for both regiments again the following September, when they once more reached maximum strength. In order to keep them within the authorized limit throughout most of 1882 and 1883, Drum usually restricted enlistments to veterans who reenlisted within a month after discharge.[27]

For the next fifteen years, the 24th and 25th Infantry had no difficulty in keeping their companies within the fifty-man limit. Although
some new recruits arrived each year, a high reenlistment rate helped the
regiments keep up their strength. The limited number of vacancies
meant that recruiters could take care to enroll only the best men. Besides,
dwindling job opportunities for black civilians during the last quarter
of the century, as the United States industrialized and all-white labor
unions drove black artisans out of the skilled trades, may have forced
more young black men to consider the army as a career.[28]

Of the two cavalry colonels, Grierson was more vigorous and active
than Hatch in badgering the War Department to provide his regiment
with enough men. While Hatch complained occasionally about manpower shortages, he seems to have resigned himself to making do with
whatever replacements the 9th Cavalry received from the Cavalry Depot.
Grierson, on the other hand, kept up a constant fire of demands, pleas,
and proposals on the subject of recruiting.

In 1876, after nine years in the Indian Territory and Texas, the 10th
Cavalry numbered just over half of its authorized strength. As a remedy,
Grierson proposed detailing three regimental officers to recruit especially for the 10th. He alleged that indifference and prejudice on the
part of Mounted Service recruiters kept black men from enlisting. "The
present manner of recruiting for the colored regiments is ineffectual,"
he wrote, because "a large majority" of recruiting officers "are prejudiced
against and feel no interest in these organizations, their only desire being
to have them mustered out of service." Grierson did not document this
serious charge, but insisted that regimental officers, "who are free from
this prejudice and who feel an interest in their work," made the best
recruiters.[29]

Just one week earlier, Congress and army headquarters had taken
steps that would bring the 10th and six white cavalry regiments up to
strength while leaving the 9th, two white cavalry regiments, and all
infantry regiments, black and white, in the lurch. In mid-August, six
weeks after news of the battle of the Little Bighorn reached Washington, Congress passed an act "to increase the cavalry force" by assigning
100 enlisted men to each company of "such regiments of cavalry as may
be employed in existing Indian hostilities" as well as others that "may
require same." Five white cavalry regiments campaigning against the

Sioux on the northern plains fell into the first category; the 10th Cavalry, with its companies scattered at nine posts across Texas, fell into the second along with the 8th Cavalry on the Lower Rio Grande. Under the new law, these regiments could be assigned a maximum of 1,202 enlisted men apiece. The 9th Cavalry in New Mexico and two white cavalry regiments in the Military Division of the Pacific—regions that had been relatively quiet for a few years—remained at an authorized strength of 845 men each. And since the "act to increase the cavalry force" kept the army's overall strength at 25,000 enlisted men, the difference came out of the infantry regiments, all of which suffered alike.[30]

Adjutant General Townsend might have granted Grierson's assertion that the recruiting system was faulty, but the claim that "a large majority" of recruiters allowed their indifference to interfere with their duty was impossible to prove. Nevertheless, Grierson's attack brought immediate results. General Sherman approved his request, and Townsend issued orders for three officers of the 10th Cavalry to enlist men only for their regiment. They concentrated on the Border States, and for a few months in early 1877 one of them recruited in Cincinnati, establishing his office as close to the city's black neighborhoods as possible. By March enough men had enlisted to bring the 10th up to strength, and regimental recruiting ceased. Fortunately, the recruiters managed to find enough men before political disputes in Washington ended in the failure of that year's army appropriation bill, which shut down all recruiting until nearly the close of the year.[31]

Meanwhile, a large number of discharges had greatly reduced the 9th Cavalry. At the beginning of 1876, after the regiment's move from Texas to New Mexico, its strength was almost equal to that of the 10th Regiment, but a year later it mustered only 538 troopers to the 10th's 800. The Santa Fe *Daily New Mexican* remarked that the 9th's "dwindled down" companies could hardly spare enough men to perform routine duties at their stations. "Our little commands take the field," the editor wrote, "fight gallantly against impossible odds, and at best can gain a costly victory." Southwestern editors usually praised Hatch and his efforts to provide military security and condemned Washington bureaucrats and politicians who seemed blind to western needs. Even staunchly Democratic editors in Texas opposed plans advanced by Democrats in Congress to reduce the strength of the army.[32]

The War Department's efforts to fill the black regiments, while not always successful, show little evidence to support claims of discrimination in the recruitment of black regulars, the personal prejudices of some officers notwithstanding. Only with larger budgets could more have been done to attract black recruits. Official encouragement and closer supervision might have improved the efficiency of the General and Mounted Recruiting Services' officers. The Adjutant General could have detailed recruiters from all four of the black regiments every year, and permanent recruiting stations in Memphis and Nashville would have brought in more black recruits. While the army may be faulted for not adopting these measures, it did not initiate special programs to raise men for equally depleted white regiments. It was the army's entire system of recruiting (along with its low standard of pay, food, clothing, and housing) that failed, not its specific response to the black regiments' need for men.

While commanding officers contended for recruits, black regulars themselves increasingly helped overcome the manpower shortage. Although their total numbers remained small, a much higher proportion of black soldiers than of whites decided to reenlist after their first term of service. Several hundred even stayed for more than two enlistments, for some black men found greater rewards in the army than they would have in civilian life. As late as 1880, the 25th Infantry's Company G had four privates who had served in all-black Civil War regiments from Kentucky, Massachusetts, North Carolina, and Ohio. By the 1890s the four black regiments contained a higher proportion of veteran soldiers than the army at large. In 1895 all of the sergeants in Company B of the 24th Infantry had more than twelve years' continuous service, and one was in his sixth enlistment, representing twenty-eight years in the army.[33]

Men with records like Corporal John H. Baily's were not uncommon in the black regiments. Baily first enlisted in July 1863 as a private in the 4th U.S. Colored Infantry. In 1891 he retired from the army, having been a sergeant in the 25th Infantry for twenty-three years. Baily's career was the subject of a regimental order on the day of his retirement; his company commander thought that reenlisted veterans were "well nigh indispensible in the great good they do the service." Veterans like Baily contributed greatly to the efficiency of the black regiments, serving as teachers and examples for the younger soldiers.[34]

These 9th Cavalry non-commissioned officers' service totaled more than 150 years when this photograph was taken at Fort Robinson in 1889 on the occasion of Colonel Hatch's funeral. Standing (from left): First Sgt. George Wilson (first enlistment, 1873); First Sgt. David Badie (1867); First Sgt. Thomas Shaw (1866); and Sgt. Nathan Fletcher (1867). Seated (from left): Chief Trumpeter Stephen Taylor (1868); Sgt. Edmund Mckinzie (1866); Sgt. Robert Burley (1868); and Sgt. Zekiel Sykes (1866). Burley, Shaw, and Taylor were Civil War veterans. *Courtesy Special Collections, U.S. Military Academy Library*

Few black veterans left any record of why they remained in the army. Perhaps the rudimentary material comforts and security kept some from returning to civilian life. Veteran soldiers, especially noncommissioned officers, enjoyed a considerable amount of prestige and power in their companies; rewards that would have been difficult, if not impossible, for a black man to attain as a civilian. First Sergeant Augustus Smith, in his fifteenth year of service, remarked during court-martial testimony that "I went to my room having some work to do." He referred not only to the paperwork that literate noncommissioned officers handled but also to the privacy of his quarters. The first sergeant was the only man in the company with a room of his own. When third-enlistment Sergeant John F. Ball matter-of-factly told a general court-martial in 1885, "I received a telephone message at 3 o'clock that two of the convicts had made their escape," his statement was one that few men of any color could have made; the telephone had only been invented nine years earlier. Black regulars suffered occasional abuse, both verbal and physical, from officers and infrequent violence from white enlisted men, but incidents like these were common in civilian life too. The black regiments' high reenlistment rate tells as much about the benefits the army offered as it does about race relations in late nineteenth-century America.[35]

In order to receive credit for continuous service, and the dollar-a-month additional pay that went with each reenlistment, a soldier had to sign on within thirty days of his discharge. Men often took advantage of this month-long waiting period to go home, visit family and friends, and sample civilian life before they made up their minds to enlist again. Some found the outside world hospitable and never came back. For others, civilian life gradually lost its appeal, and some veterans returned to the army after spending several years away. Captain Owen J. Sweet reported that one former soldier of the 25th Infantry, King Johnson, thought "that he could do much better in the Army, than in civil life."[36]

Noncommissioned officers received special consideration when it came time to reenlist. Company commanders wanted to keep these able men. Captain Louis H. Carpenter asked permission to reenlist former 10th Cavalry Quartermaster Sergeant Toney Ratcliff, calling him "a good soldier, and . . . an intelligent man," and adding that "it is very difficult to obtain soldiers of this class in the material furnished the colored regiments." When Sergeant Samuel Barnes reenlisted in 1890, the

25th Infantry's adjutant told the War Department that Barnes had served faithfully for twenty-three years. His company commander endorsed the adjutant's letter and gave Barnes a "very good" character.[37]

Veteran privates and skilled men also got special attention to assure their continued service. Private James Otey's position as the only experienced carpenter and wheelwright at Fort Missoula, Montana, the 25th Infantry's headquarters, prompted Colonel Andrews to take a special interest in his reenlistment. Officers also tried to keep qualified schoolteachers, saddlers, blacksmiths, and musicians in the army.[38]

In their search for competent soldiers, officers sometimes reenlisted men with questionable records. The 10th Cavalry's Sergeant Daniel Turner had been a model soldier before a general court-martial sentenced him to six months' imprisonment and a dishonorable discharge for stealing a uniform jacket worth $1.77. Captain Stevens T. Norvell, himself a former enlisted man, allowed Turner to reenlist on the basis of his previous good record.[39]

Many soldiers who were tired of the army refused to listen to their officers' pleas and left the service. Most never returned, and those who did were often frustrated by the army's system of recruiting, which did not guarantee former soldiers assignment to their old regiments. Unless a veteran could afford the fare to his old company's station in the West, he would have to take his chances with the recruit depots. When these men understood the situation, some wrote to their former officers for assistance. Jehu Jones, a former sergeant in Captain Charles B. Gaskill's company of the 25th Infantry, had gone back to New York City after his first enlistment, signed on again at a recruiting office there, and been sent to the depot at Governor's Island. He wrote directly to his old commander, "I have enlisted a gain and desire verry mutch to become a member of your Company if you are willing to have me." Gaskill was willing and succeeded in getting Jones sent to his old company.[40]

Other veterans, though, saw reenlistment as a chance to change companies or regiments. After their discharge at Ringgold Barracks, Texas, in 1875, several men of the 24th Infantry asked to reenlist in the 9th Cavalry. The Adjutant General approved, but added that the men would have to "apply at the station of the company they desire to join." In other words, the army would not pay their transportation costs to a distant 9th Cavalry garrison. Since five companies of the 9th Cavalry were then at Ringgold Barracks, the transfers presented no difficulty. In 1890, 25th Infantry soldier Patrick Ross got permission to reenlist in the cavalry when he agreed to pay his own fare to the 9th's closest station. The War Department had no objection to transfers, so long as they did not cost the government money.[41]

Besides reenlisting in relatively high numbers, black soldiers seldom deserted. Each year the army lost more men by desertion than by any other cause. During the post–Civil War era, with troops of the tiny regular force spread thin in the West, heavy losses in most regiments particularly impaired the army's effectiveness. In 1871, when Congress cut a first-enlistment private's pay from $16.50 to $13.00 a month, one-third of the army's white soldiers deserted, and this problem persisted until the nationwide economic depression that began late in 1873 made military life seem more attractive. Yet through good times and bad, the black regiments always had the fewest desertions in the army.[42]

This fact was widely known. Major Guy V. Henry, promoted into the 9th Cavalry in 1881, boasted to the *Army and Navy Journal*'s readers of the regiment's low rate of desertion. Army officers and War Department officials ventured opinions on why black soldiers did not desert as often as whites. A reform-minded secretary of war, Redfield Proctor, believed that the trend could be explained by most black soldiers' "previous condition in civil life"—in other words, by the limited job opportunities available to them. "To the colored man the service offers a career," Proctor suggested in 1889; "to the white man too often only a refuge." Lieutenant William D. McAnaney of the 9th Cavalry echoed the Secretary's analysis. Black soldiers, he wrote, did not "lose in social position" by enlisting and consequently "do not desert to the extent found in white regiments." It was the same reason that Ranald Mackenzie had advanced twenty years earlier.[43]

The same factors that induced many black regulars to enlist probably also kept them from deserting. For some, the service clearly offered a better existence than they could find as civilians. Another probable reason for the low desertion rate, though, was that the color of a black man's skin made him conspicuous in the West. If he ran, he could easily be identified and caught. At Fort Duncan on the Lower Rio Grande, the population in 1870 was 236 black and 58 white; in the nearby town of Eagle Pass, 1,198 white and 42 black. In El Paso County, Fort Quitman's population was 234 black and 127 white, while the city of El Paso itself had 690 white and 68 "colored" residents (not all black). In 1880, New Mexico's population was 108,721 white and 1,015 black, including the men of the 9th Cavalry and their dependents; ten years earlier, before the regiment arrived, the figures were 90,393 and 172. In 1890, black residents accounted for less than 2.5 percent of the population of any state or territory where black soldiers served. Clearly, any black soldier who attempted to desert ran a great risk of detection and arrest followed by a dishonorable discharge and the usual three-year prison sentence.[44]

Nevertheless, a comparative handful of black regulars did desert, and from time to time their officers speculated about the reasons. Colonel Grierson wrote that enlisted men's low pay made some soldiers think that they could do better as civilians, especially since labor was usually in short supply throughout the West. He also believed, with some justification, that lax recruiting standards allowed the enlistment of "unfit men" who deserted at the first opportunity. Grierson had always favored enrolling only the best men, and his suggestion that "no person should be enlisted who can not furnish undoubted evidence of good character" must have surprised no one. In 1889, while commanding the Department of Arizona, Grierson suggested that in the future recruiters should only enlist men "free from city vices," among which he numbered soldiers' favorite pastimes of drinking, gambling, and whoring.[45]

That same year, Assistant Adjutant General Chauncey McKeever avoided moralizing when he drew up a list of reasons for desertion: "disappointment at the details of the service," employment of troops as laborers without extra pay, inequality of punishments inflicted by courts-martial, oppressive treatment of the men by some officers and non-commissioned officers, and "unnecessary restraints." While McKeever's first and last reasons are vague enough to cover a multitude of causes, most black soldiers who left any record of why they deserted fit into the categories McKeever outlined.[46]

The "details of the service" probably included the incessant manual labor that was apt to be required of any private at every post. In 1883 Fort Concho's commanding officer wrote that "overwork" was a major cause of desertion at that post. The use of troops as construction workers was customary throughout the army, but although some men relished the extra-duty pay, many soldiers hated the practice and had little trouble convincing themselves that they were merely a source of cheap labor.[47]

Some men surely were fleeing from tyrannical behavior when they deserted. In 1883 Lieutenant Charles E. Nordstrom took command of Captain Nicholas Nolan's company of the 10th Cavalry while Nolan went on leave. When Nolan returned, he found morale at a very low level. After speaking to some of the troopers, he told Colonel Grierson that Nordstrom's "arbitrary and unjust treatment" had impaired the discipline of the troop and increased the number of desertions. (During Nolan's nine-month absence, his company had accounted for eight of the regiment's twenty-three desertions.) Since general courts-martial found Nordstrom guilty of abusing soldiers on two other occasions—hitting one man with a club and cursing another in front of the entire company—his exercise of command may very well have caused the deterioration of Nolan's company.[48]

A vicious first sergeant could drive men to desert, too. Nineteen men left the 10th Cavalry's Company C in July 1869, and when some of them were caught and tried, they blamed First Sergeant George Garnett. "He called me a son of a bitch, said I was not fit to be in the service," Sergeant William Gibson testified. Three men reported that Garnett said their mothers "had to do with dogs," a common sexual euphemism. Men told of being kicked and cut with a knife besides traditional punishments like carrying a log or bucking and gagging. During twenty-nine months while Garnett was first sergeant, 32 of the 10th Cavalry's 108 desertions were from Company C.[49]

Garrisons closest to cities often had the highest rates of desertion. Association with neighboring civilians served to remind soldiers of the attractions of life outside the army. In 1880 the 25th Infantry, stationed west of the Pecos River, had a lower rate than the 24th Infantry, serving in the Lower Rio Grande Valley where the men had opportunities for "drink and alliance" with the "loose population" of Brownsville, Laredo, and other border towns. The Rio Grande, besides, was the international boundary, and Mexico always offered a refuge to dissatisfied soldiers stationed there. During the early 1870s, the bimonthly muster rolls of one 9th Cavalry company stationed along the river often remarked that missing men had "deserted into Mexico." Once away from the border, though, the black regiments had the fewest desertions in the army.[50]

While reenlistments and infrequent desertions helped the black regiments maintain their strength, they lost a substantial number of men each year through discharges. After the massive dislocations that occurred from 1869 to 1872, when hundreds of first enlistments ran out all at once, attrition declined eventually to about one-fifth of a regiment's strength per year, a rate set by the five-year term of enlistment. Most discharges were issued for "expiration of term of service," and the overwhelming majority of regulars, black and white, left the army at the end of their first enlistments. Discharges "on surgeon's certificate of disability" and dishonorable discharges by sentence of general court-martial accounted for about one-fifth of discharges in the black regiments.[51]

Physical or mental incapacity was grounds for a medical discharge, whether the disability was incurred in the line of duty or not (discharges for alcoholism and venereal diseases always specified "not in the line of duty" to forestall pension claims). In April 1869 a surgeon wrote that Henry Jenifer of the 40th Infantry was "suffering from syphilis and . . . worthless as a soldier" and ordered his discharge, but Jenifer succeeded in enlisting again five months later, this time in the 9th Cavalry. Slipshod medical examinations and primitive means of identification combined with the isolation of the army's small, widely dispersed garrisons to make fraudulent enlistment easy.[52]

Officers tried to get rid of men whose sexual behavior upset their comrades. "I had noticed for several months a disposition in the Company to treat this man harshly," Captain Sweet wrote about a 25th Infantry soldier whose name and date of enlistment were later erased from the company letterbook, "and had given orders requiring respect and kindness. I now learn that . . . their contempt and disgust [arose] from his vile habit of masturbation. . . . Men in the Company loathe the man, and do not wish to sit by him at the table, or sleep near him, nor serve next to him in the ranks, when possible to avoid doing so." Although Sweet urged that the private be discharged, the erasures in the record make it difficult to trace the further course of this case.[53]

A handful of homosexual incidents resulted in court-martial charges. Richard J. Dickerson, former first sergeant of the 9th Cavalry's Company D, protested that a "clique" of his "enemies" had "laid a scheme to overthrow me" and that Sergeant Richard Miller had bullied three recruits into perjured accounts of homosexual advances because Miller coveted the first sergeant's job. Certainly, witnesses' testimony in the case seems repetitive, and Private Edward L. Baker's statement that Dickerson "caused me to ejaculate in his mouth" sounds as if it may have been coached. But the order announcing the court's decision mentioned merely that the accusations were "too indecent for publication," and Dickerson received a dishonorable discharge.[54]

Through the decades, recruiters had trouble finding enough men for the army, except during economic depressions. In good times and bad, though, black soldiers helped maintain their regiments' strength by deserting rarely and reenlisting often. That hundreds of them found military service appealing is clear, and the decision of many to remain in the army, for whatever reasons, helped form a cadre of experienced soldiers in the four regiments. Many black soldiers, particularly the noncommissioned officers, saw military service as a career. In the tiny United States Army of the nineteenth century, this professionalism did much to establish their reputation and that of their regiments.

CHAPTER FOUR

"A Minimum Number, Which Should Be of the Best"

While the army's cavalry and infantry served in the West, the War Department in Washington, D.C., lobbied to preserve as much as possible of the army's strength. The Department's decision to keep two black infantry regiments during the reorganization of 1869 showed that black soldiers figured in its plans for the future. Throughout the 1870s, though, a succession of economy-minded Congresses tried repeatedly to reduce the army's size. Many of these attempts involved doing away with the black regiments through integration, either because segregation contravened the Fourteenth Amendment or because reactionary politicians saw integration as a way to rid the army of black soldiers altogether. The decade-long debate gave Congressmen, army officers, and civilians a chance to voice their opinions of black soldiers' abilities.

Although Radical Republicans passed much of the Congressional legislation that altered politics and society in the area of civil rights, the paragraph in the army reorganization act of 1866 that called for the establishment of separate black regiments maintained a barrier between the races that had grown during preceding generations. Before the Civil War, the regular army had barred blacks from its ranks; during the war, it accepted no black recruits, although a few slipped into the state regiments of volunteers. Mounting Union casualties in 1862 and the need to draw on this untapped source of manpower, particularly after the Emancipation Proclamation added an antislavery element to the struggle to save the Union, led to the formation of the United States Colored Troops in 1863.[1]

For the first time, the federal government called on black men for military service. They were organized in segregated regiments, though, and except for about one hundred black commissioned officers, they served under the command of whites. A few of the more militant Abolitionists protested the plan of segregation, but for the most part members of the movement did not object. Frederick Douglass was glad that President Lincoln had at least approved the enlistment of black soldiers and accepted the color line as a condition of enrollment. The reorganization act of 1866 continued the practice, stipulating that a number of cavalry and infantry regiments in the regular army would be "composed of colored men."[2]

On several occasions between 1869 and 1891, the War Department and Congress considered proposals intended either to reduce the number of black regiments, to eliminate black enlistment altogether, or to destroy the color line and permit recruits to serve in all branches and regiments regardless of race. The first such proposal came in 1870, as hundreds of soldiers who had joined the four black infantry regiments in 1867 were nearing the end of their three-year enlistments. Many veterans took their discharges rather than reenlist immediately for five years, a longer term mandated by the 1869 army appropriation act. New recruits partly made up this loss by late 1870, but for about six months earlier in the year, the new 24th and 25th Infantry Regiments remained dangerously understrength.[3]

Colonel Joseph J. Reynolds of the 25th, commanding the Department of Texas, watched uneasily as the two regiments' strength dwindled. He believed that not enough men could be enlisted to fill the ranks of both and suggested to Adjutant General Edward D. Townsend that the men of the 25th Infantry be transferred to the 24th while the vacant 25th was "filled with white men." Reynolds made it clear that he offered the suggestion in the spirit of efficiency and economy. The act of 1869 had merely stated that there would be only twenty-five infantry regiments; it had not specified that any of them were to be "composed of colored men."[4]

Although Reynolds may have been ready to curtail the number of black regulars, the War Department was not. Townsend told Reynolds that the General Recruiting Service was making "renewed efforts for the enlistment of colored men" and that "only in the case of failure" would the War Department agree to consolidation of the black infantry regiments. Within the year, regimental recruiters filled the ranks of both regiments.[5]

Between 1874 and 1879, some politicians, supported by allies within the army, tried repeatedly to reduce the number of black regulars. As seceded states were readmitted to the Union, an increasing number of Democrats won seats in Congress. In 1874 voters reacted to a nation-wide economic depression by punishing the party in power, and Democrats swept to a sixty-seat majority in the House of Representatives while Northern and Southern Democrats in the Senate made a formidable coalition. Not surprisingly, the Southern Democrats brought with them into Congress their strong racial prejudices.[6]

To many Democrats, the army represented the power of the victor over the vanquished, and they were determined to harm the service whenever possible. Equally important in arousing Southern members of Congress against the army was their conviction that the Democrats stood an excellent chance of winning the presidential election of 1876. Army officers had served as election officials after the Civil War, and military detachments had policed Southern polls, but if the army could be reduced, Republicans would be hard put to marshal enough troops to oversee the voting.

Among Congressional delegations from the former Confederacy, only the Texans opposed any attempt to weaken the army. They certainly shared their colleagues' distaste for black troops, but the army maintained forts in Texas that not only guarded against Indian raids and Mexican incursions across the Rio Grande but furnished lucrative contracts for beef cattle, firewood, and hay. Political and economic factors played a role in all of the attempts to change the status and numbers of black soldiers.[7]

Another effort to reduce the size of the army began in 1874 during hearings before the House Committee on Military Affairs. The chief witness, General William T. Sherman, refused absolutely to endorse any plan that would weaken the army. Asked about eliminating one of the cavalry regiments, Sherman replied, "I do not believe that you can dispense with a single soldier in those ten regiments." The men of the 9th

Cavalry, he said, "had certainly fulfilled the best expectations entertained by the friends of the Negro people," and the Texas frontier would
be endangered if the regiment was dissolved. Sherman also praised the
10th Cavalry, and while he mentioned the two infantry regiments only
briefly, he opposed their consolidation or reduction.[8]

While Sherman praised the troopers of the 9th and 10th Cavalry,
Brigadier General E. O. C. Ord, who commanded the Department of
Texas, was less enthusiastic about their performance. Ord emphasized
the need to police the Lower Rio Grande, and he complained to the
War Department that the 9th Cavalry was incapable of performing this
duty. In June 1875 he called for reinforcements and asked that "a Regiment of white Cavalry be at once placed at my disposal for service on
the Lower river." At the time Ord gave no reason for his request to
replace the 9th with white troops, but later that year he told a Congressional committee investigating border troubles along the Rio Grande
that "there was a feeling of hostility" between civilians and black troops,
especially among the Mexicans, and the 9th Cavalry's transfer would
lessen tensions along the border. He also told the committee that he
had ordered 9th Cavalry patrols not to cross the river when in pursuit
of Indians or Mexicans. Ord concluded his testimony by claiming that
the depleted size of the 9th's companies and the slow rate of enlistment
reduced the regiment's effectiveness.[9]

Some Texans took issue with Ord. Thomas Lamb, a resident of
Brownsville, Texas, denounced the testimony in a letter to the *Army and
Navy Journal.* Lamb attacked Ord's assertion that the reduced strength
of the 9th Cavalry justified its transfer to another department. While
agreeing that the regiment had trouble getting recruits, Lamb claimed
that this was mainly due to bigoted recruiting officers who refused to
enlist blacks and implied that Ord approved of their practices. John
Vale, deputy collector of customs at Roma, Texas, wrote to Ord that the
troopers of the 9th had shielded him from Mexican bandits on one
occasion and had "given complete protection" to the town. Vale insisted
that the regiment should not be transferred under any circumstances.[10]

Reaction to Ord's comments was overshadowed by a new effort to
reduce the army. In February 1876 Henry B. Banning, an Ohio Democrat who chaired the House Committee on Military Affairs, introduced
a bill that called for the elimination of two cavalry and five infantry

regiments and set the maximum strength of the army at twenty thousand men. The bill said nothing about the black regiments, but Banning soon added a section repealing the 1866 provision for enlistment of black soldiers.[11]

When debate began, Banning, anxious to overcome stiff opposition from many Republicans, declared that the law providing for segregated regiments was "an insult to the race it was meant to compliment." Did not the very existence of such discriminatory legislation demand its repeal, he asked? But Banning's next statement revealed his true intent. Noting the army's difficulty in attracting black recruits, he declared that the few who enlisted were "of such a class that they can not be trusted or made of any benefit to themselves or the country." Banning cited reports written by Lieutenant Colonel Nelson H. Davis, who had inspected black garrisons in Texas, and Chaplain George G. Mullins of the 25th Infantry. Both described black soldiers' character and behavior in highly uncomplimentary terms. Davis mentioned theft among black troops, and Mullins claimed that black soldiers had no idea of discipline or sexual restraint.[12]

By selective quotation, Banning managed to offer a distorted picture. While Davis had reported theft in some black companies, he had found others to be in good order. Banning quoted a report that Mullins had written soon after he joined the 25th Infantry and before he became used to military life and enlisted men's amusements. The chaplain's later reports showed that he had overreacted at first and that closer acquaintance with the men had convinced him that their behavior did not differ greatly from that of white soldiers.

Banning claimed, despite the unfavorable evidence he offered, that repeal of the army's color line would allow enlistment of men regardless of race. Edmund W. Mackey, a white Republican from South Carolina, accused Banning of duplicity and told the House that an "integrated" army would be a segregated army, for few recruiting officers, given the choice, would enlist blacks. Mackey also suggested that few blacks would care to serve in integrated regiments, "subject as they must be to all the prejudices of the ignorant and uneducated men always largely composing the regular Army in time of peace." Mackey concluded that Banning's intention, "under the guise of a worthy motive," was to drive black soldiers out of the army entirely. Nevertheless, the House approved the bill and sent it to the Senate, where it died in committee. Nearly all of the House Democrats voted in favor, although the Texans stood solidly against any reduction in the army's size.[13]

Meanwhile, Banning withheld information that cast doubt on his allegations about black troops. Shortly before the House debate, Adjutant General Townsend had sent him a letter about recruiting. Banning apparently accepted Townsend's remark that it was "difficult to keep the colored regiments recruited" while ignoring the closing comment that the regiments were "now tolerably full." He also asked the Adjutant General and the Quartermaster General about cost differences in mounting and equipping a black and a white cavalry regiment for a year. Neither officer was able to furnish the information, but this did not deter Banning from asserting that black troops were more expensive to maintain than white.[14]

During the presidential campaign of 1876, Congress did not concern itself much with military affairs. In early December, though, a letter from E. K. Davies of Brownsville, Texas, to Senator Benjamin F. Butler raised the question of the black regulars' future again. Davies feared that the Democrats would try to bar blacks from the army by calling for an integrated regular force; "neither the white nor the Colored soldier desire such a thing," he insisted, dismissing arguments advanced by Banning and others who favored the elimination of all-black regiments. If these regiments were sometimes understrength, Davies claimed, it was because "a Good many of the officers on recruiting service are opposed to Colored troops and try all they can to keep them from enlisting," asking black applicants to present "all kind of credentials, also to read and write & c., which they dont require from the white recruits." Although Davies offered no evidence to substantiate his accusations, he hinted that such practices were part of a plot to allow officers to "raise the cry that the Colored Regiments cant get recruits."[15]

Davies alleged that some officers in the black regiments openly sided with Banning's plan for integration. They were ashamed of their present assignments, he wrote, and hoped that the elimination of segregated units would erase the stigma that they believed was attached to service with black troops. Davies had no sympathy for these officers and told Butler "that if a man is ashamed of the way in which he earns his bread he should look for some other means to get a living." In closing,

Davies repeated that he did not oppose the principle of integration but feared that its adoption would do away with black soldiers, except as cooks, servants, and teamsters.

These assertions provoked a controversy between Butler and General Sherman early in 1877. Butler sent the letter to Secretary of War James D. Cameron, remarking that the charges were "worthy of your attention, and investigation." Cameron asked for Sherman's comments and sent a copy of the general's remarks to Butler. Sherman characterized the letter as "simply a libel on the Army." Responding to criticism about recruiting officers, Sherman maintained that Adjutant General Townsend, who supervised enlistments, was "by nature & conviction the advocate of every lawful Right and interest of the Freedmen."[16]

Sherman also voiced his own ambivalent opinions on the value of integration and the abilities of black soldiers. "The Blacks are a quiet, kindly, peaceful race of men," he wrote. "The experiment of converting them into soldiers has been honorably & in good faith tried in the Army of the U.S., and has been partially successful, but the Army is not and should not be construed a charitable institution. Congress limits its numbers for financial reasons, and we must get along with a minimum number, which should be of the best." Sherman closed by recommending that the army should abolish its color line, just as the navy had a century before. "Contact and usage would obliterate prejudice of race," he predicted, "and all Regiments would be alike."

This reply did not satisfy Butler, who challenged the General's description of black troops in another letter to Cameron. Butler declared first that Sherman could not speak with authority, for he had never commanded black troops during the Civil War or in the West. Butler, on the other hand, had had considerable experience with black soldiers and civilians during the war and told Cameron that they were a "docile, temperate, rugged race of men, that can live on little, bear privations and . . . seem to me to be the very men for soldiers in time of peace; and if well disciplined good machines, as soldiers are, in time of war."[17]

Sherman, to whom Cameron sent a copy of this correspondence, reacted sharply to Butler's comments. The army was no place for docile soldiers, he declared. "We want and must have men of muscle, endurance, will, courage, and that wildness of nature that is liable unless properly directed to result in violence and crime, to combat the enemies of civilization, with whom we have to contend." Although Sherman believed that white men were better suited for such tasks, he declared his willingness "to take black & white alike on equal terms." Sherman always tried to avoid political involvement and, while he preferred white troops, his closing remark that integration was "certainly a fairer rule than the present one of separating [black soldiers] into distinct organizations" showed more of a faith in human equality than a hope that integration would drive all black troops out of the army.[18]

The issue arose again that October when Senator Ambrose E. Burnside called for the removal of all "color restrictions" on enlistments. His bill marked an important change in the attitude of members of Congress, particularly of Republicans. Apparently, Representative Mackey's claim that integration would, in fact, bar blacks from the army could not prevail against the logical argument that segregation violated the principles of the Fourteenth Amendment and the civil rights laws. Burnside seems to have believed that integration was the only policy consistent with the doctrine of racial equality enshrined in Reconstruction legislation.

The Senate did not consider Burnside's bill until April 1878. Meanwhile, the Military Affairs Committee heard a great deal of testimony for and against the continuation of all-black regiments. Because the committee convened to investigate affairs on the Texas-Mexican border, its members looked closely into the possibility, first raised by General Ord, that the presence of black soldiers along the border exacerbated tensions there. Asked why all four black regiments served in a region where they supposedly threatened the peace, General Sherman replied that black troops were better suited to the hot climate of the Southwest, an opinion common among nineteenth-century white Americans. He told the committee that the black troops "have done admirably, better than I had reason to expect they would do, and we are well satisfied with them." Sherman also said that they "stood up to their work as well as white troops" and praised "their courage and their fidelity," although he did admit his preference for white troops.[19]

Most of the questions that committee members put to Lieutenant General Philip Sheridan concerned black troops' efficiency. Sheridan said that he did not know whether the shortage of skilled mechanics in the black regiments kept them from repairing buildings or other necessary chores, for he had only seen the troops at inspections, where they "appeared well enough." Congressman Edward S. Bragg mentioned the lack of educated noncommissioned officers in black regiments and asked Sheridan if it would not be better, because of the "ignorance and inability" of blacks to perform clerical tasks, to consolidate the black regiments and furnish them with white noncommissioned officers. Sheridan opposed the consolidation of regiments but favored complete elimination of the army's color line. He admitted that many black regulars were uneducated but suggested that this could be avoided by refusing to enlist illiterates. Asked about relations between black soldiers and civilians, Sheridan replied that to the best of his knowledge, residents along the Rio Grande mingled "very readily with the colored troops."[20]

The next witness, General Ord, began by asserting that black regiments needed twice as many company officers as white regiments because of the workload imposed by the high rate of illiteracy among the enlisted men. Ord also declared that black enlisted men had "no idea of self-government or of the management of things for themselves," but he blamed these shortcomings on their Southern plantation background. He described some as "very effective" soldiers, while others "were rather indifferent." Ord did not blame the soldiers, though, and insisted that additional officers could correct the problem. "With proper care and proper discipline," he said, "they make good troops."[21]

Lieutenant Colonel John S. Mason, acting assistant inspector general of the Department of Texas, alleged that black soldiers were "of little or no use on the Texas frontier." Frequent contact between them and "Mexicans . . . [who] are generally of the lowest order, part Indians," led to "great demoralization" among the soldiers, who patronized "dancehouses and gambling houses" where there were "a great many lewd women." Asked if white soldiers also sought out low amusements, Mason replied, "Yes, but not to so great an extent." He suggested transferring all black troops to another department or eliminating "the distinction of color in these regiments." Mason told the committee that black troops took as good care of their equipment as soldiers in the white regiments he had inspected.[22]

Colonel Henry B. Clitz of the 10th Infantry disagreed with Mason. Clitz had commanded several "mixed" garrisons in Texas and told the committee that black troops were more costly because "they are not self-sustaining; they have no mechanics, no clerks, [and] very few of them know how to read and write." He insisted that black troops took poor care of their equipment, which they often lost or damaged unless closely supervised by their officers. This alleged carelessness did not prevent Clitz from praising their "pluck and dash" in battle, but he could not bring himself to offer an unalloyed compliment and immediately remarked that they were "not so reliable even in that respect as white troops."[23]

Three officers of the 24th Infantry appeared last before the committee. Captains John W. Clous, Lewis Johnson, and Henry C. Corbin challenged all the accusations leveled against their regiment and maintained that it was "as good and efficient as a good many white regiments." Johnson claimed that the lack of color prejudice among Mexican residents along the border improved black soldiers' morale rather than "demoralizing" them. The officers' only adverse remarks related to the quality of recruits. Clous and Johnson both agreed that the best men had enlisted immediately after the Civil War and acknowledged that some of the recent recruits made poor soldiers. None of the three commented on integration, consolidation, or the possible elimination of blacks from the army.[24]

When the Senate met to consider his bill, Burnside announced that although there was "a division of opinion in the Army," Sherman, Sheridan, and Ord favored integration. While the generals had argued in practical terms that integration would improve the recruiting system and make it easier to keep all regiments at authorized strength, Burnside preferred to dwell on the moral virtues of his bill. He told the Senate "that the colored man should be allowed to enlist in any arm of the service he may choose, if he is . . . a suitable man, and that he should be assigned . . . to the corps to which he is best suited and in which his services will most conduce to the public good." After further debate, Burnside agreed to modify the bill so that it simply ordered the War Department to fill the four existing black regiments without regard to color and allowed the enlistment of qualified black men in any branch of the army. The Secretary of War and General Sherman supported this simplified version.[25]

Other senators raised the old argument that integration would segregate the army completely, for recruiters would not enlist blacks without specific orders. Existing legislation, they insisted, while contrary to the Fourteenth Amendment, at least guaranteed black men a place in the military establishment. Senator James G. Blaine recalled that in 1866 Congress had thought it wise to maintain segregated units and suggested that consideration of Burnside's bill should be indefinitely postponed. The Senate voted for postponement, with Democrats casting nearly two-thirds of the votes in favor, thus opposing integration in any form even though support of the bill would have been an expedient way to force blacks out of the army altogether.[26]

The issue of integration remained dormant for several months after the defeat of Burnside's bill, but in January 1878 the House Committee on Military Affairs reported out a bill that called for reduction of the army from 25,000 to 20,000 men but contained no provision for disbanding the black regiments. Chairman Banning's reversal on the matter of black troops came as a surprise, for the committee had read the opinions of several officers who favored the elimination of all-black regiments. "Slavery does not beget military virtues," the 10th Infantry's Major Thomas M. Anderson had written. Anderson opposed further enlistment of black soldiers and told several committee members that "the colored men have not habits of thrift, economy, or an adequate idea of responsibility, and they are with few exceptions, thieves and liars." In the end, Banning's bill failed. General Sherman's remark that it was a plan for the "disorganization" of the army was probably an important influence. Other officers, too, strongly opposed any bill that would decrease the size of the army.[27]

The defeat of Burnside's and Banning's bills and the silence in response to Sherman's call for integration of the army marked the last significant efforts to reduce the size of the army or to change the status of black soldiers. From time to time after 1880, members of Congress introduced bills that called for the reduction or consolidation of regiments, but almost without exception these proposals received a single reading and then died in the Military Affairs Committee of the Senate or the House. Tepid Congressional interest and virtually unanimous military opposition to these measures showed that by the end of the 1870s, legislators and the War Department had agreed that the army's basic structure would remain unchanged and that the four black regiments would continue to make up about one-tenth of the entire force.

Beginning in the 1870s, soldiers devoted more time to markmanship, and regiments sent their best shots to department and division competitions. Representatives of several regiments, some of them wearing marksmanship badges on their collars, appear in a photograph probably taken at the Bellevue, Nebraska, range during the late 1880s. *Courtesy U.S. Military History Institute*

While Congressmen heard testimony and debated, a few black enlisted men managed to sidestep the army's color line because of their exceptional abilities. Whenever the question arose whether the army reorganization act of 1866, which authorized the enlistment of blacks, barred them from serving anywhere but in the designated regiments, the answer was the same: the law did not explicitly confine blacks to those regiments, but the War Department interpreted it to mean that blacks could not serve elsewhere in the army.[28]

This interpretation of the law received a good deal of publicity when a black college graduate, William H. Greene, tried to enlist in the Signal Corps, one of the most specialized of the army's staff bureaus. Besides supervising field communications and operating military telegraph stations, the Signal Corps maintained government weather stations throughout the United States. Applicants had to pass examinations in science and mathematics.

In 1884 Greene wrote to Brigadier General William B. Hazen, Chief Signal Officer (and former colonel of the 38th Infantry), asking to take the examination. Hazen, although he may have been impressed by the fact that Greene was the first black graduate of the City College of New York, told him that the law allowed blacks to enlist only in the four line regiments. It was "an expression of the public policy of the National Legislature, which I am not at liberty to violate," Hazen added.[29]

Alexander S. Webb, president of City College, a Civil War general and one of Hazen's West Point classmates, told Secretary of War Robert T. Lincoln about Hazen's reply. Webb claimed that Hazen had misinterpreted regulations and pointed out that blacks had been admitted to the United States Military Academy. Lincoln replied that although the law stipulated that four of the army's regiments were to be composed of "colored men," it did not necessarily bar black soldiers from service in the staff bureaus: the Signal Corps and the Medical, Ordnance, Quartermaster, and Subsistence Departments. The army had promoted its first two black staff sergeants from service in the line regiments in the late 1870s. Lincoln also told Webb that Greene would be allowed to take the Signal Corps examination.[30]

News of the exchange between Webb, Lincoln, and Hazen became public, and Hazen wrote to Lincoln denying newspaper allegations that he had refused to examine Greene on racial grounds. He reminded

Lincoln that although he, Hazen, had been one of the first men to command a black regular regiment, he did not believe that it was his duty
to challenge army policy regarding black enlistments. (Hazen did not
seem to be aware that the army had begun accepting staff sergeants
from the black regiments a few years earlier.) He told Lincoln that Greene
had scored high on the entrance examination and would soon join the
new Signal Corps class of instruction at Fort Myer, Virginia. Lincoln had
the last word on the matter; to avoid further complications, Hazen noti-
fied recruiting officers that the Signal Corps would reject no applicants
because of "color, or . . . African descent."[31]

After Greene completed the course of instruction (standing second
in a class of eight, of whom two failed), orders sent him to the Signal
Corps weather station at Pensacola, Florida. The sergeant commanding
the station claimed that he did not know Greene's race until he reported
for duty. When Greene arrived, though, the sergeant refused to accept
him and complained to his superiors that white residents of the town
would not tolerate the presence of a black soldier. To avoid a further
confrontation with Lincoln, Hazen put Greene in charge of the station
and ordered the sergeant's return to Washington to answer charges of
disobeying orders. Despite objections from the Pensacola's residents,
Greene remained on duty there until late 1885, when he was transferred
to the weather station at Rochester, New York. He served at Rochester
until June 1887, when a special order discharged him "without character" for undisclosed offenses.[32]

Like the Signal Corps, the Hospital Corps belonged to one of the
army's staff departments. To become a hospital steward, a noncommissioned rank roughly equivalent to commissary, ordnance, or post quartermaster sergeants, an applicant had to demonstrate ability in arithmetic,
penmanship, pharmacology, the use and care of medical equipment, first
aid, and cooking. Beginning in 1887, soldiers wishing to join the Hospital Corps as privates, whose role was chiefly to administer first aid and
carry stretchers, had to pass an examination given by the post surgeon to
assure "general intelligence and aptitude" as well as literacy.[33]

Thirty-seven enlisted men from the black regiments managed to transfer to the Hospital Corps during the new organization's first six months.
Seventeen, or roughly half of them, were young soldiers in their first
enlistment, and of these, twelve had been able to sign their enlistment

papers; that is, they had at least some schooling before joining the army. Among the older, reenlisted men, the literacy rate was exactly the opposite: twelve had marked their first enlistment papers with an "X." This was hardly surprising in the case of a fifth-enlistment man like the 9th Cavalry's Private George Johnson, whose service went back to 1867, or the 24th Infantry's Sergeant Edward Gibson, who first enlisted in 1869. All twelve, though, had learned to sign their names by the time they joined the Hospital Corps. This tiny sample only hints at the effectiveness of the army's school system and the educational opportunities that had opened up for black people in the years since emancipation. In some instances, though, the education clearly did not take. Private Isaiah Johnson had not been able to sign his name when he joined the 9th Cavalry in 1884. When he reenlisted five years later, it was in the 24th Infantry, and his shaky signature suggests a possible reason for his having left the Hospital Corps.[34]

The literacy requirement kept some men out of the Hospital Corps altogether. When Private Anson Myers of the 24th Infantry applied for a transfer in October 1887, his company commander noted that Myers was "a good cook and a good nurse, and except that he does not read and write is competent to perform all the duties of a Hosp[ital] Nurse and Cook." Myers's illiteracy kept him out of the Hospital Corps, but he reenlisted anyway a few months later in the 25th Infantry.[35]

Hospital stewards and commissary, ordnance, and quartermaster sergeants were all part of the army's staff bureaus. These noncommissioned officers were assigned to military posts to provide continuity in administration, for there were not enough officers in the bureaus themselves to furnish a commissary, quartermaster, and ordnance officer for each fort and the regimental officers who performed these duties sometimes changed frequently. Like the men of the Hospital Corps, staff sergeants came from the line regiments and had to pass an examination. Since the number of staff sergeants was fixed by law, successful candidates often had to wait, sometimes for years, for an opening.

Congress established the grade of commissary sergeant in 1873, and although the act authorized one for each military post or subsistence depot, the first two promotions from the black regiments did not come until 1879. Soon afterward, the *Army and Navy Journal* printed a letter from Fort Stockton, Texas, the home at that time of four companies of the 25th Infantry and two of the 10th Cavalry. The writer, who signed himself KNIFE, noted that "not more than two or three colored soldiers" had ever received promotion to staff noncommissioned officer, "although several have been made to perform [the duties] from time to time, with no other compensation than that of a private soldier." The men who had held these temporary, local appointments had done well and deserved the extra pay that went with sergeant's stripes. KNIFE wrote that surely the 1,700 enlisted men in the four black regiments could furnish more qualified candidates for these jobs. "I must say," he concluded, "that there is either too much prejudice against the colored man in the Army, or else his officers are not sufficiently interested in him to see that the men are justly rewarded." KNIFE hoped that black soldiers would find officers "of influence and sufficient interest" to nominate them for noncommissioned rank in the staff departments.[36]

Whether KNIFE's letter found sympathetic readers at the War Department is uncertain. He had surely found the best forum for expressing his views, though, a weekly newspaper with subscribers in Washington, D.C., and at every military post in the country. Some readers in Washington must have agreed with the general tenor of KNIFE's remarks, for five years later, when another act of Congress established the grade of post quartermaster sergeant, the general order that published the news throughout the army provided for eighty of the new sergeants "at the rate of two from each regiment, provided there are fit applicants from said regiments who deserve the position." There had been no such clause in the 1873 General Order about the selection of commissary sergeants, and the *Army and Navy Journal* soon noted that three men from the black regiments were on the list for promotion.[37]

Staff noncommissioned officers were most likely to be freeborn northern men. David B. Jeffers, one of the first two commissary sergeants, was born in Indiana and enlisted in Cincinnati. He had been a sergeant in the 24th Infantry and was serving as the 9th Cavalry's regimental quartermaster sergeant at the time of his appointment. Benjamin F. Davis, born in Pennsylvania, had served in the 32d U.S. Colored Infantry (USCI), a Philadelphia regiment. After two enlistments in the 10th Cavalry, he joined the 9th and had been its sergeant major for nearly five years when he became a post quartermaster sergeant in 1885. Richard Anderson was an exception to the rule. A Missourian, he had joined the regular army in 1866 and became a sergeant in a company of men who, like himself, had enlisted at Baton Rouge directly from the 65th USCI. After his first enlistment, Anderson had returned to St. Louis and tried civilian life for nearly a year before enlisting again and becoming first sergeant of his old company. These men were typical of the twenty-five noncommissioned officers from the black regiments who were able, eventually, to join the staff departments. It was a step that conferred better pay and long-term assignment to one post and a private dwelling, however shabby, instead of the crowded and sometimes dangerous communal life of the barracks.[38]

Strict qualifications, though, prevented most black soldiers from filling these positions. Remarks like "education quite limited" and "general fitness . . . good, as regards honesty & faithfulness, but poor as regards executive ability" abound in the reports of examining boards. One board commented that, while 10th Cavalry Sergeant Edward L. Baker was "at present only fairly qualified, . . . he is capable of becoming an expert thoroughly efficient post quartermaster sergeant." In response to General Hazen's defense of the color line and his refusal to enlist William H. Greene, one officer argued for integration in a letter to the *Army and Navy Register*. He cited the capable services of two black commissary sergeants he had commanded. The Secretary of War's annual report for 1888 mentioned that seven black sergeants were serving in the Ordnance Department and three in the Quartermaster Department.[39]

Regimental officers often made a special effort to see that deserving soldiers received these appointments. One who recommended 10th Cavalry First Sergeant David Haskins for promotion to ordnance sergeant wrote that Haskins had "served the regiment long and faithfully and has pushed himself forward from the position of an uneducated slave to that of a most efficient and very reliable First Sergeant." Even though black staff sergeants were few, the presence of even a handful of them showed that the army would promote qualified black soldiers to positions of considerable responsibility.[40]

The army's color line worked in reverse too. No white men could enlist in the black regiments, although some tried. Most were detected at once, but a few managed to get past recruiting officers. The *Army and Navy Journal* noted in 1881 that a man who "appeared to be white" had arrived at 9th Cavalry headquarters with a draft of recruits. "Upon being questioned he admitted it, and said he had served one enlistment in a white regiment, and, being a sober man, was tired of doing guard and other duties for men who got drunk—particularly pay days—and in the colored regiments there was no trouble in this respect." During their first fifteen years in the regular army, black soldiers had earned a reputation—whether deserved or not—for sobriety.[41]

Ulysses Dolby, a white man of dark complexion, passed as a black man in an attempt to take what he thought would be "the shortest route to appointment & promotion as a noncommissioned officer." Dolby joined the 10th Cavalry in 1887, but after two and a half years with no promotion ("I was not aware . . . that being a musician & printer would keep me 5 years in the ranks") he gave up hope, revealed his identity, and asked for a transfer. After Dolby's mother wrote to the War Department and verified his claim, adding that her son was "made the butt of many unpleasant remarks on account of his color," the Adjutant General arranged his transfer to the 6th Cavalry.[42]

An experiment in quasi-integration that the black regiments did not take part in was the organization of all-Indian companies at army posts near reservations during the early 1890s. With the avowed intention of "civilizing" the Indians, the army would give these young men something to do and funnel money into the reservations' economies. All eight of the white cavalry regiments and more than a dozen white infantry regiments in the West recruited an additional company of Indians, each from a different reservation—a step made necessary because many of the recruits were married and would not leave their families and because of old intertribal enmity.[43]

In January 1891, though, the army's commanding general, John M. Schofield, confided to the Secretary of War: "Whether it would be advisable to include the 9th and 10th Cavalry and the 24th and 25th Infantry, I am not now quite certain, but would like to make further inquiry upon the subject. I have never yet heard of any difficulty arising between the colored troops and the Indian scouts with whom they have served. . . . Yet, it may be possible that the colored troops would not exercise altogether the same beneficial influence over the Indians as would the white troops." Whatever "inquiry" Schofield made, the black regiments added no all-Indian companies. The idea of keeping black soldiers and Indian soldiers apart did not work, though, for men of the 10th Cavalry and 25th

Infantry in Montana shared garrisons with all-Indian companies of the 1st Cavalry at Fort Custer (recruited from the Crow tribe) and the 8th Cavalry at Fort Keogh (Northern Cheyennes) until the army disbanded the Indian companies in 1895 and gave up the experiment.[44]

Not all policy that affected the status of black soldiers was discussed and formulated at as high a level as the War Department and Congress. Post commanders in the West, free from close supervision, could observe or ignore the army's color line to varying degrees. During three decades in the West, depending on time and place, black troops were as likely to serve at a racially mixed post as at an all-black one, and interracial contact was unavoidable during guards, fatigues, and other duties.[45]

Nevertheless, some officers tried to limit that contact as much as possible. In 1867 Colonel Grierson narrowly escaped a court-martial when he challenged the right of a senior officer, the 3d Infantry's Colonel William Hoffman, to order companies of the 10th Cavalry off the parade ground at Fort Leavenworth, Kansas. Hoffman claimed that the troopers were not yet well-enough trained to take part in ceremonies, but Grierson believed that Hoffman's racial prejudice lay behind the exclusion. The 10th Cavalry's Captain George A. Armes recalled the incident in his memoirs: "I . . . was ordered to attend dress parade with my company, and after forming a line close to the white troops, General Hoffman came down and ordered them at least ten or fifteen yards to the left, saying I must not bring my nigger troops so close to his white ones. General Grierson immediately took up for the supposed right of his darkies, and he and General Hoffman seemed to have it pretty hot for a while." Grierson's decision to march his troops on parade one day while Hoffman was away from the post caused Hoffman to prefer charges against him, but the War Department quietly dropped the matter.[46]

At least one other commanding officer even tried to minimize contact between the races during routine military duties. Frances Roe, the wife of a lieutenant who had been commissioned in the 24th Infantry out of West Point but managed to transfer into the white 3d Infantry during his three-month graduation leave, noted with distaste the "daily mingling" of white and black members of the post guard at Camp Supply, Indian Territory, in 1872, which she said, "often brings a colored sergeant over a white corporal and privates." When Mrs. Roe and her husband returned there after an eight-month absence, she was pleased to learn that a new post commander had insisted on separating white and black troops on guard duty. Officers and men of the 10th Cavalry companies at the fort deeply resented the change, she wrote, but they could do little about it but sulk.[47]

Some white enlisted men shared Mrs. Roe's disgust at having to associate with black soldiers, and at least one of them could not bear the humiliation of losing an interracial contest. The most soldierly, best-drilled member of the post guard served as orderly to the officer of the day, who commanded the guard. Companies competed for this honor and put forward their best men. When the 10th Cavalry's Lieutenant Richard H. Pratt was officer of the day at Fort Arbuckle, Indian Territory, in 1868, he had to choose among men of his own regiment and those of the white companies at the post. Pratt inspected each man thoroughly and eliminated all but one black trooper and one white infantryman. Both were evenly matched in appearance and drill, and Pratt was at a loss which to choose. Finally, he ordered the men to remove their shoes, and when he saw that the cavalryman had on clean socks, selected him as orderly. Pratt recalled in his memoirs that the white soldier "could not face the ridicule of his comrades at being beaten by a Negro" and deserted soon afterward.[48]

Violent confrontations between men of different races were rare and mostly involved only small groups. In 1869 white and 10th Cavalry soldiers at Fort Wallace, Kansas, got into a brief fistfight, but the post surgeon reported no serious injuries. In 1877, when the 9th Cavalry band, on a visit to Fort Stanton, New Mexico, moved into one end of the barracks occupied by Company H of the 15th Infantry, one trooper suffered "a number of bruises and cuts" in an interracial, interregimental brawl. Later that night, one of the infantrymen was "struck on the forehead with a large stone" and died in a coma the following month.[49]

The most serious racial violence occurred at the Jefferson Barracks, Missouri, cavalry recruit depot in 1888, following the expulsion of two prostitutes from the post one afternoon. The women, one of whom was white, had been secretly brought in by some of the black recruits. When the women refused to accommodate some white recruits, the jealous men reported their presence to the post commander. That night, the disgruntled blacks punished the whites. Many soldiers from Jefferson

Barracks spent their off-duty hours at a saloon called Kelly's Ranch, and it was there that black recruits attacked the whites with stones, clubs, and bottles. The violence lasted only a short while, and only two of the whites were injured badly enough to be admitted to the post hospital. While similar volatile situations may have existed in other mixed garrisons, they never erupted into anything more serious than infrequent fights between small groups of soldiers. Evidence in scores of general courts-martial showed that most violence involved men in the same company—men who worked, ate, washed, and slept together and could therefore annoy each other far more than most outsiders, of whatever race, could.[50]

Accommodation was far more common than antagonism and violence. While examples of discrimination, segregation, and clashes between white and black troops drew official attention, soldiers far more often met without hostility or disagreement. Military necessity, more than any other factor, brought the two races together. Most officers insisted that white and black troops share equally in all military duties, and interracial contact in the performance of routine duty was the normal order of things. At mixed garrisons, the daily guard was integrated and often included black noncommissioned officers. Soldiers drawn from the several companies at a post performed fatigue without regard to race. Patients of both races recovered in the same hospitals and were attended by both black and white nurses, detailed from the companies at the post. Although the hospital stewards (noncommissioned medical officers) were overwhelmingly white, there was an occasional black hospital matron, like Amanda Baylor, who served at Fort Griffin, Texas, for two years in the late 1860s. The black regiments were represented on divisional and departmental rifle teams, whose members traveled together and competed against other teams. And at the end of some soldiers' service, neither the military prison at Leavenworth, the Soldiers' Home in Washington, D.C., or the General Hospital at Hot Springs, Arkansas, observed a color line.[51]

Outside the immediate area of military duty, it was not the army's responsibility to dictate or supervise the social relations of soldiers. Eager to use their limited leisure time to full advantage, white soldiers found it unprofitable to discriminate against talented blacks. They formed racially mixed athletic teams and minstrel groups. Although some friction developed between men of the 9th Cavalry and the 17th Infantry when judges at the 1889 maneuvers declared the infantrymen the victors in a sham battle, a newspaper reporter observed that when the picnic afterward began, "all then became amiable," and the troops mingled freely and talked over the recent exercises.[52]

When a company changed station, its arrival at a new post often prompted members of the garrison to invite the men to a dinner. Thus, 4th Cavalry troopers welcomed a company of the 10th to Fort Apache, Arizona, in 1885. After dinner, a 10th Cavalry sergeant thanked his hosts "for the cordial welcome and the friendship extended." A corporal of the 10th then commented on the harmony that surrounded him during the meal. He referred to the "past struggles" of the black soldier and was "glad that prejudice was giving way to good sense." The corporal also predicted, "the time was near at hand when men would be judged for what they were worth without regard to race, color, or creed." The writer who described the dinner in a letter to the *Army and Navy Journal,* obviously a white man, undercut his own regiment's hospitality by referring to the speakers as "Sergeant Snowball" and "Corporal Shinbones." This incident illustrates the general fairness that prevailed on the institutional level against a background of individual bigotry. It may be, too, that the 4th Cavalry had offered the dinner in a spirit of soldierly comradeship, and that the writer thought that the 10th Cavalry corporal's "race" speech was out of place.[53]

Soldiers of the 7th Infantry hosted a dinner when the 9th Cavalry's Company M arrived at Fort Washakie, Wyoming, after an eight-hundred-mile march from Kansas. One trooper, signing himself AFRICANUS, wrote to the *Army and Navy Journal:* "We cannot say too much in commendation of the spirit that prompted this preparation by one company of troops to refresh their comrades in arms upon their arrival from a long and tiresome march, albeit they are of a darker-hued skin." Dinners like this "give the lie to the oft-repeated assertion that white and colored troops won't affiliate together," he concluded.[54]

Despite enlisted men's off-duty social contacts and the admission of black soldiers to the staff departments—Medical, Ordnance, Quartermaster, Signal, and Subsistence—after 1878 the army's color line remained virtually intact during the post–Civil War era. In the black regiments, the social divide between officers and enlisted men was a racial barrier as well. Soldiers in the West found that they could bend the line somewhat, but there were always officers—and their wives—who insisted that it be observed, even at the most isolated post.

CHAPTER FIVE

"So Long a Service in the Wilderness"

The black regiments had their origin in the army's need for men. Soldiers had always been in short supply. During the 1830s, troops at half a dozen widely spaced posts had tried to patrol a "permanent Indian frontier" that stretched from Minnesota to Louisiana. The annexation of Texas in 1845 and the expansion of United States territory to the Pacific made the notion of permanence obsolete. By the mid-1850s, army posts stood scattered throughout the western states and territories. After the Civil War, the army abandoned some of these and established others, so that by the early 1890s more than 150 of them had dotted the map of the West. Called variously "barracks," "camp," "cantonment," or "fort," many guarded transportation routes like the Oregon and Santa Fe Trails or the stage road across Texas from San Antonio to El Paso. As railroads extended westward after the Civil War, the army built new posts along the Union Pacific and Kansas Pacific lines. Indian agencies on reservations that belonged to recently or potentially hostile tribes in the Plains and Southwest usually had soldiers stationed nearby. Troops also patrolled the Mexican border from a string of posts along the Rio Grande.[1]

If the West had been more thickly settled by the end of the Civil War, Congress might never have considered enlisting black men in the regular army. During the Congressional debates of 1866, several members asked whether black soldiers would help reconstruct the South or serve in the West, well removed from contact with white civilians. Several Democrats expressed the fear that black soldiers, once armed and given authority, might take advantage of their new position to intimidate whites. In Louisiana after the Civil War, the enlisted men of some regiments of U.S. Colored Troops were not allowed to buy their rifles at the time of final payment and discharge, as was customary throughout the volunteer force in black and white regiments alike. Experience in handling weapons had equipped blacks to secure their rights by force, especially in parts of the country where their numbers were large and their subjection brutal. If whites had always used violence to ensure black people's servile status, what would happen once blacks were in a position to retaliate? Fortunately for fearful politicians and their constituents, military exigencies in 1866 and the years that followed kept black soldiers far removed from the more settled parts of the country.[2]

By late 1867 more than half of the army, including four of the six black regiments, manned stations in the West. The other regiments remained in the former slave states. Generals in the South, not wishing to complicate their delicate task further, seem to have decided to minimize contact between white civilians and the two black infantry regiments in that region. During 1867 the 40th Infantry served in the Carolinas, including one company at Charleston, but by early 1868 all ten companies of the regiment had concentrated at Goldsboro, North Carolina, where they remained for the next year. Like the 40th, the 39th Infantry manned several stations during 1867, but by 1868 its companies were divided between Ship Island, Mississippi, twelve miles offshore in the Gulf of Mexico, and Forts Jackson and St. Philip, in the delta sixty-five miles below New Orleans. With the consolidation of regiments in 1869, the 40th moved to Louisiana to join the 39th as the new 25th Infantry, which sailed for Texas the following year.[3]

The other black regiments served in the West throughout the post–Civil War era. For three decades, they represented more than 10 percent of the army's strength in the West, and at some times and places they constituted more than half of the available force. By the time of the Spanish-American War, black regulars had served in nearly all the western states and territories. In sending black troops west, military planners considered which posts they should garrison, whether the regiments should serve near cities, and whether black and white soldiers should man the same stations.

The army never formed an inflexible policy, and military planners seem to have based the black regiments' assignments on the army's needs and the cost of troop movements rather than on racial considerations. In 1867, companies of the 9th Cavalry and 41st Infantry, organized in Louisiana, moved to Texas by ship and marched inland to stations west of the Pecos River and along the Lower Rio Grande. Farther north, the 10th Cavalry and 38th Infantry moved from Fort Leavenworth, Kansas, to posts along the line of the Kansas Pacific Railroad and the Santa Fe Trail, with half of the 38th's companies following the trail all the way to New Mexico. Economy and the need to protect transportation routes clearly underlay moves like these.[4]

Allegations that the black regiments suffered in these southern assignments came mostly from their white officers. The reason for this was that while an enlisted man might go to a different regiment when his five years were up or leave the army altogether, a junior officer could count on spending twenty-five or thirty years in the same regiment. By the mid-1870s, officers in the black regiments complained that the army consistently sent them to the least attractive posts and that this reflected an army-wide bias against black troops.[5]

From the end of the Civil War to the mid-1880s, Texas was the scene of incessant military activity, and more troops served there than in any other state. The 9th Cavalry and 41st Infantry were the first black regulars to arrive, but after 1870 all four black regiments served in Texas. By 1880 the 24th and 25th Infantry had been there for a decade, and some companies of the 10th Cavalry for more than five years. Although the 9th Cavalry moved to New Mexico late in 1875, it had been in Texas for more than eight years. Yet three white regiments, the 4th and 8th Cavalry and the 10th Infantry, served longer in the state. Their officers, too, had begun to complain about their long stay in Texas and to ask for a change of station.[6]

That some white troops seemed to have been banished to Texas did not deter officers of black regiments from insisting that the army had singled them out for unfavorable treatment, but a 10th Infantry officer made it clear that his regiment had served in Texas just as long. He did not deny that the black troops deserved a move but demanded that "some consideration should be shown to our white as well as colored regiments in the probability of change." Brigadier General Edward O.

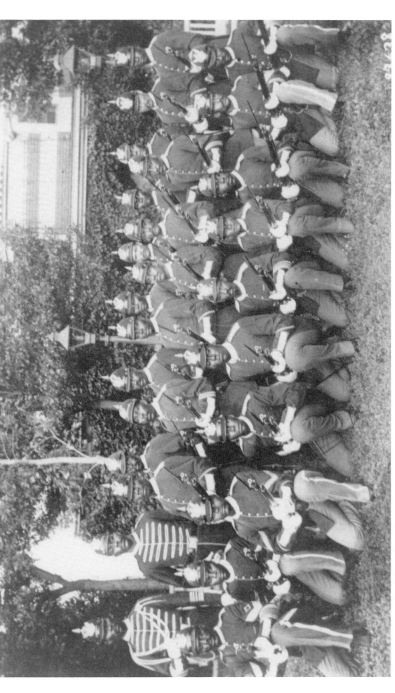

Shade trees and gaslights at Fort Snelling Minnesota, headquarters of the Department of Dakota, contrast sharply with the bare parade ground at Fort Apache (see page 103). Charles Reddick (kneeling, far left) had been first sergeant of the 25th Infantry's Company I for more than ten years when this picture was taken in the mid-1880s; he and Musician George Griffin (standing, far left) had both served continuously since they joined the 39th Infantry in October 1866. Of the nine men kneeling beside Reddick, seven show stripes on their sleeves for previous service and three of the privates look as if they were in their third or fourth enlistments. *Courtesy National Archives*

C. Ord, commanding the Department of Texas, suggested in 1878 that "it would increase the efficiency of the army to let regiments take their turn in the vicinity of civilization. . . . I refer especially to the Tenth Infantry and the colored troops."[7]

Ord and the regimental commanders kept up their agitation. In March 1880 Colonel George L. Andrews of the 25th Infantry wrote to the Adjutant General seeking a change of station for his regiment after ten years' service in Texas, adding his opinion that long service in one department demoralized both officers and men. General William T. Sherman conferred with War Department officials, who approved his suggestion to move the 25th to the Department of Dakota in the spring of 1880. Sherman thought that the 25th "deserved a change." The *Army and Navy Journal* called Sherman's action "judicious" and "beneficial" to the men and officers of the regiment and to the entire army, adding that "the turn of the 24th infantry comes next, as no doubt the programme for change will include all the colored regiments so far as the necessities of the service will permit." Tight budgets always limited troop movements. The men of the 24th Infantry and 10th Cavalry watched as companies of the 25th prepared to leave Texas and waited impatiently for orders that would send them to a new department.[8]

In the late summer of 1880, the 24th Infantry received its orders to move to the Indian Territory. Commenting on the transfer, the *Army and Navy Journal* remarked that the regiment "had been so long in Texas that they have become almost a part of the soil." In October, General Ord declared that the change would benefit both officers and enlisted men, "some of whom are depressed, if not demoralized by so long a service in the wilderness." Although Ord was gratified by the transfer of the infantry regiments, he did not fail to mention the 10th Cavalry, which was also nearly due to move. He praised the 10th's "long and severe" service "in the field and remote stations" and asked whether "it is not time that [they] should have relief by a change to some more favored district of the country?"[9]

War Department officials may have agreed with Ord's comments, but they decided to keep the 10th in Texas for several more years. In 1884 Ord's successor, Brigadier General David S. Stanley, asked that the 10th Cavalry be replaced by another regiment. He remarked that the 10th "had become localized to such an extent" during its stay in Texas that its discipline and morale had been impaired—probably a reference to Colonel Benjamin H. Grierson's land and cattle interests in the neighborhood of Fort Davis, the regiment's headquarters. The gradual cessation of Indian hostilities in Texas allowed the War Department in 1885 to send the 10th Cavalry to join the hunt for Apache raiders in Arizona.[10]

The cost of moving entire regiments from one department to another was the reason that troops stayed put for so long. In 1880, when the 1st Infantry, then stationed in Dakota, changed stations with the 25th, General Sherman estimated the cost of the move at nearly $60,000. Short funds had kept him from pulling the 25th out of Texas the year before. A tight-fisted Congress kept a firm hold on the federal purse strings, and the War Department always had to fight for its annual appropriation.[11]

Less obvious were the racial attitudes that dominated the thinking of officers who determined regimental assignments. Department commanders may have preferred to segregate their troops, and the army's dual task in Texas during Reconstruction had allowed them to do that. While white residents insisted on the necessity of defending the state's borders to counter Indian raids from across the Rio Grande as well as from reservations in the Indian Territory, Congress burdened the War Department with responsibility for administering Reconstruction programs. In 1866 General William E. Strong of the Freedmen's Bureau painted a grim picture of affairs in Texas: "In the interior of the state, . . . away from the influence of Federal troops and Federal bayonets, . . . where the citizens have but little fear of arrest and punishment for crimes committed, I assure you there is a fearful state of things; the freedmen are in a worse condition than they ever were as slaves." While Texas governors urged repeatedly that regular forces be sent from the settled eastern counties of their state to the frontier, Major General Philip H. Sheridan believed that reported Indian raids were merely a ruse to remove troops so that ex-Confederates could terrorize blacks and white Unionists and regain political control. Racial violence became common in Texas; in the spring of 1868 the Ku Klux Klan made its first appearance.[12]

Events in the settled part of the state were of little concern to the 9th Cavalry and 41st Infantry, though. Organized in Louisiana, both regiments went aboard ship at New Orleans and sailed to Texas in the spring of 1867—the cheapest, fastest means of transportation. From Indianola, the 9th Cavalry marched overland to San Antonio and posts west of the Pecos. The 41st Infantry landed near the mouth of the Rio Grande and provided garrisons along the river between Brownsville and Laredo. Both regiments were three hundred miles or more from Austin, the state capital, and even farther from the parts of East Texas where the worst racial violence was occurring. There was no question of either of them having to undertake Reconstruction duties.[13]

Before the 1870s, black soldiers in Texas rarely served at the same station with whites. This pattern began to change as more and more white companies moved to the western part of the state. In 1872 black and white regulars served together at only two posts out of fourteen in the department; by the next year, the number of mixed garrisons had increased to six. The reason was simple: the 4th and 9th Cavalry concentrated near the Rio Grande in 1873 to counter raids from Mexico, occupying six forts instead of twelve, while the 10th Cavalry moved south from the Indian Territory, taking over two posts in northern Texas that the 4th had manned. The cavalry at each post was all black or all white, depending on the regiment; the infantry companies in the garrison might come from any of the regiments, two black and two white, in the department. The army had no consistent policy of segregated duty stations; before it came to Texas, the 10th Cavalry had shared garrisons in Kansas and the Indian Territory with white infantrymen. As usual, military necessity dictated assignments.[14]

Army authorities themselves offered another reason for concentrating the black regiments in Texas and keeping them there: that blacks were better adapted to hot climates, a widespread belief throughout white America. Based on blacks' origins in tropical Africa and popularized in the antebellum era to promote overseas colonization of black Americans, this idea had taken firm hold by the late nineteenth century. In 1874 General Sherman told the House Military Affairs Committee that the 24th Infantry had been in Texas "ever since the close of the Civil War, on the theory that that race can better stand that extreme southern climate than our white troops." It would have been impolitic for generals to tell congressmen that black troops stayed so long in Texas because Congress would not give the War Department money to move them.[15]

Nineteenth-century theory linked disease as well as race with climate. Before medical researchers associated mosquitoes with malaria (thought to be caused by "bad air," as the name suggests), popular belief attributed immunity to black people because of their tropical origins. Army medical statistics, though, told a different story. In the mid-1880s Surgeon General Robert Murray reported that black soldiers suffered from malaria and related ailments at a rate more than 75 percent greater than that of white troops and offered the reasonable explanation that all the black regiments had spent years in "malarious regions"—Texas and the Indian Territory—where 20 percent of the army's total strength reported 50 percent of its malaria cases. Murray's statistics, though, were buried in tables, and by the time they were published the black regiments were scattered from Minnesota to Arizona.[16]

When the time finally came to find another station for the 25th Infantry, Quartermaster General Montgomery C. Meigs discussed the issue with Sherman, who had asked his opinion of transferring the 25th from Texas to Dakota Territory. Meigs explained briefly why he thought Congress insisted on maintaining four regiments of black troops. The reasons had to do with postwar politics, he said, and the only "non-political reason" was "their comparative exemption from the epidemics and other diseases of the Southern coast." As for moving the 25th Infantry north, Meigs remarked, "I cannot but think that orders to Dakota will prove to be the death knell of any colored regiment." He predicted that black men would not enlist to serve in a cold region and many veterans would leave the army rather than face severe winters. The average black soldier's aversion to cold would render the 25th as useless "as an army of Dormice or any other hybernating animals." Meigs believed firmly that while the biological characteristics of black people fitted them to survive in hot climates, "their constitutions will not so well resist the influence of cold." He failed to convince Sherman, though, and within a couple of years the men of the 25th Infantry were skating happily on the frozen Missouri River at Fort Randall.[17]

Throughout the 1880s, officers and men continued to complain that the black regiments received long assignments to the least desirable posts. When the army announced plans to move the headquarters of the Department of the Missouri to Fort Sheridan, near Chicago, Captain John Conline, a nineteen-year veteran of the 9th Cavalry, wrote to the Adjutant General asking to be posted there. He mentioned his company's long service in the West and stated that this was the first time he

had ever requested "what is usually called an agreeable duty station."
Officers in the 24th Infantry believed that because they commanded
black troops, they were "forced to serve at stations remote from civilization" and would never have a chance to serve "at a 'fancy' station," as
one of them wrote to the *Army and Navy Journal* from Fort Bayard, New
Mexico. Some black soldiers held similar views, but an enlisted man
always had an opportunity for change at the end of his five-year term.
When an officer asked 24th Infantry Sergeant Benjamin F. Whitley why
he wanted to reenlist in the 9th Cavalry, Whitley replied that the 24th
"had been too long" in the Indian Territory. His company had been in
the region for more than seven years and at Fort Supply for two and a
half. Whitley's enlistment in the 9th took him to Fort DuChesne, Utah.[18]

In 1891, when Colonel John K. Mizner of the 10th Cavalry heard that
the War Department planned transfers to the plains states for those regiments that had served longest in the Southwest, he wrote to the Adjutant General. "[N]o cavalry regiment in the service has been subject to
so great an amount of hard, fatiguing, and continuous field service in
a southern climate," Mizner protested, "especially during the past eleven
years, in the desert wastes of western Texas, New Mexico, and Arizona."
He pointed out that since 1885 each company of the 10th had served at
San Carlos Agency, which "was one of the most, if not the most, undesirable stations at which troops are serving." He asked that the 10th
receive "as good stations as can be assigned to it" and hoped that "no
discrimination will be made against it on account of the color of the
enlisted men, who have earned just consideration." Regardless of Mizner's
remarks about San Carlos, it was not true that the War Department
ordered an entire regiment to Arizona and kept it there for six years
simply to ensure that black troops served at an unpopular station; until
the 10th's arrival, white troops had always formed the garrison at San
Carlos, and they served at many other "undesirable" posts as well. But it
was finally the 10th's turn to move, and within a year the regiment was
in Montana.[19]

While it was evident that white and black troops alike received assignments to poor duty stations, more than sheer happenstance governed
the assignment of regiments to quiet garrisons in the East. Throughout
the post–Civil War period, the War Department sometimes moved
infantry regiments to stations in the South or on the Great Lakes. There

was no systematized program, though. While only one regiment of cavalry served in the East during the twenty-five years after 1869, seventeen of the white infantry regiments spent a few years there. (It was debatable, of course, whether Fort Snelling near St. Paul, Minnesota, where the 25th Infantry had its headquarters for more than five years, was any worse a posting than Fort Wayne, a regimental headquarters near Detroit.) Although black troops fared no worse in this regard than many whites, racial factors rather than military must have had some influence when the War Department considered the possibility of sending the black regiments east.

One instance occurred in 1879, when Brigadier General Christopher C. Augur, commanding the Department of the South, commented on a plan to transfer the 24th Infantry from Texas to stations in his department. Augur, who had earlier commanded in Texas, called the 24th "an excellent regiment" and was pleased "that it is to have a change from its long and hard service on the Rio Grande frontier; but I doubt if it would find a station at New Orleans or Little Rock agreeable either to officers or men," because of the local residents' strong racial prejudices. He thought that some "restless or drunken person may abuse or insult one or a party of these soldiers in the streets, or elsewhere. In this event there would certainly be trouble, for these troops are easily excited and thoroughly united on any question of insult to their race." Augur thought it unwise to station black troops in the South "until the relations between the two races there are settled upon a firmer and more satisfactory basis than at present" and hoped that the 24th Infantry would go to "healthier and pleasanter stations" than were available in the South.[20]

Major General Winfield S. Hancock, commander the Military Division of the Atlantic and Augur's immediate superior, agreed completely. Instead of mentioning racial considerations, though, he declared that the 24th deserved "a change of *climate*," and suggested that the weather in Louisiana was much the same as that along the Rio Grande. With Augur's and Hancock's opinions before him, Sherman added a short comment for the Secretary of War to consider, pointing out that the 10th Infantry was going to the Great Lakes after ten years in Texas and asking, "Shall one Rule apply to a White Regiment, and another to a Black?" Despite his apparent concern, though, Sherman made no explicit recommendation that either black infantry regiment go to an eastern station and, indeed, seems to have done nothing more to press the issue of equal consideration for black and white regiments with long service in Texas.[21]

The question of moving one of the black infantry regiments east arose again in 1889, when Sergeant Benjamin Brown and Corporal Isaiah Mays of the 24th Infantry won Medals of Honor in Arizona for defending a paymaster's wagon from robbers. The *New York Age*, a black newspaper, commented that such heroism proved the worth of black regulars. Noting that their regiments had served in the West for more than twenty years, the *Age* asked, "Is it not high time to give these faithful soldiers a taste of garrison duty in the East?" An officer of the 24th suggested in a letter to the *Army and Navy Journal* that the "gallantry" of the paymaster's escort might be rewarded by offering the 24th "its choice of stations." If the War Department agreed, the officer went on, the transfer could be made "notwithstanding the prejudices on the part of those to whom they [the men of the 24th] are unknown." The implication of the officer's remarks is clear: fear of angering nearby civilians kept the army from assigning the black regiments to a few years' duty in the East.[22]

There was clearly no official policy that forbade stationing black troops near civilians in the West. At various times between 1866 and 1898, black soldiers served at Brownsville and San Antonio, Texas; Fort Leavenworth, near Kansas City; and posts near Minneapolis–St. Paul and Salt Lake City. While white residents occasionally objected to having a black garrison in the neighborhood, War Department officials considered military demands, and not the wishes of the civilian population, in assigning stations.[23]

Although black regulars occasionally manned some of the worst posts in the West, there is no evidence that the War Department or department commanders adopted policies that sent them to the least attractive stations. Complaints from regimental officers and black enlisted men about the injustice of their assignments were identical in tone and substance to those that flowed into the War Department and the service weeklies from aggrieved officers and men in white regiments. Most regiments moved from one department to another three or more times between 1866 and 1898, and most soldiers, regardless of color, served at more than one post.[24]

While the War Department tended to ignore the biases of the army's civilian neighbors in assigning regiments to departments, several important nonracial factors affected decisions about the composition of garrisons. As a rule, infantry occupied stations nearest to major lines of communication, whether by rail or river. Infantry companies also served at more remote posts, but because of their relative lack of mobility they usually remained in garrison and performed tasks like stringing telegraph line or, if there was timber nearby, operating a sawmill. Cavalry companies took the field when rapid movement was necessary; if they ran out of forage, a few days' marching without oats would break down their horses.

The War Department assigned regiments to military departments; department and regimental commanders assigned companies to posts. Besides a fort's location and the number of barracks and stables it afforded, the possibility of disturbances—either by Indians off their reservation or white invaders of Indian lands, by workers on strike, or by illegal traffic across the long borders with Canada and Mexico—also influenced how many and what kind of troops the department commander would assign. In 1867 there were 138 army posts in the West. As the army's authorized strength dwindled from nearly 55,000 in the late 1860s to 25,000 by the mid-1870s, the War Department tried to compensate somewhat by concentrating troops at posts along rail lines, where they could be supplied cheaply and moved quickly. Nevertheless, General Sheridan reported in 1880 that he had one soldier for every 75 square miles in the Departments of Dakota, the Platte, and the Missouri, and one for every 125 square miles in Texas. The ratio never improved, but by 1893, when the Secretary of War announced that "Indian warfare is virtually at an end," the number of posts had declined to 60.[25]

Soldiers knew from experience that life at the more remote stations could be a waking nightmare. Veterans of the 1860s and 1870s would have hooted at the zealous recruiting sergeant who insisted in 1889 that "an inspection of our western army posts will show good, well kept barracks, with comforts which not a few of our citizens do not enjoy." During the last two decades of the century, some forts did provide a degree of comfort, but most regulars were better acquainted with more primitive quarters. A few of the older posts dated from before the Civil War and stood badly in need of repair. Most of those built since the war were the work of soldier-laborers whose engineering and mechanical skills were often rough and ready. The isolation of many posts, along with perennially small budgets, prevented the army from sending trained mechanics and necessary construction materials.[26]

Most western stations were temporary, to be abandoned when the immediate reason for their existence ceased, and War Department officials saw no reason to spend much of their meager annual appropriation on improvements. Inadequate barracks sometimes forced troops to live in makeshift quarters, in tents, or in buildings intended for other purposes. Because barracks at Fort McIntosh, Texas, were not finished by the time companies of the 9th Cavalry and 24th Infantry arrived in the spring of 1873, the cavalry moved into the storehouse and the infantry took up quarters in the post hospital, while patients bunked "in a hired building . . . in the little dirty town of Laredo, a mile distant." Three years later, the cavalry company was gone and the infantry had moved into the storehouse, making the hospital available to patients and saving the government the cost of renting a building in town.[27]

Many soldiers probably would have elected to live in tents rather than in the barracks at some places where they served. In the early 1870s, the barracks at Forts Clark, Duncan, and Quitman in Texas were in poor condition. Most were built of adobe, and spring rains had caused extensive damage at nearly all of the posts in that state. At Fort Quitman, an inspecting officer found companies of the 9th Cavalry and both infantry regiments living in low-ceilinged adobe barracks with dirt floors and roofs. "In rainy weather the quarters leak a good deal," the inspector wrote, "and are not only uncomfortable from this cause, but very unhealthful—for the water does not cease dropping from the ceiling for some time after the storm, or shower, has passed away." Appalled at such conditions, the inspector concluded that "it is a great evil to keep troops too long at any of these posts . . . where the accommodations are so bad."[28]

Other western forts rivaled the wretched condition of those in Texas. The 24th Infantry's Colonel Joseph H. Potter complained that the cottonwood walls of Fort Supply's barracks were so rotten that a severe storm or even a strong wind would endanger them. At Fort Sisseton, Dakota Territory, in 1888, "miserably lighted, poorly ventilated and overcrowded" barracks housed two companies of the 25th Infantry.[29]

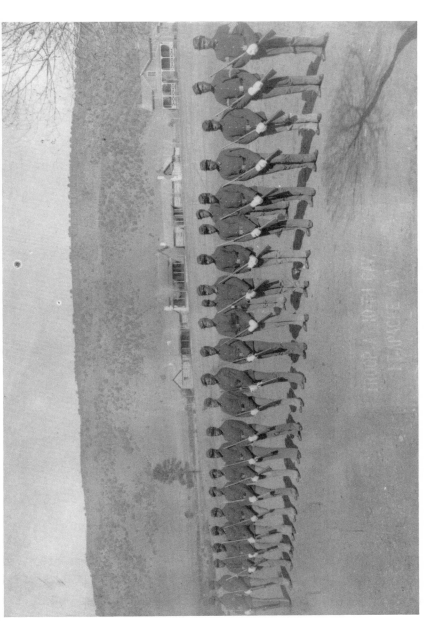

The shadow of a lone tree on the parade grounds suggests the austerity of life at southwestern posts, but the men still wore white gloves for dress parade and guard mount. It took years for the Quartermaster Department to exhaust its stock of Civil War surplus clothing, while it continually experimented with new styles and varying shades and patterns of uniform, which irritated inspecting officers throughout the army. Different colors in the men's trousers show clearly in this 1887 photograph of the 10th Cavalry's Company A at Fort Apache.

Courtesy University of Arizona Library

A bleak landscape and severe climate added to the soldiers' hardships. The post surgeon at Fort Thomas, Arizona, reported a temperature of 105 in the shade during the month of May and pleaded that an ice machine be installed for the use of the garrison. Soldiers at the notorious San Carlos Agency nearby received a supply of ice only once a week, and meat had to be eaten the day it was killed lest it spoil in the intense heat. Leonard Wood, who served there as a medical officer in the 1880s, found that the temperature of the creek that furnished the garrison's water supply was usually above 90 degrees during the day. When they went north, soldiers learned that summers on the plains could be as brutal as anything they had experienced in the Southwest. Companies of the 25th Infantry encountered 95-degree temperatures when they arrived at Fort Hale, Dakota Territory, after ten years in Texas. Northern winters were equally extreme. Ice closed the Missouri River to navigation from early November to early April, stopping most communication with the outside world.[30]

Although department commanders could do nothing about the weather, they did sometimes assign black soldiers to relatively comfortable stations. During the 1880s the army abandoned many of its smaller posts in order to concentrate troops in larger garrisons close to railroads and cities, and the Inspector General's annual reports began to mention substantial improvement in the buildings. Brick and stone had begun to replace adobe, cottonwood logs, and warped lumber. By 1887, 24th Infantry companies at Fort Sill had stone barracks complete with bath and washrooms (the former with tubs and the latter with wash basins for weekly and daily cleansing, respectively). The next year, brick barracks replaced earlier log structures for soldiers of the 25th Infantry at Fort Custer, Montana. The commanding officer called the new buildings "the finest west of the Missouri River." By the 1890s most black soldiers lived at forts that had adequate barracks as well as canteens, gymnasiums, libraries, and recreation rooms.[31]

Throughout the nineteenth century, soldiers provided most of the labor that went into improving the forts where they served. Tight budgets dictated the use of soldiers for construction at army posts. Quartermasters' fatigue parties, for which the men might earn an additional ten or fifteen cents a day, took up a great deal of their time, and most men became as familiar with a pick or shovel as they were with their weapons.

"Us sent to Fort Stockton to guard de line of Texas," former 25th Infantry soldier William Branch told an interviewer years later, "but all us do am build adobe houses." The men could see no justice, though, in doing a civilian's work for a fraction of a civilian's wage. Soldier dissatisfaction with labor details was a major cause of desertion throughout the army.[32]

Much of this labor required only strong backs and minimal skills: work of the sort that most black men performed in civilian life. When the army recruited regiments of U.S. Colored Troops during the Civil War, many officers believed that the intention was to use them as a labor corps in order to release white troops for combat, and many black volunteers did little else but work as laborers. In 1865 General Ulysses Grant recommended the temporary retention of black troops as a well-disciplined source of cheap labor. If the army, through some tacit understanding, had agreed to use black regulars chiefly as laborers, their small western garrisons would have been far from the prying eyes of Radical Republicans. That the army's leaders made no such decision is clear. The army worked its black troops, and worked them hard, but that was the rule throughout the army. Whatever the soldiers' color, infantry companies furnished most of the labor details since the cavalry were more often in the field.[33]

When black regulars first went west, new forts had to be built and older posts repaired. Scarcity of civilian laborers made officers of the 9th Cavalry and 41st Infantry set their men to work rebuilding Fort McKavett, Texas, in 1869. At its peak, construction there occupied more than one-quarter of the men in garrison. In the Indian Territory, 10th Cavalry troopers put up the first buildings at the outpost that became Fort Sill and renovated Fort Arbuckle, which had been abandoned during the Civil War. In time, soldiers learned how to patch crumbling adobe walls and replace warped or rotten woodwork in their barracks.[34]

Often, though, officers in the black regiments complained that their men were only suited for labor and that few had the skills necessary for construction work. Most companies in white regiments included men who had been carpenters, masons, or painters in civilian life. Recruiters' statistics show that few men from the building trades enlisted in the black regiments. Officers claimed that without skilled men, their companies could not carry out the constant repairs that were necessary at every army post.[35]

The shortage of skilled labor often forced officers to ask permission to hire civilian workmen. Sometimes, though, the quartermaster could not find civilians even when he offered to pay the prevailing wage. In the spring of 1890, the War Department ordered extensive repairs at Fort Apache, Arizona, where the garrison consisted of two companies of the 10th Cavalry. Unable to hire civilians and well aware of "the impossibility of finding in the colored troops of cavalry here the mechanics . . . necessary in connection with the work to be done," the commanding officer took the unusual step of asking department headquarters to send a company of white infantry to help with the project.[36]

Despite the heavy demands imposed by construction and maintenance, officers thought of their men as soldiers first, although enlisted men may have doubted it sometimes. Their ability to perform their military duties depended largely on the amount and quality of equipment they received. The supply services—Ordnance, Quartermaster, and Subsistence Departments—operated on shoestring budgets throughout the post–Civil War era, and officers kept a hopeful eye on the appropriation bill's annual progress through Congressional committees and floor debates. Hardly a year passed without some attempt, usually by Southern Democrats, to cut the army's budget.

Given the army's small size and its vast responsibilities, the War Department did not dare to reduce the effectiveness of one-tenth of its force by discriminating against the black regiments in the distribution of weapons and equipment. When the Springfield arsenal began converting muzzleloading infantry rifles to breechloaders soon after the Civil War, the new weapons became available to the black regiments as they were needed. Companies of the 38th Infantry on their way to Kansas in March 1867 received 640 of the newly altered rifles. That June, as the 41st Infantry embarked for Texas, Colonel Ranald S. Mackenzie complained that his men were still armed with the old muzzleloaders. There were no breechloaders waiting for his regiment on the Rio Grande, "and I should much prefer not moving a Regiment in this country, without arms." The next month, "forty-three cases of new arms" for the 41st arrived at Brownsville. The 39th Infantry in Louisiana and Mississippi and the 40th Infantry in North Carolina received their breechloaders by the summer of 1868.[37]

The Ordnance Department handled weapons, powder, and shot, keeping a quarterly record of the arms in each regiment's possession. The 38th Infantry was one of ten infantry regiments that had received the new breechloaders by June 1867. All of these regiments were in the Departments of Dakota, the Platte, or the Missouri—roughly from the Arkansas River to the Yellowstone—covering the main routes to the gold-fields of California, Colorado, and Montana, where there had been bloody fighting with the Plains Indians during and after the Civil War. Regiments in the occupied South, in Texas, and in the Military Division of the Pacific did not receive the 1866 Springfields as quickly. Distribution of the new weapons depended on available transportation and on the troops' immediate need for them, not on the racial composition of a regiment.[38]

During the next few years, the Ordnance Department continued to test several models of breechloading carbines and rifles and metal-cartridge revolvers. In 1871 Lieutenant Colonel John W. Davidson of the 10th Cavalry asked that some of his companies at Camp Supply be supplied with experimental weapons. The cartridge for the Sharps carbine, he explained, "is overloaded by at least ten grains. I have used the weapon frequently . . . , and after the fourth round my shoulder becomes so bruised from the recoil as to prevent further comfortable use of the weapon. This has been the case also throughout the four troops of my regiment." Davidson, in other words, was reporting the men's complaints as well as his own sore shoulder. The Ordnance Department had no qualms about issuing experimental arms to the black regiments; in 1872 two companies of the 9th Cavalry received experimental "new Colt's" revolvers for trial.[39]

When the army adopted the Model 1873 Springfield rifle and carbine and the Colt revolver, the Ordnance Department took more than a year to distribute the new weapons. All companies of the 10th Cavalry, which was concentrated at posts near the Comanche-Kiowa reservation, had their new carbines and revolvers by June 1874. The 10th was one of the first regiments to receive the new carbines because, as General Sherman wrote, it would be among "the first to have a chance to use them." That summer, four companies of the 9th Cavalry, scattered at posts in West Texas, acquired carbines and two companies had new Colt revolvers. Supplies came slowly to the 9th, but no more slowly than they did to the three white cavalry regiments in New Mexico and the Military Division of the Pacific. By March 1875 nearly all companies of cavalry had received their Springfields and Colts.[40]

Although the 1873 Springfield and its modifications remained the army's standard weapon until adoption of the Krag-Jorgenson magazine rifle in the early 1890s, the Ordnance Department continued to test other models throughout the 1870s and 1880s. Company H of the 10th Cavalry received Hotchkiss repeating carbines in 1879, and several companies of the 25th Infantry tried the long-barreled infantry model a few years later. In 1885 Company C of the 25th Infantry used experimental versions of the Lee magazine rifle, and throughout the next year some companies of the regiment used a newly designed pack that the army hoped to adopt for all infantry. Companies of the 10th Cavalry tried the experimental Whitman saddle instead of the regulation McClellan during the early 1880s.[41]

The best-known experiments in which black soldiers took part involved bicycles. By 1895 men of the Signal Corps repairing telegraph lines in Texas found bicycles "more economical than horses" and "just as good . . . , in some cases better." European armies were testing bicycles, and the Japanese had recently used them in Korea and Manchuria. "Put an Army on bicycles and their opponents would be at their mercy if they were not similarly equipped," Nelson A. Miles, the army's new Commanding General, declared. Army officers accompanied by one or two enlisted men had ridden from New York City to Washington, D.C., and from Omaha to Chicago, but by the summer of 1896 the army had not yet tried to put a body of armed men on wheels.[42]

The most persistent exponent of the bicycle's military use was the 25th Infantry's Lieutenant James A. Moss, who led seven men on a 790-mile round trip from Fort Missoula, Montana, to Yellowstone National Park and back in the summer of 1896. Two weeks later, the "wheelmen" served as scouts and couriers for the Fort Missoula garrison on its annual practice march. Private John Findley, an experienced cyclist, was chief mechanic, but every two riders shared "a complete Spalding repair kit." The next year, Moss picked twenty men from among forty volunteers for a 1,900-mile run to St. Louis. Five were veterans of the Yellowstone trip and the rest, "with the exception of five or six, were cyclists of

Cpl. John Williams stands in the foreground as 25th Infantry cyclists visit Yellowstone National Park in August 1896. A group of twenty-two traveled from Fort Missoula, Montana, to St. Louis the following year, but the Spanish-American War and the army's subsequent involvement in the Philippines ended further experiments with the bicycle as a means of moving troops rapidly.
Courtesy National Archives

more or less experience," he reported. "Some of our experiences, particularly while in the sand hills of Nebraska, tested to the utmost not only their physical endurance but also their moral courage and disposition, and I wish to commend them for the spirit, pluck and fine soldierly qualities they displayed." Moss hoped to make a trip from Fort Missoula to San Francisco, but within the year all four of the black regiments were fighting in Cuba. After the Spanish-American War, the army became preoccupied with its new overseas responsibilities, and military cycling never attained the importance for which its proponents had hoped. While interest lasted, though, the 25th Infantry conducted the most extensive field trials of the new equipment.[43]

From the late 1860s through the 1890s, the army continually tested experimental arms and equipment and adopted new models. That the Ordnance Department issued new weapons to black regiments at the same time that white regiments got them shows that the supply services did not ignore the black regiments. And while the Quartermaster Department sometimes failed to provide good horses, it was a problem that affected white regiments and black alike.[44]

Active service was harder on horses than it was on the men who rode them. Department commanders relied heavily on their mounted regiments, and cavalry troopers spent far more time in the field than did infantrymen. Hard service, poor forage, dilapidated stables, beginning riders, and a shortage of veterinary surgeons all helped wear out cavalry horses. These problems were common to all the regular mounted regiments. A lack of blacksmiths, farriers, and saddlers—skilled tradesmen all—especially plagued the 9th and 10th Cavalry.

Horse-purchasing boards in each military department convened to appraise animals that were offered for sale. A typical board included one officer from each of the cavalry regiments in the department—the 4th and 10th Cavalry, for instance, first in Texas and later in Arizona—and an officer from the Quartermaster Department. Colonel Edward Hatch himself was president of the board that bought 101 horses for the 9th Cavalry in 1883.[45]

When the 10th Cavalry's Colonel Grierson commanded the Department of Arizona in 1889, he was responsible for one and a half white regiments of cavalry besides his own, and "nearly one fourth" of the force, he complained, was dismounted. There were only 1,616 serviceable mounts for 2,134 troopers in the department. Congress had appropriated $132,000 for cavalry and artillery horses, of which Arizona got $31,731.21. The chief quartermaster thought that he might be able to buy 200 horses with that much money, "and when these are obtained there will be over 300 cavalry soldiers still dismounted in this department alone," Grierson fumed. The appropriation, he concluded, "is entirely inadequate for the requirements of the service." Problems of quality and quantity were common throughout the mounted branch and not confined to the black regiments.[46]

The army did not cripple one-fifth of the mounted troops by deliberately assigning poor horses to the 9th and 10th Cavalry. Throughout most of the post–Civil War era, these regiments served in the most active departments, and a few of their companies took part in some of the most dramatic actions of those years: at Beecher Island in 1868, at Milk Creek in 1879, and at Drexel Mission in 1890. If there had been a policy of assigning them second-class mounts, the black troopers would not have been able to venture far from their forts.

Yet officers of the 9th and 10th Cavalry complained continually about a lack of serviceable horses. The shortage was not confined to these two units, though; similar complaints came from officers throughout the mounted service. The War Department tried to provide enough mounts but often lacked the money to buy them. In 1871 the Quartermaster General authorized Colonel Hatch to purchase 218 horses for the 9th Cavalry but warned him not to spend more than $100 a head.[47]

Officers were disgusted when they received unserviceable animals after waiting months for remounts. In 1876 the 10th Cavalry's veterinary surgeon recommended the sale of horses that had been sent to three companies of the regiment at Fort Concho, Texas, "as they are utterly unfit for cavalry service." Three years later, Colonel Hatch charged that civilian horse dealers "practiced deception and in a manner not easily detected" by filing horses' teeth in order to conceal their age. Some of the horses suffered from distemper and other diseases as well. An investigation supported Hatch's claims, and a month afterward he got word that the unsound animals would be replaced.[48]

Usually, though, the remounts sent to the 9th and 10th Cavalry were fit and at least no worse than those of white regiments. The 9th Cavalry received new horses when it moved from New Mexico to Kansas in the

early 1880s, and Lieutenant Colonel Nathan A. M. Dudley reported that
"the horses of the command are excellent hardy animals almost without exception, in good, sound condition." Companies of the 9th at Fort
Hays, Kansas, "have a fine lot of horses and keep them well groomed,"
a Hays City newspaper observed.[49]

Improper care could quickly ruin the best cavalry mount. Some officers claimed that black soldiers made poor cavalrymen and treated their
horses badly. After reviewing six companies of the 10th Cavalry at Fort
Davis in 1884, one inspector reported that the men were "inclined to
be harsh with their horses, and . . . altogether too free in the use of the
spur." Most observers, though, found that with proper drill and instruction the black troopers were as good as any in the service. Five years
later, an inspector in Arizona watched all of the 10th's companies "ride
with and without the saddle; . . . at the trot, gallop, and in the charge,
and I have yet to see one of them unhorsed. . . . With judicious treatment and careful training, I believe they would make as fine cavalrymen
as any race in the world." (By "race" the inspector meant a comparison
with Arabs, Cossacks, and other famous equestrian peoples, just as ora-
tors in those years spoke of the Anglo-Saxon, Celtic, and Teutonic "races"
that made up the victorious Union army.)[50]

Frequent mounted drill helped turn the soldiers of the 9th and 10th
Cavalry into skillful horsemen. Constant training, of course, could not
compensate for a shortage of horses or the purchase of unserviceable
animals. The War Department, and particularly the Quartermaster
Department, was responsible for failures of supply. Army records show
that black troopers were sometimes poorly mounted. It is clear, though,
that these shortages were common throughout the cavalry and that the
white regiments were often no better off.

When black regulars drew poor horses, shoddy supplies, shabby living quarters, or unenviable assignments—as happened from time to
time—it was the result of army-wide policies rather than racial prejudice. Whether some War Department officials and army generals might
have preferred systematic discrimination is beside the point. What is
important is that the size of the understrength regular army, and the
scope of its responsibilities in the West, prevented any official policy that
might have created and maintained the black regiments as a separate

corps of second-class soldiers. Armed and equipped, clothed, fed, housed, and paid the same as whites, black soldiers proved themselves able to perform the same duties as those required of any men in the service.

CHAPTER SIX

"To Promote the Moral and Intellectual Welfare of the Men"

In April 1867, with recruiting for the 41st Infantry well under way, Lieutenant Colonel William R. Shafter asked that the regiment's chaplain report for duty. Shafter already had enough men to form five companies, and "the noncommissioned officers stand in pressing need of the instruction that should be given by the Regimental Chaplin [sic] as provided for by the Bill reorganizing the Army." Although all the officers of the new black regiments busied themselves to find literate recruits, Shafter was the first to summon the regimental chaplain to begin instructing the men in basic literacy.[1]

The army reorganization act of 1866, to which Shafter referred, assigned one chaplain to each of the new black regiments and broke a decades-old tradition of the regular army. Although more than 930 regimental chaplains had served with volunteer regiments during the Civil War, the peacetime army had stationed chaplains at a few scattered posts—no more than thirty, according to the 1866 legislation. But regimental chaplains of the U.S. Colored Troops—thirteen of them black men—had taught hundreds of former slaves to read and write during the war, and Congress realized that, as one representative put it, "regiments of colored troops have necessities which do not exist in the case of . . . white troops." Regular army chaplains had always run schools for enlisted men, but the act of 1866 was the first attempt to provide for a particular group of soldiers.[2]

The chaplains' first responsibility, of course, was religious. According to long-established custom, services in the army were nonsectarian but overwhelmingly Protestant. Troop movements and the annual turnover of enlisted men made it impossible to appoint chaplains who were of the same denomination as most soldiers in a particular garrison or regiment, and since the army never conducted a religious census, it is impossible to tell what church, if any, soldiers had attended in civilian life. Most black soldiers who had a religious preference, though, were probably members of either the Baptist or the African Methodist Episcopal (AME) Church. Of the sixteen regimental chaplains who served with the black regiments between 1866 and 1898, four were Baptist and five Methodist, while the rest belonged to other Protestant denominations.[3]

Army regulations required little of ministers who wished to serve as military chaplains. There were no age limits or educational requirements, and applicants had only to be regularly ordained ministers of their church, recommended for the post by "some authorized ecclesiastical body" or at least five "accredited ministers" of their own denomination. Although the army considered chaplains to be "officers without command," their pay equaled that of a captain of infantry, and they ranked similarly in order of precedence (i.e., between majors and first lieutenants). Chaplains' appointments in the black regiments, like those of the army's post chaplains, depended on political influence rather than on the applicant's ability as an educator or religious leader. Fewer than half of the sixteen chaplains who served with the black regiments had requested the assignment; most had hoped for a post, rather than a regimental, chaplaincy.[4]

All of the chaplains appointed to the six new black regiments in 1866–67 were white. Five had been chaplains during the Civil War, either in state volunteer regiments, in the U.S. Colored Troops, or in military hospitals. Only two of them had asked for assignment to a black regiment. The Episcopalian priest John C. Jacobi "had the opportunity to become acquainted with the characteristics and disposition of this class of men more fully than usually happens to an officer in the army" while ministering to wounded black soldiers in army hospitals during the war. He became chaplain of the 9th Cavalry, but ill health forced his retirement soon afterward.[5]

David E. Barr, the only other regimental chaplain who had served with black troops during the Civil War, had been chaplain of the 81st

U.S. Colored Infantry, a regiment of former slaves from Louisiana and Mississippi that entered Federal service in the summer of 1863. When Barr learned in the fall of 1866 that a large number of men from the 81st intended to join the regular army's 39th Infantry, headquartered near New Orleans, he wrote to the Secretary of War that he "could be of considerable use" if he were commissioned in the new regiment. In 1869, when the 39th and 41st Regiments were consolidated as the 25th Infantry, Barr stayed on as chaplain.[6]

Barr's fellow Episcopalian and Louisiana Unionist, Elijah Guion, did not ask for a berth in one of the new black regiments. He became chaplain of the 41st Infantry, though, and transferred in 1871 to the 10th Cavalry, with which he served until his death eight years later. Guion's successor with the 10th, Francis H. Weaver, had served as a private in the Civil War and been wounded five times. After the war, Weaver enlisted in one of the regular army's "Veteran Reserve" regiments, which were made up of wounded soldiers, but soon he began studying for the Lutheran ministry. In 1879 he applied for the vacant chaplaincy in the 10th Cavalry and served with the regiment for eighteen years.[7]

Although the War Department usually insisted that ministers commissioned in the reorganized army be Civil War veterans, John N. Schultz, chaplain of the 38th Infantry and later the 24th, had remained a civilian throughout the war. After the Confederate surrender, though, he went south and worked with the Freedmen's Bureau, establishing schools in Mississippi and Alabama. Schultz's educational experience probably helped him obtain his commission.[8]

The requirement for war service evidently relaxed as the years passed, for George G. Mullins, who replaced Barr as the 25th Infantry's chaplain, took no part in the war. Mullins had been pastor of the Church of the Disciples in Lexington, Kentucky, for several years when he wrote to the War Department that he had grown "weary of the uncertain and slavish life of a city pastor." He received an appointment to the 25th Infantry in 1875 and served for sixteen years.[9]

Only five black ministers served as army chaplains before 1898. The careers of the first two, Henry V. Plummer and Allen Allensworth, had been similar before they joined the regular army. Both were former slaves and wartime veterans of the U.S. Navy, where no color line existed below the rank of officer. Plummer labored as a field hand in Maryland until his master freed him in the late 1850s. In 1862 he joined the navy, where he learned to read and write. After the war he worked for the Post Office Department and attended evening classes at Howard University. Plummer accepted the ministry of a Baptist church in Baltimore, where he was a leader in the Republican Party. Political services helped pave the way for his appointment as chaplain of the 9th Cavalry in 1884. Plummer stayed with the regiment for ten years.[10]

Allen Allensworth was born in Kentucky and spent three years in the navy, where he rose to the rank of petty officer. After the war he attended Roger Williams University, a black school in Nashville, and later entered the Baptist ministry. Although he was "a lifelong Republican," Allensworth obtained his commission soon after Grover Cleveland entered the White House in 1885, perhaps by suggesting that his appointment would "show the colored people of Kentucky and the South that the administration is inclined to recognize them in the distribution" of jobs. In a letter to the President himself, Allensworth said that the chaplaincy "will give me an opportunity to show, in behalf of the race, that a Negro can be an officer and a gentleman. . . . I know, from past association with both Northern and Southern white men, that I can perform the duties . . . without socially embarrassing the officers of the Regiment or Army." Reassured by these remarks, and knowing that the appointment made good political sense, Cleveland approved Allensworth's commission as chaplain of the 24th Infantry, in which he served for the next eighteen years.[11]

Political influence was still important in 1891, when George Mullins retired and AME minister Theophilus G. Steward applied for the 25th Infantry's vacant chaplaincy. Steward had lived in Philadelphia intermittently since his ordination in1864 and asked John Wanamaker, department store owner and Postmaster General in Benjamin Harrison's cabinet, for an endorsement. Three months later, the man who Wanamaker called "about the best colored minister I know" reported for duty at Fort Missoula, Montana.[12]

George W. Prioleau, who taught at the Payne Theological Seminary in Ohio, assumed the duties of 9th Cavalry chaplain in 1895, and the 10th Cavalry became the last of the four regiments to receive a black chaplain when AME minister William T. Anderson arrived in 1897. Although Anderson and Prioleau served for only a few years before the Spanish-American War, the other three black chaplains, with twenty-nine years' service between them, revealed in their correspondence and reports their different interests and personalities: Allensworth, an educator who wanted to enlist better recruits; Plummer, a temperance crusader who objected to "sectarian"—Catholic and Episcopalian—services at Fort Robinson, Nebraska; Steward, who favored personal conversations with soldiers and worked closely with neighboring civilian ministers of other denominations.[13]

Lack of an army religious census or records of churches at military posts makes it hard to guess the religious interests of those black regulars who did attend services and impossible to tell why they went. Perhaps the men were merely attracted, as Colonel George L. Andrews of the 25th Infantry surmised, "by curiosity or a desire to go somewhere." The boredom of winter evenings in barracks drove nearly half of Fort Missoula's garrison to attend Chaplain Steward's temperance meetings in 1892. When springtime rolled around, Steward reported that "the base-ball fever has broken out considerably in the garrison and the Sunday afternoon games here have their effect upon our services." Two months later, he suspended the temperance meetings until fall: target practice was taking up too much of the men's time, and the heat and mosquitoes further discouraged attendance. In the winter of 1894, church attendance nearly doubled after Steward persuaded the three saloonkeepers closest to the fort to shut down during his Sunday evening services. Churches were important social and educational institutions among black civilians, but religious services also offered soldiers a change from the dull routine of garrison life. Many may have attended because they had nothing better to do.[14]

Most chaplains tried to hold services at least once a week on Sunday, if possible. David Barr offered weekly evening services at several 25th Infantry posts during the early 1870s, with special services for prisoners in the guardhouse every other week. The newly arrived George Mullins found that many of the soldiers at Fort Davis, Texas, in 1875 were "emotionally very religious" and "always crowd the chapel" during his services. Allen Allensworth's wife played the organ during services at Fort Bayard, New Mexico, and several bandsmen of the 24th Infantry formed a church orchestra.[15]

In "mixed" garrisons, black and white soldiers seem to have attended the same religious services without formally segregated military chapels.

Sunday schools with enlisted men's, officers', and civilians' children in attendance were commonplace. At Fort Clark, Texas, "all the children in the vicinity of the post" attended Barr's Sunday school in 1870. A generation later, Theophilus Steward taught "the children of officers and others" at Fort Missoula, while at Fort Robinson George Prioleau lamented that his Sunday school drew more officers' children than those of enlisted men.[16]

Army regulations required post commanders to designate a "suitable building" for religious services, but chaplains often complained of the lack of a chapel. There was none at Fort Clark, and David Barr had to conduct services "in the stable, the kitchen, & when weather permitted in the open air." Sunday horse races in nearby Brackettville must have lowered attendance further. At Fort Robinson, Henry Plummer complained that meeting in the hall used for 9th Cavalry dances "destroys much of the impressive solemnity which should characterize divine worship." As late as 1897, Theophilus Steward conducted services in Fort Missoula's post auditorium.[17]

The War Department did not provide Bibles or hymnbooks. Chaplains often found that they did not have enough to go around and turned to missionary societies, social service groups, and philanthropic organizations for help. In 1871 the "Post Library Assn. of New York" provided David Barr with a "great variety of practical & interesting reading matter." During the late 1870s, George Mullins relied on a friend who was a district supervisor of the American Bible Society. The generous response of civilian organizations helped chaplains overcome some of the difficulties caused by tight army budgets.[18]

A regimental chaplain usually served at headquarters, and unless he traveled to the stations of the regiment's scattered companies, he saw only a comparative handful of soldiers. In the chaplain's absence, some black regulars organized their own services. While inspecting Fort Clark in 1875, Colonel Nelson H. Davis noticed that many soldiers turned out for services conducted by 9th Cavalry troopers there. The gatherings resembled revival meetings and featured "loud praying, vociferous singing, shouting and harangues." Among "the most zealous," Davis added, were "the worst" soldiers at the post. Thirteen years later, Sergeant William Franklin of the 10th Cavalry conducted services at Fort Apache, Arizona, for the men of his regiment and the 24th Infantry.[19]

Civilian clergymen sometimes conducted services—Colonel Andrews of the 25th Infantry reported that the clergy of Missoula, Montana, "always cheerfully and readily complied with every request for their attendance at funerals, weddings or to conduct religious services"—and regimental chaplains returned the favor by ministering to nearby civilians. When black residents of Junction City, Kansas, lost their minister, Chaplain Charles C. Pierce of the 9th Cavalry came from Fort Riley to hold weekly services until a new pastor arrived. At Fort Bayard one Sunday in 1888, both a 24th Infantry soldier and a white civilian approached Allen Allensworth to arrange the baptism of their children. The chaplain was undecided which to baptize first for fear of insulting the other's parents as well as raising the racial issue. At last he decided that since the soldier "ranked above the civilian," the black child would receive baptism first.[20]

Most regimental officers took little interest in the enlisted men's spiritual needs. Perhaps they would have shown more concern if the chaplains had been able to prove a connection between religious instruction and military efficiency. Many probably believed that as long as the men did their duty, it mattered little if the army was composed of atheists or religious zealots. Some officers' personal conduct also worked against chaplains' efforts to bring religion to the army. While George Mullins generally approved of the 25th Infantry's officers ("I have heard but little profanity—no vulgarity, and have seen only a few instances of shameful intoxication"), he complained that "several . . . could not be called models of ambition and refined culture." Mullins thought that officers' lazy and licentious behavior set a bad example for the enlisted men.[21]

While chaplains complained that officers tended to disregard them, they could say little more of some enlisted men. Military service did not inculcate the manners of a Christian gentleman, and some chaplains never realized this. Their failure to do so began with assuming that ministering to a military garrison was no different from dealing with a civilian congregation. The least successful chaplains failed to adjust their views on religion and morality to fit the military milieu. Besides, some seem have marred their work, with black soldiers especially, by manifesting high missionary zeal and considerable paternalism. After only a short time with the 9th Cavalry, Charles C. Pierce, a strait-laced Baptist, began to complain to the Adjutant General about the troopers' drinking and the prostitutes near Fort Riley. Colonel Edward Hatch explained that, while he was pleased that Pierce took "a warm interest in the spiritual and temporal welfare of the enlisted men," the chaplain exaggerated the facts. Hatch had been with the 9th for eighteen years, since the regiment's organization, and told the Adjutant General that the incidents Pierce mentioned occurred on "unexceptionably orderly" paydays. The colonel concluded that since the chaplain came "from a quiet country community, unaccustomed to soldiers," he was "inclined to look upon a frolic as a gross outrage."[22]

Pierce's opinions did not change with time, though, and he continued to submit reports about the troopers' "vices." In early 1884 he observed that many gambled away their pay and did not "seem to appreciate the dishonor that attaches to the practice." Once again, Hatch had to defend his men in a letter to the Adjutant General. "I presume," he wrote, "that the soldiers of this Post do not gamble more than any [other] soldiers. Had the Chaplain been familiar with garrison life he would conclude the garrison of Fort Riley [was] remarkably orderly." Hatch's letter settled nothing, and the dispute with Pierce continued until April 1884, when the chaplain resigned. "I have for some time," Pierce wrote, "felt that I was accomplishing very little in my present position, and that a good pastorate in civil life would present a field of far more extended usefulness." Glad to be rid of the meddlesome chaplain, Hatch "earnestly recommended" acceptance of Pierce's resignation.[23]

Like Pierce, George Mullins subscribed to a rigid moral code when he joined the 25th Infantry in 1875. He was immediately appalled at the troops' gambling and drinking habits. "For a vile colored laundress or a filthy Mexican harlot," he wrote, the soldiers at Fort Davis would "lie, steal, or do anything. They have no conception of the sanctity of marriage—and they know not what virtue means." These impressions came from a few weeks' residence at the fort, and while the troops' conduct may have deserved some censure, the chaplain's later reports show that his first impressions were exaggerated and unduly harsh. Two months later, for instance, Mullins noted that "the moral conduct of the garrison has been such as to demand no public criticism. Order, sobriety, and peace have generally prevailed." During his years of service with the regiment, Mullins grew to accept a certain amount of drinking, gambling, and whoring as natural among soldiers. His successor, Theophilus

G. Steward, recognized at once the importance of becoming, as he put it, "more familiar to the customs of the garrison and to the habits of the men," and Mullins seems to have come to the same realization fifteen years earlier.[24]

Steward seems to have had a closer rapport with enlisted men than any of the other chaplains, black or white. He tried to find out why his congregation amounted to only about one-tenth of Fort Missoula's population, both military and civilian, and the answers he got were interesting. Some men told him that they would not make a formal profession of religion until they left the army. "They can hardly muster courage enough to stand out of the ranks of their comrades," Steward commented. Any distinguishing characteristic, either moral or physical, was a potential target for barracks raillery. "They usually say, 'I can't lead a Christian life in the army,' or 'It's no use playing the hypocrite,' and yet they are men of conscience and of fair moral habits—many of them." The pleasures of sex, liquor, and gambling, along with the conformity imposed by ribald social comment, kept church attendance low.[25]

Some chaplains themselves had difficulties with sex and liquor, and their behavior must have impaired their influence with the enlisted men. "Conduct unbecoming" certainly cost them the sympathy and cooperation of their brother officers. David Barr was "permitted to withdraw from the service with the least possible publicity" in 1872 after urinating in front of officers' row at Fort Davis while drunk. Three years later, John Schultz resigned after being seen making "lewd signs, gestures and solicitations" to a servant woman at Fort Brown, Texas, who evidently spoke only Spanish. In 1894 a general court-martial dismissed Henry Plummer, the regular army's first black chaplain, for drunken misbehavior. A few other chaplains were too old for the job: Elijah Guion and the 9th Cavalry's Manuel J. Gonzalez, both in their sixties, spent years at a time away from their regiments due to sickness.[26]

Besides the appointment of unstable, infirm, or otherwise unsuitable men, indifference at all levels of the army—from the War Department to regimental officers to the enlisted men themselves—prevented the regimental chaplains from claiming great success in bringing religion to Western garrisons. They did, at least, give some soldiers and civilians an opportunity to attend services. It was as educators that the regimental chaplains played a far more important role.

While few officers believed that the army should serve as a public school, most agreed that better-educated enlisted men would improve military efficiency. The army reorganization act of 1866 directed the commanding officer of "any post, garrison, or permanent camp" to establish a school for enlisted men in some "suitable room or building." There, soldiers would receive instruction, "especially in the history of the United States." This last provision was consonant with the role of public schools as agents of Americanization in the late nineteenth century and must have been written with the army's many foreign-born soldiers in mind. The 1866 law was the basis of the army's educational program until 1889, when the War Department established a limited system of compulsory schooling for enlisted men.[27]

Although chaplains supervised the post schools, they were not required to show academic credentials or proof of teaching experience. At least six of the sixteen regimental chaplains who served with black regulars held degrees from colleges or seminaries. Only Allensworth, Barr, Pierce, and Schultz seem to have had any practical teaching experience, but the fact that all sixteen were ordained ministers suggests an ability to instruct the troops "in the common English branches of education."[28]

A shortage of qualified teachers hurt the army's school system more than any other deficiency. Officers or enlisted men could be assigned as teachers, but most officers were too busy with other duties, while in the black regiments, especially, few enlisted men were competent to teach. Occasionally, a senior officer was able to juggle the educational services of his regimental chaplain and one of the army's post chaplains. When companies of the 38th Infantry moved to New Mexico in 1867, Lieutenant Colonel Cuvier Grover learned that a post chaplain was on duty at his new headquarters, Fort Craig. Grover ordered the post chaplain to open a school there and sent John Schultz, the 38th's chaplain, to teach at Fort Bayard. In 1869 the commanding officer at Fort Davis dipped into his post fund to hire a civilian schoolmaster for the men of the 9th Cavalry and 41st Infantry. When the money ran out after a few months, the school closed. Well into the 1880s, officers in the black regiments continued to beg the War Department for schoolteachers.[29]

The indifference of the War Department, and of many army officers, to education also reduced the success of the post schools. While few officers denied the need for more educated soldiers, almost none favored

Edward Gibson was on of the many illiterate recruits who learned to sign their names in the army. This photograph shows him as a sergeant in the 10th Cavalry during his second enlistment in the late 1870s. His collar, tie, and watch chain were nonregulation; many soldiers bought such items for off-duty occasions, especially visits to the photographer's studio. Gibson's service extended through the Spanish-American War. *Courtesy Frontier Army Museum*

a compulsory school program. Mandatory attendance, they reasoned, would only reduce the amount of time a soldier could devote to the more basic aspects of his duty. At the same time, soldiers had to be given an opportunity to educate themselves in order to be promoted. A non-commissioned officer's stripes were the principal reward the army offered to worthy soldiers, and many officers assumed that the opportunity of promotion would move ambitious enlisted men to attend school voluntarily.[30]

Officers in the black regiments probably shared these views on army education, but practical experience with their enlisted men soon forced them to revise their thinking. The high rate of illiteracy bothered officers greatly. Most military duties, of course, did not require much education, but the black regiments needed to develop a cadre of soldiers who could at least read and write. It became the responsibility of the regimental chaplains to provide the required number of literate men.

Each regiment had only one chaplain, but never were all of the regiment's companies stationed at the same post. It is not surprising that chaplains found it next to impossible to provide all soldiers with an opportunity to attend classes. Some tried to visit each of the regiment's posts in turn, but usually they only supervised the school at regimental headquarters and left the outlying posts to shift for themselves. At Fort Hays, Kansas, home to companies of the 10th Cavalry and 38th Infantry in 1867, neither regimental chaplain was present; Captain Henry C. Corbin complained that the men needed schooling, but the extreme shortage of officers prevented assigning a teacher.[31]

Even if enough instructors had been available, lack of classrooms might have doomed the school program. In 1873 Elijah Guion reported that he had held classes in barracks, mess halls, his own quarters, and even once in a stable. He complained that "the want of some more suitable and commodious arrangements . . . has rendered the establishment of my regular and systematic efforts to promote the moral and intellectual welfare of the men almost impossible." When he learned that regimental headquarters would soon move to another post, Guion hoped that "our next resting place" would afford a suitable classroom.[32]

Scarcity of teachers continued to prevent holding classes even at posts where the Quartermaster Department had built a school. Although "everything else connected with the school" was ready at Fort Randall,

Dakota Territory, in 1882, classes could not begin for want of a teacher. That same year, Colonel Joseph H. Potter had no spare teachers at Fort Supply, Indian Territory, the 24th Infantry's headquarters, to send to schools at other posts manned by companies of the regiment. In time, though, a few enlisted men became able to teach. Private Henry C. Taylor of the 24th Infantry was a company clerk who took on the job of teaching his comrades. By 1882 eight black soldiers were teaching at six posts out of 107 schools reporting. Men like these helped ease the chaplains' burden.[33]

Books and other supplies were scarce too, although army regulations authorized chaplains to use post funds for their purchase. At most western stations, though, the post garden, the bakery, and recreational equipment took precedence over the school, and chaplains had to find other sources of supply. Fortunately, some of the same religious groups that sent Bibles and hymnbooks were able to provide books, writing materials, newspapers, and magazines.[34]

Elementary instruction in reading and writing dominated the curriculum at post schools. The aim was functional literacy, to prepare soldiers for military tasks that required an ability to read and write. Chaplains also taught more advanced students other subjects. George Mullins offered American history, "practical arithmetic," and English grammar at Fort Davis. Classes met five evenings a week, with two sessions accommodating an average attendance of seventy-five to one hundred men, depending on the number of troops in garrison.[35]

Since soldiers attended school voluntarily, a chaplain's chief concern was to promote regular attendance. None ever expressed complete satisfaction with his school's attendance record, but reports suggest that the more serious students made a determined effort to come to class. About 60 percent of those enrolled at Fort Clark in 1871 usually showed up. Although David Barr complained that turnout suffered because of men's absence on fatigue and scouting parties, he mentioned with evident pride that several of his students had taken it upon themselves to "continue their studies" while assigned to duty in the field. His successor as chaplain of the 25th Infantry, George Mullins, at first complained of sporadic attendance at his school, but he claimed two years later that "a large class of the men are persistently faithful as I could reasonably ask."[36]

Mullins was the most successful educator among the regimental chaplains. A highly competent and dedicated teacher, he established a well-organized series of courses, offered instruction at hours most convenient for the men, and provided his students with sufficient books and school supplies. His activities did not go unnoticed. Colonel Andrews acknowledged that his services as a teacher "were invaluable to the regiment." The chaplain's task "was an arduous one, but it has been crowned with a great success. A great number of the men have been instructed in the elementary principles of an education, who could not either read or write when they arrived at Fort Davis," the 10th Cavalry's Captain Louis H. Carpenter recorded when Mullins had been there for three and a half years.[37]

Unfortunately, these and other comments on the progress of the soldier-students applied only to a small minority of the men. Most soldiers did not attend classes, and many of those who did came so irregularly that their exposure to education counted for little. After long, tiring hours of drill or fatigue, few wished to spend their off-duty time in the classroom. The army's reliance on voluntary attendance proved to be a great stumbling block to the successful establishment of post schools. Eventually, though, officers' complaints about illiteracy forced the colonels of the 24th and 25th Infantry to order all noncommissioned officers to attend school until they could read and write. In 1876 Lieutenant Colonel Zenas R. Bliss of the 25th submitted a transcript of Sergeant James Campbell's oral report because, he said, the sergeant was "unable to make a legible written report, or draw a map." Without seeking approval from the War Department, Colonel Andrews required regular school attendance of all noncommissioned officers, and Chaplain Mullins reported all absentees as well as any men "negligent or inattentive" in their studies. Two months later, the 24th Infantry's Colonel Potter issued a similar order.[38]

Regimental chaplains' difficulties in establishing schools and convincing men to attend classes were not unique to the black units. Post chaplains and officers in white regiments likewise reported little success in attracting soldiers to their schools, and in 1878 the War Department issued General Order Number 24, reporting the findings of a Board on the Establishment of Post Schools. Unfortunately, most of the order's provisions were those of the army reorganization act of 1866, including

reliance on voluntary attendance. Despite the War Department's failure
to institute an effective school system during the previous twelve years,
it still clung to the idea that education was not a military necessity and
should not be compulsory. An innovation was that any qualified soldier
who volunteered to teach would receive per diem pay of thirty-five
cents.[39]

Although the Board's remarks on post schools, both for children and
for enlisted men, were phrased as recommendations ("The following
rules, having given satisfactory results in practice, are suggested as a
guide . . ."), they nevertheless reflected clearly bigoted thinking by some
officers. Lieutenant Colonel Alexander M. McCook of the 10th Infantry
was the army's Inspector of Schools, and his rules for the post school at
Fort McKavett, Texas, home to companies of his regiment and the 10th
Cavalry since 1875, served as a model. McCook, for unstated reasons,
thought it best to write racial segregation into the rules for Fort
McKavett's post school, and in 1878 he furnished the Board on the
Establishment of Post Schools with a copy.[40]

According to General Order Number 24, commanding officers of
mixed garrisons might provide separate classrooms for blacks and whites.
"The teacher of the children's school taught the white soldiers, and an
assistant was detailed from the white troops to teach the colored soldiers, in an adjoining room equally well fitted up, and as comfortable
as the room used for the white soldiers." Black soldiers would thus get
instruction from the post's second-best teacher. The board's report contains no clue as to why it decided to recommend "separate but equal"
classes when no such provision existed in the earlier act. Perhaps the committee members—Adjutant General Edward D. Townsend, Quartermaster General Montgomery C. Meigs, and Judge Advocate General
William M. Dunn—believed simply that the Thirty-ninth Congress had
failed to carry the idea of separation far enough.[41]

Although the War Department's order of 1878 suggested segregated
classes, it did not prohibit the assignment of white teachers for black
troops. The thirty-five-cent per diem made teaching a form of "extra duty"
and did not contravene the regulation against enlisting white men in
black regiments. In most instances, white soldier-teachers already on
duty simply assumed the responsibility of instructing black troops. Few
of them, though, were willing to leave their companies to go on detached

service in an all-black garrison. In 1882 Colonel Hatch asked for white teachers for the 9th Cavalry companies at Fort Riley. An endorsement on one of the requests, which Hatch never saw, explained the problem: the 9th Cavalry would have to wait because of "the difficulty of obtaining [white] teachers for posts with colored garrisons." The War Department had no power to compel soldiers to teach, and a white soldier-teacher might be understandably reluctant to be the only man in an entire garrison of his own race and rank.[42]

Army records give no clue as to how widespread segregated classes were, but most evidence suggests that they were the exception, rather than the rule. In 1886 an officer at Fort Verde, Arizona, claimed that white soldiers stayed away from school because they refused to attend classes with troopers of the 10th Cavalry and suggested that attendance "would doubtless be largely increased by the detail of an additional teacher so that separate schools might be maintained for the two races." Since both the army and American society accepted segregation as the rule in race relations, it appears certain that officers would not have been reluctant to implement what was only a suggestion in the War Department's 1878 order. Segregated classes, though, would have been possible only if there had been sufficient classroom space and enough teachers. At most posts, segregation was impossible, and it is likely that most soldiers either stayed away altogether or attended integrated classes.[43]

The War Department continued to provide no direct financial support for the schools, and purchases of schoolbooks and other supplies had to come from post and regimental funds. These funds also supported libraries, gardens, recreation rooms, and gymnasiums, and post schools ranked low on the list of priorities. Chaplain Henry Plummer of the 9th Cavalry reported in 1887 that he had to conduct classes with few books and neither "maps, charts, globes, nor blackboards." At Fort Apache, "two or three" 10th Cavalry pupils had to read from the same book.[44]

Beset by numerous difficulties, chaplains nevertheless worked to keep the schools open. The mere presence of a teacher, though, was no guarantee of success. After the 1878 order, officers were reluctant to compel even the most uneducated soldier to attend school. The 25th Infantry's Chaplain Mullins remarked that Colonel Andrews had interpreted the order to mean that he no longer had authority to order noncommissioned officers to learn to read and write, and he therefore discontinued this limited compulsory schooling. With the return to an entirely voluntary system, Mullins declared, "there has been a decided falling off in the interest and ambition of about one third of the non-comm[issioned] officers; and those who most, and absolutely, need the school will not come at all."[45]

Regimental chaplains had to rely on the soldiers' own desire for self-betterment to fill their classes. Although most black regulars never showed any great interest in school, the years between 1878 and the establishment of compulsory education in 1889 did see a substantial increase in school attendance. As early as 1879, Mullins wrote that about one-fourth of the troops at Fort Davis, garrisoned by the 10th Cavalry and 25th Infantry, attended his classes. In 1880 the posts reporting the highest number of enlisted men in school were Fort Concho (seventy students) and Fort Stockton (sixty), both manned by companies of the 10th Cavalry and 25th Infantry. Average attendance of ten men per company was about the same as that in the all-white garrison of Fort Abraham Lincoln, Dakota Territory (forty), but more than three times the attendance at Fort Meade, a ten-company post with a white garrison that reported only thirty enlisted pupils in class. The only other posts reporting large school enrollments were in the East, at the recruit depots, and West Point.[46]

Of the black regulars who tried to obtain an education, many made rapid and surprising progress. Most of them were illiterate when they enlisted, and the school system's chief accomplishment was in helping these men learn to read and write. When Mullins joined the 25th Infantry in 1875, he observed that "all are discouragingly slow in learning to spell—and *not one* has been able to repeat the Addition, or Multiplication table." Nevertheless, during his four years at Fort Davis, Mullins taught some 380 men of his own regiment and the 10th Cavalry to read, write, and spell and instructed some of them in grammar, American history, and algebra. Company B of the 24th Infantry made equally impressive progress. In 1887 the company commander reported that only four—"old soldiers of more than one enlistment"—of its fifty men were still illiterate.[47]

During the 1880s some officers in the army's staff bureaus came to agree with the regimental chaplains that the post school system failed to

provide adequate education for enlisted men. At the same time, more
and more officers realized that literate soldiers would increase the army's
overall efficiency. Critics of the schools began to focus on two factors that
most impeded efforts toward education: voluntary attendance and the
shortage of qualified teachers. In 1882 six regimental commanders and
many company officers were on record as favoring compulsory education, at least for illiterates. The leading proponent of reform was the 25th
Infantry's George Mullins, who served from 1881 to 1885 as Inspector
of Post Schools, the director of the army's educational system.[48]

By 1882 Mullins had come to favor compulsory schooling for all illiterates and had gathered support for his position from many officers.
Adjutant General Richard C. Drum went so far as to suggest that a literacy test be established for all recruits and that no one who did not pass
should be enlisted. Fortunately, nothing came of it, for this plan would
have increased the difficulty of recruiting for the black regiments.[49]

Drum and other officers continued to demand a school system that
ordained compulsory attendance for all illiterates. Chaplain Plummer
found twenty-five men who could not sign the payroll in two 9th Cavalry companies at Fort McKinney, Wyoming—a rate of about 20 percent—and recommended "that it be made a part of the enlisted men's
duty, who cannot read and write, to attend school during the long winter evenings." Growing support for Drum's plan finally forced the War
Department to implement compulsory education in January 1889:
"instruction of enlisted men . . . will hereafter be a military duty." The
order applied only to men in their first enlistment, though, and to "such
young men in their second enlistment as it may be deemed necessary to
instruct." While the order did not call for the attendance of all soldiers,
its wording was vague enough that officers could use it to compel any
soldier to attend.[50]

Later in 1889 the War Department published a revised edition of
Army Regulations. Article 38, which covered post schools, contained some
of the proposals that Mullins, Drum, and others favored. Now the Quartermaster Department was responsible for providing desks, books, and
writing materials. The school term was to run from the beginning of
November to the end of April. Schoolteachers would come from the
ranks and be assigned to schools at a ratio of one to fifteen pupils. Chaplains would have direct charge of the school at posts where they served;

elsewhere, this would be the commanding officer's responsibility. An interesting omission in the new *Army Regulations* was the 1878 provision that suggested segregated classes. Perhaps experience had shown that the cost of educating the races separately was too great to justify efforts to enforce a color line in the classroom. Perhaps Mullins, while he was Inspector of Schools, had moved behind the scenes to dismantle segregation, just as McCook had done to establish it.[51]

Before publication of the 1889 regulations, a debate had flourished within the army about the advisability of permitting chaplains to continue their control of post schools. Officers complained that few chaplains were qualified teachers, adding that advanced age kept some of them from meeting their teaching obligations. Fortunately for the black regiments, their chaplains at that time were among the best ever appointed. Henry Plummer, the first black chaplain, took enough interest in the education of his 9th Cavalry students to offer the War Department his suggestions for improving the schools. Plummer, like Mullins and Drum, favored giving teachers noncommissioned rank because without it, soldier-teachers could not "command [the] respect and obedience" of their pupils. The 24th Infantry's Allen Allensworth proposed the enlistment of better-educated men. The illiteracy of many soldiers kept good officers from joining the black regiments, he thought, and more literate soldiers would alleviate this problem. "These regiments ought to be composed of the best material possible and obtainable among [black] people," he wrote.[52]

The work of able chaplains and the revised *Army Regulations* of 1889 did not, of course, bring about an immediate improvement in army education. For several years the difficulties that had plagued the army's school system between 1866 and 1889 continued to limit its effectiveness. There was still a teacher shortage in the black regiments, although officers did report greater success in finding enlisted men to act as instructors. The 25th Infantry's Sergeant George Horton taught school at Fort Shaw, Montana, "he being the only enlisted man at the post suitable for this duty." In 1891 three 10th Cavalry troopers served as teachers at Fort Grant, Arizona, and four men of the 24th Infantry at Fort Bayard qualified to teach. How many of these were products of the army's school system is uncertain; all four of the men at Fort Bayard, though, had attended Chaplain Allensworth's classes.[53]

Some commanding officers questioned the competence of the soldier-teachers. Colonel Andrews of the 25th Infantry refused to believe that the schools would be a success "until the officers are the teachers." A War Department circular in 1889 authorized post commanders to detail junior officers for this purpose. "Lieutenants of the line cannot make any valid objection to serving under the superintendency of the chaplain of the post or regiment," the circular declared, heading off any objections officers of the 9th Cavalry and 24th Infantry might have to working with their regiments' black chaplains. Commanding officers throughout the army nevertheless were often unable to relieve their juniors from other military duties to assist at the schools, and one officer suggested that the school system was a failure due to lack of interest among the officers. "If all officers had done their duty," he wrote, as "enthusiastically as . . . Chaplain Allensworth, there could be no question anywhere of shutting up a school for lack of suitable teachers."[54]

The army's new school system was never an unqualified success, and throughout the 1890s chaplains and regimental officers suggested improvements. Usually, the call was for more and better teachers, for compulsory attendance for all enlisted men, and for increased school appropriations. Concentration of troops at fewer, larger posts, for the most part accomplished during the 1890s, tended to favor army education. The reduction in the number of garrisons allowed chaplains to supervise the schools more closely. When the entire 24th Infantry assembled—for the first time in the regiment's twenty-seven year history—at Fort Douglas, Utah, in 1896, Chaplain Allensworth, following ideas developed by Booker T. Washington at the Tuskegee Institute, saw to it that the curriculum included instruction in baking, printing, and telegraphy. Less frequent field service during the 1890s enabled commanders to detail some officers as teachers, and enlisted men found themselves with more time to devote to study. Sergeant Horace W. Bivins received a four-month furlough from the 10th Cavalry in order to attend the Hampton Institute in Virginia.[55]

Army schooling was available for those who wanted it, but the program had only limited success. Responsibility for this rests equally on lawmakers, military administrators, regimental officers, and enlisted men. Congress balked at appropriating sufficient money to pay for the schools. Generals, both staff and line, often refused to see the need for compulsory schooling or for the enlistment of qualified teachers. Regimental officers were either indifferent or too busy to take much interest in the schools. Most enlisted men were less than enthusiastic about the chance to get an education. While these generalizations held true throughout the army, the history of post schools in the black regiments sometimes offered exceptions.[56]

Although some regimental chaplains were clearly not qualified to teach, most of them took an active interest in educating black regulars. Officers did not often volunteer to serve as instructors, but the extra work made necessary by widespread illiteracy in the ranks forced them to make some effort to convince soldiers to attend classes. Fragmentary evidence suggests that a greater proportion of black soldiers took advantage of the post schools than did whites. Surely, most black soldiers stayed away, but those who did attend demonstrated both their interest in learning and an ability to master the assigned subjects. Whether they went to school in order to obtain promotions, to prepare themselves for civilian life, or simply to relieve the boredom of garrison duty is uncertain; but for some black regulars, at least, post schools and the efforts of the regimental chaplains afforded educational opportunities that they might not have been able to find outside the army.

CHAPTER SEVEN

"Not So Varied and Filled with Pleasure"

Garrison life at a western army post was usually dull and uneventful. Soldiers who were not in the field—scouting, escorting surveyors or the mail, or building roads and stringing telegraph wire—spent most of their time in routine military duties. Although the daily rhythm varied slightly from station to station and according to the season of the year, the principal features were the same. Wakened each morning by the discharge of an artillery piece and the strains of reveille, soldiers followed the daily schedule until the sound of taps drifted across the post to signal the end of another day. Instruction of recruits, company drill, parades, and inspections were the common features of military life.

Fatigues (usually involving construction or sanitation) and extra-duty details (such as clerks, cooks, and hospital nurses) also kept soldiers busy. Many officers complained that these assignments prevented necessary instruction in drill, marksmanship, and riding. Little could be done to reduce the number of fatigues, but many companies also found their ranks depleted by soldiers who volunteered for extra-duty work because of the additional pay it offered. "Extra" meant outside the company rather than in addition to the soldier's normal duties, as when a carpenter worked for the post quartermaster or a baker for the commissary of subsistence. Depending on a soldier's skills and the available budget, extra-duty privates could earn from twenty to fifty cents a day beyond their monthly pay. Some men even refused the offer of corporal's stripes because few noncommissioned officers ever drew extra-duty assignments, and a promotion would have meant lower pay than they were already getting.[1]

Being an officer's servant could also bring added income to a private whose basic pay, after 1871, was thirteen dollars a month. Although federal law forbade officers from ordering soldiers to work as servants, long-standing military custom allowed them to hire privates and pay them out of their own pockets. This practice was common throughout the army and not confined to the black regiments. Soldier servants usually earned between thirty and fifty cents a day and occasionally avoided field service. When Major Guy V. Henry led a squadron of the 9th Cavalry after Apaches in 1881, he ordered all soldier servants to stay behind (at Fort Stanton, New Mexico), which the commanding officer acknowledged "was very proper and possibly necessary for the comfort of officers' families." Civilians in the middle class, to which most officers belonged or at least aspired, employed domestic servants, and officers thought that servants were necessary to their families' well being. As late as 1891, Fort Custer's site in the middle of the Crow Indian reservation made it "impossible, at times, for officers to obtain servants, or keep them, even after paying their way from St. Paul or other places where servants can be found," the commanding officer complained.[2]

While untrained and inexperienced soldier-servants plagued some officers, others were able to find men who had worked as butlers, waiters, and cooks before enlisting. Cooks and waiters were common in the black regiments, where they made up the fourth-largest occupational group, after farmers, common laborers, and men who listed their trade as "soldier." Frances Roe observed that a black soldier-cook prepared excellent meals for some of her friends when her husband's company of the 3d Infantry arrived at Camp Supply, Indian Territory, in 1872. She and her husband stayed there for several months, hiring a servant from among the men of the garrison. The only advantage of service with black troops was that "one can always have good servants," Mrs. Roe claimed.[3]

Unlike officers, enlisted men messed in company dining halls that were often uncomfortable and poorly built. Sometimes, the Quartermaster Department failed to provide cooking and eating utensils. At Fort Davis, Texas, in 1875, the lack of cutlery forced men of the 25th

Infantry and 9th Cavalry to eat with their fingers. In later years, as kitchens and dining halls improved and more men reenlisted, some companies ordered their own tableware emblazoned with company letter and regimental number.[4]

What did not change much through the decades was the army ration: bread, beans, meat (fresh or salted), coffee, and few condiments like salt, pepper, and vinegar. Gardens were a source of fresh vegetables to prevent scurvy, supplemented by produce from local farmers and merchants or canned goods from the post trader or the commissary. Until the 1890s, the army offered no special training for cooks. In many companies, officers simply chose a few enlisted men to cook, regardless of their ability, and army surgeons complained that bad cooking injured soldiers' health and led to increased desertion. When companies of the 24th Infantry garrisoned Fort Reno, Indian Territory, in 1887, the post surgeon found the culinary arrangements sadly lacking. Most army cooking was done "by rule of thumb," he wrote, and suggested that "education in this area would be of considerable help." Unfortunately for the enlisted men, the War Department long ignored these suggestions. Provision of permanent, trained company cooks would not come until the Spanish-American War awakened popular interest in the state of the army.[5]

Enlisted men constantly worked to find ways to supplement their issue ration with more appealing foods. Private William Perkins, who cooked for his 25th Infantry company at Fort Meade, Dakota Territory, had a lucrative sideline baking pies and cakes that he sold for fifty cents each, more than doubling his army pay of thirteen dollars a month. His comrades craved more substantial fare, too. "I bought three shotes [*sic*] and couldn't keep them," Perkins recalled. "The men were always after pork." Animals caused sanitation problems, though. Some 10th Cavalry troopers kept a few hogs at Fort Grant, Arizona, until the commanding officer objected to "the pools of filthy, dirty, stagnant water in the pens," which, he claimed, threatened the health of the garrison.[6]

Post and company gardens supplied the messes with a variety of fresh vegetables at many western forts. Productive gardens also brought extra revenue to the companies. In 1890, men of the 9th Cavalry at Fort Robinson, Nebraska, sold surplus vegetables from the gardens to the officers. That year, sales of vegetables at Fort Grant raised nearly two hundred

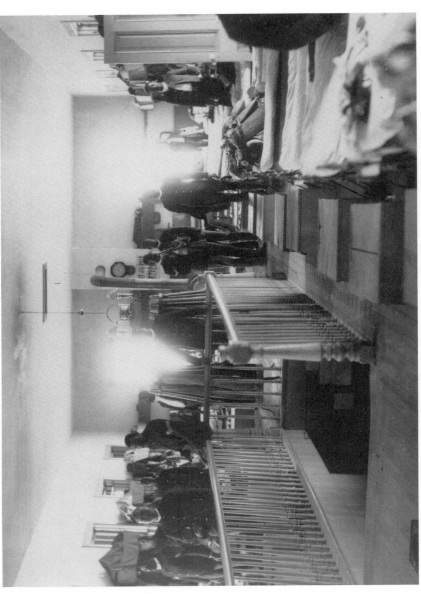

An upstairs barracks room at Fort Huachuca, Arizona, a 24th Infantry station during the 1890s. The company dining room occupied the ground floor. The door at right opened onto a balcony that ran the length of the building. *Courtesy National Archives*

dollars for companies of the 10th Cavalry and 24th Infantry. Among the crops were cauliflower, corn, onions, peppers, pumpkins, squash, tomatoes, and watermelons. Staple garden crops, though, were cabbage (an antiscorbutic), roots (carrots and turnips), and potatoes, all of which would keep through the winter.[7]

Officers were as eager as the men for fresh vegetables, often taking an interest in the gardens and encouraging the men to work in them. A company commander in the 24th Infantry wrote directly to the U.S. Commissioner of Agriculture in 1886 reporting success with peas at Fort Elliott, Texas, although the corn had been "a failure, grew very poorly, . . . and was eaten up by the worms." At Fort Meade, 25th Infantry officers asked that their men be excused from daily drill for a week so that they could harvest garden crops.[8]

Medical officers with regular-army commissions or civilian doctors on contract saw to the health of officers and men as well as their families at each army post. The post surgeon's immediate assistant was the hospital steward, a noncommissioned officer assigned to the post and similar in rank to the commissary, ordnance, and quartermaster sergeants. Until the establishment of the Hospital Corps in 1887, whatever companies happened to be at the post furnished extra-duty men to serve as nurses. Privates in the Hospital Corps, which accepted thirty-seven transfers from the black regiments during its first six months of existence, received training in the principles of hygiene and first aid.[9]

Throughout the post–Civil War period, the most common military ailments were typhoid fever, dysentery, respiratory ailments, venereal diseases, and alcoholism—the last ailment being recorded whenever a soldier brought his hangover to sick call. Although statistics showed that black and white troops did not suffer equally from the same complaints, successive Surgeons General pointed out that differences depended mainly on the region where soldiers served and had nothing to do with race. In the late 1860s, as the 10th Cavalry and 38th Infantry moved to posts in Kansas, the surgeon at Fort Wallace found that many of the men who had enlisted in Tennessee and other Southern states were "unacclimated" to the plains and often reported sick.[10]

Besides any effect that the climate of a particular region and conditions at certain forts might have had on the health of black regulars, their slightly higher rate of sickness may have been due to ignorance of the principles of hygiene. Most of them had been brought up in the country, and the Medical Department of the Union army had noted that volunteer regiments from rural areas reported more sickness than city regiments. Sanitary facilities were primitive, anyway, particularly in the early years. Post surgeons noted in the 1870s that the only soldiers who were required to bathe—once a week, according to *Army Regulations*— were the guardhouse prisoners. Later, bathing became more common, and every man in the garrison at Fort Custer, Montana, in 1893 had to sign the bathhouse register once a week.[11]

Folk beliefs probably played a part too in the rate of sickness reported among black troops. They reported to the surgeons with a variety of complaints that they claimed to have contracted supernaturally. The 39th Infantry's Sergeant Henry Adams had practiced faith healing since his youth and made good money at it in later life. "[S]uch as other doctors can't mend up, they get me to work on them and I cures them," he told a Congressional committee investigating black life in the South in 1880. Some soldiers of the regiment at Fort Jackson, Louisiana, reported that they had been "hoodooed" and could not perform their duties. Even if surgeons immediately dismissed such cases, they did enter them in their records, which in turn became the basis for the Surgeon General's annual report on the army's rate of sickness.[12]

Epidemics swept through western garrisons from time to time in spite of all precautions. One of the worst occurred in Kansas during the summer of 1867, when soldiers of the newly organized 10th Cavalry and 38th Infantry contracted cholera. Surgeons at Forts Harker and Larned believed that polluted drinking water caused the epidemic. Observers also reported that poorly prepared rations and unsanitary cooking facilities at the posts contributed to the sick list. By early August, the epidemic had run its course after killing ninety-one soldiers. Newspapers reported that regimental officers and post surgeons hoped to avoid another outbreak and that they had found new sources of drinking water and had begun to instruct the men in hygiene and proper cooking methods.[13]

The death of a comrade reminded soldiers of their own mortality and the dangers of their existence. Military funerals were solemn events, governed by both published regulations and unwritten tradition. At Fort Robinson in 1889, all members of the 9th Cavalry not on duty attended the funeral of Trumpeter William H. Carter. A horse-drawn army ambulance, flanked by an honor guard in dress uniform, carried the flag-draped coffin to the gravesite. Carter's trumpet hung on the saddle of a riderless horse that followed the ambulance. At the grave an officer read the service. A squad from Carter's company fired three volleys and a trumpeter sounded taps.[14]

The strict military routine of their lives did not cut off black regulars completely from the common joys and celebrations of life, though. Marriages also punctuated the tedium of garrison life. "Only a very few intimate friends" attended the wedding of Post Quartermaster Sergeant Benjamin F. Davis, formerly of the 9th Cavalry, at Fort Niobrara, Nebraska, in 1886. The ceremony took place in the home of 9th Cavalry Sergeant John H. Ferguson. The two men never served together in the same company or at the same post, but Davis was famous in the regiment—he had been sergeant major for nearly five years before leaving the 9th to become the first black post quartermaster sergeant in 1885—and Sergeant and Mrs. Ferguson opened their home to him.[15]

In 1887 members and friends of the 24th Infantry garrison at Fort Reno celebrated the wedding of Corporal Henry Giles. "The bride was dressed in white satin with a beautiful wreath of rosebuds and geraniums," Private Prince A. Moulton reported in the *Cleveland Gazette*. "Over 200 people crowded into our little chapel to witness the ceremony, and all the officers and their ladies were in attendance. . . . After the wedding the newly married couple and their numerous friends went over to our barracks, where they were received by music from the Fort Reno Band. . . . At about one A.M. the party broke up, and on leaving all declared it the finest thing seen in the past forty years." Moulton described the attendants and guests as visiting from all over the South: only the *Gazette*'s readers at Fort Reno would know that the best man, "Mr. A. Cook, of Nashville," was Private Alexander Cook, who had enlisted there; that "Mrs. Amanda Cooper, of St. Louis," was the wife of Private Barney Cooper, who like Moulton was a native of Warrensburg, Missouri; or that "Mrs. R. A. Cooper, of Washington," was the wife of First Sergeant Robert A. Cooper.[16]

Few soldiers were allowed to marry. Only four wives in a company could work officially as laundresses and receive army rations. This did not stop soldiers from taking wives, though; 24th Infantry Privates Ezekiel H. Hill and Zedrick L. Bird "eloped" with their brides from Fort Elliott to nearby Mobeetie, Texas, and had a double wedding performed by a magistrate. Some men who were already married lied to the recruiter in order to enlist. After four years of marriage, George Horton joined the 10th Cavalry and sent money to his wife in Washington, D.C. He came home, tried civilian life again for nearly a year, and went back to the army for two more enlistments, during which he continued to send money home. Other soldiers' wives found employment as servants and cooks for officers' families. Single women sometimes held these jobs and seldom failed to find a husband.[17]

Love could have untoward consequences in regiments full of long-service soldiers, some of whose daughters had reached the age of consent, or nearly. When Private Samuel Lundy eloped from Fort Missoula, Montana, with Etta, the sixteen-year-old daughter of 25th Infantry Quartermaster Sergeant John Williams, the sergeant's course seemed clear: "Private Johnson of the Band woke me up and said that Private Lundy had deserted and taken his horse and buggy and my daughter with him," Williams testified at Lundy's general court-martial. Johnson and Williams "went down to the depot. I then asked the [telegraph] operator which direction the trains had taken since 9 o'clock on the night of June 7th. . . . I then telegraphed to the conductor a description of the two parties to find out if they were on there. He telegraphed back that the two persons I described were on there. . . . I went to the sheriff and got him to appoint a deputy and got a warrant and had him arrested as a deserter from the U.S. Army." Convicted of desertion, Lundy could count on spending two years at either the U.S. Military Prison at Fort Leavenworth, Kansas, or the Department of Dakota's own military prison at Fort Snelling, Minnesota, more than nine hundred miles from the 25th Infantry's headquarters at Fort Missoula. But Mrs. Lundy testified that she and her husband were frightened by her father's death threats against them, and Lundy's court-martial reduced the charge from desertion to absence without leave. The court awarded Lundy three months' hard labor, which he served at Fort Missoula, close to his wife and friends.[18]

Some married soldiers like Sergeant Williams raised families in the army. Mrs. Williams bore her eighth child at Fort Sisseton, Dakota Territory, in 1887, three years before her daughter's elopement. Frequent births went hand in hand with a high infant mortality rate; memorial notices in the *Army and Navy Journal* throughout the post–Civil War era show that infant death occurred frequently in officers' and enlisted men's families. Children who survived infancy sometimes attended integrated post schools, at least in the early grades, after which officers tended to ship their children east.[19]

Other soldiers' living arrangements were not meant to produce children but came about merely because a long-term liaison was "more respectable than running around," as the 10th Cavalry's Sergeant William Johnson put it. Johnson stood trial at Fort Concho, Texas, in 1878 when a woman accused him of threatening her with a razor. Questioned by his own attorney, Johnson explained the nature of their relationship, and the cause of their falling out:

> How long had you known the woman and what were the relations existing between you?
>
> I was acquainted with her since October 1876. I was a very warm friend of hers and she were of mine.
>
> Had you been supporting her and did you furnish money to bring her from Fort Clark [when the company changed stations]?
>
> I had to a certain extent. I furnished her money to bring her from Fort Clark. . . .
>
> Do you know why she wanted to get rid of you? If so, state the cause.
>
> She had some other gentleman friends and I was in the way of them, and I would not allow such conduct to go on in my house.

Johnson told the court that he often carried a razor, for he was a barber by trade, but he had not carried one on the night he went to the house he had rented for the woman to have a serious discussion with her. Sergeant William Richardson testified that Johnson and the woman had seemed "very loving towards each other." (Richardson, who could read and write, had read her letters aloud to Johnson while the company was in the field and had written Johnson's replies for him.) Other witnesses swore that she was "a woman that keeps a disreputable house," she had paid nighttime visits to men of the 10th Cavalry at Fort Duncan months earlier, and that they would not believe her under oath. The court acquitted Sergeant Johnson of the assault charge but took his stripes for absence without leave on the night he and his "very warm friend" had met for a heart-to-heart talk.[20]

The army was supposed to muster its troops for pay on the last day of alternate months; in practice, the more remote posts had to wait several months between the paymaster's visits. With several months' pay in their pockets, soldiers could afford to enjoy themselves for a few days. A newspaper editor probably understated the mood of 9th Cavalrymen at Fort Hays, Kansas, when he wrote after one payday, "the boys are happy." Two years later, some of the same troopers were anything but happy when they learned that bandits had robbed an express wagon bearing their pay to Fort Robinson. The post commander had all he could do to keep the furious soldiers from leaving the fort to join the posse searching for the robbers.[21]

While many soldiers lived for the moment and spent their money drinking, gambling, and whoring, some banked their pay or sent it to their homes in the East. Appeals to their sense of charity or patriotism often prompted soldiers to donate to worthy causes. Enlisted men in the black regiments gave generously to the fund for widows and orphans of the 7th Cavalry after the battle of the Little Bighorn, but they donated somewhat more sparingly for a monument to the assassinated President Garfield and for a testimonial to Thomas Nast in recognition of his cartoons favoring the army against a parsimonious Congress. Corporal James Hardee of the 24th Infantry received a warm response in 1890 when he circulated a letter asking for funds to help support the surviving members of John Brown's family. "There was a great interest among the men," Hardee wrote, "to aid the family of the great man."[22]

Fraudulent schemes vied with legitimate charities for soldiers' dollars. In September 1871 Sergeant Harrison Wilson of the 24th Infantry sent a copy of a printed prospectus to the Secretary of War. "I got holt of a letter some how in this co. That I think the contents of it is unknown to the authorities at Washington," Wilson wrote with obvious effort. Private Benjamin Norman of Wilson's company had received a letter offering packages of "exact *fac-similes* of United States Treasury Notes" for a fraction of their face value. "These bills are in every particular as good as the REAL. . . . *Of course, our terms are positively Cash!* . . . Whatever you do, dont write by mail, as we will not claim or receive any letters from the Post Office. Send only by express prepaid!" Sergeant Wilson's reaction to this Gilded Age hustle was to pass it up the chain of command. The Adjutant General's Office had recently received word of a similar scheme and warned the complainant that "it was a common trick to get money on the 'confidence game.'" "Give same answer & compliment sergt. for his honesty," the Adjutant General scrawled on Wilson's letter.[23]

When the Wilberforce University Jubilee Singers toured the West in 1883, black swindlers from Manhattan, Kansas, sold worthless tickets to 9th Cavalry troopers at Fort Riley, according to a report in the Junction City newspaper. It is not clear whether the incident was a fabrication of the Junction City editor to emphasize the rascality of Manhattan residents. Newspapers throughout the West devoted a good deal of space to deprecating the abilities and morals of the residents of rival towns. If the incident was true, it shows the limited opportunities soldiers enjoyed for off-duty travel. Black Manhattanites, coming from fifteen miles away, could pose as advance agents of the Jubilee Singers; black Junction Citians, who lived just across the river from the fort, could hardly have succeeded in fleecing the soldiers.[24]

Most of the soldiers' money, sooner or later, went to the post trader. The War Department licensed these men, who enjoyed a monopoly at the forts to which they received appointments; unlicensed civilian merchants were prohibited from doing business on military reservations. The post council of administration, comprised of at least three officers, regulated the post trader's prices and hours of business. Soldiers sometimes found the trader's shelves loaded with shoddy or spoiled goods. Fort Concho's post council faulted their trader in 1878 for not stocking "either in quantity or quality the goods desired by the command." Competition was the most effective means of control. At Fort Missoula, the presence of merchants in the neighboring town forced the post trader to improve his stock and reduce prices in order to keep the trade of the 25th Infantry garrison.[25]

At many western stations, though, the post trader had no competition and very little supervision by either the council of administration or the War Department. Continued abuse of the system led in the late 1880s to the replacement of licensed civilians by government-sponsored canteens. The canteen served the same function as the trader's store, but a committee of officers and enlisted men controlled its operation. The committee drew on company and post funds to purchase merchandise, established prices, and distributed any profits. Besides offering similar wares at lower prices than post traders, many canteens operated billiard rooms, bowling alleys, and reading rooms, where soldiers could relax during off-duty hours.

Despite opposition from a few officers who did not believe that canteens were an improvement over the post trader system, soldiers and most officers warmly approved of these establishments. When the canteen opened at Fort McKinney, Wyoming, in 1889, the post trader's store "virtually closed." Although run as a nonprofit enterprise, well-managed canteens made money. The success of Fort Washakie's canteen meant profits to divide between the two companies stationed there, with the fund of the 9th Cavalry's Company E garnering just over one hundred dollars.[26]

Because soldiers spent so much of their time in onerous military duties, they needed opportunities to relax and enjoy themselves during off-duty hours. Until well into the 1880s, though, the army showed little interest in how soldiers spent their leisure time. This inattention contributed to low morale, disciplinary problems, and desertions. The unattractiveness of most western posts did not improve the situation. After watching 24th Infantry soldiers at Fort Reno in 1887, the post surgeon wrote, "Life on the frontier is not so varied and filled with pleasure, that any opportunity to amuse and at the same time improve the enlisted soldier can well be neglected." Nevertheless, the army left it to individual soldiers or to voluntary groups of officers or enlisted men to provide recreation for themselves.[27]

Soldiers lived in segregated companies, and most recreation took place within the company. Black soldiers and white did not often mix. Members of either group had little reason to like or trust the other. Most enlisted men had been wageworkers in civilian life, and black workers had a reputation among whites as cheap labor and as strikebreakers. Black workers, for their part, disliked all-white labor unions that barred them from skilled trades. In the regular army, though, black men were paid at the same rate for the same work, and white soldiers could scarcely imagine that black soldiers were out to steal their jobs. In civilian life, black people of both sexes were the butt of frequent insults and violence from whites; the army uniform usually protected black soldiers from physical, if not verbal, abuse. An inspecting officer at Fort Richardson,

Texas, in 1870 found "no trouble or bad feeling between the white and colored troops. They do not mix, neither do they quarrel." What the inspector saw was probably a wary truce made easier by military routine keeping the black infantrymen and white cavalrymen busy at different tasks and out of each other's way.[28]

Even when black and white soldiers became friendly, a third party might sour the mood. The 25th Infantry's Private William Robeson was a nurse in the hospital at Fort Meade, where Trumpeter Edward Marshall of the 7th Cavalry was a patient. Robeson and Marshall "began to play both of them was laughing and carrying on," Private James O. Cotman of the 25th, another hospital nurse, later told a general court-martial. "When Robeson got up close to Marshall's bed Marshall grabbed at him and . . . Robeson taked hold of him by the muscle part of the arm and . . . squeezed his arm"; meanwhile, another 7th Cavalry patient, Corporal Thomas Scully, watched nearby. Cotman thought that the playful Robeson and Marshall were "getting mad so I told him to come away and Robeson left the bed when I told him. Then Corporal Scully he taken it up and said 'If that damned nigger was to do me that way, I'd club him' or some such words as that." Marshall himself told the court that he was "on friendly and familiar terms" with Robeson, that "he and I had been joking most every day while I was in the hospital," but Corporal Scully summoned the Hospital Steward and preferred charges that landed Robeson before a general court-martial. The court absolved him of any wrongdoing, and Scully appeared before a garrison court-martial, which told him that if he kept on calling black soldiers "niggers," he could expect unpleasant consequences.[29]

Soldiers of either race seldom associated singly with those of the other. Simple prudence dictated having a few trusty friends along. In 1885 the 25th Infantry's Sergeant Albert Ray played a game of pool in a nearby saloon with a white soldier from the artillery battery stationed at Fort Snelling, but Ray had gone to the saloon and returned to the fort in the company of half a dozen men from his own regiment. In organized groups, though, the races could safely mix. When Company M of the 9th Cavalry reached its new station at Fort Washakie, Wyoming, in August 1885, Company G of the 7th Infantry welcomed them with "one of the best dinners I ever saw prepared for troops," one of the cavalrymen wrote, "and the troopers of the Ninth did it full justice."[30]

Sports provided another setting in which black soldiers mingled with whites. Although the army had no formal physical training program, enlisted men took part in athletic contests at every opportunity. Officers viewed sports as beneficial to the troops' physical and moral well being and encouraged the men to participate. Some soldiers enjoyed individual competition, like foot racing and boxing, but more of them joined in team sports, with most companies and posts fielding a baseball nine and, increasingly in the 1890s, a football eleven.

Baseball was by far the most popular team sport. Soldiers and officers used company funds or individual donations to purchase uniforms and equipment. Teams of black soldiers sometimes played against other all-black clubs, but more often played against whites. In the West, there were simply more all-white teams to play against. Ball players of the 9th Cavalry at Fort Robinson lost to an 8th Infantry team during Independence Day celebrations in 1889. A writer for the Valentine, Nebraska, *Republican* called it "an exciting game of ball . . . resulting in victory for the white men." (Valentine was the town closest to Fort Niobrara, the 8th Infantry's regimental headquarters, so the writer had a hometown, as well as a racial, interest.) White teams from nearby Valentine and Chadron often met the troopers from Forts Niobrara and Robinson. When members of Coxey's Army camped near Missoula on their way east in 1894, the 25th Infantry baseball team obliged them with a game. The 24th Infantry's 1897 schedule at Fort Douglas, near Salt Lake City, included visits by civilian clubs from Park City, Utah, and Evanston, Wyoming, as well as a 9th Cavalry team from Fort DuChesne.[31]

Although segregated regiments and companies necessarily fielded segregated baseball teams, some mixed garrisons organized integrated post teams. In 1887 five 24th Infantry soldiers and four from the 5th Cavalry made up the Fort Reno nine. The men from Fort Reno visited Fort Supply and defeated a 5th Cavalry team "who said not long ago that 'Negroes could not play ball,'" an anonymous 24th Infantryman told readers of the *Cleveland Gazette*. Supporters of the 5th Cavalry team "lost hundreds of dollars backing them" against the visitors, but each company at Fort Supply, whether 24th Infantry or 5th Cavalry, had the Fort Reno players to supper in its mess during their four-day stay.[32]

At Fort Missoula in the 1890s, four University of Montana students occasionally joined 25th Infantry players on the fort's team, as did a few officers. The Lieutenant Burt on Fort Missoula's 1897 roster was the son of Colonel Andrew S. Burt, who commanded the 25th. "I was one of the first, if not the first, commissioned officer to step over the line and play ball with the men," Colonel Burt recalled years later about his days as a company commander and shortstop in a white infantry regiment. By the time he came to the 25th, the old Civil War veteran had long since hung up his spikes, but his remark about "the line" is a reminder that rank, as well as race, divided black soldiers from their white officers.[33]

Throughout the 1870s and 1880s, officers suggested that the army should provide and equip post gymnasiums. Without athletic exercise, they argued, soldiers grew fat and lazy, especially during winter. The War Department, as usual, was slow to respond, and individual officers and enlisted men took the initiative. Company officers and troopers of the 10th Cavalry donated funds to purchase a complete gymnasium set for Fort Grant as well as two billiard tables and equipment for a ten-pin alley. By the late 1880s, the War Department had accepted the advantages of physical training and authorized construction of gymnasiums at most posts. This so pleased 9th Cavalry troopers at Fort Washakie that many of them volunteered to help build the gymnasium during their off-duty hours.[34]

Officers began to organize track-and-field events as well and used the nation's new rail network to bring troops together for competition, just as they did for training exercises. One track-and-field meet, at Denver in 1896, featured a participant from each company in the Department of the Colorado (Arizona, Colorado, New Mexico, and Utah), including the entire 24th Infantry and two troops of the 9th Cavalry at Fort DuChesne. The two 9th Cavalry entrants attracted particular notice. Blacksmith Patrick Ross finished first in three events, including tent pegging (with a saber, a variation on the exercise practiced by lancers in India), scored the highest number of points of any competitor, and won the General's Medal. Corporal William Morris won both the 100- and 220-yard dash with the 24th Infantry's Sergeant Alonzo Scott placing second in each. Department headquarters issued an account that called Morris's running "probably the most sensational feature of the contests." A banquet and dance awaited Ross and Morris when they returned to Fort DuChesne.[35]

Some soldiers enjoyed boxing, and an officer who visited Fort Quitman in 1871 found several men of the 9th Cavalry and 25th Infantry sparring and practicing with gloves (though in those days bouts were fought bare-knuckle). Years after his discharge, in his pension application former 9th Cavalry trooper Benjamin Watkins explained that a hand injury occurred "while sparring . . . not done in any fight just boxing in fun." Most soldiers, though, preferred watching fights to taking part in them. Men of the 24th Infantry witnessed a contest between the champion of the regimental band and a member of one of the line companies at Fort Bayard in 1889. After eleven bitterly contested rounds, Private John Johnson of Company A defeated the bandsman and received a prize purse of forty dollars.[36]

The countryside surrounding most western posts was a paradise for hunters and anglers. In the 1880s, parties from the 25th Infantry at Fort Snelling enjoyed duck-hunting expeditions to the Minnesota lakes. Near Fort Sill, Indian Territory, Private Isaac J. Wilkes of the 24th Infantry bagged turkeys, rabbits, and other small game. The poor army diet made hunting more than a pastime, though, and officers sent their best marksmen out whenever possible, armed sometimes with shotguns purchased by the company fund.[37]

Soldiers spent much of their leisure time in less strenuous ways. They looked forward eagerly to national holidays, when officers excused the men from nearly all duties and the day was devoted to athletic events, band concerts, banquets, dances, and theatrical performances. New Year's Day, Washington's Birthday, Decoration Day, Independence Day, Thanksgiving, and Christmas were the official holidays; others were celebrated less formally.

Independence Day was a major event at army posts. The day usually began with a thirteen-gun salute. Additional salutes punctuated the day's activities, and toward evening a final salute, one discharge for each state, would resound across the fort. After the morning salute, the commanding officer might read the Declaration of Independence or deliver an address on some patriotic theme, but more often the officers quickly dispensed with formalities in order to get on with the day's festivities. Besides a baseball game, there were usually sack races and a greased-pig contest, with a dance and fireworks in the evening. In a sparsely settled country, the soldiers' celebration drew neighboring civilians as well. Fort Robinson's Independence Day festivities in 1888 included not only

9th Cavalry and 8th Infantry soldiers and their families but also "cowboys, grangers and Indians . . . eating at the same table."[38]

The army observed Decoration Day in more reverent fashion. The rites held special significance for those officers and men who had served in the Civil War. At most posts, an officer delivered a formal address, which was followed by a service for the Civil War dead and a dress parade. Nearby towns often called on commanding officers to furnish a few troops to add a martial tone to their observances of the day. Regimental bands played and officers frequently urged their men to take part in civilian as well as military ceremonies.[39]

Christmas was especially welcome in drab western garrisons. In 1890 each company of the 10th Cavalry at Fort Bayard prepared a buffet supper, and on Christmas Day soldiers went from one barracks to the next sampling the food and observing the decorations. Warm weather in Arizona allowed companies of the 10th Cavalry and 24th Infantry at San Carlos Agency to celebrate Christmas 1890 with a baseball game.[40]

A shortage of women prevented soldiers from dancing as often as they might have liked, so a dance always drew a crowd. Committees of enlisted men organized these events in behalf of companies, voluntary organizations like baseball clubs, or entire garrisons. The 24th Infantry string band played for dancing after Corporal Henry Giles's wedding at Fort Reno in 1887. Soldiers could contrive ingenious excuses for a dance too: the 24th Infantry's Company H held one to celebrate its recall from an extended fatigue, cutting blocks of ice out of a frozen river for the Fort Supply quartermaster. Social clubs also sponsored fund-raising dances. The Fort Elliott Mutual Aid Society invited "soldiers and civilians, black and white" to its annual ball.[41]

Excessive drinking at the dances and competition for the few available women could lead to ugly, violent incidents. One 10th Cavalry trooper received a prison sentence for hitting and wounding another soldier with a whiskey bottle during a dance at Fort Grant. Responsible enlisted men usually tried to supervise these festivities and prevent untoward occurrences. When noncommissioned officers of the 10th Cavalry's Company H chaperoned a dance at Fort Davis, "the best of order and decorum" prevailed. But in a mixed gathering—black and white or soldier and civilian—a racial insult might mar the amity at any moment. In

1873 the 24th Infantry's Corporal Logan Goodpasture faced a general court-martial at Ringgold Barracks, Texas, for assault and battery on Appolenos Romero, a servant of the 9th Cavalry's Colonel Hatch. Romero had been peering through a window at a dance in the company barracks, and Goodpasture had invited him, in Spanish, to come inside and take part. The civilian replied, also in Spanish, that "he did not dance with niggers," and Goodpasture ordered him, in English, to "clear out." Words soon led to blows that landed Romero in the post hospital and Goodpasture in the guardhouse. The court acknowledged Goodpasture's "just cause and provocation" for the assault and fined him five dollars— about one-third of a month's pay but still far less than other sentences that it might have imposed.[42]

Fraternal orders and clubs also provided entertainment for soldiers. Several national organizations, including the Odd Fellows, had chapters in the black regiments. Prominent among them was the Regular Army and Navy Union, a fraternal order founded by veterans in the late 1880s, which swept the army during the next decade. By 1898 there were 146 "garrisons," as the chapters were called, in cities and at military posts across the country. The Union proposed reducing from thirty to twenty-five the number of years an enlisted man had to serve before retirement and instituting civil-service preference for veterans. It drew no color line, and men of the 25th Infantry and 9th Cavalry established garrisons at their regiments' headquarters posts. The Union at Fort Missoula "seems to be very strong," Chaplain Theophilus Steward remarked in 1892, "and I trust is doing some good."[43]

Even in earlier years, and at some of the more isolated posts, soldiers took the initiative and formed their own clubs. The 9th Cavalry garrison at Fort Stanton formed the Northern Liberty Singing Association. Chaplain Henry Plummer took considerable pride in the troopers he had taught to read who formed a literary club.[44]

Minstrel troupes enjoyed great success wherever they appeared. The veneer of burnt cork afforded enlisted men a sanction for whatever humorous remarks they might direct at otherwise unassailable authority. Some of the soldier-minstrels had belonged to civilian troupes and brought a degree of professionalism to their shows. Sergeant Jacob C. Smith of the 24th Infantry claimed to have had some theatrical experience before enlisting and organized "a dramatic and minstrel troupe" from members of his own regiment and the 3d Cavalry at Fort Elliott in 1885. Another integrated troupe, with members from the 9th Cavalry and 20th Infantry, entertained audiences at Fort Hays and at the Hays City Opera House. At the urging of Chaplain Plummer, a mixed troupe from 9th Cavalry and 21st Infantry companies at Fort McKinney in 1889 performed to raise money to buy books for the post school and an organ.[45]

While most black regulars must not have considered reading as a form of recreation, some found it a relief from the routine of their daily lives. Regulations provided for reading rooms and libraries, but a survey of all military posts conducted by the Medical Department in 1870 mentioned a post library at only one of the ten stations occupied by black troops that year. At Fort Clark, Texas, the 25th Infantry's 900-volume library was still in boxes, having just come from Louisiana with the regiment, while the post library of 184 volumes was kept in an officer's quarters. The report did not name titles or subjects, noting only that the books were "generally in good condition."[46]

A post council made up of enlisted men and officers selected reading material, although the contents of some post libraries suggest that officers wrote most of the acquisition lists. The library at Forts Jackson and St. Philip on the Mississippi River below New Orleans contained works of "history, biography, science, [and] belles lettres." The Fort Davis library in 1879 subscribed to *Popular Science* and the *Scientific American.* Many posts where black soldiers served had libraries of several hundred volumes. Even some smaller forts had impressive collections. The three-company post of Fort DuChesne listed 790 works "of miscellaneous literature" in its library, and Fort Duncan, a two-company post, had 355.[47]

Reports from regimental chaplains and other officers suggest that the more literate soldiers did considerable reading in their off-duty time. In 1881 Fort Randall's commanding officer estimated that a weekly average of 75 of the 184 men in the 25th Infantry garrison used the reading room. Relatively few black regulars were avid readers, though, and most never set foot in the post library. The post surgeon at Fort Gibson, Indian Territory, noted in 1872 that while the library was "well furnished," it "was not much patronized by the men" of the 10th Cavalry and 25th Infantry companies there.[48]

Post libraries subscribed to a wide variety of newspapers and magazines. Most took more than one New York newspaper, at least one from Chicago (headquarters of the Military Division of the Missouri), and a paper from the city nearest to the post's department headquarters such as the Leavenworth *Times* or the St. Paul *Pioneer Press*. The Huntsville, Alabama, *Gazette* claimed to be the first black newspaper subscribed to by a post library, thanks to the suggestion of Paschal Conley, regimental clerk of the 24th Infantry at Fort Supply. Posts with black troops in garrison often subscribed to the Cleveland *Gazette* or the Washington *Bee* besides the ubiquitous service weeklies, the *Army and Navy Journal* and *Army and Navy Register*. Most post libraries subscribed to a few monthly magazines like *Harper's, Scribner's, Harper's Weekly,* and *Frank Leslie's Illustrated Newspaper.*[49]

The subscription lists indicate a strong possibility that enlisted men had some say in which newspapers the post library would take. Black newspapers kept soldiers up to date on racial news. The men could read about their campaigns in illustrated papers like *Harper's Weekly* and see their likenesses sketched by Frederic Remington. In the pages of the professional military press, black regulars could follow developments throughout the army and better understand the overall meaning of their service. As reproduction and illustration techniques improved toward the end of the 1880s and newspapers and magazines carried more pictures, even illiterate soldiers could enjoy the reading room.

Soldiers often looked to nearby towns for recreation and amusement. If civilian proprietors of dance halls, theaters, and saloons harbored any racial prejudice, they quickly learned that black soldiers were free spenders when they came in search of entertainment. Economic considerations alone helped open many doors to black soldiers that might have remained closed to them in more settled regions.

Traveling theater companies and circuses attracted soldiers and civilians alike. When Robinson's Circus arrived at Willcox, Arizona, in 1890, the 24th Infantry's Captain Henry Wygant allowed his men and 10th Cavalry troopers at Fort Grant to go to town, even providing army wagons for the fifty-four-mile round trip. Officers needed diversion too and wanted as much as the men did to see the circus.[50]

Civilian entertainment was noteworthy because of its rarity, though, and for the most part soldiers had to provide their own. A 25th Infantry minstrel troupe at Fort Meade in 1882 was accomplished enough to entertain civilian audiences in nearby towns, and another from Fort Missoula toured the state of Montana in 1894. And throughout the army, soldiers could rely on one group that always strove for a high degree of professionalism: the regimental band.[51]

The band was an important part of every regiment. Resplendent in distinctive and often elaborate uniforms, bandsmen made an impressive showing at dress parades and outdoor concerts. Although federal statutes made no provision for bands, *Army Regulations* authorized the commanding officer to appoint a chief musician and to appoint as many as sixteen musicians from the companies. Funds for the purchase of instruments and uniforms came from voluntary contributions of officers and men.

Recruiters often made special efforts to find musicians. In 1874 the War Department assured the 9th Cavalry's Colonel Hatch that the government would pay for the transportation of several players from Evansville, Indiana, to St. Louis, the nearest recruiting station of the Mounted Service. Competition between regiments could be keen. In Lexington, Kentucky, 10th Cavalry Lieutenant Robert G. Smither requested authority to enlist musicians specifically for his regiment, to prevent any that joined through the Mounted Recruiting Service from being assigned to the 9th Cavalry instead.[52]

The War Department allowed regimental commanders to hire civilians as music instructors with the title of principal musician. Because of the principal musician's civilian status, there could be no official objection when black regiments hired a white man, often a European. Army records are unclear as to how many white men signed on as principal musicians in black regiments, but they numbered at least three and probably as many as six. The principal musician served primarily as an instructor, and outside of his official duties he had little to do with the troops, living apart from them. He usually received an extra forty to sixty dollars a month beyond the twenty-two-dollar monthly stipend authorized by the War Department. This pay, along with free housing and rations, probably helped white musicians overcome any qualms they might have had about service with black troops.[53]

Principal musicians joined their regiments from civilian life, but some of them were former soldiers too. When Gustav Oechsle received his discharge from the 21st Infantry band in 1886, he wrote to Colonel Hatch asking to be appointed principal musician of the 9th Cavalry and providing several recommendations from officers of his old regiment. Hatch was delighted to secure an experienced military bandsman as well as a

Soldiers at an army logging camp near Fort Bayard, New Mexico, in 1892.
Courtesy Museum of New Mexico

A 10th Cavalry group in Montana in 1894. The man standing center with his hand on the bottle appears to be the one sitting in front of the tent facing the camera in the photograph of soldiers in New Mexico, Pvt. Edward Crouch, the only man whose name appears on both rosters. *Courtesy Montana Historical Soceity*

Frederic Remington's 1888 picture of 10th Cavalry troopers in Arizona may include some of the men who were photographed at Fort Bayard's logging camp in New Mexico in 1892 (opposite). Seated and standing figures show that Remington accurately recorded the postures of black regulars off duty. *Courtesy Frederic Remington Art Museum, Ogdensburg, New York*

good musician, but warned Oechsle that while the 9th's musicians were proficient, they had little formal musical education and that his job would require considerable work and patience.[54]

The regimental band usually performed at least twice a day: at "Guard Mount," when the new guard formed to relieve the men of the previous day's guard; and at "Retreat," the evening dress parade during which the colors were lowered. Bands usually offered open-air concerts once or twice a week as weather permitted. A typical program might include selections from Rossini, Verdi, Wagner, or Weber; a march or two; and perhaps a composition by the principal musician himself. Concerts often drew a crowd of civilian listeners from nearby towns. Bandsmen, on their own time, also played at dances. Musicians of the 25th Infantry band furnished music for social dancing at Scottish games near Missoula, Montana, in 1894.[55]

The regimental bands were in great demand among western towns, particularly on national holidays. Residents of Santa Fe held the 9th Cavalry band in high esteem and called on its services often: between 1876 and 1880, the band played at every municipal observance of Memorial Day and Independence Day. The bands of the other black regiments enjoyed similar success elsewhere. When the headquarters of the 25th Infantry arrived at Fort Snelling in 1882, its band took up the tradition of playing for graduation exercises at the Shattuck Academy in nearby Faribault, Minnesota. They were invited back year after year, despite Private Thomas Johnson's getting drunk and insulting a civilian during the band's first appearance there. The band also furnished music for the Minnesota Industrial Exposition in 1886 and on special occasions for the Minnesota National Guard and the Grand Army of the Republic.[56]

Because the bands usually remained at regimental headquarters and seldom visited the companies at other posts, soldiers in those companies often formed their own musical groups. At Fort Washakie, which one soldier described as being "one hundred miles from nowhere," monotony prompted seventeen 9th Cavalrymen to form a brass band. Few of them had any previous experience, but the long Wyoming winter allowed them plenty of time to practice. By spring, the group had made enough progress to present a much-applauded concert for the garrison. Three years later at Fort DuChesne, six troopers of the same company formed a string band to provide music for dances there.[57]

The soldiers' own musical groups were an important source of entertainment in isolated western garrisons. These and other voluntary organizations—literary, social, and athletic—helped the men avoid the kinds of commercial entertainment in nearby towns that might impair their health or endanger their lives. But baseball, dances, and theatrical performances came too infrequently to relieve entirely the tedium of garrison life, and many soldiers took to saloons and brothels for amusement. Veteran officers, who were used to soldiers' tastes and habits, usually tolerated behavior that did not affect their troops' discipline, efficiency, or morale. Efforts by the chaplains and other officers, and by some enlisted men themselves, to get the men out of the saloon and into the schoolroom varied in intensity and effectiveness and were never more than partially successful.

CHAPTER EIGHT

"Serious Breaches of Discipline and Morality"

Post surgeons sometimes remarked that soldiers' behavior, as evidenced by drunkenness and venereal disease, varied according to the amount of money in circulation. The army scheduled paydays every other month, but traveling paymasters often arrived less frequently than that and disbursed several months' pay at one time. After a paymaster's visit to Fort Riley, Kansas, in the fall of 1883, "the men have been found at their worst," 9th Cavalry Chaplain Charles C. Pierce complained. A loan shark from nearby Junction City arrived to collect his debts and had to be run off the post. Civilian gamblers, "who seem to defy the authorities, so long as the Post Trader's room is open to them," took up residence at the fort. "A company of white and colored prostitutes has been encamped just beyond the bounds of the reservation. . . . Tardy action was taken by the civil authorities, and they were allowed to escape. This is no new thing." Still, although "serious breaches of discipline and morality have occurred, . . . they are few in comparison to the number of men in garrison," the chaplain admitted.[1]

Soldiers, like other populations of young, single males, enjoy forms of recreation that a Surgeon General nowadays would label "harmful to their health." Some of the amusements available in the nineteenth-century American West certainly promoted what the Articles of War called "conduct to the prejudice of good order and military discipline." On the other hand, one of the more understanding chaplains dismissed periodic outbreaks of licentiousness as "the hilarity incident to Pay-days and Holidays."[2]

Officers soon learned that there was little they could do to eliminate or even to curtail these activities. When Chaplain George G. Mullins arrived at Fort Davis, Texas, in 1875, he observed that soldiers of the 25th Infantry liked to spend their money on women and on whiskey "of the most poisonous and abominable kind," or to gamble it away. Twenty years later, Theophilus G. Steward inveighed against the brothels that stood just outside the military reservation at Fort Missoula, Montana, and expressed alarm in the spring of 1896 at "an epidemic of gambling" that "seems to have broken out quite recently" in the 25th Infantry companies stationed there. In fact, soldiers' rough amusements persisted throughout the decades. Charles Pierce, posted at Fort Riley in the 1880s, repeatedly condemned the liquor traffic in supposedly "dry" Kansas and the prostitutes and civilian gamblers that visited the fort at payday. The troopers "get wild over their games," Pierce reported ruefully.[3]

In western garrisons, soldiers did most of their gambling in the company barracks. The post surgeon at Fort Duncan, Texas, noted that despite officers' efforts to catch gamblers, 24th Infantry soldiers persistently held games in their barracks. Lieutenant Henry O. Flipper of the 10th Cavalry found that more than a dozen men of his company had loosened the ceiling boards and crawled up under the barracks roof for their games. Men who possessed what General William T. Sherman called "that wildness of spirit that is liable unless properly directed to result in violence and crime" showed considerable ingenuity in their pursuit of pleasure.[4]

Some officers set poor examples for the men by gambling in their quarters and betting on horse races. In 1879 the straitlaced President Rutherford B. Hayes asked Congress to add an antigaming clause to the Articles of War, but although the House approved the measure, it failed to pass the Senate. In 1889 a regulation finally outlawed gambling in the newly established post canteens but did not name other places where soldiers might or might not gamble.[5]

At some posts, commanding officers tried to make up for the lack of an antigambling clause in *Army Regulations* with specific post orders that forbade all gaming. In 1873 the 25th Infantry's Major Zenas R. Bliss instructed officers and company noncommissioned officers at Fort Davis to report any men they found gambling. Other commanders issued similar orders but apparently seldom succeeded in enforcing them. Most probably believed that they had little cause to interfere with soldiers' off-duty activities.[6]

Captain Alfred C. Markley of the 24th Infantry subscribed to this view. Although standing orders at Fort Thomas, Arizona, in 1891 prohibited gambling, Markley allowed games in the barracks. His indifference to regulations went unnoticed until one man complained that he had been cheated. This complaint led to a general court-martial that tried thirty-two enlisted men in Markley's company and levied substantial fines. Although the Captain was not on trial, the reviewing authority delivered him a sharp reprimand for allowing gambling "daily in the company barracks, from early in the morning until late at night, for about two months. . . . This gambling which was so freely indulged in, resulted in . . . ruining the discipline and efficiency of the company. Had [Markley] complied with regulations and orders, . . . the unusual spectacle of nearly half a company being tried" at once might have been avoided.[7]

When soldiers found that prying officers made it unsafe to gamble in their barracks, they simply moved their games to other buildings. Troopers of the 10th Cavalry let a corporal in a white infantry regiment at Fort Wallace, Kansas, set up his roulette wheel in their cookhouse. At Fort Sill, Indian Territory, Lieutenant Flipper discovered men gambling in the room of an officer's servant. "They ran for the barracks and beat me to them," he recalled years afterward. "When I entered every bed was occupied, every man was asleep and snoring. Of course, if I had turned the bedding back I would have found my men, but I did not disturb them." The young lieutenant knew that determined gamblers would always find some place to play.[8]

Away from officers' supervision, men could even gamble while on duty. The 9th Cavalry's Captain Ambrose E. Hooker preferred to post a five-man guard over his company's grazing horses because "with a larger guard a portion of the men occupy themselves with gambling under a shade tree if the weather is warm, or around a fire if cold." The gamblers posted one man on the lookout for officers with another couple of men keeping the herd nearby "without being given proper opportunity to graze, the balance of the men being engaged in the game and the noncommissioned officer in charge probably the Banker." Hooker's mention of a "banker" indicates that the game was three-card monte, a favorite of soldiers from Arizona to Montana, as general court-martial transcripts attest.[9]

Soldiers often drank when they gambled, and since the post traders were the only authorized sources of recreational alcohol on military reservations, allowing men to gamble was shrewd business practice. Attics, basements, and storerooms in post trader's stores were favorite haunts of gamblers. At Fort Elliott, Texas, in 1882, the post commander threatened to close the trader's store if he continued to allow gaming among men of the 9th Cavalry and 24th Infantry. In 1890 the trader at Fort Grant, Arizona, rented a "club room" to men of the 10th Cavalry. When the officer of the day reported the "new club room in full blast" after midnight, the post commander reminded the trader that gambling was forbidden. Even if zealous officers had succeeded in breaking up all the games on post, nearby towns provided soldiers with ample opportunities to risk their pay at the tables.[10]

Drink offered as much escape from the drab routine of garrison life as did gambling. "The peculiar isolation" of Fort Davis, the 25th Infantry's headquarters, "surrounded by a vast, desolate and uninhabited country," Chaplain Mullins wrote, "creates a cheerless atmosphere—which render[s] temptations to intemperance very strong." Some soldiers drank little or not at all, while others spent all their pay on whiskey. Chronic alcoholism caused some medical discharges, and many dishonorable discharges resulted from drink-inspired misbehavior. Officers knew from experience that heavy drinking impaired morale and discipline and often led to violence, crime, and desertion.[11]

While the number of cases of "alcoholism"—the post surgeon's diagnosis whenever a soldier reported sick because he was too hung-over to perform duty—remained high throughout the army during the post–Civil War period, the incidence was clearly lower in the black regiments than it was in the army as a whole. While the annual rate of "alcoholism" per 1,000 men in white regiments varied from a high of 76.00 in 1883 to a low of 32.16 in 1895, the yearly rate in black regiments usually remained below 5.00 per 1,000 men; only once did it reach as high as 6.47. During the decade 1884–93, the average annual rate of "alcoholism" among white troops was 48.56 per 1,000 men, but only 4.45 among blacks. Recruiting Service statistics confirm this pattern. Of the 2,063 whites and 131 blacks whom recruiters rejected as unfit for service in 1882, 63 whites, but none of the blacks, were turned away because of "evident chronic alcoholism." Three years later, recruiters turned away white applicants for "alcoholism and its results" at a rate nearly four times higher than that of black applicants.[12]

Post surgeons, regimental officers, and civilians recorded impressions of black troops' drinking behavior, some of which support the Surgeon General's findings. A correspondent of the Santa Fe *Daily New Mexican* observed a payday at Fort Davis in August 1875. Although the soldiers could easily get whiskey within a few hundred yards of the post, no one seemed to get drunk. "Could I make the same statement," the writer asked, "if the five companies were white soldiers?" When twelve companies of the 9th and 10th Cavalry took the field during the Red River War, Brigadier General Christopher C. Augur, commanding the Department of Texas, wrote that he did not "see or hear of a drunken soldier or one even under the influence of liquor. This is the more remarkable in the case of the column from Fort Sill, as they were paid but a short time before leaving the post." Augur called the black troopers' restraint "a very gratifying and hopeful exhibition of discipline and good morale." The post surgeon at Fort Missoula reported in 1891 that while 25th Infantry soldiers frequented a brothel near the post, "little drunkenness" came to his attention.[13]

Other observers painted a different picture. When Chaplain Mullins organized a temperance society at Fort Davis in 1876, he claimed that most of its sixty members—in a garrison of about two hundred—were "of the class addicted to intoxication, and habitues of the guard house." At Fort Concho, Texas, the surgeon recorded little heavy drinking in November 1877 but suggested that it was because the troops had not been paid for several months. In March 1890 the post surgeon at Fort McKinney, Wyoming, mentioned "considerable demoralization among the men" after payday.[14]

These conflicting reports preclude any conclusive remarks about the black regulars' drinking habits. That some of them drank frequently and to excess is certain, yet the number who reported sick afterward, and therefore became statistics, remained very small compared to the rest of the army. Pride kept 24th Infantry Private Charles W. Day from shirking a work detail when "the little I did drink . . . put me in the condition I was in." Day became a legal statistic, instead, after he told the sergeant in charge of the detail: "Put me in the guard house and be God damned to you. You can't put me in none too soon." The dozens of army doctors who served with black troops across the West, whose records provided the data contained in each annual report of the Surgeon General, could hardly have falsified their reports consistently for three decades. Regardless of the number of black soldiers who drank, few of them reported sick because of it.[15]

Boredom and dissatisfaction with military life were probably the leading causes of soldiers' drinking. It is possible that the much lower rate of "alcoholism" among black troops reflects their relative contentment with the army. True, some of them had little love for the service, but for many the army represented a better way of life than they had known before enlisting. Limited employment opportunities in civilian life—an overwhelming majority of black recruits listed their occupations as farmer or laborer—may have convinced them that they were better off in the army than outside it.

Heavy drinkers, though, found that their indulgence could result in heavy punishments, even a dishonorable discharge. Drinking was not a military crime in itself; only disorderly or insubordinate conduct, drunkenness on duty, and "conduct to the prejudice of good order and military discipline" (a catch-all charge akin to "conduct unbecoming an officer and a gentleman") were forbidden. Company commanders enjoyed some latitude in sentencing. When 10th Cavalry Captain Louis H. Carpenter found that his company first sergeant drank too much and set a bad example for the men, he reduced the sergeant to private and recommended his transfer to another company, "in order to break up his connections here." Privates, already at the bottom of the military hierarchy, could only be punished with fines or imprisonment. When Major Guy V. Henry found four men of the 9th Cavalry drunk during a campaign in New Mexico, he fined each of them five dollars of their thirteen-dollars monthly pay, the same punishment the court awarded to two white privates in the 15th Infantry who had also managed to get drunk in the field. Private Andrew Raily of the 9th drew six months in the guardhouse at Fort McKavett, Texas, for being drunk on duty. This was a general-court-martial sentence; company officers' discretion

extended only to fines of as much as one month's pay and imprisonment in the post guardhouse for one month or less.[16]

Most officers favored the discharge of troublesome drinkers. Although
Captain Owen J. Sweet conceded that 25th Infantry Private John
Boughton was "good when sober," he asked for the man's discharge
because Boughton was "addicted to periodical inebriation," during which
he became "wholly unreliable and irresponsible." If immediate discharge
of habitual drunkards was not possible, officers could refuse to reenlist
them. In 1882 the 10th Cavalry's Captain Robert G. Smither had "one or
two drunkards" in his troop, "whose term of enlistment expires in a few
days." He intended to "let them stay out, especially [of] my troop."[17]

Men convicted of drunken offenses could sometimes secure remission of their sentences if they agreed to sign a temperance pledge. Private Jacob Wilson of the 10th Cavalry got out of the guardhouse at Fort
Stockton by promising to abstain for one year. Unfortunately, he was
back inside three months later for being drunk on duty. Henry Johnson had more perseverance. In 1874 he was discharged from the 25th
Infantry for his drinking, under the provisions of an order to reduce
the size of the army by getting rid of "worthless" men. Two years later,
Johnson wrote to the Adjutant General and asked permission to reenlist. He admitted that in 1874 "the habit of drinking had so grown upon
me that I was at that time unfitted to perform the duties of a soldier."
Despite this, Johnson liked the army, and after his discharge he had
remained with his company as a cook without pay. His former company
commander thought that Johnson deserved another chance, and the
Adjutant General noted that "this seems to be a case worthy of favorable consideration" and approved the enlistment.[18]

Most binge drinking occurred during the week after payday. Money in
hand, the men headed for the post trader's store, toward saloons in a
nearby town, or to the "whiskey ranches" just outside the military reservation. Experienced officers considered payday as a holiday and ignored what
they thought was a reasonable amount of drinking. At Fort Robinson,
Nebraska, in 1889, the post commander confined drunken soldiers in the
guardhouse but released them afterward with no additional punishment.
Despite drinking, payday passed in an orderly manner at many posts. Even
Chaplain Pierce, once he became accustomed to life at Fort Riley, acknowledged that payday came and went without undue excitement.[19]

Military reformers suggested that all paydays would be orderly if more soldiers were able to save their money. In the years after the Civil War, the army helped soldiers remit part of their pay to their wives or families but did little to promote savings. In 1872, 25th Infantry Chaplain David E. Barr recommended the creation of a National Military Savings Bank, modeled on the Freedmen's Savings Bank, that "would be of great assistance in encouraging thrift, stimulating ambition & guarding against the tempter's power" exercised by the "Mexican Traders, Gamblers & Sunday Horse Racers who . . . hover around the Post like evil birds of prey." While basically sound, Barr's plan did not consider the soldiers' immediate desires. Fifteen years later, Lieutenant Colonel James J. Van Horn of the same regiment wrote that soldiers were "like all citizens[,] money earned by them they feel they can dispose of as suits them best." Van Horn thought that his men preferred to spend their money on drink and women and that few of them would show any interest in saving their pay.[20]

A small minority of them did, though. The year after Barr made his suggestion, Congress authorized a savings plan for enlisted men that, ten years later, had deposits totaling $1,046,568.51. By 1890, twenty-nine hundred enlisted men (14 percent of the army's strength) held accounts. Participation varied widely from company to company, probably influenced by the advice of officers and the example of noncommissioned officers. The 24th Infantry's Company B averaged fewer than five depositors a month during the first half of 1896; in Company D of the 25th, the average number of depositors during the last quarter of 1895 was more than eleven. (Both companies numbered about sixty men.) The difference may have been that Company D, in the Department of Dakota, began receiving its pay once a month—a practice that many officers hoped would promote sobriety and savings—in September 1888. Company B, in the Department of Arizona, had only begun monthly paydays in November 1895. The men of Company D had had seven years in which to acquire the savings habit. Sergeant Hayden Richards had put aside $216.50 by the time of his discharge in March 1896. Another of the company's regular depositors, Private William H. Gooden, left the army a few months later with $506.50.[21]

Some soldiers took it upon themselves to control their drinking, and temperance groups flourished in many garrisons. Chaplain Mullins claimed considerable success with a temperance society at Fort Davis. During the first two months, only one of the abstainers broke his pledge, "and none of them have been in arrest or in the guard house." Other officers and chaplains throughout the army took an interest in promoting such organizations.[22]

The post trader's presence in every western garrison proved to be the greatest impediment to any military temperance movement. Traders enjoyed a monopoly of the sale of alcoholic beverages on military reservations, and soldiers could purchase liquor by the bottle until President Hayes forbade the practice in 1878. After that, army regulations prohibited the sale of intoxicating liquors at military posts until the establishment of post canteens in the late 1880s. (Beer and light wines could be sold, but only by the glass.) The 1878 regulation was not strictly enforced, though, and some traders continued to provide soldiers with whiskey. The commanding officer at Fort Stanton, New Mexico, in 1880 only forbade the trader from selling spirits to enlisted men "showing signs of intoxication."[23]

Even before 1878, a few commanding officers had ordered their post traders to stop selling liquor. As early as May 1868, Lieutenant Colonel William R. Shafter of the 41st Infantry warned the Fort Duncan trader that no liquor would be sold to any soldier within the limits of the military reservation. The next year, Colonel Benjamin H. Grierson gave similar orders at Fort Gibson, Indian Territory. He also warned civilian bootleggers that "all whiskey found on unauthorized persons, except for medicinal purposes, would be confiscated." In these instances, the colonels may have exceeded their authority, but the traders seemed unwilling to jeopardize their licenses and made no formal complaints to the War Department.[24]

If the post trader refused to obey regulations after repeated warnings, the commanding officer could close the store. Before suspending the Fort Concho trader's license in 1878, the post commander conducted a thorough investigation of his business practices. A board of officers found that the trader sold whiskey to soldiers and civilians "in sufficient quantities to cause drunkenness"; that his store was open after hours and on Sunday; and that he allowed gambling in his store. The board also charged was that the trader's whiskey was "of a very inferior quality." The post council of administration considered the board's findings and recommended that the commanding officer close the trader's store.[25]

Most towns close to army posts were little more than crude villages offering crude amusements. A military garrison attracted whiskey peddlers, gamblers, and prostitutes. Brackettville, Texas, near Fort Clark, "was a great gambling place," former 24th Infantryman Robert H. Harper recalled, "and they used to shoot and fight a good deal." An officer at Fort McKinney wrote that because of "the existing state of society" in nearby Buffalo, Wyoming, "the name of the place should be Bordello." A white cavalryman recalled that saloons in Willcox, Arizona, accommodated customers of all sorts during the 1880s. "Chinamen, cowpunchers, Mexicans, Indians, colored troopers, and men from our own troop, [were] all taking a chance" at the card tables.[26]

Given too much to drink, soldiers could become rowdy. When 25th Infantry Sergeant Nevel T. Henderson caused a disturbance in San Angelo, Texas, Fort Concho's commanding officer sent a patrol to arrest him. They brought the Sergeant back to the fort, but he afterward returned to town ("arrest" for a noncommissioned officer meant restriction to quarters rather than confinement in the guardhouse), where the guard had to arrest him a second time. Private Henry Chase of the 9th Cavalry, "in a frolic" in Crawford, Nebraska, rode his horse into a saloon. Not all drunken escapades were amusing, though. While returning to Fort Gibson from a spree in January 1873, 10th Cavalry Saddler Sergeant Henry C. Miller "fell or laid down in the road and was found next morning, . . . nearly frozen to death." He died in the post hospital the next day.[27]

Soldiers often did not even have to travel as far as the nearest town in order to obtain drink. They could purchase whiskey from entrepreneurs who set up "whiskey ranches" (road houses) that thrived just outside the boundary of the military reservation. In 1874 civilians at stage stations on the Concho River sold liquor not only to passengers but also to soldiers detailed as station guards. The 9th Cavalry's Lieutenant Colonel Wesley Merritt complained of "the demoralization of the detachments at these stations . . . resulting from the license allowed the station keepers," but he was powerless to prevent the sales. Several liquor vendors set up shop on a strip of land between Fort DuChesne and the nearby Ute Indian reservation, land to which the government did not have title and where federal regulations, including those of the army, did not apply.[28]

Toward the end of the 1880s, War Department officials and regimental officers accepted the fact that while they could not prevent soldiers from drinking, they could at least provide more wholesome surroundings in which to imbibe. Many officers favored the establishment of post canteens. Besides helping to reduce drunkenness, they urged, canteens would provide soldiers with approved recreation and a place to relax during off-duty hours. Those who criticized the shady business practices of some post traders also pointed out that canteens offering the same goods but run instead by the post council of administration would greatly improve discipline and morale.

Officers at some of the smaller posts, especially, believed that the canteen would do much to improve the enlisted men's lives. Captain Charles L. Cooper, commanding a company of the 10th Cavalry at San Carlos Agency, Arizona, in February 1889, thought that a canteen would soften somewhat "the unusual hardships incurred by service at a camp well known as probably the most disagreeable and undesirable of any in the army." That month, other men of the regiment at Forts Grant and Verde petitioned for canteens. Although few expressions of opinion from most of the black regulars have survived, the canteen's lower prices and the opportunity for billiards, bowling, and other amusements must have generated considerable support.[29]

Even before these requests arrived in Washington, the Secretary of War had authorized commanding officers to establish canteens at posts with no licensed trader or at the request of a majority of the officers and men of the garrison. Besides "supplying the troops, at moderate prices, with such articles as may be deemed necessary for their use, entertainment, and comfort," canteens would provide "the requisite facilities for gymnastic exercises, billiards, and other proper games." The latter, of course, excluded gambling, and canteen regulations prohibited betting "money or [any] other thing of value." Post commanders could authorize the sale of beer and light wines by the glass, but regulations forbade "the sale or use of ardent spirits." A council made up of three company officers and a steward chosen from among the enlisted men administered the canteen. This council drew on post and company funds for the initial purchase of supplies and equipment after which all additional purchases would be made with the canteen's profits. The council had authority to set all prices.[30]

Canteens appeared at many western posts after 1889 as both officers and enlisted men realized the advantages of the system. From Fort McKinney, an officer of the 9th Cavalry wrote that "the canteen became more popular with the enlisted men as they began to realize that in fact it was their own club." The canteen's success depended on the support and enthusiasm of the troops in each garrison. Some were little more than crudely furnished rooms, but at many posts they were large, comfortable, and well supplied. At Fort Washakie, Wyoming, 9th Cavalry troopers enjoyed a canteen that included a barroom measuring twenty-one by seventeen feet, a forty-one-by-twenty-one-foot combination billiards hall and lunchroom, and a kitchen. Besides billiards tables and a ten-pin alley, the Fort Grant canteen offered men of the 10th Cavalry and 24th Infantry a well-equipped gymnasium.[31]

Beer and wine, tobacco, canned goods, and other comforts made up the stock of the typical post canteen. Fort Grant's was particularly well stocked in 1890, offering "beer, porter, claret, sherry, . . . cigars, cigarettes, tobacco, pipes, . . . matches, condensed milk, pickles, sardines, cranberry sauce, canned oysters, mustard, crackers, canned deviled ham, canned salmon, canned baked beans, canned corned beef, canned peas, metal polish, . . . candles, clothing brushes, button brushes, combs, soap, and heel ball [wax for polishing leather]." Not all canteens carried such an extensive inventory, though. The officer who inspected a detachment of the 24th Infantry at Fort Selden, New Mexico, summed up the diversions available there: "Beer is the only item kept for sale. Cards furnish the games."[32]

Approval of the new system was virtually unanimous. Many officers believed strongly that canteens had reduced intemperance and improved discipline and morale. Colonel James Brisbin, who commanded companies of the 1st Cavalry and 25th Infantry at Fort Custer, claimed that the canteen had "greatly improved the discipline of this command . . . [and] decreased drunkenness more than 50 per cent." Brisbin remarked that the lower canteen prices attracted many soldiers, adding that he planned to raise the price of beer by five cents a bottle to curb excessive drinking. At Fort Grant, the commanding officer also found that the troops greatly appreciated the reduced prices at the canteen; at the same time, he acknowledged that it had not been in operation long enough for him to notice a decline in the men's drinking. The virtual end of Indian campaigning by the late 1880s permitted administrators to devote more attention to improving the living conditions of enlisted men. By the mid-1890s, nearly all army posts were operating fully equipped canteens.[33]

Unlike alcoholic beverages, recreational sex was an amenity that the government did not provide. Venereal diseases ranked sixth, just behind alcoholism, on the Surgeon General's list of reasons for medical discharges and the rejection of recruits. Medical reports show that the rate of venereal diseases among black troops was slightly higher than that of whites. Between 1884 and 1893, about seventy-five of every thousand white soldiers reported sick with venereal diseases; among black troops, the annual rate was eighty-five per thousand. The men seemed to accept disease stoically as a natural part of life. "I had a private disease," the 39th Infantry's Hamilton Jackson recalled years later. "I suppose I got it like all the other men by messing around the women." Other soldiers expressed a similar attitude in discussing other diseases. When 25th Infantry veteran Samuel Bias applied for a pension, one of his Civil War comrades mentioned "a touch of yellow fever" Bias had contracted in Florida. "Most of us had [yellow fever]. . . . I had it. Very few men escaped having it in some degree." Given the state of medical knowledge at the time, stoical acceptance was as sensible as any other attitude.[34]

Black civilians were few in the parts of the West where black regulars served. Even in Kansas and Texas, black farmers and laborers settled in the eastern counties, where rainfall and cities promised greater opportunities, while soldiers' duties tended to take them west. Black soldiers did find sexual partners among black prostitutes and other civilian women, but court-martial transcripts, medical reports, and routine military correspondence show that black soldiers often had sexual relations with women of other ethnic groups. In Texas and New Mexico, for instance, Mexican American women received black soldiers more hospitably than did the Anglos, which did not endear the soldiers to Latino men. The 24th Infantry's Musician George McKay discussed this with his companion, Faustina Sanchez. "I says to her," McKay later told a court-martial, "How is it that when a colored man marries a Mexican woman that the Mexican men dont like it and tries to kill him; and she says, I dont know the reason but that is the truth." This conversation, and occasional mentions of marriages in pension and court-martial records, suggests that long-term liaisons between black soldiers and Latinas were not uncommon. Where black soldiers served on Indian reservations, in the Dakotas, Indian Territory, and Montana, they became acquainted with Indian women.[35]

Army records contain material that reveals both sexual indulgence and abstinence. The post surgeon reported a large increase in the number of syphilis cases after companies of the 24th Infantry arrived at Fort Supply, Indian Territory, in 1880. Other army doctors, though, claimed that black troops under their observation were relatively free of venereal disease. The Fort Custer surgeon reported no cases in companies of the 25th Infantry during the last half of 1888, and surgeon's reports at Fort McKinney show that, for several months in 1889, none of the 9th Cavalrymen there contracted a disease.[36]

Conflicting reports like these rule out general conclusions about black regulars' sex lives. The major influences, though, seem to have been those that affect the sexual behavior of all soldiers: the proximity of towns, the presence of prostitutes in or near the garrisons, and the soldiers' ability to pay. At Fort Concho in 1877, an army doctor connected the low venereal disease rate with the paymaster's failure to visit the post for several months. Without money, the men could not visit the prostitutes of San Angelo.[37]

A few black women lived in the western garrisons. The army generally refused to enlist married men, although regulations allowed soldiers to marry with their company commander's permission. Most soldiers' wives conducted themselves well, but some were certainly adulterous if not outright prostitutes. There was no way to determine the moral character of women when they first arrived at a post, and the presence of some wives who paid more attention to other soldiers than to their husbands created problems. In 1894, 24th Infantry veteran Maxillary Wallace moved from New Mexico to the Soldiers' Home in Washington, D.C., and his former comrades in Company F took up a collection to pay his wife's fare. Mrs. Wallace took the money and set up housekeeping with a man in Company D. She tried to accompany the regiment when it moved to Salt Lake City in 1896, "But She Was not allowed By the commanding officer on accont of not Beeing married," one veteran recalled. "She did have the ill Will of great many Ladie of the post Because they gave for the same purpose She was a Sporting Woman after she Left there."[38]

Soldiers were also able to bring women into the garrison by claiming them as members of their family. In order to remove what he called "camp followers" from Fort Davis in 1878, 25th Infantry Captain John W. French posted a notice listing the names of women who were entitled to live at the post. Fifteen years later, twenty-five 9th Cavalry troopers had families living at Fort Robinson, and in 1894 a census of the post counted 117 women and 126 children connected in one way or another to the 500 men of the 9th Cavalry or the 8th Infantry. "Camp followers" were an army-wide phenomenon and not restricted to the black regiments.[39]

Until 1878, regulations allowed the assignment of four laundresses to a company. The army preferred to hire soldiers' wives for this work, providing quarters for the laundresses, who were supposed to augment the family income by washing and mending soldiers' clothing. Occasionally, women served as nurses or matrons at post hospitals: Louisa Conner, the wife of 24th Infantry Sergeant Charles Conner, was a hospital matron at Fort Duncan during the 1870s.[40]

Although laundry and homemaking engaged the energies of most soldiers' wives, some also found time for prostitution. In 1870 Fort McKavett's surgeon pointed to the laundresses as the cause of several cases of venereal disease among soldiers of the 24th Infantry. The 10th Cavalry's Captain Nicholas Nolan requested the removal of three laundresses from Fort Concho because of their "utter worthlessness, drunk[en]ness, and lewdness."[41]

Soldiers were as adept at bringing unauthorized women into the post as they were at obtaining whiskey or convening a card game. When 9th Cavalry Sergeant Alexander Jones accused First Sergeant Jason J. Jackson of bringing "his whore" in the barracks at Fort Sill, Jackson replied that "when she would be going to prayer meeting, she would always stop and ask me to go with her as escort." At Fort Grant in 1889, the post surgeon charged that men of the 24th Infantry brought prostitutes into their barracks, and Lieutenant Colonel Edward P. Pearson ordered company officers to press charges against the men involved. The soldiers' practice of inviting prostitutes to dances at the post caused Pearson to issue a warning that there be "no lewd women admitted to the hall."[42]

Officers at posts near Indian agencies tried to keep soldiers from visiting Indian women in order to prevent possible violence. Standing orders at Fort Washakie in 1889 forbade 9th Cavalry troopers from visiting the neighboring Shoshones, and no Indian women were permitted on the post. The post surgeon hoped that strict enforcement of the order might reduce the venereal disease rate.[43]

A few of the more literate black soldiers wrote letters to convey their intentions to the women of their choice. This tactic may have brought satisfactory results to some, but love letters from a black man to a white woman, whatever their wording, always caused a stir. Private William Eckler of the 41st Infantry "was corresponding with" a white woman near Fort Concho in 1869. A white man named Finley "was at the same time paying his addresses," Captain George H. Gamble explained, "but as she preferred the soldier to him, Finley made many threats that he would kill Eckler at sight." According to Finley, "no damned nigger had a right to correspond with a white girl." Gamble reported that "Finley is a man of low character and can not tell the truth," and added that local whites were "much prejudiced against colored soldiers and fired on them several times," killing Private Boston Henry of the 41st. "I consider [Finley]'s complaint arises entirely from prejudice," Gamble concluded, "and has no foundation whatever." What is most remarkable about Gamble's report is the complete lack of indignation at a black soldier's addressing a letter to a white woman. Far more offensive were white civilians who sniped at black soldiers.[44]

Most black regulars, though, patronized the women who set up shop near every military post, where prostitution thrived as it did in mining towns and railroad division points throughout the West. Regimental officers, army surgeons, and chaplains condemned lewdness, claiming that it led to an increase in venereal diseases and a breakdown in discipline. The convenience of brothels, though, made the traffic hard to suppress. "Mexican shanties, trade stores restaurants &c. which shelter thieves and prostitutes in great measure" stood just outside the boundary of the Fort Davis reservation, inviting the men of the 25th Infantry and 9th Cavalry. "When the soldier has no greater distance to go than to the stables from his quarters to reach a disreputable district, it is nearly impossible to control the morals of the post," the 9th's Colonel Edward Hatch complained in 1870. Twenty years later, men of Fort Grant's 24th Infantry garrison could easily walk the three miles to the nearest brothel, and 9th Cavalry troopers at Fort DuChesne, Utah, patronized one near there. "Every night immediately after retreat numerous groups of [25th Infantry men] were seen headed for these houses," Fort Missoula's surgeon reported in 1891.[45]

The brothel and dance hall run by a black man named Abe Hill enjoyed huge popularity among men of the 25th Infantry at Fort Meade, Dakota Territory. In the mid-1880s, army officers and residents of nearby Sturgis tried to close Hill's business, but he had been careful to build outside the city limits as well as off the military reservation and continued to operate with impunity. Hill's place was on the road between the fort and the town, and passersby were "subjected to the vilest insults in the shape of open acts of indecency which . . . [it] is in most cases impossible to avoid seeing," the commanding officer complained. The brothel may have disgusted officers and civilians, but enlisted men loved it and visited the women whenever they could.[46]

While most western prostitutes were white or of Mexican ancestry, some black women were in the business as well. Where they came from or why they came west is uncertain, but these women could be found near many of the posts manned by black soldiers. Although some worked in brothels, others seem to have been independent businesswomen who operated in private dwellings near the garrisons. These prostitutes were highly mobile and sometimes followed their customers from post to post. In the spring of 1878, enough of them followed a company of the 24th Infantry from Fort Clark to Fort Duncan to earn mention in the post surgeon's report. Distance did not deter two others who moved from Texas to Dakota Territory when the 25th Infantry changed stations. The remarkable mobility of these independent operators, as well as their attachment to their customers, contrasts sharply with the popular nineteenth-century image of the prostitute as a morphine-addicted wretch.[47]

A soldier's visit to a prostitute could end in violence, injury, or death: occurrences often connected with enterprises that operate outside the law or on its margins. Private George Williams of the 25th Infantry received a clawhammer-blow on the head when he kicked in the door of a house operated by two women near Fort Meade. Not all injuries in brothels resulted from animosity, though. When the post surgeon at Fort Shaw, Montana, asked 25th Infantry Private Jefferson Talton how he had developed an acute hernia, Talton replied, "sky-larking with women."[48]

Violent quarrels about women could erupt in barracks too. In 1877 two men of the 24th Infantry at Ringgold Barracks, Texas, David Lyons and John Ewing, got into a fight in their company dining room that began with crockery and a stick of firewood as weapons and ended with a carving knife and a pocket pistol. Their disagreement concerned several women at a nearby "ranch"—not their attractiveness, but whether one of them "could whip two others." The dispute intensified when Ewing called Lyons a liar. Lyons wound up cut and bleeding, and Ewing received a dishonorable discharge and three years' imprisonment. In 1880, after 25th Infantry Private Thomas C. Dyson hit Private Joseph Hale "about [Dyson's] whore," Hale came looking for Dyson in their company barracks at Fort Stockton armed with a bayonet. Dyson hid under his bunk, and Hale got six months' hard labor and a seventy-two-dollar fine. Contentious, violent men also quarreled about women other than prostitutes. Sergeant Barney McDougal fired three or four pistol shots at 24th Infantry Private Jefferson Weedon because of a rumor that Weedon intended to "see if he could not get a little from McDougals wife."[49]

Army officers continually pointed to prostitution as the cause of venereal diseases, which they tried to prevent by any means possible. Although Fort Grant's surgeon lectured the troops several times in 1888, he believed that the absence of proper bathing facilities contributed to the rate of venereal infection. "Most of the men were not able to clean themselves" after visiting prostitutes, he wrote. "The men rarely find the means of making the necessary ablutions after a debauch at these places, on account of the scarcity of water, and the facilities are so poor at the post that many of them neglect to do so after returning to it." Some medical officers tackled the problem directly. At Fort Brown in 1874 and at Fort Concho in 1879, surgeons ordered all soldiers to attend inspections for signs of disease.[50]

After he had served for nearly two years with the 25th Infantry, Chaplain George Mullins was no longer aghast at the men's behavior. He gradually came to understand their standards of conduct and decided that if he could not turn them into good Christians, he could at least try to save them from the more unpleasant consequences of their vices. By 1877 Mullins had reluctantly accepted the facts that "soldiers will and always have been a strong, passionate animal" and "harlots have been and will ever be an irrepressible evil." In what must have been a difficult letter for a chaplain to write, Mullins suggested to the Adjutant General that the army license prostitutes and subject them to medical examinations at regular intervals. In this way, he believed, the problem of venereal disease might be eliminated. The Adjutant General did not reply; apparently, he did not find the chaplain's idea worth serious consideration.[51]

"Public houses of prostitution follow the law of supply and demand," Surgeon George W. Adair reported from Fort Robinson in 1889, "and are the constant attendant of soldiers from the recruiting rendezvous to the most remote frontier station." Since brothels were "not subject to military control," Adair proposed that the army might be wise to consider lifting the ban on married soldiers. He believed firmly that there "was no substitute for marriage," and that if soldiers married they would have little need to visit prostitutes, but the War Department turned a deaf ear to Adair's proposals too.[52]

The army never discovered an effective way to control soldiers' vices, and throughout the post–Civil War period, enlisted men continued to gamble, drink, and whore. These pastimes were common to all soldiers regardless of color. Harmful or not, they helped alleviate the stupefying boredom that attended military service in the West.

CHAPTER NINE

"A Trial Will Bring out the Whole Matter"

Colonel George L. Andrews had to draw up charges against two of his men. It was 1882, and 25th Infantry recruits Edward Mack and Robert Lincoln stood accused of raping an Indian woman, one of the Sioux prisoners of war at Fort Randall, Dakota Territory. "I am entirely satisfied the men are guilty," Andrews told Department of Dakota headquarters, "but of course the Indian woman is the principal witness and her competency depends entirely upon her comprehension of the obligations of an oath." Nevertheless, Andrews determined to press forward with a court-martial rather than let the case go before a civilian jury. "As the frontiersman generally considers that an Indian has no rights which a white man is bound to respect it does not seem advisable to place these men in the hands of the Civil Authorities, certainly not until they have been made amenable to military law for their military offenses." A general court-martial, Andrews thought, would be the proper way to try this unusual case.[1]

In parts of the West where clear patterns of social order and control were not yet established, military garrisons must have seemed like islands of stability. A constantly changing population and the West's vast distances contributed to the region's image as a wild and lawless country. The soldier, on the other hand, found his entire life ordered by regulations. The code governing military behavior remained unaffected by geographic distance or local conditions and governed soldiers whether they served in the harbor defenses of a great city or at a remote Indian agency. Discipline lay at the foundation of military authority and was central to the army's existence.

Military discipline began at the company level and depended largely on the ability of officers and noncommissioned officers to supervise and instruct their men. Each year, officers of the Inspector General's Department visited nearly all of the western garrisons. Their reports, giving the inspectors' impressions and judgments in narrative form, show a direct relation between discipline and the diligence of company officers and noncommissioned officers.[2]

Lieutenant Colonel James H. Carleton inspected the 25th Infantry at San Antonio in 1870 while the regiment was on its way from Louisiana to posts west of the Pecos River. He reported favorably for the most part, praising especially the companies commanded by Captains Charles Bentzoni and George L. Choisy. Both men were strict but fair disciplinarians, Carleton wrote, as the appearance of their companies showed. Choisy's was "probably the finest company in the regiment." The Captain himself was "prompt, attentive, and soldierlike," and "the men as is usual in such cases, take their captain as a pattern." Not all of the 25th's companies had such good officers, though. Carleton believed that although Companies F and K had good men, their slack discipline could be traced to the officers. To correct this, he suggested that "a strict commanding officer" would improve Company F and that a "sharp quick Captain" like Choisy should be assigned to Company K. The enlisted men of both companies, Carleton noted, seemed to be "quite up to the average," and he found little fault with them.[3]

Officers relied heavily on their sergeants and corporals to instill and maintain discipline. In some companies, officers preferred to leave nearly all disciplinary matters in the hands of noncommissioned officers. While a wide official and virtually unbridgeable social gap existed between officers and enlisted men, the same barrier rarely appeared in relations between privates and noncommissioned officers. Despite their rank, sergeants and corporals were still enlisted men. Soldiers might easily view officers as a separate class, but—the matter of race aside—they knew that their noncommissioned officers had been privates once, themselves. Noncommissioned officers who reenlisted in another company began again as privates, and it was not uncommon for one to commit some infraction or other and lose his stripes.[4]

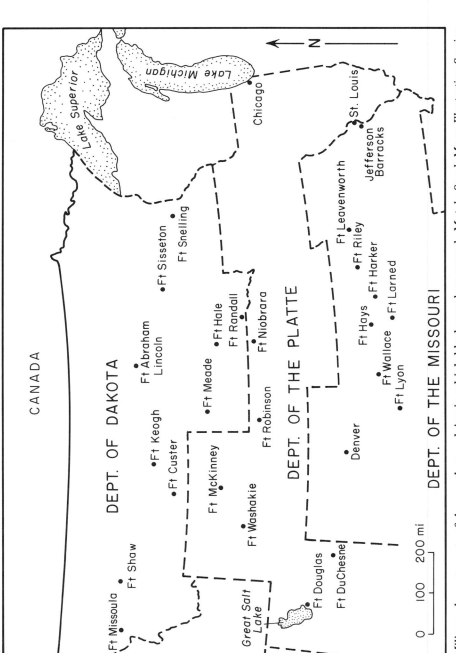

Military departments of the northern plains in which black regulars served. *Map by Sarah Moore Illustration Services, Pullman, Washington*

Sergeants and corporals had to walk a fine line between forfeiting the respect of their comrades by siding too often with officers and losing their officers' confidence by failing to exercise firm control over the men. Officers had to judge carefully in selecting men to promote, and bad choices led to disciplinary problems. The same year Carleton submitted his report on the 25th Infantry, Captain James Curtis inspected companies of the 24th Infantry and 9th Cavalry elsewhere in Texas. He found the soldiers well disciplined "in the immediate presence" of their officers, but that "as far as my experience goes very little respect is paid to the authority of the non com[issioned] officers, generally, in colored organizations." Nine years later Lieutenant John Bigelow of the 10th Cavalry entertained similar thoughts. "A colored man cannot command the respect of another colored man. It is no wonder; they were all slaves together," he concluded. Opinions like these sound patronizing, but they did not arise only from ignorance and prejudice. Angry soldiers sometimes revealed their feelings, as when 9th Cavalry trooper Evan Shanklin, "excited and insubordinate," told his captain "that Sergeant [James] Williams was no better than he was and that he would not take orders from him."[5]

While discipline meant adherence to certain standards, it also implied penalties for infractions of the rules. Most punishment took place at the company level. Often, it took the form of extra fatigue duty, but some officers preferred physical punishment. This often occurred without the knowledge of the regimental commander—who may have been at another post a hundred miles or more away—and the severity of the sentence depended on the nature of the offense as well as the officer's temperament. Before and during the Civil War, the army sanctioned brutal, painful, often sadistic punishments, but by 1866 several reforms of military discipline had taken place. The army abolished flogging at the beginning of the war, and early in 1866 General Order Number 7 promised an investigation of the "state of discipline of companies, and treatment of enlisted men by commissioned officers, . . . with a view to preventing harsh and arbitrary treatment and illegal punishments."[6]

Many reports, though, show that brutal, cruel punishments did not cease. When the 9th Cavalry's Private William Seward faced a general court-martial for sleeping while on sentry duty, witnesses told that he "had been made to walk, without intermission, carrying a saddle, from retreat to reveille" the night before. Seward's falling asleep, the reviewing officer commented, was "not as remarkable or criminal as the act of detailing him for guard after such an unusual punishment." While incidents like this seem to have occurred no more frequently in black regiments than in the rest of the army, some officers may have resorted to physical punishment in the belief that their men responded more readily to force than to reason. A civilian visitor to Fort Stockton, Texas, in 1868 sympathized with this viewpoint when he wrote to the San Antonio *Herald* that although some punishments in the 9th Cavalry and 41st Infantry might seem harsh to the "superficial observer . . . , it must be remembered that Negroes are wanting in that sense of honor or shame, which to some extent restrains the white race from evil practices."[7]

Although traditional, extralegal physical punishments developed during generations before the army accepted black recruits, they reminded black regulars of conditions under slavery, aroused fierce resentment, and inspired several mutinies and near-mutinies during the early years of the black regiments. Some officers maintained that these punishments were traditional in the army—General Order Number 7 of 1866 was proof of that—and not unnecessarily harsh. Common extralegal punishments were for a soldier to carry a knapsack full of rocks or a heavy log, or to stand on a barrelhead for a certain length of time. Carleton noted that company commanders at Fort Quitman, Texas, in 1871 used both methods.[8]

The official basis of military discipline was the volume generally known as *Army Regulations* and the Articles of War, a chapter that specified offenses and their punishments. The Articles of War embodied most of the disciplinary code for enlisted men. In order that soldiers become thoroughly familiar with the articles, regulations directed that they be read aloud to the men at least once every six months. Most army posts also displayed a copy of the Articles of War in some prominent place, but widespread illiteracy in the black regiments made oral recitation the most important means of publishing the articles. In 1871 Fort Clark's commanding officer had them read at Sunday church services and company first sergeants of the 25th Infantry took attendance.[9]

The army's emphasis on discipline appeared in the opening paragraphs of *Army Regulations*. The first required all soldiers to obey and execute promptly the "lawful orders" of their superiors. The next adjured officers to exercise their authority with "firmness, but with kindness and justice," while the third paragraph forbade officers "to injure those under them by tyrannical or capricious conduct, or by abusive language." When officers noted an infraction, disciplinary action was to begin "as promptly as circumstances will permit." (Distance and travel conditions in the West often prevented strict adherence to this provision, and accused soldiers sometimes had to wait in confinement for weeks before the members of a court could assemble.) If the court found the defendant guilty, the sentence passed had to be in accordance with military law.[10]

If officers or noncommissioned officers ignored regulations, the Articles of War allowed a soldier to make a formal complaint of mistreatment by bringing charges through his commanding officer—who might, at many of the army's tiny posts, himself be the subject of the complaint. The commanding officer would then convene a court-martial. The burden of proof rested on the plaintiff, though, and if the court declared the charges to be "groundless and vexatious," the soldier was liable to punishment at the court's discretion. This provision undoubtedly kept many soldiers with real grievances from making formal complaints. Regardless of the article's intent, soldiers knew well enough that unless they could present an airtight case, a court composed of officers would most likely accept the word of the accused and punish the man who had brought the charges.[11]

Beginning in 1884, every enlisted man received a pocket-sized guide entitled *The Soldier's Handbook,* which included a list of fifty-eight of the Articles of War that applied to the rank and file. They covered a wide range of offenses, from mutiny and striking a superior officer to selling or wasting government ammunition. Although the articles stated briefly and explicitly the nature of the various offenses, they did not specify the severity of the possible punishments. In most instances, the articles simply declared that guilty parties would be fined, imprisoned, or both at the discretion of a court-martial.[12]

Some articles stipulated clearly the punishment for a particular offense. According to one, any soldier who sold or lost his horse, arms, or clothing could have up to one-half of his monthly pay withheld until the loss was made good. Two others, which dealt with striking a superior officer and mutiny, authorized the death sentence. *Army Regulations,* which supplemented the Articles of War, detailed "legal punishments." These ranged from fines ("forfeiture of pay and allowances") and, for noncommissioned officers, reduction in rank; through imprisonment (and its refinements—bread-and-water diet, solitary confinement, hard labor, the ball and chain); to death.[13]

Although the army did not codify a list of specific punishments for most offenses until 1891, precedents and long-established judicial traditions had led to a considerable degree of consistency in sentencing. Tradition and custom, though, were poor guarantees that all soldiers would receive equal punishment for committing similar crimes. The vague wording of the Articles of War and *Army Regulations* enabled the members of a court-martial to dispense justice in an inconsistent, arbitrary, and often capricious manner. Nearly all of the articles that related to enlisted men left punishment to the discretion of the court.[14]

Enlisted men appeared before either a general court-martial or a garrison court, depending on the nature of the crime. General courts-martial dealt with major offenses, including those that civilian law recognized as felonies, as well as the purely military crimes of desertion and gross insubordination. A typical court sat for days on end, "for the trial of such prisoners as may properly be brought before it," in the usual wording of the order. The acting judge advocate, a staff officer at the headquarters of each military department, reviewed every court-martial's proceedings, verdicts, and sentences. He could disapprove any part of each case, overruling the court with the words, "The prisoner will be released from confinement and returned to duty."[15]

Garrison courts, which tried infractions like missing roll calls and work details or simple drunkenness, could not impose punishment more severe than thirty days' confinement in the post guardhouse with a fine of one month's pay. In the West, this meant that many soldiers had served time equal to a garrison court-martial sentence before their paperwork reached the department judge advocate. Sometimes, though, review was quicker. While four companies of the 25th Infantry were serving at Fort Snelling, Minnesota, headquarters of the Department of Dakota, Private Robert Frager pleaded guilty to a charge of absence without leave and received a sentence of twenty days' hard labor. The department acting judge advocate decided that since the court had not cleared the room while it deliberated Frager's punishment, its proceedings were invalid and ordered Frager released just a week after he began serving his sentence.[16]

Privates charged with a breach of regulations were kept in the guard-house, while a noncommissioned officer's "arrest" usually meant confinement to barracks. When the defendant finally appeared before the court, he could challenge the fitness of any officer to serve on it. The 25th Infantry's Private George E. Freeman claimed that Captain Jacob Paulus "said he would like to get a chance to sit on my court, as he would like to send me to Huntsville [site of the Texas State Penitentiary] for one or two years." The defendant and the challenged officer left the room while the court considered, usually sustaining the challenge, as happened in Freeman's case. Privates Horace W. Ramsey and George Wiles, both of the 24th Infantry, may have set a record when each had four challenges sustained in a general court-martial. Often, the challenge was sufficient to make an officer ask to be excused, for few officers, if any, enjoyed sitting for hours listening to testimony.[17]

Rarely were soldiers represented by counsel of their own choosing, civilian or military. Instead, a member of the court, the trial judge advocate, was responsible for protecting the rights and interests of the accused. This appointed officer did not discuss legal strategy with the accused, but regulations dictated that after the plea, he would "so far consider himself counsel for the prisoner as to object to any leading question to any of the witnesses, and to any question to the prisoner, the answer to which might tend to criminate himself." While providing these important but minimal legal safeguards, the trial judge advocate's chief responsibility was to serve as prosecutor for the army. The judge advocate was usually a lieutenant in a line regiment (cavalry or infantry in the West, where black regulars served), few of whom had much legal training. Both the prosecution's success and the protection of the rights of the accused therefore rested on the same officer.[18]

Bringing formal charges against capricious and brutal officers was a risky business, for it pitted a soldier's word against that of an officer. In the summer of 1867, a 10th Cavalry officer reported from Fort Riley, Kansas, that Captain John B. Vande Wiele "has had more trouble in his company. Two men whom I *know* to be *good men* have come in on foot to report ill treatment, brutality, on the part of Capt. V. and bring a written complaint from men of the company. The Captain sent in 5 men mounted after them, wanting them arrested and summarily punished as deserters—but it would be impossible to prove any intention on their part to desert—so I keep the 2 men here—and think they better stay till 'B' Co. comes in—then a trial will bring out the whole matter." Three months later, Privates Monroe Gabbard and Thornton Hampton stood trial for absence without leave, rather than desertion, as well as the catchall charge of "conduct to the prejudice of good order and military discipline." A general court-martial sentenced each man to three months' hard labor and loss of all pay.[19]

The trial took place in the Department of the Missouri, and that department's General Court-Martial Orders during the late 1860s afford a handy view of the army's treatment of deserters and absentees, showing how soldiers black and white fared in the military justice system. Two months before Gabbard and Hampton received their sentences, a court at Jefferson Barracks, Missouri, had tried three privates of the Engineer Battalion for desertion, found them guilty of absence without leave instead, and sentenced them to three months' hard labor and ten-dollar-a-month fines, roughly similar to Gabbard's and Hampton's sentences and lighter than those handed out to men convicted of desertion.[20]

During the late 1860s, six months' hard labor was a typical sentence for desertion without aggravating circumstances. At Fort Harker, Kansas, in September 1867, the 38th Infantry's Private Samuel Stewart got that and a fine of fourteen dollars a month for six months. A month later, three 7th Cavalry troopers at Fort Wallace, Kansas, who had taken along their carbines, revolvers, and other equipment when they deserted, began six months' hard labor, each man wearing a twenty-pound ball on a three-foot chain. The court sentenced them to be marked with a letter "D," but the reviewing authority commuted that part of the sentence, as it almost always did in the years after the Civil War.[21]

A court at Fort Lyon, Colorado, sentenced three deserters from the 7th Cavalry who had taken their horses (worth $165 each) as well as their carbines ($100) to dishonorable discharges and one year in a state penitentiary. The reviewing authority, though, found the trial record "fatally defective" because the court did not cite the department order that authorized its existence. "The proceedings, findings and sentences are therefore disapproved," the reviewer fumed. "The prisoners will be released from confinement and returned to duty. Thus from an oversight," three men, "evidently guilty . . . , escape the just punishment of their offences, and the example is lost in deterring others from the commission of similar crimes." At Fort Hays, Kansas, the next month, this legal game of "Simon Says" worked to the advantage of the 10th Cavalry's Private Edward Batties, who avoided four months of wearing a ball and chain and the loss of half his pay (he had deserted, taking along his horse, carbine, and other equipment) when the trial record failed to note that the court's members were duly sworn. In the Department of the Missouri in the fall of 1867 and throughout the West in the decades that followed, general courts-martial subjected black and white soldiers alike to similarly severe sentences and similarly erratic procedures.[22]

If soldiers failed to prove accusations of abuse and brutality, a general court-martial followed, as happened to troopers Gabbard and Hampton. The most notorious application of the "groundless and vexatious" complaint clause occurred at Fort Stockton in 1873. That fall, twenty-one men of the 9th Cavalry and 25th Infantry, including sixteen noncommissioned officers, signed a round-robin petition charging that the post surgeon had effectively killed Private John Taylor by refusing to admit him to the hospital. Taylor died of an enlarged spleen, and an investigating board had cleared the surgeon of wrongdoing. The army dropped the case, but the soldiers at Stockton continued to press their claims. When they began to threaten the surgeon, the post commander arrested the men who had signed the petition on charges of "mutinous conduct, to the prejudice of good order and military discipline"—one step short of outright mutiny. A general court-martial found all of the defendants guilty, declaring that they had verbally threatened the life of an officer and had signed a petition containing false charges. The court, with the approval of the Judge Advocate General, sentenced all of the accused except one to dishonorable discharges and either one or two years' imprisonment.[23]

Soldiers often complained of real, exaggerated, or imagined instances of ill treatment by officers and noncommissioned officers. Many petitions complained of physical or verbal abuse. The War Department undertook formal investigations only when plaintiffs identified themselves. Boards of inquiry and courts-martial were reluctant, anyway, to convict officers because of soldiers' allegations. Three separate complaints charged Captain Henry Carroll of the 9th Cavalry with striking enlisted men. "An officer of your experience," the post adjutant at Fort Stanton, New Mexico, told him, "ought to know the responsibility you assume in

knocking a recruit senseless to the ground for an imperfection in drill."
Each time, though, Carroll escaped censure when no soldier would
openly testify against him. Not all officers got off so easily, though. A general court-martial sentenced Lieutenant Charles E. Nordstrom of the
10th Cavalry to suspension from rank and command for six months, forfeiture of seventy-five dollars a month of his pay, and confinement to the
limits of the post for six months for beating First Sergeant James E.
Parker with a club.[24]

The War Department's practice of not responding to anonymous
complaints and the provision in the Articles of War that left soldiers
liable to prosecution if they could not prove their charges must have kept
some enlisted men from reporting legitimate grievances. In rejecting
anonymous accusations and punishing false witnesses, military law differed little from civilian law. Only a few of the unsigned letters that
reached the War Department listed specific complaints, while most
described bad treatment only in the vaguest terms, failing even to
include the name of the abusive party. Some letters, though, were
extremely detailed and graphic. In 1871 an anonymous 24th Infantry
sergeant at Fort Davis, Texas, claimed that Lieutenant Colonel William
R. Shafter "haes not no Respect of the troopes of his Command." Officers were "calling the Soldiers Dam Black negros" and saying that they
would rather serve with white troops. "We Colerd troopes can Command
our[selves] if the officers of White Dont Want to Do it," the sergeant
concluded.[25]

Six months later, the War Department received a similar letter from
Fort Bliss, Texas. The author, a 25th Infantry soldier who signed himself "Justice O.K.," announced that he was speaking for members of his
own company and of the 9th Cavalry and listed some of the abuses they
endured:

> I do not think it becomes a Soldier to work . . . from 8 o'clock in
> the morning untill 6 o'clock in eving and then to get redy for Per-
> rade, witch we do not have time to clean nothing if we do not com
> out clean we are Punished. . . . I think it is verery hard for us to get
> along as we are doing now we are working harder than any labor-
> ing men are working for five dollars Pear day and I think it is Poor
> incurdgement for us to do the duty as good Soldiers ought to do

> . . . for thirteen dollars Pear mounth. . . . I do think it dos not
> becomes a U.S. office[r] to Kick and Beat and to driv us about as
> we was not Beter than dogs witch is don in this comperney. . . . We
> have not Seen the benifit of our Comperney fun[d]s onley of the
> holer days betwen thoes days we are fed on Soup witch is not fit
> for a hog to eat . . . and we are fed on hard bread witch is full of
> wormes . . . and if we say any thing about our food we are sent to
> the Guard House. . . . The old Soldiers of Comperney H, the 9th
> Cavlary they are . . . geting thare Dischardge for the Experration
> of time and not one of them will reenlist for the Reason of the il
> treatment at this Post. We are not treated as . . . Soldiers but as a
> lot of dogs, and I think . . . it is Poor Encur[age]ement for any Sol-
> dier to Stand up for the Defence of his counterey is to be treated
> as we are, we are all the time in trubel in this Comperney.[26]

Unfortunately, most of the conditions that "Justice O.K." complained
of—long hours of manual labor, bad rations, arbitrary and even violent
punishment, and the small deductions for necessary items of equipment that ate away at soldiers' scanty pay—were common throughout
the army and took decades to improve.[27]

Unsigned letters and petitions claiming mistreatment reached the
War Department from time to time, but the next detailed letter did not
arrive until 1888. In July of that year, a 25th Infantry soldier at Fort
Shaw, Montana, voiced his grievances in a letter to the Secretary of War.
The immediate cause of the letter was the lynching of a black soldier by
civilians, but the underlying complaints were long-standing:

> [T]he Officers treat them like dogs it is a shame the way the Offi-
> cers carry on at this post they treat enlisted men worse than slaves
> because they are colored and the Officers think they have not
> sence enough to write to the proper authoritys the Commanding
> Officer says openly he don't like a blackman and his conduct has
> shone that he mean what he says. . . . [H]e has made all sorts of
> remarks in our presence about our color and our prevous serve-
> tude as slaves and that is where we should be to day. . . . [T]here
> are not a man here that will reenlist here and as soon as we are
> here long enough to save a little money they will three fourths of
> them desert the Service. no humane will stand the treatment they

receive here while Canada is so nere. but you know the Colored
Soldier does not like to desert. for god sake and ours too please
do some thing for us and receive the thanks and prays of your
Humble Servants.[28]

By adhering to the policy of ignoring all anonymous letters, the War
Department undoubtedly subjected soldiers to continued unjust and
brutal treatment. The army did not have enough officers to investigate
every charge of abuse, but in the case of letters like those from "Justice"
and the soldier at Fort Shaw, investigators might have made an effort to
find the writers and convince them to come forward and prefer charges.
A signed letter, though, could circulate at the highest departmental levels. When Sergeant Major James W. Sullivant of the 24th Infantry wrote
to discuss black soldiers' status in the army, General Sherman passed
his letter along to the Secretary of War, who sent it to the Joint Committee on the Reorganization of the Army (see chapter 4). Unfortunately, the committee did not print the letter in its report and threw
away its manuscript records, so Sullivant's words are lost.[29]

At least once, though, an anonymous allegation of homicide led to
the investigation of a complaint. All five members of a herd guard died
when Apaches ambushed them and ran off the horses, leaving the 9th
Cavalry's Company E on foot in New Mexico in 1879. Eighteen of the
dead men's comrades composed a letter, blaming Captain Ambrose E.
Hooker for the deaths. They charged that the size of the guard had been
too small; the men were armed with revolvers, accurate only at a few
yards' range, instead of carbines; their horses had been equipped only
with saddle blankets and halters instead of saddles, stirrups, and bridles;
and no officer ever visited the horse guard to see that all was well. Accusing an officer of responsibility for five deaths, the anonymous letter
received more respectful attention than the Fort Stockton round robin
had six years earlier, and an investigating officer visited Company E's
camp.[30]

He interviewed all fifty-one surviving enlisted men as well as Captain
Hooker, Lieutenant Frank B. Taylor of Company E, an army surgeon,
and a neighboring civilian. Hooker was "responsible for the killing of
the herd guard," Privates George W. Hance and Evan Shanklin said in
almost identical statements. Twelve other men, including all but two of

the company's noncommissioned officers, criticized the guard's lack of saddles and carbines. "They had no show the way they were armed," Private Royal Wilson told the investigator.[31]

Most of the men expressed no opinion about the deaths of the herd guard, but they complained unanimously of Hooker's verbal abuse. He called them "damned negro sons of bitches," Private Luther Craven recalled, "not one of us fit to be a soldier," although Craven told the investigator that the Captain "has never called me individually by a bad name." According to Private Abraham H. Booth, Hooker remarked that the Apaches "did not think enough of the god damned black sons of bitches to even take their scalps" after killing the guard.

Hooker defended his horse-herding practices. A detail larger than five men was inefficient, he said, for two men watched the herd and another kept an eye out for prowling officers while the rest of the guard gambled. Carbines were useless in a running fight with horse thieves, while his men were accomplished pistol shots. Use of saddle blankets instead of saddles meant fewer sore backs, and halters instead of bridles enabled the guards' horses to graze along with the rest of the herd. Hooker admitted that the board of officers who inquired into the loss of the herd had taken a different view.

"Black sons of bitches" was "an expression I have never used," Hooker told the investigator. He "carefully avoided," he claimed, language that raised "any question as to distinction on account of race or color." Yet Hooker went on to say that he was "in command of a treacherous, conspiring race, utterly devoid of anything like honorable or truthful instincts," and that he "endeavored to impress upon them that there was a great difference between soldiers in the United States Army and cornfield niggers." Hooker found that "there has always been a spirit of insubordination . . . which has required the most rigid discipline." He would not even allow his men "to wear all sorts and shades of headgear and clothing" while on campaign, which was the usual practice throughout the army. "Rigid" was the only kind of discipline Hooker knew.

It was unfortunate, the investigating officer concluded, that an officer "with a conscientious sense of duty, whether mistaken or not," should command "men so recently and suddenly lifted from the deepest possible degradation" whom he so obviously despised. "Anger like any other passion increases when constantly indulged and will hardly ever become the proper agent for increasing the efficiency of an Army, whatever material its soldiers may be composed of." Hooker's own remarks proved the allegations of verbal abuse, but the investigator absolved him of any responsibility for the deaths of the horse guards. "Nobody but an imbecile would have ever brought a herd into such a place, in an Indian country. . . . White soldiers would . . . have met with the same fate, and would probably have committed the same error, if left to themselves," the investigator concluded after visiting the canyon where the ambush occurred.

In the course of the investigation, Hooker's men complained of the punishments he inflicted during their months-long periods of field service. Hooker countered that extralegal punishments were necessary when the company was far from a garrison where a court could convene. Enlisted men "carried a log" for galloping the horse herd in from grazing, which caused the animals to be too overheated to go to water. (The men had "probably been gambling and the time had slipped away unawares," Hooker suspected.) Private Thornton Jackson had marched dismounted for five days, handcuffed to the company wagon. Like the others, Jackson did not mention what misconduct had led to his punishment. Hooker explained that he had Jackson disarmed and handcuffed after the trooper threatened him with a revolver.

While incidents of ill treatment occurred in white as well as in black regiments, officers usually handed out punishments in accordance with regulations and accepted army practice. The army's judicial system, with no uniform code of punishments, might have allowed officers to vent their ill will by repeated trials of black soldiers, guilty verdicts, and harsh sentences, but officers had to keep uppermost in their minds the efficiency of their own companies and regiments: on the most basic level, how many men would be available for guard duty; how many for necessary fatigues? The 25th Infantry soldier who wrote from Fort Shaw claimed that the large number of garrison courts-martial there reflected the officers' dislike of their men more than it did lax discipline, but the Adjutant General's statistics show no such overall pattern in the black regiments or even throughout the army. Although the records are incomplete, they do give an idea of how the army's judicial system worked on black regulars. Statistics cover only general and garrison courts-martial; company commanders did not keep accounts of extralegal punishments.

The statistical record of general courts-martial throughout the army and a sampling of garrison trials at several posts show that black soldiers landed in serious trouble less often than did their white comrades. During the years 1880–83, the average number of general courts-martial in the 24th and 25th Infantry was 69 percent of that for white infantry regiments; for the 9th and 10th Cavalry, the average was 78 percent of trials in white cavalry regiments.[32] Garrison courts-martial show a similar pattern. Records from the Department of Texas in 1872, the Department of Dakota from 1884 to 1887, and the Department of Arizona in 1887 and 1890 show that general and garrison courts tried proportionally fewer cases that involved black soldiers. Garrison courts during 1877 at Fort Stanton tried 36 cases from one company of the 15th Infantry, but only 23 from two companies of the 9th Cavalry at the post. Of almost equal numbers of 1st Infantry and 10th Cavalry soldiers at Fort Davis, garrison courts between April 1881 and May 1882 tried 130 cases involving whites and only 50 that involved blacks.[33]

Courts convicted black defendants no more often than they did whites. In Texas in 1880, there was no substantial difference in the proportion of convictions and acquittals. Setting aside desertion, for which the white 8th Cavalry had fourteen convictions and the 10th Cavalry one, each cavalry regiment had five men convicted of serious crimes during the year. The three white infantry regiments in the department had five convictions for serious crimes other than desertion, while the 24th and 25th Infantry combined had four. In 1881 the rate of convictions overturned by reviewing authorities was 35.37 percent in the black regiments and 31.44 percent in the white cavalry and infantry regiments. Between 1876 and 1891, black inmates in the U.S. Military Prison at Fort Leavenworth, Kansas, which housed soldiers convicted of serious crimes, were fewer than whites, proportionally as well as in absolute numbers.[34]

As the reversals of decisions show, courts staffed by regimental officers were more rigid in their interpretation of regulations than were the reviewing authorities. At the regimental level, officers often preferred to apply the utmost rigor of the law to show their men that discipline would be enforced. Reviewers at department headquarters often spotted procedural errors that set prisoners free. Automatic review of all general court-martial sentences worked to protect soldiers against procedural errors and too-harsh penalties.

Not all soldiers received the same sentences for apparently identical offenses. Sentencing was largely at the court's discretion, and its members no doubt considered a wide range of factors such as the defendant's past record as well as military custom and judicial precedent. Enlisted men must have hated such arbitrary power, and many probably despaired of ever receiving justice before a military court.

Some officers undoubtedly allowed personal biases to influence what should have been impartial verdicts in cases involving black soldiers, some of whom received inordinate sentences. But the same latitude in sentencing extended to courts trying white soldiers, and the Judge Advocate General's review applied to all. While some soldiers did receive harsher sentences than were usual, caprice or military necessity might mitigate a sentence or lead to its remission altogether. Zenas R. Bliss recalled a general court-martial in 1869 that sentenced two of three 39th Infantry defendants to six months' hard labor for stealing from the post trader's store but dismissed charges against the third defendant because he, the bugler, could not be spared. Lieutenant John L. Bullis of the 24th Infantry persuaded his commanding officer to drop charges of disorderly conduct against Private French Hickman because of Hickman's "extreme youth."[35]

Mention of crime brought out white observers' worst fears about black people. When the cavalry officer and novelist Charles King, who never served with black troops, called Captain Nicholas Nolan's Company A of the 10th Cavalry "sixty of the best darkies that ever stole chickens," he expressed a view common in the late nineteenth century. When Frances Roe suspected 10th Cavalry troopers of stealing her commissary stores at Camp Supply, Indian Territory, she wrote, "I can readily believe that some of them . . . can possibly be good soldiers, and that they can be good thieves too." Most army officers and literate civilians came from the middle class or aspired to join it, and crime represented a threat to the stability that they valued so highly.[36]

Pilfering military stores was common throughout the army. Inadequate and unpalatable rations; the absence of a post garden and a supply of fresh vegetables or the garden's failure due to drought, frost, hail, or other natural calamity; and the post trader's high prices all moved some enlisted men to steal from commissary warehouses. Others stole for profit. Private William Scott of the 10th Cavalry stole a sack of corn from the stables at Fort Concho, Texas, in 1876 and sold it to a neighboring civilian. Government ammunition and weapons fetched good prices too, and some enlisted men found in this market a way to supplement their meager incomes. A clever soldier might convince his superiors that he had lost equipment in the line of duty and have the government replace what he had sold. In 1868 the 41st Infantry's Lieutenant Colonel William R. Shafter, commanding Fort Duncan, Texas, suggested impounding all items of uniform worn by civilians. "The soldiers are constantly selling their clothing," he explained, "and Mexicans when found wearing what is evidently new clothing invariably declare that it was purchased in San Antonio." Given authority to strip civilians of military garments on the spot, Shafter was sure that he could put an end to the illicit trade.[37]

Weapons were the most marketable commodities, and officers had to take strict measures to prevent their sale. The Colt revolvers and Springfield rifles and carbines that the army adopted in 1873 fired metallic cartridges and were prized by civilians, many of whom still carried percussion cap weapons. Companies kept their small arms in locked racks in the barracks when the men did not need them for drill or target practice, and at Fort Brown, Texas, a light was kept burning at night to discourage thieves. In 1876 the 9th Cavalry's Colonel Edward Hatch ordered each company commander to select a noncommissioned officer and a "reliable private" to guard the weapons. Locked arms racks were standard throughout the army, because civilian demand for revolvers and breechloaders made theft a frequent occurrence in white regiments too.[38]

A few soldiers did not limit themselves to theft. In 1877 the 25th Infantry's Private Perry M. Webber was released to "civil authorities"—the state of Texas—to be tried for forging paymaster's certificates of deposit and using them as security for his own debts. Webber was an unusual soldier. He had joined the 10th Cavalry in 1867, deserted the following spring, and reenlisted a year later under a false name; was assigned to the 10th again; and recognized, tried, and sentenced to three years' imprisonment for desertion. After serving his time, he enlisted yet again, under his own name but at a station of the General Recruiting Service rather than the Mounted Recruiting Service (which had landed him back in the 10th and then in the Fort Sill guardhouse), and wound up with the 25th Infantry.[39]

Reports of rape and sexual assault were everyday reading fare in American newspapers during the late nineteenth century. Metropolitan dailies and rural weeklies alike thrived on sensational news and promoted the image of the black man as sexual predator. The writer might express himself in the most genteel terms as when Major Guy V. Henry, who was full of praise for his 9th Cavalry troopers, admitted their "one weakness, for the fair sex, which the white soldier, from his superior intellect, finds easy to overcome." More often, editors characterized an accused rapist as a "negro fiend."[40]

A soldier on trial for rape in a military court was charged under the all-inclusive provision covering "all disorders and neglects . . . to the prejudice of good order and military discipline." In 1872 a court-martial at Fort Davis awarded 25th Infantry Musician Martin Peede a dishonorable discharge and seven years' imprisonment for attempting to rape the wife of another soldier in his company. The reviewing authority deleted Peede's dishonorable discharge and reduced his imprisonment to one year's hard labor, to be served at Fort Davis, along with a twelve-dollar-per-month fine—nearly all of a private's monthly earnings. Not long after Peede's trial, the wife of Lieutenant Frederic A. Kendall shot and killed 9th Cavalry Corporal Daniel Taliaferro when he tried to break into the Kendalls' quarters. She told investigators that she had fired only after Taliaferro ignored her warnings to halt, and she had no doubt that he intended to rape her. Reporting the incident, Colonel Andrews emphasized that married officers were "reluctant to leave their families for any purpose after dark" and that "these feelings [were] shared" by married enlisted men.[41]

Married soldiers resented other men's interest in their wives, and competition for female attention was always a major cause of violence. The 24th Infantry's Private William D. Manson told his wife that "her conduct had created jealousy," and he wanted a separation. "Later in the day thinking over the matter I commenced drinking," he told his general court-martial. "I went to my wife's quarters after Tattoo and finding the door closed, discharged my shot gun through it." Despite Manson's hope that "sentence will be light" since "no one was injured in the least," the court levied a fine of ten dollars to be taken from each month's pay while he served a year at hard labor.[42]

Chaplain George Mullins estimated that one-third of the general courts-martial at Fort Davis in the mid-1870s stemmed from squabbles over women. A few years later in San Antonio, 24th Infantry Private George Steele told his military judges why he had been absent for five months before turning himself in:

> What first occurred was that Sergt Wm Foster had a woman in the company, and him and her busted up, and she went off and left him and he laid it all on me and he reported to the Company Commander that . . . he caught me out in town with her, in bed with her or something like that, and the Captain told me he didnt want me to go about her any more, and I didnt go any more . . . and the Sergeant came down and raised a fuss with me about it again afterwards, and I tried to reason with him that I wasnt interfering with her any more, and he . . . kept on after me, saying I was still running after her. . . . After that he threatened to shoot me, about this same affair. I got frightened, and I started off and he told me I'd better go and not come back there any more,—if I did he'd make trouble for me.

The court must have believed Steele, for after hearing another private corroborate his story and an officer call him "one of the most valuable men in the regiment," it levied an eighty-dollar fine to be taken from Steele's pay in four bimonthly installments, unusual leniency toward a man charged with desertion.[43]

Enlisted men's appetites for sex and liquor have always drawn providers to towns near military garrisons and helped set the tone of life there. Officers and civilian visitors came away with the impression that these towns were markets of sin where money-hungry degenerates pandered to every debauched taste imaginable. The residents of Maxey, Arizona, were "nothing but cock-suckers, whores, gamblers, cut-throats and thieves," Captain Alfred C. Markley warned soldiers of the 24th Infantry.[44]

Alcohol often sparked confrontations. Drink loosened tongues and bigotry became more open. On Christmas Day, 1882, three 9th Cavalry troopers tried to thrash a white soldier who insulted them in a Hays, Kansas, saloon. Too much drink could also strain old friendships. A black bartender named Overman shot and killed 25th Infantry bandsman Charles Wheeler at a saloon near Missoula, Montana. According to a newspaper account, Wheeler and the barman "were in the habit of fooling in a rough manner, but were on friendly terms." Police arrested the killer, but the *Missoulian* reported that "feeling at the post is . . . bitter against Overman, and if he is discharged he will have to get out of the country in a hurry." The men of the 25th were ready to lynch any civilian who murdered one of their comrades, whatever the murderer's color.[45]

Drunken, rowdy soldiers worried residents of nearby towns, who felt unsafe on the streets, feared for their property, and resented any threat to the peace of their communities. Most towns relied on a city marshal or a few police officers to keep order. Some 9th Cavalry troopers celebrating payday in Hays had "a difficulty" with "an officious constable," as their commanding officer later reported, which ended with the soldiers taking the policeman's pistol from him. Soon afterward, another townsman, chasing the soldiers, shot and killed the unoffending Corporal Thornton Jackson. When word of the shooting reached Fort Hays, about a dozen of the dead man's comrades seized their carbines from the arms rack and headed for town. Sergeant John Fields, who reached Jackson first, ordered the angry troopers back to barracks and brought the body back to the post. His prompt action, and the post commander's disarming the men of Jackson's company until the next day, averted further bloodshed.[46]

As early as 1874, the Surgeon General noted the black regulars' larger number of violent crimes and the incidence of homicide. Of the army's 163 deaths by homicide between 1869 and 1874, 42 (slightly more than 25 percent) occurred in the black regiments. This rate was more than double their proportional strength in the army and three times the rate among white troops. Regimental officers also noticed this, and some attributed the death rate to the soldiers' practice of carrying concealed weapons, usually razors. In 1875 the post surgeon at Fort Griffin, Texas, commented that men of the 10th Cavalry "were in the habit of carrying razors and small pistols on their persons" and that several had suffered "accidents and injuries during their pay day." A newspaper editor in Valentine, Nebraska, remarked in 1889 that 9th Cavalry troopers at Fort Niobrara "were used to carrying guns and knives and flashing them for real or imagined reasons." There is no doubt that concealed weapons were common in the black regiments, but the reasons for carrying them were real. Full-scale riots in Memphis, New Orleans, and other cities after the Civil War and the constant possibility of assault had taught black men to go armed.[47]

Although black soldiers had learned before they joined the army to carry weapons for protection against unprovoked assaults by white civilians, they were most likely to use these weapons on their comrades. Violent episodes, like all social relations in the army, took place mostly within a soldier's own company. In a Christmas fracas at Fort Bayard, New Mexico, in 1889, Dick Richardson of the 24th Infantry opened up Private Lee Chrisholm's face with a pocketknife. Chrisholm managed to produce a razor before friends parted the two men. Richardson, who drew blood, got two months' hard labor at the post; Chrisholm, who merely kept a razor handy, served one month.[48]

Some men carried weapons for show and were less than adept in their use. Private John Anderson of the 9th Cavalry wounded himself in the leg while trying to stuff a small pistol down his boot. "When Anderson was brought to me," his company commander recalled, "I asked him what he was doing with a pistol and why he carried it in his boot leg. He replied he had bought the pistol and he thought the boot leg a Cavalryman's holster." At other times, though, black regulars used their weapons with brutal skill. In 1873 the 25th Infantry's Private Amos Anderson died at Fort Quitman of an abdominal razor wound "received in a drunken brawl." Even guardhouse walls could not protect inmates from the wrath of their fellows. Private William Grant of the 10th Cavalry was beaten and stabbed to death while confined at Fort Davis in 1878.[49]

Officers tried to keep their men from carrying privately owned weapons. At Fort Davis in 1873, the 25th Infantry's Major Zenas R. Bliss "prohibited carrying personal weapons, especially knives, razors, slung shot, and pistols." Bliss told soldiers to surrender their weapons and warned that anyone found with an unauthorized weapon would face punishment, but orders like these did little to curb violence. Noncommissioned officers also recognized the problem and tried to control it. "Your razor will send you to prison if you fool around here with it," Sergeant Lewis Finney warned 25th Infantry Private George W. Newman.[50]

Although most homicides and serious injuries resulted from personal quarrels between soldiers and few killings seemed premeditated, the men could make a particular target of a tyrannical noncommissioned officer. On Christmas Day, 1887, Sergeant Emanuel Stance, a twenty-year veteran of the 9th Cavalry and a Medal of Honor winner, was ambushed and shot to death near Fort Robinson, Nebraska; a patrol discovered his body, with seven gunshot wounds, the next day. The killers had not taken Stance's watch or wallet, and his medal was still pinned to his uniform. Investigating officers could not discover the culprits, but they guessed that Stance had been killed by his own men because he was a brutal disciplinarian.[51]

Black soldiers resorted to murder to rid their companies of undesirables on at least two other occasions. The 10th Cavalry's Captain Phillip L. Lee faced a general court-martial for making false reports to conceal the lynching of a suspected barracks thief by members of his company. Some time on the morning of November 28, 1876, several enlisted men had pistol whipped Private John L. Brown to death and left his body hanging from a tree near Fort Griffin. Lee entered "suicide" as the cause of death in his company records. Prostitutes who lived outside the post had witnessed Brown's abduction, but a vigilance committee warned them to leave town before the county grand jury convened. Lee's court-martial acquitted him, and although the reviewing authority disapproved the verdict, it could not reverse an acquittal. An investigator's report named Brown's murderers, but by the time Lee's trial was over, one of the killers had died, another had deserted, and the others had been discharged and were beyond the reach of military justice.[52]

In the summer of 1889, black soldiers murdered another of their own. That July, 10th Cavalry Private Will Flemming had complained to the commanding officer at San Carlos Agency, Captain Lewis Johnson, that First Sergeant James Logan used profane language in addressing his men. Johnson investigated the charge and sent his findings to the department judge advocate. He admitted that Logan had used profanity but insisted that the sergeant was "a soldierly man of 20 years service, zealous in performance of his duties," although "inclined perhaps to be a little severe," while Flemming was "a poor excuse for a soldier, . . . stupid, negligent, and dirty" and "suspected of secret indecent practices." The incident appeared to be closed, but three weeks later Johnson had to report that Flemming had been murdered. Four members of his company had lured him away from a dance and killed him. Two of the accused soldiers confessed to having led Flemming into an ambush, named his murderers, and hinted that the idea originated with Sergeant Logan. A U.S. Marshal took Logan and the four privates into custody, and they went to Tucson for trial. After two years of legal proceedings, a civilian court acquitted all of them of the charges. By that time, the enlistments of three defendants had expired, and the army did not pursue the case against Sergeant Logan and Private Primas Douglass, who were still in uniform.[53]

Black regulars usually received fair treatment from military tribunals, and civilian juries that tried soldiers seem to have handed down just verdicts. Nevertheless, flaws in the army's legal system could work to enlisted mens' detriment. The most glaring weakness in the system of military justice was the War Department's refusal to investigate unsigned petitions and complaints submitted by soldiers. The anonymous writers may have been describing legitimate grievances, and the army allowed these injustices to persist by not conducting formal investigations.

Despite the vague language of *Army Regulations* and the Articles of War and the discretionary power vested in military courts, the overall record shows that black soldiers did not receive harsher punishments than whites convicted of similar offenses. That black soldiers committed a proportionately higher number of violent crimes is clear. Perhaps the most unfortunate effect of these offenses was to reinforce the stereotype of the violent, criminally inclined black man, allowing bigoted civilians and officers to extend the generalization to all black soldiers.[54]

CHAPTER TEN

"The Result of Outrageous Treatment"

Mutiny was the most serious military crime a soldier could commit, one of the few for which the Articles of War prescribed the death sentence. It was rare in the post–Civil War army, but when it occurred, or even when officers detected the intent to mutiny, the army moved quickly to punish offenders. Mutiny was the black regulars' reaction to officers' brutality and to the imposition of some traditional extralegal military punishments that reminded them of those inflicted on slaves. Regular-army mutinies by black soldiers built on a tradition of group protest that had developed in the U.S. Colored Troops (USCT) during the Civil War.[1]

More than three thousand—about half—of the men who joined the new black regiments during the first two years had served in the USCT. During the Civil War, USCT regiments had recruited locally. Because the new regular regiments did the same—the 38th Infantry concentrated on Nashville, for instance—many of their companies included men who had served in the same regiment during the war, sometimes even in the same company. These old associations portended special disciplinary problems for black regulars.[2]

Company commanders in the new regiments increased Civil War veterans' influence by awarding them warrants as noncommissioned officers. With fifty or more unfamiliar men to pick from, an easy method of selection was to promote veterans. At least thirty-six of them became noncommissioned officers in the 40th Infantry alone, but their influence went far beyond numbers. Benjamin Helm, former sergeant major of the 6th U.S. Colored Cavalry, enlisted at Louisville in February 1867 and became first sergeant of Company C of the new 10th Cavalry. The 41st Infantry's regimental quartermaster sergeant was David Bentford, a veteran of the 111th U.S. Colored Infantry (USCI) who had survived seven months in a Confederate prisoner-of-war camp. Men like these helped shape the regular regiments and set standards of behavior. Part of the standard was to resent, and in some instances to protest, the infliction of corporal punishment.[3]

The men of the USCT had been subject to the same disciplinary system as white volunteers and to most of the forms of corporal punishment that had existed in the all-white regular army before the war. Although Congress had abolished flogging in 1861, two of the most common punishments were still "tying up" (suspension by thumbs or wrists) and "bucking and gagging" (binding the ankles and wrists in an extremely uncomfortable position, with the soldier's mouth gagged). Punishments like these rankled many black soldiers, thousands of whom had known corporal punishment as slaves. When two men of the 109th USCI were tied up in June 1865, First Sergeant Samuel Green approached the company commander "at the head of a party." "Captain," he said, "those men must be released, if they are not released it will raise the devil. . . . We came from home to get rid of such treatment as this." Green and eleven others were tried for mutiny for their action. The court-martial acquitted Green and one other man, but the rest received sentences ranging from one month to the balance of their enlistments, all at hard labor. Similar cases occurred elsewhere. "No white son of a bitch can tie a man up here," vowed Private George Douglas of the 38th USCI aboard a transport ship bound for Texas. In these instances, the men of the USCT showed that they were not disposed to suffer the same kind of treatment that they had borne during slavery.[4]

Nor were the black regulars, who resisted brutal punishments in the same way, which the army called mutiny. Several times during the black regulars' first decade, men in the new regiments were charged with this crime. Two of these cases are worth considering for several reasons. The rarity of a charge of mutiny points up the significance of the incidents, and the conditions that inspired them offer valuable glimpses into some soldiers' experiences in the army. These cases also serve as tests of military justice as meted out to black soldiers, especially regarding those offenses that the army considered most serious and for which it ordained the harshest punishments. The first and by far the most violent resistance by black regulars occurred in Company E of the 9th Cavalry in April 1867. It resulted in the deaths of one officer and a sergeant and the court-martial of nine enlisted men.[5]

In the fall of 1866, the 9th Cavalry began recruiting in Louisiana. Early the next year, the regiment had almost reached full strength and was under orders to move to Texas. Colonel Edward Hatch realized that many of his troopers were poorly trained, for fewer than two-thirds of the regiment's officers had reported for duty. Some companies of the 9th had only one officer present when they took ship for Texas that spring.[6]

Lieutenant Edward M. Heyl had commanded Company E since February. During the war, he had risen from the ranks to become a captain in a Pennsylvania cavalry regiment and was one of the first officers commissioned in the 9th. The company's only officer, the lone white man among nearly eighty black men, and probably unsure of the assistance he could expect from his noncommissioned officers, Heyl quickly proved himself a brutal disciplinarian. Witnesses recalled seeing him beat soldiers with his fist or the flat of his saber during drills and inspections.

Landing at Indianola, Company E marched overland toward San Antonio. At San Pedro Springs, it joined a battalion of the 9th commanded by Lieutenant Colonel Wesley Merritt. Instead of an authorized strength of more than fifteen officers, though, the battalion had only four lieutenants and its commander. The only other troops nearby were two companies of a white regiment, the 35th Infantry, at San Antonio.

The night before the violence, Heyl visited a saloon near the camp, and several soldiers saw him drinking in his tent the next morning. At morning stable call, Heyl put Sergeant Harrison Bradford in charge of grooming and watering the horses. About an hour after Bradford formed the men and marched them off, Heyl left his tent to inspect their progress. He found that three troopers had failed to remove the feedbags from their horses' heads. This minor infraction so enraged Heyl that he ordered Bradford to hang the soldiers by their wrists from a tree-branch about one hundred yards from the company tents. The sergeant apparently did not object to this, for he and several other men tied the prisoners "so that their feet swung more than a foot from the ground." After the men were tied, Heyl mounted his horse and rode off for another visit to the saloon.[7]

He was gone only a short time, but during his absence one of the three troopers managed to untie himself and flee the camp. When Heyl returned and discovered the prisoner's escape, he galloped around the camp looking for him, cursing loudly and nearly trampling several soldiers. In the meantime, one of the prisoners had managed to rest a foot on a tree stump to relieve the pressure on his arms. Heyl walked over to the tree and beat the soldier several times with the flat of his saber.

Sergeant Bradford and the men were returning from watering their horses when they saw Heyl beating the helpless man. Bradford maintained his composure and ordered his twenty soldiers to fall in line. Drawing his saber, but holding it at the carry (on his shoulder), Bradford told the men that he intended to march them to Lieutenant Colonel Merritt's tent to present a formal protest against Heyl. Since the company had not yet received revolvers, their only sidearms were sabers, which all except the sergeant carried sheathed.

At Bradford's command, and in good order, the detail began to march down the line of tents toward Merritt's headquarters. As the party approached Heyl's tent, the lieutenant stepped forward, ordered Bradford to halt, and demanded to know where he was taking the detail. Bradford halted the men and told Heyl that he was taking them to speak to Merritt, "as I don't like to see the men done so," adding that "he could not serve under an officer without he would treat him like a man." When Heyl asked Bradford, mockingly, "I do them so, hey?" the sergeant replied, "Yes, you do them so."

The lieutenant then fumbled in his pockets for a small revolver, which he pointed at Bradford, twice raising and lowering it without saying a word. When he raised it a third time, quickly, Bradford lunged forward and attempted to knock his arm aside. Heyl sprang back and tried to fire, but the pistol jammed. Bradford made several wide sweeps with his saber, trying to knock the pistol out of the officer's hand. Heyl managed to fire a shot, striking Bradford in the mouth. Bradford did not waver but moved forward, swinging his saber and pressing Heyl against the wall of his tent. Heyl got off another shot, wounding Bradford in the chest, before he tripped and fell over a tent rope. As the lieutenant went down, Bradford swung wildly and cut him severely on the hand.

At the sound of the first two shots, Lieutenants Frederic W. Smith and Seth E. Griffin, who had been sitting in Griffin's tent, rushed outside and saw, as they thought, Bradford attacking Heyl. Griffin was armed and moved to assist Heyl while Smith ducked back into the tent to get his revolver. Griffin fired at Bradford but missed. Bradford turned from Heyl and advanced on Griffin, who fired from about twelve feet away. The sergeant sliced Griffin's head open with a swing of his saber and struck him again as he lay on the ground. Smith, who had just come out of the tent, fired two shots that hit Bradford in the head and chest, killing him.

While Bradford was advancing on Smith, the mortally wounded Griffin tried to rise but was struck down by a soldier who broke from the detail, which still stood halted in front of Heyl's tent. After striking Griffin several times with his saber, the man fled back to the company tents. His decision to attack Griffin apparently jolted several other soldiers out of their immobility. Private Irving Charles and four other troopers drew their sabers and rushed at Lieutenant Smith. Smith turned to fire at them, but his pistol was fouled from an exploding percussion cap and the cylinder would not revolve. He threw up his arms for protection as they cut him several times with their sabers. When Charles saw Smith begin to topple, he turned and ran and the four other men followed.

The whole incident, from the time Bradford assembled his men to the wounding of Lieutenant Smith, lasted no more than ten minutes. During that time, no officer, noncommissioned officer, or private called for the camp guard, which was stationed less than one hundred yards from the scene. Only a handful of Bradford's men drew their sabers and attacked the officers, the rest remained in ranks throughout the incident. After Lieutenant Smith collapsed, Private Charles and eight other soldiers left the camp, while the rest returned to their tents.

Soon after the soldiers dispersed, and probably only a few minutes after Smith fell, Lieutenant Colonel Merritt reached the scene. Captain George A. Purington, who had reached Smith just before Merritt arrived, reported that the men of Company E had mutinied. Merritt ordered Purington to form his company quickly to preserve order in the camp and try to catch the deserters. In order to learn the number of fugitives and their names, Merritt ordered Company E's sergeant to assemble the men. They obeyed promptly. The good conduct of the remaining members of the company so soon after the attack prompted

Merritt to mention in his report that the soldiers still in camp had been "perfectly subordinate." When he learned the number of deserters, he dispatched Captain Purington and a mounted patrol to capture them.[8]

In his report Merritt condemned Heyl's "cruel, not to say brutal," behavior, although he did not excuse any of the soldiers who attacked the officers. He noted especially that most of the men of Company E stayed in camp after the incident and continued to obey orders; this, he suggested, showed that the outbreak was not premeditated and that only Bradford and a few others took part in the attack. Merritt closed with a plea that his command "*must have more Officers.*" Griffin's death and the wounding of Heyl and Smith had left the battalion with "but one Officer for duty."[9]

A general court-martial assembled in Austin to hear the cases of Corporals James Lock and Charles Woods and Privates Ephriam Bailey, John Bushwar, Irving Charles, Frank Handy, Henry Johnson, Walker Jones, and Charles Stapleton, each charged with mutiny and desertion. The court first heard the case against Private Charles, who pleaded guilty to the charge of desertion but not guilty of mutiny. Lieutenant Smith was the first prosecution witness. Although he was an officer in Company K and admittedly not familiar with the men of Heyl's company, he identified Charles as one of the five men who had attacked him with sabers. Smith also insisted that he had seen a number of soldiers, whom he could not identify, attacking Lieutenant Griffin but that as soon as he emerged from his tent five of the attackers, led by Charles, turned on him.

The company clerk, Private James Williams, who had watched the outbreak from near the company headquarters tent, testified that he could not be certain that Charles called upon his comrades to mutiny. Several other men from Company E identified Charles as one of the participants, but none accused him of inciting the men. All of the enlisted witnesses declared that Sergeant Bradford had intended to make a peaceful complaint to Lieutenant Colonel Merritt and that he told the men not to draw their sabers. All who had heard the exchange between Bradford and Heyl in front of the officer's tent agreed that the Lieutenant had been rude, and some swore that they were certain he was drunk or had been drinking. "I never saw him go on as he did that morning before in my life," Private Louis Brown testified. "I knew he was drunk

from the way he carried on." They also pointed out that Bradford attacked
Heyl only after the lieutenant had pointed his revolver for the third time.
All of the witnesses agreed that neither Heyl nor any other officer had read
them the Articles of War as prescribed by *Army Regulations.*

In the face of these reports on his conduct, Heyl took the witness
stand and claimed that Bradford had attacked him without provocation
or warning. When the judge advocate asked him if he knew any reason
why Bradford had formed the men to report to Merritt, Heyl replied
that Bradford was angry because Heyl had mentioned replacing him as
first sergeant. Heyl could not even identify the defendant, Irving
Charles, as having been present at the mutiny.

Charles, at the trial's end, offered a statement in his defense that
resembled the testimony of his comrades until he described the moment
when he stepped out of ranks to attack Lieutenant Smith. He insisted
that he remained in ranks when Heyl fired at Bradford and did not
move until Smith emerged from his tent and fired at him. Charles maintained that the firing frightened him and that he merely broke ranks
and ran by Smith to the safety of the company tents without striking a
blow. This attempt to clear himself ran counter to the evidence already
offered. Charles explained that he had deserted after the outbreak
because he was "afraid to go back to camp."

The next case to be tried was that of Corporal Woods. Like Charles,
Woods pleaded guilty to the charge of desertion but not guilty to mutiny.
The court again called Lieutenant Smith, who said that he had seen the
corporal strike Lieutenant Griffin with his saber. Smith was unsure,
though, if Woods had attacked Heyl or had been among his own attackers. Several men of Company E and Captain Purington's black civilian
servant, who witnessed the mutiny, acknowledged that they had seen
Woods break ranks and strike Griffin with his saber. Some of his other
comrades, though, swore that they had neither seen him break ranks
nor strike Griffin. Woods's defense closed with a brief statement in which
he again denied the charge of mutiny but admitted to having deserted.
Like Charles, he explained that he deserted "because I was frightened."

The court then considered the cases of the other defendants, who
also pleaded not guilty to the charge of mutiny but admitted that they
had deserted. In each case, except that of Private Jones, the judge advocate asked the court to drop the charge of mutiny because of insufficient

evidence. Lieutenant Smith testified that he was fairly sure that Private Jones had been one of the men who attacked him, but the uncertain identification and the statements of other witnesses who claimed that Jones took no part in the attack convinced the court to drop the charge of mutiny against him too.

During the second week of June, the court announced its verdicts. For desertion, the court sentenced Privates Bailey, Bushwar, Handy, Johnson, Jones, and Stapleton to six months' imprisonment at hard labor in the military prison on Ship Island, Mississippi. Corporal Lock received the same sentence and was reduced to the ranks. The leniency of the sentences clearly suggests that the court was impressed by the extenuating circumstances surrounding the San Pedro Springs outbreak and the prosecution's failure to prove that any of the defendants had mutinied. Major General Philip H. Sheridan approved the proceedings and the sentences without comment and forwarded them to Washington for consideration by the Judge Advocate General.

The court extended no such consideration to Corporal Woods and Private Charles, though. It found both men guilty of desertion and mutiny and recommended death sentences. Lieutenant Smith and other witnesses had identified both Charles and Woods as active participants in the outbreak, and the court based its verdict primarily on this testimony. The members were not unanimous in their decision for the death penalty; two of them urged clemency for Charles because of "mitigating circumstances," citing Heyl's "harsh and cruel treatment" of his men and the fact that Company E had never heard the Articles of War read.

The transcript of Charles's trial reached General Sheridan during the last week in June. On the same day he approved the sentences of most of the prisoners, Sheridan sent his views on the Charles case to the War Department. He asked that the death sentence be reduced to "imprisonment for a term of years," citing Heyl's "outrageous and cruel" behavior and the men's ignorance of the Articles of War.

After nearly two weeks of deliberation, Judge Advocate General Joseph Holt sent his evaluation of Charles's case to the Secretary of War. He began with a long, scathing indictment of Heyl's conduct, pointing to the Lieutenant's "savage" misbehavior as "the immediate occasion" of the mutiny and recommending a general court-martial for him. Holt decided that Charles had acted in ignorance of the Articles of War and in self-defense, for Charles had feared that his and Sergeant Bradford's lives were in danger. The Judge Advocate General agreed entirely with Sheridan's plea for mercy.

He then listed several factors for the Secretary of War and the President to consider when they passed judgment on Charles: the men of Company E were orderly when Bradford assembled them; no evidence showed that any of the soldiers had planned the mutiny; "and their natural terror on seeing Lt. Heyl draw his pistol and without warning shoot" Bradford. "In view of these circumstances," Holt suggested, "it may well be questioned whether any punishment should be inflicted." In conclusion, he "earnestly advised" the Secretary of War to make any further punishment "extremely light."

On August 16 the Adjutant General issued an order that approved the court's proceedings and verdict in Charles's case. "But in view of the extraordinary circumstances developed by the testimony, showing that there was no disposition on the part of the prisoner either to mutiny or to desert, but that his conduct and that of his company was the result of outrageous treatment on the part of one of the commissioned officers, and in view of the suffering he has already endured, the sentence is remitted, and the prisoner will be restored to duty." The remittance also applied to the sentences of Corporal Lock and Privates Bailey, Bushwar, Handy, Johnson, Jones, and Stapleton, who had not yet left Austin for Ship Island to begin serving their time.[10]

When Judge Advocate General Holt received the transcript of Woods's trial, he repeated much of what he had already said about Charles's case, but he also included his strongest condemnation of Lieutenant Heyl: "The sense of cruel wrong which must have governed these men after the acts of Lieutenant Heyl's brutal tyranny which they had experienced and witnessed, and the terror which must have inspired them when their Sergeant fell, would go far to mitigate punishment for any offense committed while they were so influenced." Holt closed by asking that the charges against Woods be dropped. On October 16 the Adjutant General issued an order similar to his earlier one, directing that Woods be freed and restored to duty.[11]

The actions and decisions of the general court-martial that met in Austin were blameless, for the most part. The trial judge advocate and the court's individual members diligently questioned witnesses, and the number who testified for the defense shows that the court wanted to hear both sides of the story. At least once, in the case of Private Jones, the court accepted the testimony of enlisted men called for the defense over that of Lieutenant Smith. When it found no evidence to connect most of the defendants with the crime of mutiny, the court unanimously agreed to try them only on the charge of desertion. The circumstances of the outbreak, and the deserters' fear of being attacked by white troops, prompted the court to approve moderate sentences for all except Woods and Charles. Only the identification of these two as active participants in a mutiny moved the court to recommend death sentences, a verdict strictly in accordance with military regulations.

While a majority of the court believed that Charles and Woods deserved death sentences, two of its members insisted that "mitigating circumstances" justified leniency. The court, of course, did not have the authority to carry out its sentence, and final approval rested with higher military and civilian officials. Clearly the provision of army regulations that required review of all general court-martial decisions played an important part in the San Pedro Springs trial. General Sheridan's plea, and most particularly the reports of Judge Advocate General Holt, saved the defendants from what might have been a monumental miscarriage of justice.

The San Pedro Springs case is also especially noteworthy because of the attacks on Lieutenant Heyl's conduct by his commanding officer, Lieutenant Colonel Merritt, as well as by Sheridan and Holt. In the end, though, these denunciations had no effect. Heyl never had to account for his actions before a court of inquiry, as Merritt recommended, and in July, while the deserters' sentences were still under review, the organization of the regiment's last companies assured Heyl's promotion, along with three other first lieutenants, to captain. Seniority was the only consideration for advancement through the grade of colonel, and all promotions through captain took place within a regiment. Heyl stayed with the 9th Cavalry until 1870, when he transferred into the 4th Cavalry. After nearly eighteen years as a captain, he became a major in the Inspector General's Department in 1885. Promotion came fast after that, and Heyl was a full colonel when he died ten years later.

On July 14, 1867, less than four months after the San Pedro Springs incident, some soldiers in Company A of the 39th Infantry engaged in a brief, violent protest at New Iberia, Louisiana. More than four-fifths of the company's fifty-eight men were Civil War veterans, nearly half of them coming from the 10th U.S. Colored Heavy Artillery. Officers were scarce, though, and since the company's organization in December 1866 it had had only one officer, Lieutenant Brainerd P. Blanchard of the 116th USCI. On July 12 Lieutenant Lucius H. Warren arrived to replace him. Warren had served for nearly two years as a lieutenant in a Massachusetts regiment before accepting an appointment as major in the 38th USCI. Along with the rest of the all-black Twenty-fifth Army Corps, the 38th USCI moved from Virginia to the Rio Grande at the end of the Civil War, and Warren stayed with it until he received a first lieutenant's commission in the regular army.[12]

When Warren joined Company A, Blanchard told him that some of the men were used to leaving camp without permission during the night to visit the nearby village of New Iberia. To let the men know that he would not tolerate unauthorized absences, Warren called the roll without warning just before midnight on July 12. He found two corporals and one private missing. When the three soldiers turned up the next morning, Warren ordered them confined in the guardhouse. He held another surprise roll call the next night and again found several men absent. Acting on Warren's orders, the guard arrested them as they returned from New Iberia early on the morning of Sunday, July 14, and took them to the guardhouse.

The three men who had been arrested Saturday morning spent the rest of the day policing the camp, a usual sort of company punishment. On Sunday morning, Warren ordered the most recent guardhouse arrivals to join in this work, telling the sergeant of the guard, James Bishop, to make the prisoners "pick up everything bigger than a fingernail." At about nine o'clock, Bishop reported that some of the prisoners had refused, saying, "It is a damn sight better to put us in a cornfield at once and whip us to make us work." Bishop apparently told Warren that he sympathized with the men, who claimed that they were being worked too hard. Warren's response was to pick up his revolver and ask Bishop if he would obey an order to return the prisoners to work. Bishop consented, but while he was reforming the work detail one of the prisoners, Private James Wilburn, cursed Warren in a loud voice, adding, "We might as well be slaves as policing three times a day in Camp."

Hearing Wilburn's outburst, Warren stepped from his tent, waved his revolver in the air, and ordered Bishop and the company first sergeant, Alfred Goings, to assemble the entire camp guard. When the guard formed, Warren ordered Bishop to have Private Charles Williams tie up Wilburn. Williams refused to do this. While Warren pondered his next step, Leon Joseph, who had been a corporal until his arrest on the morning of the 13th, stepped out from among the prisoners. "Goddamn you, you can not tie us up," he said. "If the lieutenant wants us tied up, why don't he come out and tie us up himself."

Warren ignored Joseph for the moment and instead approached Private Williams and ordered him to tie up Wilburn. When Williams again refused, Warren raised his revolver and fired in Williams's direction. The startled soldier dropped his rifle and started to run from the camp. Warren tried to get another shot at him but another member of the guard, Private Westley Wiggins, suddenly broke ranks and diverted his attention. At almost the same time, Private William Robinson, a prisoner, picked up Williams's rifle and advanced on Warren. Another member of the guard, Private Baleford Ward, also moved toward the lieutenant with his rifle raised. In the confusion, Warren managed to get off several more shots, wounding Robinson and another soldier. In return, he received one bayonet wound and several severe blows from rifle butts. During the melee, according to Warren, several prisoners, soldiers, and members of the guard had urged their companions to attack him. Neither of the sergeants, Bishop or Goings, came to his assistance.

Only a small number of soldiers actually took part in the attack, and the other men of Company A did not take the assault on Warren as a signal to riot or desert. Some of them even helped their wounded officer to his tent and one went into New Iberia to fetch a doctor. Only two soldiers, Williams and Robinson, ran from the camp after the attack, but Williams surrendered later in the day and the corporal of the guard arrested Robinson. By noon, Warren had recovered sufficiently to send a civilian messenger with a request for reinforcements. A company of the 1st Infantry arrived within forty-eight hours. Witnesses later reported that the men of the 39th Infantry were still angry and uttering mutinous remarks. Other than verbal threats, though, the soldiers maintained good order and did not try to leave their camp.

A general court-martial convened in New Orleans two weeks later to try the accused mutineers. Twenty men of Company A stood charged with offenses that ranged from inciting a mutiny to failure to come to an officer's assistance. Lieutenant Warren was the principal witness for the prosecution.

The first defendant, Private Leon Joseph, stood accused of inciting mutiny with "incendiary and insubordinate language." He pleaded not guilty, but Warren testified that he believed Joseph to be one of the mutiny's ringleaders. Warren admitted that he was not sure if Joseph had been among those who attacked him but declared that Joseph's remarks were largely responsible for the entire incident. A neighboring civilian who was at the camp when the mutiny took place recalled that although Joseph did tell the soldiers that they should not let Warren shoot them down without defending themselves, he stayed near the guardhouse throughout the attack and took no active part in it. A member of the guard supported the civilian's testimony. The court must have believed Warren's assertion that Joseph led the mutiny, though, for it sentenced him "to be shot to death by musketry."

Private Baleford Ward pleaded not guilty to charges of joining a mutiny and of striking a superior officer. Questioned by the court, Warren admitted that he could not be sure that Ward had struck him but recalled seeing him advance with his rifle raised. Two other prosecution witnesses failed to confirm that Ward had actually struck the officer or had even used mutinous language. Ward claimed that, far from hitting Warren, he had moved away when Warren fired in his direction, adding, "I did not invite anyone else to kill or shoot the lieutenant." Despite a lack of evidence that Ward had injured Warren, the court sentenced him to death too.

Like Ward, Private William Robinson denied the charge of mutiny, although he admitted stabbing Warren with his bayonet. The lieutenant testified that Robinson had urged the men to mutiny and that when Private Williams dropped his rifle and fled, Robinson picked it up. Warren also told the court that he managed to wound Robinson and that the private had kept up a steady stream of mutinous remarks until reinforcements arrived from New Orleans. Robinson said that he used the bayonet only after Warren had shot him: "The moment the ball struck me I stabbed him." Regardless of his claim, the court found him guilty and sentenced him to death.

Warren swore that Private Eli Winters, one of the camp guard, refused to move to tie up Private Wilburn and later moved against Warren with his musket raised, although Warren was not sure that Winters had landed a blow in the melee. While waiting for help to arrive, Warren heard Winters and others making comments like, "It is a damned shame boys to see men shot down like dogs in this way, and not prevent it, and you are not men if you allow it." Although two witnesses testified that they did not see Winters join in the assault on Warren, the court sentenced him to death.

Other defendants received lighter sentences. Private Westley Wiggins, a member of the guard, denied inciting mutiny. Warren testified, though, that Wiggins was among the first of the guard to refuse to tie up Wilburn and that he continued to make mutinous remarks during the two days after the incident. Several witnesses testified that Wiggins had broken ranks in an effort to distract Warren from shooting at the fleeing Charles Williams, and Wiggins claimed that his intent was only to protect Williams, but the court sentenced him to fifteen years' hard labor.

For refusing to obey a direct order to tie up Private Wilburn and for running away, the court gave Charles Williams ten years' hard labor. Williams pleaded guilty but explained that he did not tie up Wilburn because Warren did not give a direct order to him or any other member of the guard. He pointed out that he fled the camp only after Warren opened fire and came back as soon as the camp became quiet.

Two of the prisoners who refused to police the camp that Sunday morning received sentences of nine years' hard labor. Paul Mitchell, like Leon Joseph, had lost his corporal's stripes the day before the outbreak for missing Warren's midnight roll call. His comment on the attempt to tie up Private Wilburn was that if anything like that had happened in his old regiment, the 81st USCI, "the Lieutenant would have been killed." Warren heard Private Frederick Collins, another of the prisoners, remark "that he would be damned if he would work any longer, . . . that he was treated like a slave." Collins "exhibited the same mutinous spirit as the rest of the company," Warren told the court.

Five-year sentences went to two of the corporals who had been on duty that morning. Sylvester Newson's punishment was for "inaction . . . while serving as Corporal of the Guard." Newson made no effort to protect Warren or to control his men. "I could not assist the lieutenant," he told the court, "because I was afraid of being shot myself, he was firing, and I was afraid to run up near him for fear he would mistake and shoot me. I discouraged the mutiny as much as I could without endangering myself." Warren claimed to have seen Corporal James Waslem "with other men of the company, who were making use of mutinous language, and he was talking in an excited manner." Warren heard someone say "that it was a damn shame to have men punished in this way, that it must be stopped," although he was not sure who spoke. Far from joining in the outbreak, Waslem told the court, he was most concerned with avoiding the lieutenant's fire.

Two privates also received five-year sentences. Warren identified Albert Jeffrey as "one of a crowd of soldiers making use of mutinous language" but could not swear to having heard him say anything, although he guessed that Jeffrey "sympathized with the mutineers from the gestures of his hands and the motions of his face." Jeffrey swore that he had been "asleep in bed with my wife as I had just come off guard," but his protest was to no avail. In the trial of John Williams, Warren told the court that although Williams stayed by his tent throughout the incident, he made mutinous remarks. "It is a damned shame," Warren said he heard Williams tell another soldier, "you ought to have killed him."

Warren reserved special condemnation for Sergeants Goings and Bishop. Goings denied failing to "use his best endeavor" to put down the disturbance, but it was clear that he had done nothing until after Warren was wounded. Goings tried to avoid responsibility for the incident by insisting that supervision of prisoners was Bishop's duty as sergeant of the guard. The court sentenced Goings to five years' hard labor. Although Bishop pleaded not guilty to the same charges, the court sentenced him to twenty years' hard labor. The difference between the two sentences was due to Bishop's having been in command of the guard and therefore in a better position to have averted the outbreak.

The court learned more about Company A and Warren's version of its history. Lieutenant Blanchard, the previous commanding officer, had assembled the company several times and read the Articles of War. While some of the newer recruits may never have heard the articles, Warren claimed that most of his men, especially the noncommissioned officers, were familiar with them. He believed that the incident had been thoroughly planned and suggested several times that it was the result of a conspiracy between the prisoners and members of the guard. Warren failed to produce any evidence to support his charge, but no questions from the court could shake his belief. Despite the nature of his unsupported assertions, he never made any statement that clearly reflected racial bias, nor did he once refer to the race of the men he commanded.

Throughout the trials, members of the court rarely questioned Warren and apparently accepted his testimony as fact. Like Warren, none of them openly exhibited any racial prejudice or appeared to take special notice of the defendants' race, but the sentences demonstrate a clear intention to punish the accused severely. Nevertheless, the court acquitted three of the defendants: one who had been on guard in another part of the camp, another who had been getting cleaned up for inspection, and a third who had been out of camp on a pass visiting an old friend who had "waggoned with me in the Quartermaster Department" during the war. That these three men faced the court at all shows Warren's haste in pressing charges as much as did his hesitant or evasive answers during the other trials.

The speed with which the court moved also suggests that its members may have agreed on guilty verdicts beforehand. In their zeal to convict, they accepted as fact testimony that consisted only of the assumptions and unsubstantiated statements of the prosecution's chief witness, Lieutenant Warren. These tendencies, rather than any clear evidence of racial discrimination, marred the court's proceedings (hearing testimony), findings (verdicts), and sentences, and guaranteed close scrutiny by the reviewing authority.

The trials' most glaring fault was the conviction of some defendants who may not have joined in the outbreak. Although Warren had been at the New Iberia camp for less than two weeks and had commanded Company A for only two days, no member of the court challenged his ability to single out the men who took part. Warren was certain that Leon Joseph and William Robinson were involved in the incident; as to the other defendants, though, his memory was not so clear. For instance, he claimed that Albert Jeffrey had made several mutinous remarks during the two days before the arrival of reinforcements from New Orleans. On this basis Warren assumed that Jeffrey had taken part in the mutiny. Although the lieutenant could not swear that Baleford Ward had struck any blows at him, the court ignored his uncertainty and sentenced Ward to death.

The court seemed concerned only with establishing the fact of mutiny and never tried to determine its cause. There was no attempt to determine whether Warren overworked the prisoners, as some of the defendants claimed, or whether the order to tie up Private Wilburn was justified. That some of the defendants feared for their lives when Warren began to fire his revolver seems not to have troubled the court. Also ignored was Warren's testimony that the outbreak lasted for only a few minutes, that only two of the soldiers fled from the camp, and that despite verified "mutinous remarks" from some of them, the soldiers of Company A behaved well during the two days between the disturbance and the arrival of reinforcements from New Orleans. The maintenance of order should have been even more noteworthy because the company's only officer, Lieutenant Warren, was incapacitated by wounds and unable to command.

After announcing its verdicts and the sentences, the court sent the trial record to the department commander, General Sheridan, who read it and passed it on to Judge Advocate General Holt in Washington. By the end of August, Holt had reviewed the proceedings, verdicts, and sentences and sent his recommendations to the Secretary of War. In every case he urged a reduction in the sentence or the dismissal of charges altogether.

In Charles Williams's case, Holt found that the court had charged him under the wrong article. Article 8, under which Williams was charged, required soldiers to use their "utmost endeavor" to put down a mutiny. Williams had dropped his rifle before the shooting began and therefore "took no part in the mutiny other than to refuse to tie up a prisoner." Because of the error in the charge, Holt recommended Williams's release. The court had also tried Goings under the wrong article. He had been charged with a violation of Article 99, which contained the catchall phrase "conduct to the prejudice of good order and military discipline" that covered infractions not specifically mentioned elsewhere. Holt maintained that Goings should have been charged under Article 8 and advised that the case against him be dropped. He also recommended the release of Private Jeffrey since the trial judge advocate had failed to prove that Jeffrey had made inflammatory remarks or taken part in the outbreak.

Because the court recommended the death sentence for Private Joseph, Holt devoted special attention to his case. There was little doubt that Joseph had helped to cause the trouble, but aside from making inflammatory and insubordinate remarks, he had stayed near the guard tent during the entire incident and never assaulted Warren. In connection with Joseph's case, Holt mentioned the trial of 9th Cavalry trooper Irving Charles, who had recently been restored to duty when the President had disapproved his death sentence. Holt cited the mitigating circumstances in Charles's case, particularly Lieutenant Heyl's "extreme cruelty," and regretted that the court did not collect testimony about Warren's treatment of the men during the days before he took command of Company A. Although he did not dwell long on the similarity of the two cases, Holt clearly believed that Warren's behavior had sparked the incident.

Referring again to the San Pedro Springs cases, Holt observed that the 9th Cavalry outbreak and the one at New Iberia "were equally free from the suspicion of premeditation." Neither Warren nor the court could establish that the soldiers "had a preconceived design to resist" the officer's authority. Only after Warren opened fire with his revolver, and then only out of "terror and excitement," did some of the soldiers assault him. Holt also believed that the "unhesitating obedience of the men" before Warren began shooting "and their submission to his authority" afterward effectively countered allegations of a "general spirit of mutiny."

Although Holt pointed out errors in the trial proceedings, he did not criticize the court's members directly. All of them were line officers "who were probably without much experience, though with abundant zeal." It was unfortunate, Holt added, that Lieutenant Warren was "in several cases the only witness, and in all of them the only important witness. . . . The prisoners were undefended by counsel, and were too ignorant to frame a defense, or to know how to elicit facts." The Judge Advocate General came close to declaring the trials a miscarriage of justice.

Within a week, Holt submitted his views on the trials of Privates Ward and Robinson, whom the court had also condemned to death. He began by reviewing the conduct of all of the defendants. Clearly, only three or four men took an active part in the outbreak. The rest "were governed in their conduct by a sudden terror" when Warren began shooting. Since the lieutenant had commanded Company A for only two days, Holt found it hard to believe that he could identify the accused soldiers with any certainty. Citing Warren's confessed inability to name Ward as one of his attackers, Holt advised reducing Ward's death sentence to two years' hard labor. He agreed that the court was on firmer ground in sentencing Robinson to death, but he noted that Robinson bayoneted Warren only after the lieutenant had shot him. Because Holt believed that the mutiny "was the result of an unforeseen and momentary passion" caused by Warren's "want of judgment," he suggested that Robinson's death sentence be commuted to ten years' hard labor.

The President approved Holt's recommendations. All of the defendants except Alfred Goings, Albert Jeffrey, and John and Charles Williams received dishonorable discharges and served their sentences at the military prison on Ship Island. Goings, Jeffrey, and Charles Williams returned to duty at once, and John Williams came back to Company A after a month on Ship Island.

There was no investigation of Lieutenant Warren's conduct. Instead, he went on regimental recruiting service to Norfolk, Virginia, where he stayed until January 1868. While in Virginia, he received promotion to captain of Company G, which he commanded until the consolidation of 1869, when he requested a discharge.[13]

Protest never again became as violent or involved as many soldiers in an incident as it did in 1867. Black Civil War veterans, like whites, adjusted to life in the regular army. Most later protests in the black regiments involved only a few men, and the charge was usually "mutinous conduct," which did not carry the death penalty, or the catch-all "conduct to the prejudice of good order and military discipline." The outbreaks of 1867, though, tell a great deal about the post–Civil War regular army and its new black soldiers.[14]

The actions of the courts and reviewing authorities in the San Pedro Springs and New Iberia cases reveal several important points about the army's judicial system. First, the race of the defendants played no discernible part in the decisions of either the court or the reviewing authorities. The defendants were treated as soldiers, not as *black* soldiers. Only once did the subject of race arise. In reviewing Irving Charles's case, the Judge Advocate General referred to Lieutenant Heyl's "contempt for and hatred of men of color," although there had been no mention of it during the trial. Under military law, black witnesses testified in all the

Defendants and Sentences in the New Iberia Mutiny

NAME	USCT SERVICE (CO./REGT.)	GCM SENTENCE	REDUCED TO
Pvt. Leon Joseph	D/10 H. Art.	Death	10 years
Pvt. William Robinson	"soldier"	Death	10 years
Pvt. Baleford Ward	none	Death	2 years
Pvt. Eli Winters	D/81 Inf.	Death	Term of service
Sgt. James Bishop	K/80 Inf.	20 years	6 months
Pvt. Paul Mitchell	D/81 Inf.	20 years	2 years
Pvt. Westley Wiggins	none	15 years	3 years
Pvt. Robert Mackey	D/10 H. Art.	10 years	*
Pvt. Charles Williams	none	10 years	Released
Pvt. Frederick Collins	C/10 H. Art.	9 years	1 year
Pvt. Joseph Bambrick	F/81 Inf.	5 years	n.a.
1st Sgt. Alfred Goings	E/10 H. Art.	5 years	Released
Pvt. Albert Jeffrey	D/10 H. Art.	5 years	Released
Cpl. Sylvester Newson	F/10 H. Art.	5 years	1 year
Cpl. James Waslem	D/117 Inf.	5 years	6 months
Pvt. John Williams	D/10 H. Art.	5 years	1 month
Pvt. James Wilburn	C/10 H. Art.	**	n.a.
Pvt. Praley Scott	D/82 Inf.	Acquitted	n.a.
Pvt. Thomas Thompson	none	Acquitted	n.a.
Pvt. Peter Word	none	Acquitted	n.a.

* Mackey's general court-martial file does not contain a letter from the JAG recommending a lighter sentence.
** The court found Wilburn guilty but was deadlocked on the sentence (three for a firing squad, two against). There is no letter from the JAG in this case file.

trials, an innovation then under heated discussion in state legislatures, south and north; their comments were considered along with those of whites; and in some instances the courts agreed with enlisted men who spoke out against their officers.[15]

Another point is that regimental officers who made up the tribunals tended to be harsher in their judgments and adhered more closely to the letter of *Army Regulations* than did the reviewing authorities. Transcripts show too that presentation of evidence depended largely on the officer who served as trial judge advocate. Few of them had much legal knowledge, and this fact alone could easily influence the nature of the testimony. Although officers' lack of legal knowledge did not drastically affect the outcome of these three trials, it must have often worked to the disadvantage of soldiers who appeared before other courts.

These trials also show that the power of review was the most important safeguard in preventing a miscarriage of justice. The Judge Advocate General possessed extensive military and legal knowledge. Although his recommendations were subject to approval by the Secretary of War and the President, they bore considerable weight, as shown in the San Pedro Springs and New Iberia cases.

The most striking facts that these cases demonstrate are the defendants' reasons for acting as they did. Arbitrary, brutal punishments surely existed in other companies at other times and places during the years after the Civil War, and men objected but were not goaded to violence by their officers' stupidity. The unanswered question, though, is how prevalent such conditions were. Most black regulars seemed to have accepted their lot without overt objection or protest.

CHAPTER ELEVEN

"The Colored Troops Have Made a Favorable Impression"

From the very first, white people worried about how black soldiers would get along with white civilians. "Their very presence would be a stench in the nostrils of the people from whom I come," declared Delaware's Willard Saulsbury during Senate debate of the army reorganization act of 1866. "A negro soldier riding up and down the streets . . . , dressed in a little brief authority, to insult white men!" Not surprisingly, his concern was for the whites' well being. During the Civil War, black volunteers had served both as fighting troops and as laborers, but black regulars, Saulsbury reminded the Senate, would be part of an army of occupation. He and other Democrats feared for the about-to-be-reconstructed South.[1]

Although Saulsbury objected especially to using black troops in the South, his remarks reflected a bias shared by most Americans. Many must have asked whether black people hated all whites for having kept them in bondage; whether black men were "beasts" prone to violence and lawlessness; and, if they were unreliable, what sense it made for the national government to place them in a position of trust and authority, providing them weapons with which to enforce that authority. Whites, north and south, had often used force to subjugate black people: if blacks were armed, some asked, would they not be in a position to counter that force? Fear of slave revolts had been peculiar to the South, but Northerners now had to consider the possibility that black people might use violence to challenge barriers of discrimination on their side of the Mason-Dixon line.

Most members of the Thirty-ninth Congress did not concern themselves with these questions, though. Republican politicians were secure
in the knowledge that no black troops would patrol the streets of northern cities and no parties of armed black soldiers would supervise elec-
tions there. In 1866 the South and the West posed the nation's military
problems. While Republicans could smugly announce that soldiers would
serve wherever they were needed, regardless of the wishes of local residents, some tried to appease Saulsbury and his Democratic allies by pointing out that most of the regular army, and with it the black regiments,
would go west, where troops would have little to do with white settlers.

Until the Spanish-American War, black regulars served almost entirely
in the West. Duty there minimized but did not completely eliminate
contact with white civilians. While many western posts were far from settlements, some lay close to county seats and even state and territorial
capitals. Supply contracts and wage labor with the Quartermaster
Department at even the smaller posts attracted settlers, and towns often
grew up nearby. Economic dependency on the army aside, there was
no reason to believe that westerners would be more receptive toward
black troops than were residents of more populous regions. Settlers
brought racist sentiments with them when they moved west.

Western newspapers displayed a degree of racial intolerance that was
common throughout the United States. Not surprisingly, many Texas
editors consistently referred to black soldiers as either "niggers" or
"coons." Elsewhere, 9th Cavalry troopers might have come across a column, "Jokes on Sambo," that appeared in the *Daily New Mexican* in 1881.
The same men might also have seen a story in the *Pueblo Chieftain* about
a mob in Maryland lynching a "negro beast." The *Kansas City Times*
printed a long account of "gambling hells" in Philadelphia, which it
headed "A Curse of Colored Men." Men of the 25th Infantry probably
did not appreciate a humorous sketch about "common traits . . . of the
negro race" in the *Helena Daily Herald* a few years later. Pieces like these
reflected many white westerners' attitudes.[2]

Racial patterns in the West did not exactly mirror those in the East,
though. Black residents were seldom numerous enough in western towns
to make whites worry about "keeping them in their place." The need
for laborers forced many employers to disregard the color of a worker's
skin. Merchants in a cash-starved region could not afford to exclude

customers on the basis of race alone. Perhaps most important in the development of race relations in the West, black people who moved there found themselves in a unique position. Although they could not escape incidents of intimidation and discrimination, black westerners quickly discovered that they were not the only targets of racism. Mexicans, Chinese, and Indians often suffered worse treatment. These other, more numerous minorities were a far greater worry to the dominant whites than were the region's few black residents.[3]

An army garrison—enlisted men, their families, and civilian employees of the quartermaster and contractors—always constituted the largest concentration of black people for miles. Their white neighbors' reactions are difficult to determine, though, because only a small number expressed their feelings either in word or in deed. Although civilians' actions cannot be viewed as conclusive evidence of the attitudes of most white westerners, a few examples afford some insight into black-white relations in the West.

Merchants, saloonkeepers, and the owners of gambling halls and brothels usually ignored a soldier's race. Warnings like the sign in a Las Vegas, New Mexico, pool hall, "Colored men and women not allowed to play at this table," were so rare that the editor of the *Daily New Mexican* mentioned it only as a curiosity. Black soldiers mingled freely with white soldiers and civilians in most nearby towns. Reports in 1882 that "scenes of riot and disorder between white and colored soldiers" were "a daily occurrence" in Hays, Kansas, prompted prominent residents, including a state senator, county officials, and businessmen, to declare that "both white and colored" soldiers "behaved themselves," deserved "the respect of the citizens, and disorderly conduct among them has been . . . very rare." The color of a man's money was more important than that of his skin and dictated tolerance. When a Kansas editor lamented the departure of the 9th Cavalry, "because the entire command, officers and men, are very popular with our people, in social and business circles," he underlined the economic basis of relations between soldiers and civilians.[4]

While westerners depended on the army as a source of income, they also looked to it for entertainment. When the 25th Infantry moved to Montana in 1888, the *Weekly Missoulian* was apprehensive about the arrival of "colored troops." First to show up was the regimental band. "This is

one of the famous bands of the Northwest," the *Weekly's* editor acknowledged, "and Missoula is fortunate . . . from a musical point of view, if no
other." The band marched in Missoula's Decoration Day parade and
played at the fort each week, a ceremony that attracted an audience from
town. A few years later, when a company of the regiment arrived at Fort
Missoula, it was "met at the depot by the regimental band and an immense
throng of plain, every day citizens," drawn, no doubt, by the prospect of a
free concert to alleviate the boredom of life in a small western town.[5]

Civilians mingled with black regulars at band concerts and parades,
and many of them went home with favorable impressions. A white Texan
who saw 9th Cavalry and 24th Infantry companies at Fort Sill, Indian
Territory, wrote to his hometown paper that their appearance would
"convince the most prejudiced that the darkey makes a good soldier,
and is able to compare very creditably with the white troops." Newspapers
across the West echoed these sentiments, though not the Texan's choice
of words.[6]

Whether the occasion was a ceremony or a routine troop movement,
the black regulars were always on display. When the 25th Infantry arrived
in Dakota Territory in 1880, the men's manners and discipline impressed
residents of Yankton. The "novelty of a regiment of colored troops"
drew hundreds of people to watch them embark on the riverboat that
would carry them up the Missouri River. When the 1st Infantry had
passed through town a few weeks before on its way to Texas to trade
places with the 25th, an armed guard had been necessary to round up
some of the strays. The men of the 25th Infantry, though, left their train
and quietly boarded the steamer while the regimental band played for
civilian onlookers. After the troops had gone, the *Press and Dakotaian*
praised their behavior. "There was no straggling or running up town
after whisky. . . . In regard to discipline and good conduct the colored
troops have made a favorable impression." Nearly fifteen years later, residents of Missoula remarked that "the men of the 25th are not only
orderly but quite *gentlemanly*. Certainly they do not suffer in comparison
with other soldiers," Chaplain Theophilus Steward reported.[7]

Time spent on tasks that were not strictly military also helped the black
regulars' reputation. Soldiers labored long on construction projects
besides those required for maintenance of their posts. Most construction
was of roads and telegraph and telephone lines, basic infrastructure that

promoted economic development. When these projects were complete, the government opened them to civilian traffic, and western civilians were not blind to the benefits they received from the troops' labor.[8]

Railroads were central to western growth, and the 10th Cavalry and 38th Infantry began guarding construction crews in Kansas as soon as companies could be organized at regimental headquarters and sent west in the summer of 1867. Four years later, Company A of the 10th Cavalry escorted the chief engineer of the Atlantic and Pacific Railroad across western Texas and New Mexico. In 1880 several companies of the 9th Cavalry protected crews of the Denver and Rio Grande from attack by Ute Indians. Express and freight companies also called on troops to escort their wagons. Soldiers often rode the stages or followed behind on horseback.

Residents of El Paso demonstrated the stagecoach lines' reliance on military protection in 1877, when they sought to prevent discontinuance of guards furnished by the 25th Infantry. Petitioners claimed that without soldier escorts, "the mails cannot be carried with safety; . . . life will be in constant danger and the business interests of this section of the country will be very materially impaired." An agent of the Texas and California Stage Company wrote directly to Colonel George L. Andrews of the 25th, admitting that the company's civilian employees had mistreated soldiers in the past but promising reform. The company would even allow soldier guards to occupy quarters built for its employees, and the civilians would live in tents originally intended for the guards. Andrews assented but told at least one sergeant in charge of a station guard to report any civilian "who insults, maltreats, abuses, or in any way treats a United States soldier improperly," adding that "escorts and station guards furnished by the government are hereby ordered not to put up with any abuse whatever from stage men." The Colonel's black soldiers represented the authority of the United States, and their white antagonists were probably ex-Confederates anyway.[10]

The livestock industry was important to the Texas economy, and military escorts sometimes accompanied trail herds. The 9th Cavalry's Company D rode with a cattle drive to New Mexico in the summer of 1872. The next spring, the company's commander told department headquarters that "if the same number of herds are driven over the road this season that have passed in previous years, it would take half a regiment"

The first assignment for the newly organized 10th Cavalry and 38th Infantry was guarding railroad construction and stagecoach routes in Kansas. Alexander Gardner photographed these infantrymen, identifiable by their rifles and bayonets, at Fort Hays during his western tour in 1867. *Courtesy Kansas State Historical Society*

to guard them. Trail drivers relied "alltogether too much on the protection . . . furnished by the troops. Last year I saw a party of 15 or 20 men in charge of about 1,000 cattle who had in addition to their pistols only 2 or 3 worn out muskets in their party." Five of the 9th Cavalry's companies patrolled the Lower Rio Grande to deter rustlers from driving stolen cattle into Mexico and sometimes escorted wagon trains that carried supplies to the enormous King Ranch. All of the black regiments performed similar duty at one time or another during the 1870s.[11]

The army also carried the mail on some routes. When white Texans questioned whether black soldiers could do the job, the 25th Infantry's Captain Charles Bentzoni spoke out "in justice to the troops which I have the honor to command." In October and November 1875, Bentzoni reported, riders of the 25th Infantry and 9th Cavalry traveled more than 2,100 miles in Texas, delivering the mail "punctually, and . . . in good order." The duty was sometimes dangerous. "Mail rider killed yesterday morning going from here," Colonel Andrews telegraphed to district headquarters in April 1878. "Have three scouts out each with an Officer—and a fourth has gone for the body and to look for the mails." To say that a job was routine or commonplace does not imply that it was boring or safe.[12]

Civilian officials sometimes looked to the army to uphold law and order in their towns. Although *Army Regulations* forbade the use of troops to enforce any laws but those named in a carefully detailed list of federal statutes or as part of a posse comitatus, local commanders interpreted these prohibitions very flexibly. Once, 25th Infantry soldiers from Fort Bliss had to patrol the streets of El Paso to forestall a threatened duel between two residents. In 1877, again in El Paso, a battalion of the 9th Cavalry suppressed a political disturbance known as "the Salt War." Companies of that regiment also intervened in violent political and economic disputes in Lincoln County, New Mexico, during the late 1870s, and in Johnson County, Wyoming, in 1892.[13]

Black soldiers' conduct during labor disturbances sometimes earned them a kind word in local newspapers. When workers struck the Northern Pacific Railroad in 1894, a battalion of the 25th Infantry went to Anaconda, Montana, to protect railroad property. They remained there for several weeks until the railroad reached a settlement with the workers. The soldiers' presence annoyed the strikers, but the local editor thought "that if the soldiers had to be called out there could have been none better than the companies of the 25th Infantry who were encamped here. The prejudice against the colored soldiers seems to be without foundation, for if the 25th Infantry is an example of the colored regiments, there . . . are no better troops in the service." Earlier that year, men of the regiment had played an exhibition game of baseball to benefit marchers of Coxey's Army who were passing through Missoula. The black regulars' behavior, on and off duty, often inspired favorable opinions among neighboring civilians.[14]

Terms used to identify black soldiers also showed some change over the years. Uncomplimentary labels never vanished, and some westerners always referred to them as "niggers," particularly in Texas soon after the Civil War. Elsewhere, though, civilians used less opprobrious language, at least in print. "Brunettes," a ponderous bit of Victorian whimsy, appeared as early as 1867 and came into common use. Plains Indians coined the term "buffalo soldiers" to describe black soldiers in Indian Territory. At Camp Supply in 1872, the antipathetic Mrs. Roe noted that Indians compared "their wooly heads" to "the matted cushion . . . between the horns of the buffalo." The next year, a correspondent of *The Nation* at Fort Sill credited the Comanches with noticing that "like the buffalo" the men of the 10th Cavalry and 25th Infantry were "woolly." The expression gained wide circulation through Frederic Remington, who used it in the title of a magazine article in 1889. Its popularity seems to have been limited to journalists, though. Soldiers who described army life in letters to black newspapers did not mention the term, and the men seem to have used "buffalo" only as an insult.[15]

Whatever names their white neighbors applied to black regulars, many western civilians welcomed soldiers, whatever their race, solely for economic reasons. Military posts offered an important market for merchants, farmers, and cattlemen. Army contracts for beef, fuel, and forage pumped much-needed capital into local economies. Moreover, the relative isolation of many posts left the troops with few places to spend their pay, and local entrepreneurs were quick to realize the advantages of this captive market. In 1872 Lieutenant Colonel William R. Shafter of the 24th Infantry wrote that in the neighborhood of Fort Davis, Texas, "the entire community depends on the post and stage line for their support and . . . nothing is being done toward a permanent settlement of the Country and were the troops removed probably every person except those connected with the stage line would leave." No more troops were needed at Fort Meade, Dakota Territory, the editor of the *Sturgis Weekly Record* wrote in 1884, "but if the [War Department] sees fit to ship two or three hundred more out here the people of Sturgis will not rebel. . . . Three additional companies will make that much more pay to be distributed." Businessmen saw that the market provided by a military garrison attracted new residents and helped their town, and their businesses, grow.[16]

Many western civilians could easily name ways in which the army's presence benefited them directly. More than any other factor, though, the black regulars' field service determined the praise or abuse they received from their white neighbors. Civilians might have initial misgivings about black troops' presence near their communities, but they felt justified in demanding that the soldiers provide security for their lives and property. Although the black regiments served throughout the plains and Rockies, they spent their hardest years of campaigning in the Southwest, particularly in Texas and New Mexico, and the newspapers there applauded or damned them according to the fortunes of war.

Except for Union sympathizers and a quarter-million former slaves, few Texans cheered the arrival of the U.S. Army after the Civil War. The presence of uniformed and armed black men intensified the bitterness and hatred that former Confederates directed at all agencies of the federal government. Meanwhile, Texans kept up a loud and constant cry for more military protection on the frontier. Appeals for more troops and frequent reports of Indian raids filled the state's newspapers well into the 1870s. Civilians, especially editors, never tired of vilifying army officers and their troops for not doing enough to protect the state.

During Reconstruction, though, black regulars received an occasional bouquet from Republican editors in Texas. In the spring of 1868, a correspondent of the *San Antonio Daily Express* declared that 9th Cavalry troopers in the western part of the state had "won golden opinions from all who have needed military protection." The paper went even further in reporting the 9th's first major Indian fight in September 1868. A correspondent at Fort Davis wrote that the "many sufferers . . . from these ruthless savages will be pleased to see the glad tidings of the heavy punishment inflicted on the redskins" and pointed out that "while the deluded slaveocrats are moving Heaven and earth to deprive them of manhood and their very life," men of the 9th Cavalry "gallantly exposed their lives for the sake of their oppressors."[17]

While the editor of the *Express*, like many Republicans, used black people as a stick to beat the South in particular and the Democratic Party in general, pro-Democratic opinion predominated in most of the rest of the state's press. The Express's rival, the *Daily Herald*, often led the assault. When the 25th Infantry passed through the city in 1870 on its way west, the *Herald*'s editor pronounced them "as common looking niggers as we have ever seen, and as they are infantry, . . . the frontier will not receive much protection from their sort." Two years later, when a 9th Cavalry patrol blundered into an ambush, the *Herald* was quick to call the skirmish a "terrible disaster," insisting that the incident amply demonstrated that "the negro is not reliable for the defense of our frontier." Nineteenth-century editors had no scruples about "objectivity," and party doctrine was only slightly less important to them than promoting their towns.[18]

Besides Texans, residents of New Mexico were the only westerners who had seen garrisons of black soldiers before the regulars arrived. The 125th U.S. Colored Infantry, the last volunteer regiment to muster out, had marched there from Fort Leavenworth, Kansas, in the spring of 1866. Although newspapers in New Mexico were not as uniformly hostile as the Texas press, one army officer found residents of the territory "much disgusted at the idea of Negro troops being sent down there," fearing that they would not afford "any protection from the Indians." The 125th stayed in New Mexico for nearly a year and a half. While the regiment was preparing to leave in the fall of 1867, companies of the newly organized 38th Infantry were arriving. They stayed until 1869, when they moved to Texas and joined the 41st Regiment to form the consolidated 24th Infantry. Black soldiers did not serve again in New Mexico until the 9th Cavalry marched there from Texas late in 1875.[19]

A few months after arriving in Santa Fe, the 9th's Colonel Edward Hatch remarked to the *Daily New Mexican* that "good and abundant food given to the Indians is much less costly than grape shot," a variant of the usual army saying that it was "cheaper to feed them than to fight them." Some New Mexicans may have doubted Hatch's resolve and his regiment's ability, but newspaper reports soon allayed their fears. Less than three weeks after Hatch spoke, the *New Mexican* praised the "meritorious manner" in which 9th Cavalry troopers "discharged their arduous duty," pursuing Apache raiders for two days and nights and recovering five stolen horses and a mule. The paper never claimed that the army had pacified the far reaches of the territory; merely that Hatch and other commanders used their available forces efficiently. "The record of this command . . . is unexcelled for fortitude, courage, and discipline, tempering justice with mercy in its dealings with the common foe." While praising the 9th, the editor called on the army to assign more troops to New Mexico.[20]

The Apache leaders Loco and Victorio had returned to their reservations by late 1877, and the *New Mexican* applauded "the untiring activity of gallant troops in Hatch's command." The next summer, Victorio and his followers left their reservation again and crossed into Mexico. The *New Mexican*, along with most territorial newspapers, declared that only a shortage of men kept Hatch from preventing the Apaches' escape. Several months later, Victorio crossed again into New Mexico and began raiding isolated settlements, and in September 1879 his band defeated four companies of the 9th Cavalry on the Las Animas River in southwestern New Mexico. The troopers suffered four men killed and one wounded, and lost twenty-seven horses. Even the *New Mexican* could not ignore this reversal and acknowledged that the Apaches had beaten the soldiers for the time being.[21]

The Las Animas defeat dimmed the 9th Cavalry's reputation briefly, but events on the Ute Reservation in Colorado a month later did much to restore it. Exasperated beyond endurance by their inept agent, the Utes opened fire on a small force of soldiers that came to his support. At the end of the first day's fighting at Milk Creek near the Ute agency, 11 soldiers and 10 white civilians, including the agent, lay dead and the remaining 167 were surrounded; twenty-three Utes had been killed. Three days later, Company D of the 9th Cavalry, led by Captain Francis S. Dodge, rode in to join the besieged soldiers. Tactically, this accomplished nothing: four companies rather than three were now surrounded, and Company D's horses were all killed or wounded in a short time; but the black troopers' arrival lifted the survivors' spirits. In another three days, reinforcements reached Milk Creek, and the Utes withdrew into the mountains.[22]

Western newspapers ran the story on their front pages, and nowhere did Captain Dodge and his men receive higher praise than in the New Mexico press. The *Daily New Mexican* cheered their "plucky manner," noting that "fidelity and courage are requisite of good soldiers, and are virtues possessed in an eminent degree by these colored troops." Most residents of the territory, the editor wrote, "did not share the prejudice entertained by some . . . towards the Ninth Cavalry." A month later, the *New Mexican* devoted four columns to a history of the regiment and of the service of the U.S. Colored Troops during the Civil War. The black troopers could "rest assured that there are few people in New Mexico who do not appreciate their merit. . . . The people of this territory are proud of the Ninth Cavalry. It is well officered, and made up of as brave and efficient soldiers as can be found in the service."[23]

Throughout the early months of 1880, New Mexico newspapers refrained from any criticism of the 9th Cavalry. Many of the territory's residents probably would have agreed with a correspondent in Silver City who announced that the 9th's services "have won the respect and regard of all our people, and the prejudice existing against them at one time has entirely disappeared." The next year, when Mexican troops in the state of Chihuahua attacked and killed Victorio and more than seventy of his followers, the *New Mexican* insisted that most of the credit should go to the 9th Cavalry. Several other territorial papers, as well as the *Denver Tribune* and the *Cheyenne Leader*, agreed and printed accounts of the regiment's service during the campaign.[24]

Press comment on black regulars in other parts of the West shows that editors' attitudes depended on the imminence of hostilities and the troops' performance. During the late 1860s, companies of the 10th Cavalry and 38th Infantry served in Kansas. When the *Leavenworth Conservative* reported a skirmish in which men of both regiments took part, it declared that the troops "behaved handsomely. In fact, the general impression here seems to be that properly officered, they are better at fighting Indians than white soldiers." The correspondent then off-handedly undercut the qualification "properly officered" by noting that the 10th Cavalry's Corporal William Turner had commanded the detachment. When men of the regiment encountered Indians on the Saline River a month later, they and the Kansas volunteers who accompanied them "displayed the greatest bravery," a Junction City editor wrote.

"There was no distinction, colored and white; all did their duty nobly
and courageously." Western editors, being businessmen and town pro-
moters themselves, appreciated the army's role in opening the country
to settlement.[25]

On the other hand, the nearest town was likely to harbor many residents who liked soldiers, and black regulars especially, less than did newspaper editors and army contractors. Rabid Negro-haters could be found
in many places, particularly in Texas. Enlisted men's tastes in entertainment attracted civilians who operated on the edge of the law and catered
to any young, single males who had money to spend. Peace officers had
difficulty restraining the behavior of the buffalo hunters, drovers, and
freighters who, like soldiers, sought amusement in towns like Dodge City
and Jacksboro. Some policemen were bigots themselves, while others
would beat and arrest soldiers regardless of their color. If these men harbored strong racial prejudices, they rarely encountered any civilian willing to object.[26]

This atmosphere did not lead to smooth race relations, and army officers and civic-minded townspeople tried to minimize the chance of violence. Many commanding officers, like Fort Robinson's in 1888, forbade
troops to carry sidearms (cavalry revolvers or infantry bayonets) during
their off-duty hours and tried unsuccessfully to ban privately owned
weapons altogether. Civilians helped these efforts by urging lawmen to act
with equal firmness against all those, either black or white, who disturbed
the peace. When a policeman in Valentine, Nebraska, arrested a 9th Cavalry trooper for being drunk, the *Republican's* editor called the action
unjust. He declared that white civilians "could get drunk and paint the
town red" without fear of arrest. "The right thing to do," he insisted, "is to
serve all alike, and not the least partiality should be shown to anyone."[27]

Civilian violence toward soldiers invited retaliation, and confrontations occurred that might have developed into full-scale race wars. Several times, civilians' fears were realized when black regulars responded
violently to indignities. On other occasions, prompt action by army officers and civil authorities averted a clash. Four instances during a twenty-
year period show the circumstances in which black soldiers were willing
to seize their weapons to avenge a wrong.

In August 1873, Brigadier General Christopher C. Augur, commanding the Department of Texas, moved the 25th Infantry's Company A

away from his headquarters at San Antonio, a one-company post where Company A was the only garrison, to avoid what he feared would be "a serious conflict between the colored soldiers—most of the colored people in the city would also have joined them I think—and the white citizens of this city." A man named Tobin, who owned one of the city's largest hotels, abducted and flogged Private James White, who had written offensive letters to Tobin's daughter. White's comrades thought that he had been murdered and went in a body, unarmed, to Tobin's hotel. Their company commander ordered them back to barracks, and they obeyed. Meanwhile, Tobin's white friends and sympathizers began to gather at the hotel. Twenty of them were deputized and stood guard for the next two nights. When some soldiers took their rifles from the arms racks and prepared for a shootout, an officer formed the company and marched it to the outskirts of town while Augur prepared orders for its transfer to Fort Clark.[28]

In a letter to General Sheridan, Augur explained why he removed Company A from San Antonio. He had seen "nothing like a spirit of mutiny among the men" there, but at Fort Stockton, where twenty-one men faced mutiny charges for circulating a petition, there was "a great feeling of anxiety . . . particularly of the officers who have wives and families," and Augur had reinforced the garrison there with a company of white infantry. "The fact cannot be disguised, that there is anxiety at every post garrisoned exclusively by colored troops. They are so clannish, and so excitable, turning every question into one of class, that there is no knowing when a question may arise which will annoy in a moment the whole of the garrison against its officers not as officers, but as white men." Although the men of Company A were "perfectly quiet and obedient" at the time he wrote, Augur thought it best to put them where white civilians could neither insult nor injure them—and where civilians would be safe from the soldiers' retaliation.[29]

Although the Democratic *Herald* had reported the story in lurid tones— Private White was "a bright mulatto man . . . known to have been a regular reader of the obscene literature published in New York, and, by correspondence, a dealer with such parties as advertise the sale of 'love powders'"—the editor took a different view when Company A's transfer removed fifty men from the army's local payroll. Before the incident, he wrote, there had been no evidence of insubordination among the black

238 THE BLACK REGULARS, 1866–1898

soldiers, and the officers had kept their men "in excellent discipline." Residents of San Antonio had never complained about the troops, whose conduct "might have been taken for an example by many of our . . . negroes, and, indeed, by some other of our citizens." Not for another nine years, though, until companies of the 25th Infantry arrived at Fort Snelling, Minnesota, would black soldiers again serve at a departmental headquarters or near a city of any size.[30]

In the winter of 1881, relations between Fort Concho's garrison (four companies of the 10th Cavalry and four of the 16th Infantry) and residents of nearby San Angelo became more violent than usual. A civilian shot dead Private Hiram E. Pindar of the 16th Infantry while Pindar was trying to stop a fight. The killer "was furnished with a fast horse," Colonel Benjamin Grierson, commanding the post, reported to department headquarters, "and has not been arrested." Just twelve days later, another civilian killed the 10th Cavalry's Private William Watkins when Watkins, who had been entertaining a saloon crowd to earn drinks, said he was too tired to dance any longer. This time the gunman wound up in San Angelo's jail.[31]

Grierson strengthened the guard and ordered extra roll calls. The first roll call showed that about seventy men, most of them from Pindar's and Watkins's companies, had left the fort and taken their weapons with them. A soldier's company was the focus of his loyalty—just as it was the setting for most violence—and the men, black and white alike, had set out to avenge their dead comrades. Grierson sent the guard after them, the drummers beat the long roll as a signal to assemble, and the missing men returned about a quarter of an hour later.[32]

On February 3 a printed handbill appeared on the streets of San Angelo:

> We, the soldiers of the U.S. Army, do hereby warn Cow-Boys &c., of San Angela [sic] and vacinity, to recognize our right of way, as just and peaceable men. If we do not receive justice and fair play, which we must have, some one will suffer—if not the guilty, the innocent. It has gone too far. Justice or death.
> (Signed) U.S. Soldiers
> One and All.[33]

Grierson quickly discovered that the author was a soldier of the 16th Infantry and that the post printers, Private Frederick Mitchell of the 10th Cavalry and another infantryman, had run the handbills off on the fort's printing press.

A garrison court-martial tried the three men later that month. The handbill's author lost an entire month's pay—the maximum fine a garrison court could award. Private Mitchell lost three dollars—nearly one-quarter of his month's pay—and the other printer apparently got off without punishment. All three men were extremely fortunate, for a charge of "conduct to the prejudice of good order and military discipline" might have brought them before a general court-martial, which could award prison terms and dishonorable discharges.[34]

Two nights later, there was another raid on San Angelo when about seventy men in the companies that had not taken part in the earlier excursion doused the lights in their barracks, broke open the arms racks, and headed for town with their weapons. "A good many shots were fired" before Grierson could assemble a force large enough to pursue the absentees. By the time the patrol reached San Angelo, the soldiers were returning to the fort.

The reason behind the second raid is obscure. The men may have been annoyed by civilians sniping at the extra guards Grierson had posted to keep his men from sneaking into town, or they may have decided to find and lynch a policeman who had once killed a soldier and was notorious for beating and robbing soldiers, arresting them on the slightest pretext. Whatever the cause, twenty-one Texas Rangers arrived in San Angelo the next day, and an uneasy truce prevailed during the following weeks while a grand jury in the county seat tried to sort out matters.[35]

One of the most violent confrontations between black soldiers and neighboring civilians occurred in 1885 at Sturgis, Dakota Territory, near Fort Meade. Companies of the 25th Infantry and 7th Cavalry garrisoned the fort. During their off-duty hours, the men frequented saloons and brothels in Sturgis. Since some white prostitutes objected to black patronage, there were a couple of brothels staffed by black women, but black soldiers did not encounter a great deal of bigotry in town. When companies of the 25th had arrived several years earlier, the *Black Hills*

Daily Times greeted them by observing that "times are lively" for "they brought money with them," a frank admission of the basis for nearly all civil-military relations in the West.[36]

Corporal Ross Hallon of the 25th Infantry's Company A was attached to a woman named Minnie Lewis. When he beat her severely, she went for treatment to H. P. Lynch, a druggist in town, which further angered the Corporal. Unable to contain his rage, Hallon went into Sturgis on the night of August 22, found the druggist reading in his office, and fired several shots, one of which killed Lynch. Hallon returned to Fort Meade afterward, but the post commander, Colonel Samuel D. Sturgis of the 7th Cavalry, ordered his arrest. The next morning, the Colonel surrendered him to civil authorities for trial.

On the night of August 25, a mob broke into the jail, took Hallon to the edge of town, and hanged him. Some members of Company A took their rifles and headed into town to avenge their murdered comrade. They did not doubt that Hallon had murdered his rival, but they wanted revenge for the lynching. When Colonel Sturgis heard of this, he sent a cavalry patrol to head off the infantrymen.

An atmosphere of extreme tension prevailed during the following weeks. Soldiers still visited town, though, and on the night of September 18 several infantrymen were drinking in a saloon owned by a black man named Abe Hill. The 25th Infantry's Private John Taylor got into an argument with Hill himself and left the saloon, vowing, "You will hear from us again tonight." Soon afterward, more than a dozen armed infantrymen left Fort Meade and went into Sturgis. They formed a line in front of Hill's saloon, called out to any soldiers still inside to leave, and fired between sixty and one hundred rounds into the building. Two witnesses heard them inquire after the town policeman, who had allowed the mob to take Hallon, saying that they wanted to see him "up at Fiddler's tree," a local landmark where a mob had hanged a man by that name the year before. The soldiers then returned to the fort, leaving a white civilian named Robert S. Bell dead on the floor of the saloon.

Next morning, Colonel Sturgis appointed a board of officers to investigate the whole affair. The officers examined the scene of the shooting, viewed the corpse, talked to witnesses, and finally arrested four soldiers whom civilian witnesses identified as members of the party. Several Dakota newspapers praised the Colonel's efforts to find the guilty; some took the opportunity to heap obloquy on all black soldiers. "A Squad of Drunken Colored Soldiers Shoot Promiscuously and Kill a Cowboy," the *Deadwood Pioneer*'s headline blared.[37]

In their report the officers noted that the shooting had involved only a few members of one company of the 25th Infantry. They did not connect Bell's death with those of Lynch and Hallon and offered no explanation for the soldiers' violent behavior. The report seemed to imply that no riot had occurred, that the incident involved only a few soldiers, and that it reflected no discredit either on the residents of Sturgis or on most of the garrison at Fort Meade.

Bernard G. Caulfield, one of the town's founders and a member of the territorial Democratic committee, expressed a decidedly different view in a letter to President Grover Cleveland. Caulfield claimed to know a great deal about the incident, for he had been at Colonel Sturgis's house on the evening of the shooting. He called the men of the 25th Infantry "a set of reckless desperadoes" and asked if it would not be best to send them to a more isolated post. Caulfield acknowledged that soldiers "have met sometimes with outrages from a class of scoundrels . . . fleecing & robbing the soldiers about pay day," but he was careful not to include "the good citizens" of Sturgis in this category.[38]

Cleveland sent a copy of Caulfield's letter to Brigadier General Alfred H. Terry, commanding the Department of Dakota, who refused to countenance the regiment's removal. In his reply, Terry insisted that only a few men from one company had fired into two of the town's saloons and that the troops at Fort Meade posed no threat to the residents of Sturgis. "I have had much experience with colored troops," Terry wrote, "and I have always found them well behaved and as amenable to discipline as any white troops, that we have." Certain "evils" were always present near military posts, Terry maintained, and the town of Sturgis offered an abundance of them. He blamed the violence on the town's many saloons and brothels. "Until the people of the town shall have suppressed these dens, which equally debauch the troops of the post and threaten their own safety," Terry concluded, "they will not be in a position to ask the government to change its garrison." The "evils" remained unabated, and four companies of the 25th stayed at Fort Meade until 1888, when the entire regiment moved to Montana.[39]

Gunfire broke out again in the spring of 1892, when six companies of the 9th Cavalry camped near an end-of-track town in Wyoming's Powder River country after the Johnson County War. One of the new state's senators asked the Secretary of War to send the 9th to patrol the rangeland after an inconclusive shootout between resident homesteader-ranchers, many of them former cowboys who had come from Texas with the trail herds, and gunmen hired by the Wyoming Stockgrowers' Association. "The colored troops will have no sympathy for the Texan thieves, and those are the troops we want," members of the association had urged Senator Joseph M. Carey.[40]

Whether Texan or not, Johnson County residents were prepared to dislike soldiers, whom they saw as agents of the Cheyenne cattle barons. Captain John F. Guilfoyle, who had marched hundreds of miles with the 9th Cavalry through the homesteaded lands of Kansas and Nebraska, and now into Wyoming, observed that "on our march here the citizens generally avoided us, contrary to their usual habits. . . . There was also a prejudice against the colored soldiers." That these troops were black offered opportunities for "open hostility" and "gross insult" that offended even the officers.[41]

Many residents of Suggs, a town that one officer called "a collection of tents occupied by the class usually found along the line of a new railroad," treated the men of the regiment as though they were the Stockgrowers' Association's hired guns: they boycotted them. Within days of their arrival, troopers had been refused service at the hotel, by a barber, and by at least one prostitute. But the factor of race entered too. "Ain't your mother a black bitch?" a white man with a drawn revolver asked one trooper, who prudently retreated and rode out of town to an accompaniment of gunfire.[42]

After dark the next evening, about twenty soldiers stole out of camp and walked into town. They announced their arrival with a fusillade and continued firing. Some townspeople returned the fire. The commanding officer ordered two companies to ride into Suggs, restore order, and bring back the missing troopers. When the patrol reached town, it found Private Willis Johnson dead, shot in the head, one civilian wounded in the arm, and many residents scattered in the nearby hills, where they had fled from the firing.

Companies of the 9th Cavalry remained in Johnson County until fall. When they returned to Fort Robinson, Nebraska, a general court-martial tried three men, the leaders of the raid on Suggs, for conduct to the prejudice of good order and military discipline; all three pleaded guilty and received fifty-cent fines. Members of the court reasoned that the men had already been locked up for three months, since the night of the raid, and some of the officers may have remembered the insults that they themselves had suffered in Wyoming.[43]

These violent incidents span most of the post–Civil War era. That they occurred in such widely scattered places shows that black regulars never escaped prejudice and that racial hostility could always erupt into violence. Each time, though, soldiers were prepared to respond with force. Regardless of the legality or the wisdom of their acts, some of them were ready to seek justice in perhaps the only way many westerners—indeed, many Americans—understood.

White civilians' reactions to black soldiers, as expressed in newspapers, followed a fairly predictable course. Initial apprehension gave way to a realistic appraisal of the soldiers' military worth in times of active campaigning. During spells in garrison, the troops' reputation depended entirely on avoiding violence: baseball games and the regimental band made for smooth relations with neighboring civilians; brawls and killings did not. And although white troops were just as likely to be shot at and to shoot back, a violent response from black soldiers might earn the remark that they were "fit subjects for a cannibal island."[44]

Civilians' economic motives were everywhere apparent. Nearby residents who profited directly from the soldiers' pay—tavern owners and brothel keepers especially—provided potentially violent settings where the soldiers' conduct was most likely to draw the wrath of "respectable" townspeople—newspaper editors and army contractors among them—whose complaints could reach high up the army's chain of command. Although a military post furnished its civilian neighbors with several kinds of income, lethal violence gave a town a bad name, and civic leaders might ask for a change in the garrison.[45]

It is virtually impossible to learn which factor, fear or greed, most affected civilians' attitudes. How highly did black soldiers' neighbors value their military protection? They certainly prized the economic addition of an army post to the neighborhood. Was black soldiers' behavior, both on duty and off, more influential than civilians' preconceptions about their inferiority? What is certain is that, despite the continued existence of bigotry, black regulars helped create an atmosphere in which many white civilians learned to tolerate, and even appreciate, their presence. Frequent contact did not erase all racial hostility (at times, contact clearly intensified hatred), but black regulars and their civilian neighbors often achieved a kind of racial truce that allowed them to live, most of the time, in relative tranquility.

CHAPTER TWELVE

"Some Regular Army Prejudice to Overcome"

In 1866 Colonel Edward Hatch, on his way to New Orleans to begin organizing the 9th Cavalry, met Samuel L. Woodward, a lieutenant assigned to the 10th Cavalry. They chatted for a while—both men had served during the Civil War in a brigade commanded by Benjamin H. Grierson—and before parting Hatch remarked that he and Grierson, both of them high-ranking officers whose only military training had come in the volunteers during the war, would "have some regular army prejudice to overcome." Although Hatch was referring to the well-known rivalry between West Pointers and officers whose commissions came from Civil War service, his observation also applied to the new black regiments that he, Grierson, and others led during the decades that followed. Just as the black regulars had been second-class citizens in civilian life, in the army they never escaped reminders that many observers, military and civilian, considered them second-class soldiers.[1]

Never had men entered the army under such a handicap. That many regiments of U.S. Colored Troops (USCT) had done well in the Civil War did little to alter commonly held views about the race. Deep-rooted beliefs about the innate character of black people permeated white American society and the army, where many officers and enlisted men refused to acknowledge that black men could ever become competent soldiers.

Some of the criticism was justified. Most black soldiers were uneducated, only a few were literate, and not many possessed skills beyond those of a common laborer or field hand. The USCT's performance during the war should have proved that with proper instruction and leadership these disadvantages could be overcome. That their service record seemed to count for little demonstrates the strength of racist sentiment within the regular army.

Most officers, had they been polled, would probably have rejected any plan to enlist black troops. General Grant wanted to retain the USCT regiments temporarily, although not as part of the regular army; but when President Andrew Johnson signed the reorganization act of 1866, the army had no choice but to recruit the stipulated number of black soldiers. If Congress had created a large enough army and not kept it on a tight budget while reducing its strength repeatedly, black soldiers might have been discreetly swept under the carpet. Given enough troops, the army might have stationed the black regiments in its most remote, isolated posts. It could also have issued picks and shovels instead of weapons to black troops and used them as laborers. Strict legal limits on the army's size and composition, though, prevented any such action. As it was, black troops along the Rio Grande were no more isolated than were white troops near the Canadian border, and white soldiers as well as black often spent more time on construction fatigues than they did at drill. Ordered to enlist black soldiers, hamstrung by a parsimonious Congress, and faced with recurring emergencies in all parts of the country, the army could only use its black and white soldiers alike.[2]

While critics debated the army's success in turning recruits into competent soldiers, few openly questioned the troops' fighting ability. Officers seemed to accept their men's courage as a fact and urged only that their instincts should be channeled in the proper direction by training and instruction. The peacetime army's ethnic composition supported this position. Native-born recruits made up more than half of the enlisted strength; the rest were predominantly British, Irish, and German. These were the ethnic strains, or "races," that had made up the victorious Union army, which writers of the day liked to call Anglo-Saxon, Celtic, and Teutonic. The late nineteenth-century army was overwhelmingly northern European in character. But the same men who believed firmly in the virtues of the "Anglo-Saxon race" entertained a very low opinion of the "African." Many Americans were prepared to believe that while not all white men might be warriors, all black men were cowards. Stripped of one of the most essential traits of a soldier, black men entered the army under a severe handicap.[3]

Other widely accepted ideas did little to improve their situation. While a soldier's life did not require a towering intellect, many whites supposed that blacks were of such low intelligence that they could never develop military qualities. Some officers advanced popular stereotypes of blacks' subservience, laziness, and unreliability to suggest the impossibility of turning them into soldiers. Others argued that blacks' supposed docility made them more susceptible to discipline and urged their employment as a labor corps, but even these critics agreed that submissiveness would be a drawback in combat.[4]

These beliefs persisted throughout the post–Civil War era. Most officers, including those in the black regiments, never completely abandoned the racial yardstick, claiming that they could never be sure that an individual soldier's competence was not simply exceptional. When Lieutenant John Bigelow joined the 10th Cavalry, fresh from West Point, he found that First Sergeant Jacob Young was "an intelligent darkey who has been in the Regiment ever since its organization," a man who could help to guide a shavetail's uncertain steps. Five weeks with the regiment, though, only confirmed prejudices that the young lieutenant had brought with him. "There is no word I can think of that better expresses . . . a colored soldier's shortcomings than—childishness," he wrote. "He is ignorant, illiterate, careless, heedless, . . . variable in his character and in fact in every other respect. No exhibition of stupidity or thoughtlessness by a colored soldier surprises me now." Black soldiers always found themselves judged by two standards: one military, the other racial.[5]

Prejudice and theory aside, most of the War Department's information about its troops, black and white, came from annual reports by officers of the Inspector General's Department. Inspectors paid particular attention to drill and appearance, but also inquired into rations, living quarters, and other aspects of military life. Through the decades, inspecting officers sometimes found some black soldiers careless of their appearance, deficient in drill, poor shots, and clumsy—even cruel—horsemen. These reports, though, described only specific posts and companies in certain years and were not intended to characterize all black soldiers or even an entire regiment. In 1868 the horsemanship of two 10th Cavalry companies at Fort Arbuckle, Indian Territory, made

Major George A. Forsyth reflect that "it is a difficult undertaking to make good cavalrymen of colored men and requires labor, patience, and time." A few days later, though, he received an entirely different impression at Fort Gibson. The black troopers there had been in the army for only a year, but Forsyth thought that theirs was "one of the very best companies of colored cavalry in service." He praised their appearance and noted the instruction provided by company officers. The men at Fort Arbuckle, he wrote, could be brought to the same degree of proficiency.[6]

Inspectors found the same faults in white troops, but prejudiced readers could take unfavorable reports and generalize. Out of context, some of the remarks supported claims that blacks made poor soldiers. When Congressman Richard Banning attempted to legislate blacks out of the army in 1876, he read two inspectors' adverse comments into the *Congressional Record.* Banning had selected the documents to further his cause and did not quote reports by the same officers that praised black troops at other posts. Many inspections found that black soldiers could equal whites in all areas of military proficiency; like the unfavorable evaluations, these dealt only with individual companies at certain times and places and were not meant to affect the reputation of all black soldiers.[7]

Although reports criticizing and praising black troops continued to reach the War Department throughout the post–Civil War era, a marked increase in favorable comments began in the mid-1880s. By that time, the black regiments had seen almost twenty years' service; nearly all of the company commanders and many of the senior noncommissioned officers had been present since the regiments' organization. These cadres of veterans trained the newer soldiers, and inspecting officers gradually began to notice an increased level of professionalism. An inspector at Fort Hale, Dakota Territory, remarked in 1883 that companies of the 25th Infantry "seem to be in excellent discipline; their appearance and bearing is exceptionally good . . . and in fact . . . Captain Schooley's company presented the best general appearance of all the companies I have yet inspected." The next year, another inspector found companies of the 9th Cavalry and 24th Infantry at Fort Sill, Indian Territory, "very soldierly." Arms, clothing, and equipment were well cared for and the troops proficient in drill. The cavalry horses were "in excellent condition" and remained calm when the men fired blank rounds during skirmish drill.[8]

Reports of field service also influenced generals' opinions of black soldiers, and the language of annual reports conveys the esteem the troops had earned. Late in 1875 the 9th Cavalry moved from Texas to New Mexico. During the next five years, the regiment not only fought Apaches and Utes, but also became embroiled in the Lincoln County War between rival factions of white settlers. "Everything that men could do they did, and . . . their services in the field were marked by unusual hardships and difficulties. Their duties were performed with zeal and intelligence, and they are worthy of all consideration," the department commander wrote in his 1880 report. The next year, when the 9th was about to leave New Mexico, a joint resolution of the territorial legislature declared that the regiment's conduct had "added fresh luster to the reputation of the United States Army."[9]

Official "appreciation of gallant services in the field" could bring a few soldiers, at least, to a choice station. A 9th Cavalry battalion from Fort Robinson, Nebraska, was part of the force that gathered in 1890 to quell the Ghost Dance disturbance at nearby Pine Ridge Reservation. Afterward, the regiment received orders to send one of its companies to Fort Myer, just across the Potomac from Washington, D.C., where a squadron made up of companies from different cavalry regiments served. The 9th's Company K, filled to maximum strength with men who had distinguished themselves in earlier campaigns as well as at Pine Ridge, went east. Fort Myer was "under the direct eye of the government," the Adjutant General cautioned, "visited by distinguished and critical people, both home and foreign," and the regiment sent its best men.[10]

Company K's arrival marked the first time in more than twenty years that black soldiers had served east of the Mississippi River. The *Army and Navy Register* called Fort Myer "an honor station" and proclaimed that the 9th's troopers "deserved the assignment." In a long account of the regiment's service in the West, the editor concluded that white soldiers could not view one company's assignment to Fort Myer "as an act of unmerited favoritism, based on race and color." The *Cleveland Gazette,* a black newspaper that often criticized the army for not properly rewarding the services of black soldiers, declared that the troopers were finally in a position "where they may be admired by the residents of the national capitol and paraded before the thousands who annually visit

Men of the 9th Cavalry had to spread straw so that their horses could lie on snowy ground near Pine Ridge Agency, South Dakota, during the winter of 1890–91. Black soldiers' performance at northern stations confounded the expectations of racial theorists who thought that they were better suited to warm climates. *Courtesy Denver Public Library, Western History Collection*

the city." Company K remained in the East for more than three years until military planners decided to replace the "honor" squadron drawn from different regiments with one from a single regiment.[11]

Fort Leavenworth was another station where representative companies from both black cavalry regiments served. The school for cavalry and infantry officers, founded there in 1881, required a body of troops for the students to maneuver, and a squadron of cavalry with one company from each of the Military Division of the Missouri's four departments and a similar force of infantry assembled at Fort Leavenworth. One company of the 9th Cavalry, then serving in the Department of the Platte, took its turn from 1886 to 1893 and one of the 10th Cavalry, in the Department of Dakota, from 1892 to 1894. To officers, Fort Leavenworth offered the social and political life of a large post and a department headquarters; to enlisted men, few construction fatigues and no sudden calls to suppress an Indian outbreak or labor strike; all a thirty-minute train ride from Kansas City.[12]

Newspaper accounts of the black regulars' campaigns reflected the public attitude toward the men and their regiments. Two military weeklies, the *Army and Navy Journal* and the *Army and Navy Register*, frequently printed pseudonymous letters from their own readers and copied stories from the civilian press. In 1881 both papers reprinted a *New York Herald* correspondent's account of a skirmish between Apaches and a 9th Cavalry detachment, in which the writer included what he must have thought was a characteristic remark by a wounded soldier: "Damn my black hide!" Private Norman E. Gaines reportedly exclaimed. "Who says the colored sojers won't fight?" The remark may never have been uttered; what is important is that the writer included it. If he had held a low opinion of black soldiers, he would not have taken the trouble even to invent a comment or to record the names of Gaines and Corporal Monroe Johnson, the two wounded troopers. What affect the report had on white soldiers' attitudes is impossible to calculate, but every post library in the army and many officers subscribed to both the *Register* and the *Journal*. In their pages, many soldiers learned about the black regulars, and it may be that favorable accounts altered some people's thinking.[13]

From time to time, articles about black soldiers also appeared in the national press and in magazines. The best-known artist of military life,

Frederic Remington, furnished *Harper's Weekly*, *The Century*, and other journals with illustrations of the soldiers' exploits, notably *Captain Dodge's Colored Troopers to the Rescue*, which portrayed the 9th Cavalry's Company D at Milk Creek in 1879. Black newspapers, on the other hand, seldom mentioned the activities of black soldiers or printed reports about them, unless it was a letter from a subscriber that the paper could print without charge.[14]

Black regulars took considerable pride in their own deeds and were sensitive to any criticism of their bravery, as a petition signed by members of the 24th Infantry in 1886 showed. Robbers had held up a train in Kansas. Among the passengers were a sergeant and two privates of the regiment, armed with revolvers while taking two military convicts from Fort Elliott, Texas, to Leavenworth. The three men gave up their weapons to the robbers without resistance. A Fort Worth newspaper, learning of this, ignored the soldiers' protests that other passengers urged them not to fight and called them cowards. When the news reached Fort Elliott, Company F, to which the sergeant and one of the privates belonged, convened "a rousing meeting . . . for the purpose of expressing contempt" for their conduct. They passed a resolution and sent copies to both service weeklies.[15]

Enlisted men's meetings were everyday occurrences throughout the army. Hardly a week went by without the *Journal* and the *Register* printing a resolution from a company in one regiment or another mourning a dead comrade or wishing an officer well on his promotion and transfer. The resolution's form was the same as that used by fraternal orders and labor unions throughout the country. But Company F's meeting and resolution, having to do with official misconduct, was definitely "to the prejudice of good order and military discipline." A general court-martial took First Sergeant William Rose's stripes and fined him sixty dollars for allowing the meeting and helping draft the resolution. Fort Elliott's commanding officer seemed embarrassed. "The negro soldier is very sensitive to any reference to his color," he explained to the Adjutant General. "Incited by the abuse in the newspapers, some men . . . organized themselves into a town meeting, passed resolutions denouncing the conduct of . . . the guard, and sent copies of their resolutions to newspapers for publication. The un-military conduct of these soldiers was not known by any officer at this post until after the newspapers arrived here." From the tone of letters in the *Army and Navy Journal,* it is hard to tell whether officers were more aghast at the guards' cowardice or at the indiscipline of the meeting that followed.[16]

Behavior like that at Fort Elliott, with one discreditable incident leading to another, allowed detractors to cling to their notions about black men's military ability despite plentiful evidence to the contrary. There were always high-ranking officers ready to condemn black troops in one way or another. In 1873, for instance, General William T. Sherman told a reporter that he had ordered changes of station between the 4th and 9th Cavalry in Texas because "the Ninth Cavalry is not quite so efficient for scouting purposes as the Fourth." Sherman never bothered to outline the 9th's particular deficiencies; perhaps he believed that patrols led by black noncommissioned officers were less reliable than those of a white regiment. Two years later, Brigadier General E. O. C. Ord, commanding the Department of Texas, forbade the 9th's patrols to cross the Rio Grande into Mexico, explaining that he could not "trust their detachments without officers—who are not always available."[17]

A disaster that received wide press coverage and exposed the black regulars to adverse criticism occurred in July 1877, when Company A of the 10th Cavalry, led by Captain Nicholas Nolan, lost its way on the Staked Plains of Texas. In the course of a day, the troopers drained their canteens. Nolan dispatched a civilian scout to find water, but the man did not return. To relieve their thirst, the captain had his men kill several horses and mules and drink their blood. "Previous to this the command were suffering so much for water, they were compelled to drink their own and their horses' urine," according to one account. "Having sugar along Capt. Nolan issued a liberal supply to the men, which tended to make the urine palatable." Several men deserted, trying to find their way back to their supply camp instead of pushing on with the rest. Nolan's command reached water on the afternoon of the fourth day, and the next morning another company of the 10th, also on a scout, discovered them. The four-day ordeal took a heavy toll. Two men crept off during the last night and disappeared; two more died the next day after eighty-six hours without water. At the end of August, three men were still in the Fort Concho hospital.[18]

The immediate reaction was sympathetic. Newspapers and army officials at first praised Nolan and his men for sustaining so few casualties.

As weeks passed, though, stories began to circulate accusing some of the soldiers of cowardice. Although half of the men in Company A—and all of those who died—had been in the army for less than a year, some detractors alleged that the troopers' lack of stamina proved their worthlessness. Others suggested that white soldiers would not have suffered as much in similar conditions. When the Department of Texas ordered Colonel Grierson to prosecute the men who had left Nolan's column, Grierson replied that although the men were technically deserters, the "hardships endured, mental sufferings and punishment already undergone" mitigated their offense, and he had released them from the guardhouse. Nevertheless, in obedience to orders, he convened a court-martial. A sergeant, a corporal, and two privates of Company A received dishonorable discharges and sentences of from four to fifteen years' imprisonment, which was reduced to one year for the privates and two years for the noncommissioned officers. In reducing the sentences, General Ord wrote that "perhaps, the class of troops to which these men belong have not yet had the opportunity, as citizens, to acquire that sense of responsibility . . . which would enable them to appreciate the military principle that the greater the danger or distress to which their commands are exposed the greater the crime of deserting them, and the greater the necessity for maintaining discipline." In other words, the black soldiers did not deserve stiff sentences because their crimes were the result of ignorance.[19]

One of the most widespread beliefs about black regulars was that they depended heavily on their white officers. Many military documents, including monthly returns from posts and regiments as well as bimonthly company muster rolls, show black noncommissioned officers and privates delivering mail, guarding isolated outposts, and performing other tasks without an officer's supervision. Despite this, the belief in black soldiers' dependence on their officers would not die. It was part of the dogma of black inferiority, and incidents sometimes occurred that furnished ammunition to the black regiments' critics.

The 9th Cavalry's First Sergeant Moses Williams earned the Medal of Honor partly because he rallied the men when they believed that their officer, Lieutenant George R. Burnett, had been killed or wounded in a skirmish with Apaches. Burnett had not been hit; leading the column in single file, he had dismounted in order to steady his carbine on his horse's saddle while he took aim at what turned out to be an Apache in ambush. "Immediately the Indians opened on us from all along the ridge," Burnett wrote, supporting Williams's application for a medal. "I at once ordered my men to dismount and take shelter among the rocks, but in the excitement my horse broke away and started to the rear riderless on the dead run." Some of the men panicked and began to leave the firing line, the lieutenant explained, "with this the whole outfit proceeded to follow suit, with the exception of 1st Serg't Williams. . . . I called to Sergt Williams to go after them and bring them back." Williams "quickly succeeded in rallying" the scurrying troopers, and it was for this, besides "coolness, bravery and unflinching devotedness to duty," that he received the medal. This tale of flight and recovery, of fear and courage, could provide evidence for both critics and supporters of the black regulars.[20]

Some of the most scathing observations came from the black regulars' own officers. Lieutenant John Bigelow had served with the 10th Cavalry for eight years when a national magazine published his Arizona campaign diary. Although his comments included all enlisted men, he had special criticism for the men he commanded. In August 1885 Bigelow had had to send out a patrol of ten troopers and three Indian scouts because one of his sentries had not been able to point out where he had noticed some fires in the distance the night before. "The intelligence of our enlisted men, especially the colored, and more especially the colored cavalry, is not up to the military requirements of our age," he fumed. "Work is required of them . . . which they must either fail to do or do very imperfectly. What is more important, especially in a cavalryman, than ability to render a clear and correct account of what he sees?" This was not the first time that Bigelow had difficulty understanding black speech patterns. "Questions have to be put to them almost in monosyllables," he had complained years earlier, while serving as recorder of a court-martial, and "their answer is in such bad english that it is almost impossible to punctuate them and to get at their meaning."[21]

A month after the sentry's incoherent report of fires in the night, Bigelow described what had happened as he led his company through a small town. Looking back, he saw that two privates and a sergeant had left the column and were standing in front of a saloon. "The sergeant's deportment was more reprehensible than that of the privates, and would have been more vexatious had I not been prepared for it. As it was, I hardly gave it a thought, and said nothing to him about it. The great difficulty in the government of colored troops is the securing of efficient non-commissioned officers. I find, as a general thing, not more than two or three efficient ones to a troop. It is only up to a certain point, and that not a high one, that colored troops are more easily disciplined than white. To attain high or even proper discipline they require more training than white men."[22]

Many officers believed that black soldiers required a strong guiding hand because of laziness or lack of initiative. When Bigelow compiled a history of the 10th Cavalry, he collected anonymous officers' opinions that exemplify these sentiments. "These men . . . , if properly officered, and properly handled, will prove second to none," declared an officer who said he had helped organize the regiment in 1867. They would "follow wherever led" and "never desert" their officers. Another informant said that black regulars were "good soldiers only with good officers. . . . Being less used to thinking for themselves, or inheriting from their slave ancestors a disposition to look for guidance or orders, they require more attention from their officers than white troops. . . . [L]eft to themselves, white troops will do better than colored, but when led, directed, and driven by capable energetic officers, colored troops will do better than white." Both of Bigelow's informants claimed to see black soldiers' need for a firm guiding hand.[23]

Army records contain many allegations about black soldiers' deficiencies, ranging from prejudiced opinions of their general abilities to frank appraisals of new recruits. Surgeon William M. Notson at Fort Concho commented on the "impracticability of making intelligent soldiers out of the mass of negroes," adding that several officers of the 9th Cavalry and 41st Infantry at the fort privately agreed. In 1875 Lieutenant Colonel Nelson H. Davis of the Inspector General's Department wrote that, of seventy-eight recruits for the 9th Cavalry at Fort Clark, "about one half were fair to good—the other half were indifferent, and 50 per cent of them were in my opinion unfit for the Cavalry service." Notson clearly disliked black soldiers ("This was the end of the colored garrison of Fort Concho, and I hope the end of my service with such troops," he remarked when the last company of the 9th Cavalry left there), but the inspector's comments may well have been a fair estimate of the recruits he saw.[24]

There is no question that some of the black regulars made very poor soldiers and should never have been enlisted. Officers did their best to weed out incompetents, either discharging them whenever one of the army's periodic reductions allowed or refusing to reenlist them. Some men's discharge papers show their officers' forthright, even vehement, opinions: "deficient in intellect and generally worthless" was Private Arthur Jackson's farewell from the 25th Infantry. When a surgeon pondered Private James A. Reeder's disability discharge because of "nervousness," Captain Patrick Cusack offered his own evaluation: "Were I tomorrow ordered with my Company into action . . . I would certainly not allow him in the firing line as he would be likely to do more harm than good." Reeder "would likely create a stampede owing to his having no confidence in himself," Cusack added, and the "nervous" private had to leave the 9th Cavalry.[25]

White officers brought with them into the army notions of black indolence and subservience, and held on to these ideas even after years of experience commanding black troops. Bigelow, who served with the 10th Cavalry for twenty-five years, asserted that while a black trooper would endure hardships "without grumbling," he would "exert himself less of his own accord." Chaplain George Mullins claimed to see a similar lack of initiative among soldiers of the 25th Infantry. Black soldiers liked a "go-easy and unambitious life, free from care and restraint," and therefore needed exceptionally able and determined officers. A former 6th Cavalry trooper, who probably knew more about enlisted men's needs than either Bigelow or Mullins, took a different view from those officers. Harry McConnell had seen 38th Infantry soldiers at Fort Richardson, Texas, in the summer of 1869 and thought that "their volatile, devil-may-care characters fitted them for the ups and downs of the army" and so worked in their favor; perhaps an example of the "wildness of nature" that General Sherman thought was required to make a soldier.[26]

It is hard to ignore the judgment of men who had extensive experience with black regulars and accuse them of forming their opinions only because of racial bias. Certainly, these officers were not free of prejudice, and decades-long service in the same regiment afforded little basis for general comparisons between black and white soldiers' behavior, but officers were in a position to judge their own men's behavior. An officer's ability to do his job—sometimes even his life—depended on the accuracy of that judgment. Enlisted men relied on these leaders, and some of the men must have fit Bigelow's and Mullins's descriptions. In making such sweeping assessments, though, officers often ignored or discounted a great deal of contrary evidence. The most noticeable contradiction of their derogatory remarks lay in the distinguished performance of some black regulars.

Through the years, official reports mentioned dozens of black soldiers by name, often for leading small detachments in the field without an officer's supervision. In the summer of 1872, Sergeant Pierre Rock led eleven 9th Cavalry troopers on a two-hundred-mile scout along the Rio Grande. Sergeant John Denny of the same regiment led eight men on a five-week scout in the Magdalena Mountains of New Mexico during the winter of 1877. Two years later, Denny chased some deserters from Fort Bayard, New Mexico, to the town of Hillsborough, a trip that took him and his party of seven men one hundred fifty miles. Although noncommissioned officers constituted only a fraction of the entire strength of the regiments, their accomplishments showed that not all black regulars could be called lazy or passive; and if some men showed energy and good sense, many of their comrades must have had the same traits.[27]

Foot soldiers were less mobile than cavalry, but they too occasionally garnered some official praise. When Sergeant Joseph Luckadoe led three 25th Infantry privates in defending a Texas mail station against an attack on New Year's Eve, 1873, his company commander praised his "soldierlike conduct" and forwarded a copy of Luckadoe's report, which eventually reached the War Department in Washington:

> [W]hile sitting in the Station our attention was attracted by the dogs barking at what we at the time, supposed to be a Cayote, to be sure, I told Newby to get his gun and to see what they were barking at. When he got near the Haystack, he was fired upon by some one, the ball merely passing him and imbeded itself in one of the Corral posts. We seized our guns, and rushed out of doors when they discharged some 8 shots at us, the balls striking the stone and flatt[en]ing out with the exception of two, one is imbeded in one of the uprights for our Arbor, the other, as I turned around, struck

my Cap brim, cutting away a portion of the cloth and pasteboard but did not hurt me. . . . I told Williams to fire on them, this he done, when one of them fell at the second shot—at daybreak we found that he had bled all over the stones at least a half gallon of blood. they taken him off with them. . . .

I do not realy think they were Indians they were to[o] bold and defiant although there are plenty of Moccasin tracks in the gulch. I think that more than one of the party was hurt. I think we killed the one that bled so much—we did not sleep any on the 31st, we are all well, and on the lookout.

Please ask the Col. to send some more ammunition we have 130 rounds . . . , and please send those Beans to the station keeper and some vegetables, if you have some to spare.

The men had provided for their comfort by building an arbor, or *ramada,* fought off a night attack by parties unknown and reconnoitered afterward, and needed more ammunition and rations. Sergeant Luckadoe gave a concise sketch of outpost duty in Texas during the 1870s.[28]

In garrison, though, most noncommissioned officers' duties centered on drill or the supervision of fatigues. Occasionally, sergeants traveled on official business, escorting prisoners to state penitentiaries or the U.S. Military Prison at Fort Leavenworth or delivering insane soldiers to the government hospital in Washington, D.C. These tasks fell frequently to the four companies of the 25th Infantry that served at Fort Snelling, Minnesota, headquarters of the Department of Dakota, from 1882 to 1888. Sergeants of the 25th supervised parties of recruits en route from department headquarters to their regiments and traveled to small towns in Minnesota and Dakota Territory to pick up deserters who had been arrested by local officials. In the spring of 1884, Sergeant Joseph Pendleton accompanied an insane soldier of the 11th Infantry to Washington. At the end of the year, he traveled to St. Paul and Hastings, Minnesota, to serve subpoenas on civilian witnesses in a general court-martial. Sergeant James D. Cooper delivered another patient to Washington in between assignments as post librarian and school overseer.[29]

In the performance of their duties, Pendleton, Cooper, and others like them won their officers' respect, and black regulars who left the army with character references of "excellent" or "very good" far outnumbered those who earned unfavorable remarks. Some men, of course, took slowly to the service. When William H. Myers joined the 25th Infantry he was, his company commander wrote, "at first a dirty careless fellow." Myers managed to adjust to army life, though, and by the end of his first year had become "a clean tidy soldier." He reenlisted and earned promotion to corporal. When Myers left the army after ten years, the same officer called him "above the average in intelligence." Another soldier who enjoyed the trust and respect of his officers was the 24th Infantry's First Sergeant John H. Thomas. In 1887 Thomas's death moved his company commander to insert a memorial notice in the *Army and Navy Journal:* "Died of Typhoid at Fort Elliott, Texas, . . . John H. Thomas, . . . after a continuous service of nearly 23 years, more than twenty as a sergeant and about eighteen years as first sergeant. The service loses one who during a long and faithful service in war and peace, by his honesty, fidelity, and zeal had won the respect and applause of his superiors and subordinates alike." It was a standard military obituary notice of a kind that appeared in both service weeklies through the years whenever a long-service officer or enlisted man in any regiment died. That the language was formulaic made the sentiments no less sincere.[30]

Although army officers venerated bravery and personal honor, the racial attitudes that they shared with nearly all white Americans characterized many of their observations about black regulars. To a bigot, the praiseworthy actions of an individual always appear exceptional, while the misdeeds of a few discredit an entire group. Yet officers, while rejecting absolutely the notion of "social equality," were prepared to recognize the bravery of black soldiers under their command.

Recognition could mean a Medal of Honor, a Certificate of Merit, or mention in orders. During the nineteenth century, criteria for awarding medals and certificates changed through the years, sometimes being restricted to privates, sometimes to all enlisted men, and sometimes to all soldiers. Bravery in battle, saving lives or government property, or performing some other hazardous duty were all worthy of one distinction or another.[31]

Fourteen black regulars won the Medal of Honor; the 10th Cavalry's Sergeant William McBryar for his part in a skirmish with Apaches in 1890. Only three years into his first enlistment, McBryar was already a sergeant; the citation commended his "coolness, bravery and good marksmanship." Sergeant Thomas Boyne of the 9th Cavalry earned the medal for his courage on two occasions in the spring and fall of 1879. "I have seen him repeatedly in action," the 9th's Major Albert P. Morrow wrote, "and in every instance he distinguished himself. I cannot speak too highly of his conduct." Remarks like these typify officers' endorsements of the black regulars' bravery in action.[32]

The army recognized exemplary courage, even in a losing fight. In May 1889 robbers in Arizona wounded eight members of a paymaster's escort during a half-hour gun battle and made off with $28,000 in gold. The paymaster wrote that he "never witnessed better courage or better fighting than showed by these colored soldiers," and within months Medals of Honor arrived for the 24th Infantry's Sergeant Benjamin Brown and Corporal Isaiah Mays, while eight other members of the escort, men of the 24th and the 10th Cavalry, received Certificates of Merit. Not all decorations came so quickly, though.[33]

Half of the black regulars' Medals of Honor came as the result of a bureaucratic process begun by the men themselves years after the heroic acts that the medals were meant to commemorate. The 9th Cavalry's Company I fought Apaches in the Cuchillo Negro Mountains of New Mexico in August 1881, but Augustus Walley did not apply for a medal until nine years had passed. Lieutenant George R. Burnett, who had been wounded in the fight and was retired by 1890, wrote a letter praising Walley's "gallantry and bravery," as he did again the next year, when John Rogers applied for a Certificate of Merit. Rogers had carried a message from Burnett to Lieutenant Gustavus Valois, the other officer present that day. Burnett praised Rogers's "courageous and intelligent action," and Valois (who, like Burnett, was retired by this time) added an endorsement to the file.[34]

It was several more years before word of these awards reached Moses Williams, Company I's former first sergeant. Williams had left the 9th Cavalry and in 1896 was an ordnance sergeant stationed at the mouth of the Columbia River. He asked for and received a letter from Burnett attesting that his "skill and ability" had averted disaster at one point in the Cuchillo Negro fight, and Williams got his medal fifteen years after the event.[35]

The 9th Cavalry's incessant campaigning during the late 1870s and early 1880s meant that commendations, like other paperwork, sometimes got lost. In 1894 an assistant adjutant general complained that Sergeant Brent Woods's conduct during one fight in New Mexico "should have been deemed worthy of official report or notation on rolls and returns, at the proper time, thus to support the claim now made" in applying for a medal. Woods had taken charge of a patrol when its officer was killed and had shown "excellent skill . . . in getting out of an ambush" and defending his position until a force led by Lieutenant Charles W. Taylor arrived. "Why this recommendation has not been made before is a matter of conjecture," Taylor answered the assistant adjutant general's quibble, thirteen years after the fight. "Had I been this man's troop commander in 1881 I certainly would have made my recommendation then. . . . I earnestly hope that Justice long delayed may now be accorded this soldier." Taylor, Burnett, and other officers who led black soldiers readily acknowledged exceptional bravery in battle.[36]

In the late 1880s, the army began publishing the names of enlisted men and officers who performed "gallant or specially meritorious acts" that did not quite qualify for a Medal of Honor or Certificate of Merit. The 9th Cavalry's Private James Settlers "risked his own life without a moment's hesitation" to rescue Fort Washakie's commanding officer from drowning and earned a place in the annual list. Sergeant William Chambers of the 25th Infantry, on the trail of a deserter, "displayed great coolness and bravery" while fighting off a night ambush intended to rescue his prisoner; Private Calvin Kimblern, also of the 25th, had "a severe struggle" to capture another deserter after pursuing him from Fort Custer to Sheridan, Wyoming.[37]

Sergeant Luckadoe's report of outpost duty, quoted earlier, gives a hint about why black regulars received fewer decorations for bravery than their numbers—roughly one-tenth of the army's enlisted strength, and sometimes half the troops in a department—would suggest. As was often the case, Luckadoe and his men formed a small detachment and there was no officer present who could have written a citation. Throughout the army between 1870 and 1890 in battles where more than a dozen soldiers earned Medals of Honor, the average number of companies engaged was eight, enough to assure that plenty of officers were present. During those years, black soldiers took part in only four actions of that size, and in three of them no soldier, black or white, won an award. The black regulars seldom operated in great force, and while this may have placed greater responsibility on junior officers and helped attract better West Point graduates to the black regiments, it lessened men's chances of having an official witness to their good conduct. Once the recommendation was submitted, no officer, from company and regimental commanders to the War Department in Washington, seems to have objected to or refused to endorse black soldiers' citations for valor. It is impossible to tell whether officers' prejudices ever prevented them from recommending their men, but in any case this would have reflected only individual bias rather than an official policy of refusing to grant awards to black soldiers.[38]

Officers' ability to praise their men for efficiency, valor, and leadership, while at the same time believing them to be dependent and incapable of initiative, demonstrates the power of racial stereotypes in American thought. Certainly, the record showed that not all black soldiers were stupid, lazy, and docile. Many officers must have believed that the actions of competent soldiers were exceptional and did not constitute a challenge to their overall impression of the men's limited abilities.[39]

Racial prejudice can be blatant and undisguised or subtle and hard to detect. What may appear on the surface to be a clear example of discrimination may in fact be nothing of the kind. Most nineteenth-century whites took a dim view of black people, and it would be foolish to assume that white officers did not hold many of the same beliefs. Certainly, some allowed their opinions to cloud their vision when they reported the activities of black soldiers. Others who may have called themselves objective were not aware that bias influenced their reactions too. They may have claimed that they harbored no prejudice, but few of them, if any, were able to judge black soldiers free from the influence of racial views.

Although most officers who recorded their impressions of black soldiers served at the regimental level and never made policy decisions about the status of black troops, they nevertheless voiced their opinions in official reports that others used to formulate policy. Few could write about black troops without injecting some qualifying remark. Nearly all of their observations, however complimentary, contained the inevitable "but," showing that the writer connected black soldiers to traditional racial stereotypes. This is clearly apparent in memoirs that did not appear until well into the twentieth century. While at Fort Sill in 1870 and 1871, Assistant Surgeon Robert H. McKay had considerable contact with men of the 10th Cavalry and recorded his impressions in a diary. "I did not see that they were very different from other enlisted men," he recalled in 1918. "If anything they seemed to take more interest in their appearance than the white soldiers but they were accused in the army as they are out of it, of petit larceny." James Parker of the 4th Cavalry had served often with black troops and claimed that "they had very estimable qualities." Yet, they "must be officered by whites else they are of no account," Parker wrote in his memoirs. Black soldiers' dependence on their officers was the most commonly invoked qualifier.[40]

Some officers who spoke their minds (although anonymously, as in Bigelow's unpublished history of the 10th Cavalry) were forthright, even defiant, in praise of their men. According to one: "[T]he colored soldier needs no defender or apologist. His incomparable record made against difficulties and prejudice such as no other race ever had to combat, speaks for itself." Another concluded that "the colored man is not excelled in bravery in action and other qualities of a soldier, by men of any other race." A third declared, "My opinion of the colored man as a soldier is that he is as good as any other man that I have ever served with." While these remarks display a good deal of regimental pride, they probably reflect their authors' honest views of black men as soldiers.[41]

Praise of the black regulars, though, failed to erase widespread doubts about them. Their generally commendable record would have gone unchallenged in the absence of racial prejudice, but acknowledgement of their abilities had to overcome mistrust and ill will. The way in which their defenders cited the black regiments' low desertion rate showed this clearly.

Throughout the late nineteenth century, the army lost more men each year by desertion than from any other cause. In the summer of 1889, the *St. Louis Globe Democrat* printed War Department statistics showing that 2,811 men had deserted during the previous year, costing the government about $600,000. When an anonymous 10th Cavalry officer (almost certainly John Bigelow) saw the article, he observed that "it would seem sensible and economical" to recruit more black soldiers "and eliminate the lawless, insubordinate . . . class which . . . is picked up from the foreign and low-born part of the population and assigned to the white regiments."[42]

Later that year, Secretary of War Redfield Proctor mentioned the desertion rate in his annual report when he proposed raising at least one regiment of black artillerymen. Advances in naval weaponry—armored ships and rifled cannon—meant that the country's harbor defenses needed improvement, and the War Department asked Congress for two new artillery regiments to help man the new fortifications. Proctor maintained that black soldiers had shown themselves capable of learning gunnery, but he also stressed the low desertion rate in the black cavalry and infantry regiments. The existing artillery regiments lost more men by desertion than did the army's cavalry or infantry, and Proctor thought that black soldiers' low desertion rate justified the creation of at least one black artillery regiment.[43]

While Bigelow and Proctor did not say it in so many words, each implied that black soldiers' low desertion rate was at least as important a reason to include them in the artillery as any ability they might have to learn how to fire cannon. A 24th Infantry officer expressed this when he wrote to the *Army and Navy Journal* that it "should be a factor in removing some of the prejudice" against black servicemen. Here again is the qualifying statement, the inescapable "but." Certainly, the black regiments' rate of desertion was minuscule and saved the government a great deal of money; but it was typical of the low-budget army that the black regulars' proficiency was not enough to recommend them. Their services had to cost less than those of white soldiers too.[44]

From the end of the Civil War to the beginning of the Spanish-American War, black regulars faced the dilemma of meeting the same military standards as white soldiers while having their abilities and behavior prejudged on racial grounds. The army furnished all its soldiers alike with the same food, clothing, housing, and equipment and expected them to accomplish the same tasks. Meanwhile, racial stereotypes allowed some officers to disregard their men's abilities and to insist that they would never make good soldiers. When a black soldier truly failed to meet expectations—through dishonesty, stupidity, or violence—critics quickly seized on his example as proof of their position. In this respect, officers' thinking reflected predominant white American attitudes toward black people. Throughout their first three decades in the regular army, black soldiers always had to satisfy two sets of criteria, the professional and the racial. From the outset, they managed to meet professional standards. Prejudice, on the other hand, dogged them and their successors for generations.[45]

CHAPTER THIRTEEN

"Just Chored around and Did Whatever He Could Get to Do"

The army did little for discharged soldiers except provide the able-bodied with free transportation to wherever they had enlisted and the disabled with a place in the Soldiers' Home at Washington, D.C., or in one of the National Military Homes founded mainly to care for Civil War veterans. During most of the post–Civil War era, men joined the army for a term of five years with the option of reenlisting as long as they could pass a physical examination. Most soldiers, black and white alike, left the army after one enlistment, although many returned to it after weeks, months, or even years of civilian life. In 1885, Congress provided retirement at three-quarters pay for enlisted men with thirty years' cumulative service, and in 1894 the army shortened enlistments to three years in order to attract younger, better-educated men. An American soldier's service, War Department officials decided, "should be an incident, and not the business, of his life."[1]

Agreement came from an unexpected source. "Look carefully through the ranks of the soldiers, scan well the forms and faces of the men . . . who defend the property of the millionaire," labor leader Terence V. Powderly advised members of the Knights of Labor who might confront the regular army during a strike as when the itinerants of Coxey's Army and the Coeur d'Alene miners faced the men of the 25th Infantry during the 1890s. "They are all workingmen, sons of workingmen."

American soldiers had been workers in civilian life, and it was to that world that they returned from the army. What jobs were waiting for discharged soldiers—particularly for the black regulars?[2]

Most immediately, army posts sometimes offered employment to veterans. John H. Jackson spent the rest of his life near Fort Davis, Texas, where he left the 24th Infantry in 1870, farming and occasionally driving a team for the post quartermaster. Crawford, Nebraska, and Junction City, Kansas, both supported colonies of black veterans who had served at nearby Fort Robinson and Fort Riley. Former 10th Cavalry trooper Jeremiah Harris found work for a year with the blacksmith at Fort Sill before moving on.[3]

Fort Sill, in the southwestern corner of Indian Territory, was unique in the opportunities it afforded discharged soldiers, at least for a few months during the early 1870s. Established in 1869 by the recently organized 10th Cavalry to protect the U.S. Indian agency for the Comanche, Kiowa, and Wichita tribes, the new post was still under construction when most of the troopers' five-year enlistments expired in 1872. Discharged soldiers found themselves in the civilian labor market again, and the Fort Sill quartermaster needed hands.[4]

Nothing like this had occurred before in the short history of the black regiments, nor would it happen again. When the 9th Cavalry's enlistments ran out in 1871–72, its companies manned nine different posts in western Texas and the Rio Grande valley. Two years earlier, when the black infantry's three-year enlistments expired, the 24th Regiment was scattered at ten different Texas posts, and the 25th Infantry was in well-populated Louisiana. Veterans from the other black regiments did not affect local labor markets as the men of the 10th Cavalry did, nor did military construction at small posts offer the opportunities that were available at Fort Sill.

During the first three months of 1872, with discharges averaging only 34 a month, Fort Sill's garrison—ten companies of the 10th Cavalry—stood at about 650 men. That summer the monthly average rose to 83 men, and by October 452 troopers had taken their discharges at the fort. Sixty-nine of them, or 15 percent, reenlisted within thirty days and received a dollar-a-month pay increase for continuous service. Most of the others left for parts unknown, but post quartermaster's monthly reports show that at least 54 discharged soldiers quickly hired

Companies of the 10th Cavalry made up most of Fort Sill's garrison during the early 1870s, when this picture was taken. More than fifty discharged veterans of the unit joined the post quartermaster's construction crews that built the fort. *Courtesy National Archives*

on as civilian employees of the army. Nearly one veteran in eight, then, was able to ease his return to civilian life with a job at Fort Sill.[5]

Private William Baker became the first, a week after his discharge on January 9. He and the other eight "laborers" earned twenty-four dollars a month; four carpenters worked for two dollars a day. Two former cavalrymen joined Baker in February and two more in March. By early spring, the quartermaster's common laborers included four 10th Cavalry veterans in a crew of twenty-six, with new men joining and quitting every week.[6]

Spring always brought a renewal of campaigning. Comanche and Kiowa young men left their reservation to raid as far south as Mexico; meanwhile, unlicensed traders, horse thieves, and other outlaws preyed on those Indians who remained. As Fort Sill's commanding officer put it, his men would "have to march to the Cheyenne and Arapahoe Agency, . . . the Western portion of the Chickasaw Agency, and the Kiowa Comanche and Apache Agency for the purpose of removing unauthorized persons." (The 10th Cavalry, in other words, was responsible for the western half of present-day Oklahoma.) With troopers leaving the regiment at the rate of nine a week in April 1872, department headquarters authorized Fort Sill's quartermaster to hire fifty civilian teamsters. Ten of them were recently discharged men of the 10th Cavalry.[7]

Teamsters and laborers earned thirty dollars a month that summer as demand for their services increased. Veterans of the 10th Cavalry never numbered more than a dozen during any one month in a work force that averaged 145 men, and all of them worked as teamsters or laborers except the blacksmith Wade Hampton. No relation to the South Carolina grandee, Hampton was the son of a Choctaw father and a black mother, had enlisted at Fort Gibson in June 1867, and had spent most of his time as a company farrier and blacksmith. He earned eighteen dollars a month during his last year in the army; as a civilian his daily wage was $2.75, with monthly earnings as high as $82.50 in July and August. Hampton spent the rest of his life in the country where he had been born. He died at Okmulgee in 1932.[8]

Although the vast majority of black veterans came from east of the Mississippi River, with lesser numbers from Louisiana, Missouri, and Arkansas, several thousand settled in the West after they left the army. James Martin, a freeborn native of Alexandria, Virginia, drove trail herds north out of Texas. "I drove cattle for big outfits," he told an interviewer fifty years after his military service ended, "and drove two or three thousand head sometimes from South Texas clean up to Dakota. . . . There wasn't no trails and no fences. The Indians would come and ask for meat and we knew if we didn't give it to 'em, they'd stampede the cattle." Most veterans, though, found more prosaic employment. After First Sergeant William H. Goldsborough's disability discharge at Fort Supply in 1883, he headed for Caldwell, Kansas, where he "worked at different little jobs. . . . I owned a one horse wagon and horse and drayed on my own account." When Oklahoma, the part of Indian Territory from which the 9th Cavalry had tried so often to eject the Boomers (illegal white settlers), finally opened for settlement in 1889, Goldsborough took up a claim there.[9]

Many discharged soldiers, though, took advantage of the army's offer of free transportation and returned to their old hometowns. A survey of 418 black regulars' pension files showed 37 living in Washington, D.C.; more than in any other place. San Antonio with 23 resident veterans was second; always the headquarters of the Department of Texas, the establishment of Fort Sam Houston during the 1880s gave it a sizeable garrison too. Following those two cities were New Orleans (21); Leavenworth (15), another military town; and Baltimore (14). No other city—not even New York, Chicago, St. Louis, or Nashville—attracted even ten of the 418 veterans. Seventy-four lived in the South—outside Baltimore, New Orleans, and Washington—and the same number in Texas. Another 129 settled in the West outside of Texas in towns from San Diego to St. Paul (Fort Snelling), Missoula to Silver City, New Mexico (Fort Bayard). Clearly, the army had taken these men places that they would not have gone otherwise.[10]

Whether former soldiers found their military background a help or a hindrance in civilian life is almost impossible to tell. Except for the post school system and what little technical training the army might afford, military service did not prepare soldiers for work in the civilian world. It may be, though, that the discipline and sense of responsibility that some black regulars gained from the army impressed potential employers and helped veterans enjoy greater success in the marketplace.

The federal government continued to sustain some discharged soldiers in different ways. William H. Green, a Civil War veteran who served in Kansas with the 38th Infantry, returned to Marietta, Georgia, where he had enlisted, and worked at the National Cemetery there. Some veterans became post office janitors: among these former 10th Cavalry troopers Thomas J. Dilwood and John A. Howard in San Antonio; and George Brummsick, who served three enlistments with the 25th Infantry, in Sioux City, Iowa. As late as 1913, the Civil War veteran Alexander Stepney, who had ended his military career in the 9th Cavalry, carried the mail from the Crawford, Nebraska, railroad depot to Fort Robinson.[11]

Most black regulars found jobs of the kind that black men had done before the war and continued to do far into the twentieth century. Anthony Toombs, one of the first to be discharged (he had enlisted in September 1866), stayed on with Company A of the 25th Infantry as the captain's personal servant. The Civil War veteran Allen Downs, after his discharge from the 24th Infantry, worked as a cook in Denver and Pueblo, Colorado, and Las Vegas, New Mexico. David Lacey, another Civil War veteran, ran the barbershop in Chicago's Hyde Park Hotel for twenty-five years after he left the army. The railroads' growth during the last third of the century opened a new career for black men, and former cavalry troopers Henry Harrison, James H. Massey, and George Sperlin became Pullman porters.[12]

Other discharged veterans did not fare so well. In Austin, Texas, David Dickerson, minus his left thumb after a shooting accident while serving in the 25th Infantry, could do only "light work" for thirty-five cents a day. Stricken with hemorrhoids, former 10th Cavalry trooper William Garrett reported "Jobing a round Best I can" in Silver City, New Mexico. After serving in all four of the black regiments, George Thomas moved to Leavenworth, Kansas, and "just chored around and did whatever he could get to do." Even after Congress legislated Indian Wars pensions in 1917, eligibility depended on whether a man's regiment had taken part in a particular campaign in certain states and territories at a specific time. Veterans of 9th Cavalry companies that had spent the Ghost Dance winter of 1890–91 at Fort DuChesne, Utah, could not draw Indian Wars pensions, which were only for men who had actually gone to Pine Ridge. Similarly, troopers of the 9th who served in New Mexico from 1876 to 1881 had no status as "Indian campaigners." That was reserved only for the men of D Company for their role in the Ute War of 1879. Infantrymen who had served along the Rio Grande during the 1870s received no recognition at all.[13]

Although the army's arbitrary list of Indian campaigns did not prevent disabled regulars and Civil War veterans from getting pensions, former members of the U.S. Colored Troops had other difficulties. Many of them had served under one name and adopted another in civilian life. One 10th Cavalry veteran explained to a pension examiner that he took the name George Washington during the Civil War and was known by that name in the army, but that while he was working in the Indian Territory afterward, "an uncle of mine . . . came . . . hunting me up. He is the only one of my folks that I can ever remember seeing. When he . . . saw me he told me I ought to take my father's name of Robinson. My uncle told me that by taking my father's name I might some day run on to some of the rest of my folks. . . . So I took the name of Wash Robinson. I took part of my father's name and part of my own." Just as common were the problems caused by the names of former masters. The widow of one 24th Infantry veteran told a pension examiner that "he was married under the name of Cicero Starks. He had found his father then who was Moses Starks, and took his father's name of Starks. But until he took his father's name he went by the name of Cicero Cummings. He served in the army as Cicero Cummings, as he had belonged to a Cummings when made free, and . . . kept his master's name until he found his father Moses Starks." Veterans, like many black Americans in the nineteenth century, endured the torment of family separation and the labyrinth of legal difficulties caused by multiple surnames.[14]

Another problem, particularly for those black regulars with Civil War service, was that the U.S. Colored Troops recruited its regiments locally but numbered them nationally. Old men's failing memories led to confusion. George Bruce, who served in the 40th Infantry and 9th Cavalry after the war, had his Civil War pension held up because investigators could not find his name on the rolls of the 32d Pennsylvania Infantry. Bruce had joined the 32d U.S. Colored Infantry, which organized at Philadelphia, and had called it the "32nd Pennsylvania" on his pension application. Black veterans' pension applications contain references to the "3 Pa. Inf," "7 Meriland," "60th Iowa," and other regiments that were raised in different states but numbered consecutively as U.S. Colored Infantry. Local affiliation was important to the regulars too in the early days. Former infantryman John Pettit's pension application said that he had served in the "25th Louisiana Regiment," which had been formed from the "39th Louisiana and the 40th South Carolina." Thousands of veterans, some barely able to sign their names, others completely illiterate, faced the perplexities of official paperwork. "The colored men dont get much show these days no how," former 9th Cavalry trooper Henry Johnson told the Commissioner of Pensions in an unusual outburst of annoyance.[15]

The calendar played a cruel trick on at least one black regular. Edward Somerville joined the army in 1866, when infantry enlistments were for only three years. Soon afterward, the term became five years for all branches. In 1894, after five more enlistments in the 25th Infantry, Somerville needed two more years to qualify for retirement, but the examining surgeon discovered shortness of breath and "heart trouble" and refused to accept him. The month before Somerville's last army physical, he had fallen out of a practice march and ridden back to Fort Missoula in an ambulance. If his first enlistment had been for five years instead of three, he might have been able to scrape by until retirement. As it turned out, Somerville had to enter the Soldiers' Home in Washington, D.C., and begin applying for a disability pension.[16]

Founded before the Civil War, in the nation's capital yet rural enough that Abraham Lincoln used the site as a summer White House, the Soldiers' Home was supported by a levy on enlisted men's pay of 12.5 cents a month ($1.50 a year) and, until army reforms in the late 1880s, by court-martial fines. The qualification for residence was twenty years' service or a disability discharge. As hundreds of Civil War veterans came to require care, National Military Homes arose all across the country. More than 10 percent of black army pensioners spent some time in the Soldiers' Home or a National Military Home, brought there by age, disability, or indigence.[17]

The story of one Soldiers' Home resident's string of unsuccessful pension applications illustrates the difficulties that many black regulars faced late in their lives. Henry Washington enlisted in the 40th Infantry in Boston in 1867, transferred to the 25th two years later, and reenlisted in 1870. The spring of 1875 found him at Fort Davis, Texas, where he enlisted in the 9th Cavalry and served with that regiment for ten years. In 1885, Washington traveled from the Indian Territory, where he left

This photograph of Henry Washington accompanied his unsuccessful 1912 application for a pension based on his Civil War service in the 5th Massachusetts Cavalry. Washington's twenty-three years in the 9th Cavalry and 25th Infantry were not enough to gain him a pension, since the companies in which he served did not take part in any officially recognized Indian campaign, nor could he demonstrate a service-connected disability. *Courtesy National Archives*

the 9th, to Minnesota in order to sign up again with his old company of the 25th Infantry. He served for another five years and, after living in Missoula and Minneapolis, entered the Soldiers' Home in 1904.[18]

The next year, Washington applied for a disability pension. Rheumatism had forced him into the hospital twice, once in the winter of 1885 at Fort Reno, Indian Territory, and again in 1886 at Fort Sisseton, Dakota Territory, while he was serving with the 25th. (It may be that the Fort Reno hospitalization led to Washington's trip north to find his old regiment, because he thought that it would be too difficult to reenlist in the 9th.) The Pension Bureau interviewed six of his comrades from both regiments who recalled that Washington "complained of his leg and hip a good deal" and "was quite lame and limped about the Post." A year after leaving the army, though, Washington developed running sores on his leg, which a doctor who treated him in Minneapolis called "tubercular abscesses," that prevented him from working and confined him to bed for more than a year. Two of his lodge brothers in a fraternal order there cared for him, until he could travel to the Soldiers' Home, and submitted affidavits. But although the rheumatism that twice sent Washington to the hospital was clearly incurred "in line of duty," he could not persuade the Pension Bureau that his abscesses were a result of his military service, and the Bureau refused his application.[19]

It had taken four years to sift the evidence. Meanwhile, Washington continued to live at the Soldiers' Home, and in 1912 he applied for a Civil War pension for his service in the 5th Massachusetts Cavalry. Pension examiners wanted to know why he never mentioned Civil War service while applying for his disability pension. He had lost his discharge from the volunteers, Washington explained, and the lawyer who handled his application "knew nothing of my volunteer service. . . . He never asked me about it and I didn't think it was necessary as I wanted a pension for my regular service." Since his earlier claim had been rejected, Washington decided to try again without a lawyer: "I am going to take my chances with the Pension Bureau," he told the examiner. There were discrepancies in his narrative, though, and four veterans of the 5th Massachusetts Cavalry, when shown a recent photograph, were unable to say whether it was the man they had known nearly fifty years earlier. The Bureau of Pensions ruled that Washington was "unable to establish [his] identity" and again refused his application.[20]

When Washington applied for an Indian Wars pension five years later, the rejection was even swifter. His company of the 9th Cavalry had not served in the Ute War of 1879, the Bureau found, and the regiment's service in New Mexico from 1876 to 1881 was not covered by the pension act of 1917. It was Washington's last application. He died at the Soldiers' Home on April 18, 1927, just forty-six days after Congress finally provided pensions for soldiers who "served . . . in any Indian war or campaign, or in connection with, or in the zone of any active Indian hostilities in any of the States or Territories of the United States" between 1817 and 1898. By that time, Washington had been rejected first because he could not prove a service-related disability, then because he could not prove his Civil War service, and finally because he had not taken part in a "recognized" Indian campaign during his twenty-three years in the regular army. Many black veterans suffered rejection for one or more of these reasons as well, but few had the perseverance to try three times, much less the bad luck to fail in all.[21]

Beginning in 1911, the National Indian Wars Veterans lobbied for extended pension benefits, and black veterans along with their spouses and widows joined the organization and sent letters to its monthly newsletter. Mrs. Nannie L. Mure's husband, John, who had served in both the 9th and 10th Cavalry, "was fighting for a pension when death overtook him. Now the government is paying me $12 per month, and that is very little to live on, as I am 79 years old and cannot go out to service," she told readers of *Winners of the West*.[22]

Black veterans occasionally held office in local chapters of the National Indian Wars Veterans, and former 10th Cavalry trooper Frank P. Fielding was the organization's national chaplain in 1929. Race relations were not always smooth, though. Black veterans in Washington, D.C., founded the Colonel Charles Young chapter, named after West Point's third black graduate, in the spring of 1929. Photographs in *Winners of the West* suggest the reason: an all-white party of veterans decorating graves in Arlington Cemetery in 1927; a delegation of veterans in Herbert Hoover's inaugural parade, with former 10th Cavalry trooper William Hawkins posed among twenty-nine white men. Black veterans in the nation's capital needed a chapter of their own.[23]

Wherever they lived and however poor they were, most veterans seem to have received decent funerals. Well into the twentieth century, the

Grand Army of the Republic played an important part. When David Morgan, a veteran of the 24th Infantry, died in 1917, forty-six years after his discharge and "wholly without means," army officers at Fort Brown and the Brownsville post of the G.A.R. bore the expenses. In Sioux City, Iowa, lodge brothers of the "U.D., A.F.&A.M. (colored masons)" buried George Brummsick "in the Grand Army lots at Floyd cemetery." John Sims, who joined the 40th Infantry at Washington, D.C., and returned there after eight years in the army, got a place in Arlington National Cemetery in 1928. The Bureau of Pensions settled undertakers' accounts too, as shown by the bills in some veterans' files. Whether through the offices of the federal government, a fraternal order, or their neighbors' charity, black veterans could be fairly sure of a respectable burial.[24]

They died as obscurely as they had lived. Black newspapers did not feature their obituaries. Few Americans, black or white, noticed the regular army in peacetime, apart from sensational incidents like the 9th Cavalry's fight at Milk Creek in 1879. There was a brief surge of interest during the Spanish-American War, as several thousand black Americans joined state and federal regiments, and just after the war when the army raised two all-black regiments of U.S. Volunteer Infantry for service in the Philippines. Public attention soon lapsed, though, just as it had thirty-five years earlier when the U.S. Colored Troops mustered out.

During the years after the Civil War, the black regulars—fewer than twenty thousand men in all—had made a place for themselves in the army. Those who recalled their service in letters to *Winners of the West* told a story that Frederic Remington and John Ford had made familiar to millions. Scott Lovelace summarized the 10th Cavalry's activities during the late 1870s as "chasing the redskins to help blaze a right of way for the settlers of the wild west." Another 10th Cavalry veteran, former sergeant George W. Ford, wrote more soberly: "Our sacrifices and hardships opened up a great empire to civilization." Like the rest of the army, black soldiers had sometimes endured tumbledown barracks, Civil War surplus clothing, and outbreaks of scurvy. In the West, they had guarded stagecoaches that carried the mail and built and repaired the roads the stages used. To perform tasks like these, Congress had created the black regiments, and their duties were the same as those required of white regiments: no more, no less.[25]

Sgt. William Chambers and Commissary Sgt. Dalbert P. Green flank Sgt. Maj. Anthony A. Marrow in 1899, during the 25th Infantry's first tour of duty in the Philippines. Chambers, who first entlisted in 1875, had served with the 25th in Texas, Dakota Territory, Montana, and Cuba. He left the army in 1900 and applied for a disability pension two years later. Marrow and Green both joined the regiment during the 1890s and served through the First World War. Green had been one of Lt. James A. Moss's cyclists on the Yellowstone trip in 1896 and served as captain, manager, and historian of the regimental baseball team. These men typify the long-service soldiers who helped bring the black regiments into the twentieth century. *Courtesy National Archives*

Although Congress would ignore the black regulars when it provided for ten new infantry and cavalry regiments in 1901, the army's high command had accepted them as early as 1869, when it created the 24th and 25th Regiments of Infantry. That year's appropriation act merely required that the number of infantry regiments be cut from forty-five to twenty-five; the choice to keep two of the regiments black was the War Department's. In 1884, when General Order Number 89 announced the rank of post quartermaster sergeant, it stipulated that the eighty successful candidates should come, "so far as practicable, . . . two from each regiment, provided there are fit applicants from said regiments *who deserve the position.*" Eleven years earlier, the general order that announced the new rank of commissary sergeant had included no such encouragement to black applicants. The Hospital Corps accepted applicants from black regiments at the time of its founding in 1887 and afterward, although the number varied from place to place since the post surgeon had to approve candidates and there were few means for an enlisted man to dispute an officer's judgment. For this reason too the number of black commissary, ordnance, and quartermaster sergeants was never as high as the author of General Order Number 89 might have wished.[26]

The black regulars faced racial prejudice from individuals both inside the army and out. In the army, though, they found an organization that needed their services and that could not afford to discriminate against them in the matters of food, housing, clothing, and equipment. However poor these might be, they were the same that the army issued to white troops. The question of equal pay had been settled during the Civil War, and army courts-martial were ahead of some civilian jurisdictions in admitting the testimony of black witnesses. The United States Army was one of the most impartial institutions of the day, and it attracted men whose ability and endurance assured their regiments' survival and a place, however small, for black Americans in the nation's public life.

Abbreviations Used in Notes

AAAG	Acting Assistant Adjutant General (a staff officer at the district level)
AAG	Assistant Adjutant General (a staff officer at the department and division level, or at the AGO in Washington, D.C.)
ACP	Appointments, Commissions, and Personal Branch of the AGO (it kept officers' personnel files beginning in 1871; these files are designated by a number, the initials ACP, and a year [e.g., 5397-ACP-1883 is Nicholas Nolan's file])
adj.	Adjutant
AG	Adjutant General
AGO	Adjutant General's Office
ANJ	*Army and Navy Journal*
ANR	*Army and Navy Register*
AR [date]	Army Regulations [edition] (e.g., *AR* 1861)
BRFAL	Bureau of Refugees, Freedmen, and Abandoned Lands
Cav.	Cavalry
CB	Commission Branch of the AGO (established in 1863 to collect correspondence bearing on officers' careers; forerunner of the ACP Branch; these files are designated by the initial of officer's surname, a number, the initials "CB" and a year [e.g., G-553-CB-1865 is Benjamin H. Grierson's file])
CG	Commanding General
CMSR	Compiled Military Service Record
CO	Commanding Officer
DB	Descriptive Book
Dept.	Department
Dist.	District
Div.	Division
EB	Enlisted Branch of the AGO
FB	Fund Branch of the AGO
FO	Field Order

FS&B	Field, Staff, and Band
GCM	General Court-Martial
GCMO	General Court-Martial Order
GO	General Order
GRS	General Recruiting Service
HQA	Headquarters of the Army
IG	Inspector General
Inf.	Infantry
ISHL	Illinois State Historical Library
JAG	Judge Advocate General
LB	Letter Book
LC	Library of Congress
LO & RR	Letters, Orders, and Reports Received
LR	Letters Received
LS	Letters Sent
LS&R/RO	Letters Sent and Received, Recruiting Officer
Mil	Military
MRS	Mounted Recruiting Service
n.s.	new series
OAR	*Official Army Register*
OB	Order Book
PMH	Post Medical History
PRD	Principal Records Division, AGO
QMG	Quartermaster General
RG	Record Group
RLR	Register of Letters Received
RPAH	Reports of Persons and Articles Hired
RQM	Regimental Quartermaster
RTR	Register of Trimonthly Returns
RD	Recruiting Division
RS	Recruiting Service
SB	Scrapbook
SO	Special Order
SW	Secretary of War
SWAR	*Annual Report of the Secretary of War*
TS	Telegrams Sent
USAMHI	U.S. Army Military History Institute
USCHA	U.S. Colored Heavy Artillery
USCI	U.S. Colored Infantry
USCT	U.S. Colored Troops
USMA	U.S. Military Academy (West Point)
VA	Veterans' Administration

A capital letter in quotation marks, followed by a regiment ("E" 9th Cav., for example) refers to a company of that regiment when muster rolls or letters are cited. Documents from military posts are cited, for instance: LS/Cummings (Letters Sent, Fort Cummings); PMH/Riley (Post Medical History, Fort Riley); GO 21 Davis, [date] (General Order 21, Fort Davis, [date]); and so on.

Notes

INTRODUCTION

1. In nearly every year from 1866 to 1897, the Secretary of War's annual report announced either the number of "colored recruits" enlisted that year or a suspension of enlistments because the black regiments were full. The only exceptions were 1878 and 1879, when reports did not mention this subject. The published total of "colored recruits" in thirty-one years was 19,621. The real number was smaller; enlistment papers, muster rolls, and pension files show that an indeterminate number—certainly hundreds—of veterans waited more than one month before reenlisting and therefore reverted to "recruit" status.

The term "regulars" distinguishes soldiers in a nation's standing army from members of state militias or wartime volunteers or conscripts.

Recent histories of the black regulars are Fowler, *Black Infantry in the West*, and Leckie, *Buffalo Soldiers*, which covers the cavalry regiments. Billington, *New Mexico's Buffalo Soldiers*, deals with black soldiers' service in that territory, and Kenner, *Buffalo Soldiers and Officers*, studies one regiment, the 9th Cavalry. Schubert, *Black Valor*, has as its subject Medal of Honor winners and their lives before and after their heroic acts, while the same author's *Outpost of the Sioux Wars* tells the story of one fort and the black soldiers who made up a large part of its garrison. *Black Frontiersman* is the memoir of the 10th Cavalry's Lieutenant Henry O. Flipper; Seraile, *Voice of Dissent*, is a recent biography of Theophilus G. Steward, the 25th Infantry's first black chaplain.

2. Redkey, *Grand Army of Black Men*, is an anthology of letters from the *Christian Recorder*. Litwack cites the *Christian Recorder* often in *Been in the Storm So Long*.

3. *New Orleans Tribune*, October 13, 1866.

4. Gatewood, *"Smoked Yankees,"* is a collection of letters from black soldiers in Cuba, the Philippines, and the United States to black newspapers.

5. Most colonial, state, and territorial militias—with the exception of Louisiana—limited membership to white men. Jordan, *White over Black*, 125–26, 411–12; on Louisiana, see Tunnell, *Crucible of Reconstruction*, 69–70.

6. In 1863, as the regular army's strength declined due to casualties and the inability to compete with state enlistment bounties, it began to enlist black cooks, as many as four to a company, but this was a wartime measure. Kautz, *Customs of Service*, 90.

7. *ANJ,* January 13, 1866; *New York Times,* January 11, 1866.

8. Grant to Sherman, October 31, 1865; and Grant to Wilson, January 12, 1866, Grant Papers, LC. At the time, officers' promotion in the staff departments—engineers, ordnance, quartermasters, and other—was within the corps. In the artillery, cavalry, and infantry, promotion for lieutenants and captains was within the regiment; for majors, lieutenant colonels, and colonels, within the branch. For instance, if a cavalry colonel died, retired, or was appointed brigadier general, the senior lieutenant colonel of cavalry would become colonel of his regiment, the senior cavalry major would take the lieutenant colonel's place, and the most senior of all cavalry captains would take the major's place. This usually, but not always, meant transfers between regiments. Grant's proposal would have diminished the chances of promotion for officers serving with black troops.

9. *Congressional Globe*, 39th Cong., 1st sess., 1866, vol. 39, pt. 2:1385.

10. *ANJ,* March 24, April 7, 1866.

11. *Congressional Globe*, 39th Cong., 1st sess., 1866, vol. 39, pt. 3:2027; *ANJ,* May 5, 1866.

12. *Congressional Globe*, 39th Cong., 1st sess., 1866, vol. 39, pt. 4:3668. Desertion was so troublesome for a year after the war that the army instituted the first of its two amnesties. Under the terms of the first amnesty, deserters who surrendered "will be returned to duty without trial or punishment, on condition that they make good the time lost by desertion and forfeit all pay and allowance for the time of their absence." GO 43 AGO, July 3, 1866, RG 94. The second amnesty came in 1873 after one-third of the army deserted when privates suffered a 20 percent pay cut. GO 102 AGO, October 10, 1873, RG 94.

13. All four new regiments of cavalry—the 7th, 8th, 9th, and 10th, two white and two black—carried two veterinary surgeons on their rolls; the six older, white regiments had only one each. That the black infantry regiments had lower numbers—38th through 41st—than those of the Veteran Reserve Corps suggests that the army always intended its new black troops for active service rather than as an auxiliary garrison or labor corps. The black regulars always received equal pay, unlike the USCT, whose pay was less than that of white soldiers until late in the Civil War. Cornish, *Sable Arm*, 192–95; Glatthaar, *Forged in Battle*, 174–75.

14. Besides long-standing social custom, practicality dictated segregation. The New York Draft Riots in 1863 and riots at Memphis and New Orleans in the spring of 1866 strongly indicated that black recruits would be in grave danger scattered throughout the army and outnumbered ten-to-one by whites in barracks, kitchens, stables, and other settings of everyday military life. Black

applicants began to be accepted as noncommissioned officers in the Ordnance, Quartermaster, and Subsistence Departments during the late 1870s and 1880s.

15. Leckie, *Buffalo Soldiers*, 15, 259; Grierson to Dear Alice, April 27, 1867, Grierson Papers, ISHL.

16. Steelhammer to AAAG, December 11, 1879, 2434-1879 LR/Dist. New Mexico, RG 393; Carpenter to Grierson, May 22, 1870, Grierson Papers. In 1869 an army officer wrote to the *Army and Navy Journal* from Camp Supply, Indian Territory, "Two [10th Cavalry] companies, H [Carpenter's] and I, are well mounted, the other companies expect horses in a few days." Carpenter himself was absent on leave at the time. *ANJ*, July17, 1869.

17. Gatewood, *Black Americans and the White Man's Burden*, 42; Stiles, "Buffalo Soldiers," 85.

18. For whites' use of "buffalo soldiers," see *Nation*, October 30, 1873; Remington, "Scout with the Buffalo Soldiers"; and *ANJ*, November 8, 1873, April 3, 1880, August 25, 1894. Quotations from GCM transcripts of Private Robert Hopkins, PP4575, and Private Peter White, RR825, RG 153. "Buffalo soldiers" does not occur in soldiers' letters to the *Cleveland Gazette*, the *Huntsville Gazette*, or other black newspapers cited here or in letters from Spanish-American War regulars that Gatewood quotes in *"Smoked Yankees."* Black veterans who wrote to the monthly *Winners of the West* during the 1920s did not use the term either. As for the black regulars' racial pride, the 25th Infantry's Chaplain George Mullins wrote that they were "possessed of the notion that the colored people of the whole country are more or less affected by their conduct in the army." Mullins to AG, January 1, 1877, 5053-ACP-1874, RG 94. In 1869, with the regular army's first black chaplain about to face a court-martial, Commissary Sgt. David B. Jeffers, himself a former 9th Cavalry trooper, counseled a potential witness, "I would advise you as a matter of race pride to avoid being a witness against the chaplain, you know the general feeling against the few colored officers we have and that there are always those who are ever ready to take any advantage of the leaders of the race." Stover, "Chaplain Henry V. Plummer," 39.

19. Marszalek emphasizes that order was the essence of the army's being in Sherman, 377–400; Dobak, "Fort Riley's Black Soldiers."

20. Woodward, *Meet General Grant*, 372.

21. *Congressional Globe*, 39th Cong., 1st sess., 1866, vol. 39, pt. 4:3669.

CHAPTER 1

1. *Statutes at Large* 14 (1866): 332. The enlarged army included ten regiments of cavalry, five of artillery, and forty-five of infantry.

2. CG to SW, August 2, 1866, LS/HQA, RG 108.

3. AG to Sherman and Sheridan, August 3, 1866; and AG to Miles and Thomas, August 7, 1866, LS/AGO, RG 94. Of the four generals, Miles alone did

not hold a regular commission—he was a wartime general of U.S. Volunteers—and later accepted a regular appointment as colonel of the 40th Infantry.

4. AG to Sherman, Sheridan, and Thomas, August 13, 1866, LS/AGO, RG 94; AG to Sickles, September 25, 1866, LS/RD, RG 94.

5. Brisbin to Forsyth, October 15, 1866; and Forsyth to AG, October 16, 1866, 685-F-1866 LR/RD, RG 94.

6. Swayne to Hazen, February 6, 1867; and Hazen to Leet, February 11, 1867, 87-H-1867 LR/RD, RG 94.

7. AAG to Sheridan, June 18, 1867, LS/RD, RG 94; Hazen to AAG Dept. Missouri, February 6, 1867; Hazen to AG, February 6, 1867; and adj. to Ezekiel, February 26, 1867, LS/38th Inf., RG 391.

8. CO to AG, March 15, 1867; and CO to Caziare, November 15, 1867, LS/40th Inf., RG 391; AAG to Hinks, April 29, 1868, LS/RD, RG 94; muster rolls, "A" and "B" 40th Inf., December 1866–June 1868, RG 94. Stanley finished his enlistment as first sergeant of Company B and reenlisted, the only member of the recruiting party to do so. Miles had been a major general of U.S. Volunteers during and after the Civil War, but became a colonel in the regular army with the expansion of 1866. He spent most of his time while colonel of the 40th away from the regiment on Reconstruction duty.

9. Conner to AG, April 6, 1867, 87-C-1867 LR/RD, RG 94.

10. Spurgin to AG, February 12, 1867, 75-S-1867 LR/RD; and Quimby to AG, September 21, 1867, 45-Q-1867 LR/RD, RG 94.

11. Penney to AG, April 8, 1867, 84-P-1867 LR/RD; and Penney to AG, May 10, 1867, 96-P-1867 LR/RD, RG 94; AAG to Johnson, June 5, 1867, LS/RD, RG 94. Walking and hopping were tests that every recruit had to pass during the mid-nineteenth century. Bartholow, *Manual of Instructions*, 171; Tripler, *Manual of the Medical Officer*, 18. These primitive methods of gauging health were not much different from those that had been common at slave auctions before the Civil War. Bankole, *Slavery and Medicine*, 71, 78.

12. Pension files of Leonard Scott, SC676266; Lorenzo George, SC518011; Lafayette Mundy, SC841482; and William Henry, SC749554, RG 15. Hasty medical examiners may even have accepted a woman, Cathay Williams, who later claimed to have spent nearly two years in the 38th Infantry before being discharged as "feeble, both physically and mentally, and much of the time quite unfit for duty." Pension file of Cathay Williams, SO1032593, RG 15; Blanton, "Cathay Williams."

13. Grierson to Pettee, May 23, 1867, LS/10th Cav., RG 391; Mackenzie to AG, December 11, 1867, LS/41st Inf., RG 391; regimental returns, 10th Cav., May 1867, and 41st Inf., June 1867, RG 94.

14. Mower to AG, April 4, 1868, 96-M-1868 LR/RD, RG 94. On antebellum literacy, see Berlin, *Slaves without Masters*, 303–6; Genovese, *Roll, Jordan, Roll*, 561–66.

15. Miles to Clous, September 11, 1867, LS/40th Inf., RG 391; AG to Purington, May 30, 1867, LS/RD, RG 94.

16. Adj. to Danielson, January 7, 1867, LS/40th Inf, RG 391.

17. Hatch to AG, November 4, 1866, 1070-H-1866 LR/RD, RG 94. The education that northern cities offered their black residents was rudimentary and segregated. Boston's schools had integrated formally in 1855, but de facto segregation still prevailed there, as well as in Philadelphia and elsewhere. There was no public education for black residents of Washington, D.C., until the mid-1860s. Detroit ended legal segregation in 1867, but the practice continued for years. Litwack, *North of Slavery*, 142–50; Pleck, *Black Migration*, 34; Lane, *Roots of Violence*, 17; Johnston, *Surviving Freedom*, 170–73; Katzman, *Before the Ghetto*, 22–25, 50, 84–90.

18. Schofield to Hood, January 6, 1867, LS/41st Inf., RG 391; Grierson to Pettee, May 23, 1867, LS/10th Cav., RG 391; Wheaton to AG, June 28, 1867, LS/39th Inf., RG 391.

19. Brisbin to AG, January 25, 1868, 53-B-1868 LR/RD, RG 94; Cooper to adj., October 12, 1867, LS&R/RO, 39th Inf., RG 391.

20. Endorsements, RLR/39th Inf., 43, 75, RG 391; Kirby to AAG Dept. Gulf, March 2, 1867, LS/39th Inf., RG 391; AAG to Broatch, April 16, 1868, LS/RD, RG 94.

21. Hatch to AG, February 1, 1867, 77-H-1867 LR/RD, RG 94; AG to Hatch, February 19, 1867, LS/RD, RG 94.

22. Adj. to Badger, March 28, 1867, LS/10th Cav., RG 391; Mackenzie to AG, November 27, 1867, LS/41st Inf, RG 391.

23. Pension files of Noah Spiller, SC489276, and Joseph Luckadoe, SC871158, RG 15.

24. Hinks to AG, April 10, 1869, 264-H-1869 LR/AGO, RG 94; QMG to AG, June 2, 1869, 271-Q-1869 LR/AGO, filed with 264-H-1869.

25. AG to Brisbin, February 23, 1867, LS/RD, RG 94; Kinney to Grant, January 2, 1867, 2-K-1867 RLR/HQA, RG 108; Alvord to Badger, June 5, 1867; and Alvord to Carpenter, June 10, 1867, LS/10th Cav., RG 391. "Lance" meant a probationary, unpaid rank. Speakes soon became a sergeant in Company E of the 10th.

26. Pension file of Hector Preston, SO1084669, RG 15; Miles to AG, December 22, 1866, 1154-M-1866 LR/RD, RG 94; Hinks to AG, July 3, 1868, RLR/RD, RG 94; Miles to Robinson, January 9, 1867, LS/40th Inf., RG 391.

27. Pratt, *Battlefield and Classroom*, 7; Woodward to Grierson, July 19, 1867, Grierson Papers, ISHL. Although a company of cavalry was called a "troop" long before 1883, when the name became official, this book uses the older term throughout since "troops" is also a synonym for "soldiers."

28. Regimental returns, 10th Cav. and 38th Inf., June–October 1867 (the 10th Cavalry also listed five dead of unknown causes and three of "disease"), RG 94; adj. to Armes, July 18, 1867, LS/10th Cav., RG 391; adj. to Cooper, September 14, 1867, LS&R/RO 39th Inf., RG 391; regimental returns, 39th Inf., September–October 1867, RG 94.

29. Company muster rolls, 40th Inf., 1866–67, RG 94; 40th Inf., "Organization List to Pension Files" (microfilm); CMSR of Rodolphe Bayne [*sic*], 99th USCI, Carded Records, RG 94; GCM transcript of Sergeant Major Rudolph Bacquie [*sic*], MM3017, RG 153. Being a natural leader, Baqui was once tried for inciting a mutiny and spent several months as a prisoner at Fort Jefferson in the Dry Tortugas. On the trades open to free blacks and the competition from white labor, see Berlin, *Slaves without Masters*, 230–39.

30. Wheaton to AG, December 23, 1866, LS/39th Inf., RG 391; Mackenzie to AG, May 27, 1867, LS/41st Inf., RG 391.

31. Regimental return, 39th Inf., February 1867, RG 94.

32. Merritt to AAG Dist. Gulf, July 20, 1867, 75-A-1867 LR/HQA, RG 108; Hazen to AG, May 4, 1867, LS/38th Inf., RG 391.

33. Mackenzie to AG, July 12, 1867, LS/41st Inf., RG 391.

34. GO 101 AGO, November 26, 1867, RG 94.

35. *Statutes at Large* 15 (1869): 318.

36. Butler introduced a bill in the House that specified the number of black regiments in the reduced army, but his version did not survive to the final vote. House debaters were more interested in the size of the appropriation for the Rock Island Arsenal, and the Senate, where the subject of race did not arise at all, concerned itself mostly with a paragraph that settled a claim that dated from a British coastal raid during the War of 1812. Both houses discussed at length the size of the army's officer corps and how to reduce it. *Congressional Globe*, 40th Cong., 3d sess., 1869, vol. 40, pt. 2:970, passim.

A week after the appropriation bill passed, Rawlins and Sherman had a list of which infantry regiments would merge, and a few days later they issued an order for the movements necessary when these regiments had to travel from one part of the country to another, as when the 40th Infantry went from North Carolina to Louisiana to consolidate with the 39th, making the new 25th Infantry. GO 16 AGO, March 11, 1869; and GO 17 AGO, March 15, 1869, RG 94. Although the army reorganization act of 1866 continued to guarantee the existence of the black cavalry regiments, the black infantry regiments seem to have had no legal status until they appeared in section 1108, *Revised Statutes of 1873*, page 204. The authorities cited in *Revised Statutes*, though, were the army reorganization act, which specified *four* black infantry regiments, and the appropriation act of 1869, which did not mention race at all. How the 1869 act came to be interpreted as confirming the existence of *two* black infantry regiments is a mystery; the fact remains that Rawlins and Sherman retained these units on their own initiative.

37. Discussion of all-black artillery regiments in the 1890s came to nothing (see chapter 12). When Congress authorized ten new regiments of cavalry and infantry in 1901 and reorganized the army's artillery, it created no new all-black organizations.

38. GO 17 AGO, March 15, 1869. The consolidation of 1869 affected the entire infantry force and left the army with twenty-three white infantry regiments instead of forty-one.

39. Hinks to AG, June 8, 1869, 121-H-1869 LR/RD, RG 94; AG to Hinks, June 24, 1869, LS/RD, RG 94.

40. Hinks to AG, February 1, 1870, 58-H-1870 LR/RD, RG 94. This file contains Hinks's report and those submitted by the company commanders of the 25th Infantry.

41. In 1870, New Orleans employed 182 black policemen in a force of 647 officers. The number declined sharply with the end of Reconstruction. Rousey, *Policing the Southern City*, 135–42. Black farm ownership was rare but not unheard of; Duprie's purchase was made easier by a 70 percent decline in the value of Louisiana farmland after the Civil War. Ransom and Sutch, *One Kind of Freedom*, 51, 81–87.

42. Lawson was not alone in his preference for soldiers of obviously mixed ancestry. Descriptive rolls of the four black infantry regiments in 1866–67 list 962 recruits as having a "black" complexion out of a total of 1,544 (a little more than 62 percent); of 181 sergeants in those regiments in 1867, only 83 were "black" (almost 46 percent). Lighter-skinned soldiers stood a better chance of becoming noncommissioned officers. Muster rolls, 38th, 39th, 40th, and 41st Infantry, RG 94.

The officers' prejudice had a historical basis. Before the war, Southern planters often extended benefits to their slave children in the form of better jobs, educational opportunities, and even freedom, conferring great advantages on them. Genovese, *Roll, Jordan, Roll*, 415–16. About half of the slaves manumitted in Richmond, Virginia, between 1831 and 1860 were mulattoes. Berlin, *Slaves without Masters*, 151n.

43. General Sherman, commanding the army since March 1869, when Grant entered the White House, read Hinks's report and added remarks of his own. He approved of allowing the 39th's officers to sign up white recruits at the regiment's stations, "for thus each man . . . would know with whom he was to associate, but I would not send . . . white men, from the General Rendesvous for this Regiment, as I know it would be offensive to the White Recruits, and . . . would discourage General Enlistment everywhere." This was a surprising suggestion from Sherman, who five years earlier had called the inclusion of black men in the Civil War draft "an insult to our Race," adding, "A nigger is not a white man, and all the Psalm singing on earth won't make him so." Sherman's years in the South before the war had shaped his views on race relations, although he later came to appreciate the black regulars' service in the West. In any case, neither he nor the Secretary of War could abolish the color line without Congressional approval, and the regiments remained segregated. Quotations from Sherman's endorsement, February 18, 1870, 58-H-1870

LR/RD, RG 94; Sherman to "J.A.R.," September 12, 1864, quoted in Marszalek, *Sherman*, 271.

44. Mackenzie to AG, December 6, 1869, and AG's endorsement, January 5, 1870, 2-M-1870 LR/RD, RG 94.

45. AG to Mackenzie, January 7, 1870; and AG to Hinks, May 28, 1870, LS/RD, RG 94; Mackenzie to AG, June 4, 1870, 93-M-1870 LR/RD, RG 94; and Mackenzie to AG, June 16, 1870, 101-M-1870 LR/RD, RG 94.

46. Schwenk to Mackenzie, July 27, 1870; and Mackenzie to AG, August 1, 1870, 101-M-1870 LR/RD, RG 94.

47. Mackenzie to Williams, October 21, 1867, LS/41st Inf., RG 391; he repeated this view in Mackenzie to AG, December 11, 1867, LS/41st Inf.

48. Foner, *Reconstruction*, 262–64; Church to Davis, July 14, 1866, Box 6; and Watkins to Howard, March 13, 1866, Box 17, LR/Commissioner, RG 105.

49. Pension file of Edward Smith, SC303061, RG 15; Wayne, *Reshaping of Plantation Society*, 63–64; monthly inspection report, Lake Providence, La., August 1866, RG 105; muster roll, "E" 9th Cav., December 31, 1867, RG 94. On economic dislocation and violence in southeastern Louisiana parishes that contributed more than 200 recruits to the 9th Cavalry and the 39th and 41st Infantry, see Hyde, *Pistols and Politics*, 147–49, 160–63; similarly, floods and racial violence occurred near Wilmington, North Carolina, where 87 men joined the 40th Infantry during the winter of 1867. Alexander, *North Carolina Faces the Freedmen*, 120, 130–38; regimental returns, 40th Inf., December 1866–March 1867, RG 94. On the other hand, drought prevailed in northern Georgia (Hahn, *Roots of Southern Populism*, 139–41), where a tour by 38th Infantry recruiters in May 1867 netted 75 men in Atlanta and 26 in Dalton, Marietta, and Rome. DB/38th Inf., RG 391.

50. Hardwick, "'Your Old Father Abe Lincoln,'" 111–13; Green, *Washington*, 277–78, 302–3; Bureau of the Census, *Statistics of the Population*, 231; Santmyer, *Ohio Town*, 90–92.

51. Madison Bruin interview in Rawick, *American Slave*, vol. 4, pt. 1:171; Cashin, *Under Fire*, 58. Quotations from interviews with former slaves conducted during the 1930s by the Federal Writers' Project are quoted here as they were transcribed by the interviewers.

52. Pension file of Hector Preston, SO1084669, RG 15; Jenkins to Bullis, January 6, 1870, 81-B-1870 LR/RD, RG 94.

53. For population movement during the last years of slavery, see Genovese, *Roll, Jordan, Roll*, 450–58, and Gutman, *Black Family*, 151–56. Between 1841 and 1852, the number of slaves on Louisiana sugar plantations more than doubled, from 50,000 to 125,000. McDonald, *Economy and Material Culture*, 4. For population movement during the war years, see Berlin et al., *Slaves No More*, 63–67, and Litwack, *Been in the Storm So Long*, 30–36.

54. DB/"K" 40th Inf., RG 391. Twenty-seven out of sixty-four men in the company (42 percent) had enlisted in Boston, New York, and Philadelphia; most of the rest were from Baltimore, Norfolk, and Washington, D.C.

55. The figure 533 comes from examining descriptive books and muster-out rolls of the 10th USCHA and the 65th, 80th, 81st, 107th, 116th, 117th, and 125th USCI regiments. More names probably lie concealed under the tape that holds some of the muster-out rolls together. Comparison of regular-army enlistments in Lexington and Louisville, Kentucky; Nashville, Tennessee; and Philadelphia, Pennsylvania, with descriptive books of USCT regiments raised in or near those cities yielded 274 names; the rest came from regular-army pension index cards for the 9th and 10th Cavalry and the 38th, 39th, 40th, and 41st Infantry.

CHAPTER 2

1. *Congressional Globe*, 39th Cong., 1st sess., 1866, vol. 39, pt. 3:2006. On the variety of men's reasons for accepting commissions in the USCT, see Glatthaar, *Forged in Battle*, 39–42.

2. Adj. to Harris, November 7, 1866; and CO to AAG Dept. Gulf, October 22, 1866, LB/10th USCHA, RG 94. The files of the Freedmen and Southern History Project at the University of Maryland contain eleven complaints about payroll fraud and deadbeat officers in nine regiments stationed from Camp William Penn near Philadelphia to Ringgold Barracks on the Rio Grande and covering the period from March 1865 to April 1867. FSHP files A2325, B113, B214, B251, B318, B321, C604, G44, G178, CC8, and CC14. Glatthaar describes officers' abuses and their consequences in *Forged in Battle*, 54–55, 109–12.

3. *Congressional Globe*, 39th Cong., 1st sess., 1866, vol. 39, pt. 1:265; *ANJ*, January 13, March 17, May 5, 1866.

4. GO 56 AGO, August 1, 1866, RG 94, published the text of the army reorganization act, which prescribed the selection procedure. "Regular army commissions" by no means implies a West Point background. The army added nine infantry regiments at the beginning of the Civil War, nearly trebling the number of infantry captains and lieutenants. Almost all of the new officers came directly from civil life.

5. Stanton to Grant, October 11, 1867, Stanton Papers, LC; for Grant's lists of officers, see Grant to Stanton, August 7, 17, 22, 1866, Grant Papers, LC.

6. Sheridan to Stanton, April 4, 1866, Sheridan Papers, LC; Grant to Stanton, August 2, 1866, Grant Papers.

7. Higginson, *Army Life*, 28; Stanton to Miles, August 3, 1866, Stanton Papers. Miles did not mention his postwar service with black soldiers in either his *Personal Recollections* (Chicago: Werner, 1896) or *Serving the Republic* (New York: Harper, 1911). Henry C. Corbin's unpublished memoir mentions that he was colonel of the 14th USCI during the war but does not explicitly mention the race of the soldiers he led during nearly fourteen years' peacetime service with the 38th and 24th Infantry. Corbin Papers, LC.

8. Biographical information from the alphabetical entries in volume 1 of Heitman, *Historical Register*.

9. The 3d Cavalry's Marshall S. Howe, who failed to win a brevet, does not even have an entry in Boatner's *Civil War Dictionary*. Information about the colonels of 1866 is from Boatner, *Civil War Dictionary*, and Heitman, *Historical Register*, 1:55–136 and individual entries.

10. Benteen's experience during the war as colonel of the 138th USCI may have influenced his decision. When his promotion to major finally came in 1882, it was to a vacancy in the 9th Cavalry, after all.

11. Grierson's petition is in his personnel file, G-553-CB-1865, RG 94. Coxe's personnel file is 4781-ACP-1873, RG 94. LR/AGO (RG 94) and LR/HQA (RG 108), 1866–67, contain many applications for commissions.

12. AG to Sherman and Sheridan, August 3, 1866, LS/AGO, RG 94.

13. Hale to Grant, August 14, 1866, S-481-CB-1867, RG 94; Carpenter to AG, August 23, 1866, 1562-ACP-1881, RG 94.

14. Corbin to Eckart, July 26, 1866, 1710-ACP-1876, RG 94; Pratt to AG, March 26, 1867, 713-ACP-1874, RG 94; Granger to Nelson, August 14, 1866, G-35-CB-1870, RG 94.

15. This survey of officers whose names appeared in the *Official Army Register* for 1867 and 1868 counted only those whose war service was in the volunteers, not former USCT officers who already held regular-army commissions like James S. Brisbin and Louis H. Carpenter. The total number of black regiments in the Union army included several state organizations like the 5th Massachusetts Cavalry and the 29th Connecticut Infantry that never received a Federal number. Several of the infantry regiments never completed organization, and their men were assigned elsewhere.

16. In four large batches (February 23 and July 28, 1866, and January 22 and March 7, 1867), the army awarded former volunteer officers 719 commissions, 106 of which went to veterans of the USCT. On selection of USCT officers, see Glatthaar, *Forged in Battle*, 35–59.

17. Copies of examination questions are in the personnel files of Nicholas Nolan, 5397-ACP-1883, and Charles E. Nordstrom, 179-ACP-1872, RG 94.

18. Personnel files of Theodore A. Boice, B-212-CB-1869, and Edwin A. Rigg, 3435-ACP-1872, RG 94.

19. Cooper to AG, December 27, 1870, 4224-ACP-1879, RG 94; Schooley to Shoemaker, November 24, 1870, S-149-CB-1866, RG 94.

20. Grierson to AAG Dept. Missouri, November 29, 1870, 4070-ACP-1879, RG 94; Viele to AG, September 24, 1870, 4564-ACP-1877, RG 94. Captain Henry C. Corbin of the 24th Infantry wrote to his friend and patron, the Cincinnati newspaper editor Murat Halstead: "I have got tired of hunting the noble 'Red Man' on foot. I want to leave the Infantry and am an applicant for an appointment to the Pay Department of the Army. I have in five years marched over 5000 miles and want a change." Corbin to Halstead, December 12, 1871, in Maus-Halstead Family Papers, USAMHI. Corbin eventually managed a transfer to the Adjutant General's Department and had become AG by the time of the Spanish-American War.

21. By the late 1890s, only one of the sixteen field-grade officers in the black regiments—Major William C. Forbush of the 9th Cavalry, a West Point graduate of 1868—was not a Civil War veteran. Army-wide, 43 percent of infantry captains were age fifty or older; twenty-two of them were sixty or older. The youngest infantry major was fifty-three years old. *ANJ*, April 10, 1897.

22. *ANJ*, March 3, 1888.

23. *ANR*, February 16, 1884; Brechemin, "Promotion in the Line"; Hein, *Memories*, 110. Brechemin's seventy-six year-old colonel was an arithmetical construct; sixty-four was the statutory age of retirement.

24. Bliss, "Autobiography" (5 vols.), 5:48, Bliss Papers, USAMHI; AG to Purington, May 30, 1867, LS/RD, RG 94; Hatch to Crosby, November 4, 1866, 1070-H-1866 LR/RD, RG 94.

25. McConnell, *Five Years a Cavalryman*, 213.

26. *ANJ*, August 8, October 10, 1868.

27. *ANJ*, March 3, 1883. See also *ANJ*, December 4, 1875, April 1, 1876, September 10, 1881; *ANR*, March 5, 1887; and *New York Times*, March 10, 1888.

28. Scott, *Some Memories*, 25. While 92 percent of West Point graduates assigned to the 9th Cavalry during the years 1869–76 stood in the lowest quarter of the class, by 1887–91 the figure had dropped to 16 percent (total number of graduates during these years, eighteen). The corresponding decline in the 10th Cavalry was from 100 percent to 13 percent (total number of graduates, nineteen). *OAR*, 1869–76 and 1887–91.

29. *ANJ*, November 30, 1889.

30. *ANJ*, February 7, May 15, June 12, August 14, October 2, 1880; *First Class Annual of the Class of '86*, 93.

31. Clarke to Mother, March 19, 1886, October 1, December 19, 1884, Clarke Papers, Missouri Historical Society; Order 217, December 10, 1884, OB/Davis, RG 393; muster rolls, "D" 10th Cav., December 31, 1884, and "K" 10th Cav., October 31, 1884, RG 94; enlistment papers of Phillip Jones, RG 94.

32. Clarke to Father, May 4, 1886, Clarke Papers.

33. Clarke to Mother, May 11, 1886, ibid.; muster rolls, "K" 10th Cav., June 30, 1886, and "D" 9th Cav., October 31, 1879, RG 94; enlistment papers of Edward Scott, RG 94.

34. CG Dept. Texas to AG, July 14, 1874, N-105-CB-1867 (Robert Neely), RG 94; Grierson to AG, January 7, 1878, LS/10th Cav., RG 391; GCMO 64 AGO, August 24, 1887, RG 94. Each year's *Official Army Register* listed "casualties" (deaths, dismissals, resignations, retirements). Between 1871, when officer assignments to the consolidated infantry regiments were complete, and 1890, captains and lieutenants in the four black regiments—company officers who had direct contact with the men—numbered 140 in a total of 1,180 cavalry and infantry captains and lieutenants (for thirty-five regiments). They represented less than 12 percent of officers but more than 26 percent of dismissals. Dismissals decreased across the board in the years from 1891 through 1897, with only

eleven captains and lieutenants of cavalry and infantry dismissed, only one of them in the black regiments—although 1894 also saw the dismissal of 9th Cavalry Chaplain Henry V. Plummer.

35. Sherman to Lugenbeel, May 20, 1881, LS/HQA, RG 108. Batchelor retired as a captain in January 1902 and died seven months later. As an example of how seniority varied among regiments, Walter L. Finley and Charles H. Grierson both graduated from West Point in 1879, but Finley's promotion to first lieutenant in the 9th Cavalry came only four years later, while Grierson, in the 10th, remained a second lieutenant for seven years. Finley became a captain in the 9th in 1891, while Grierson had to wait until 1897.

36. Conline to his father, July 2, 1872, 1055-ACP-1873, RG 94.

37. *ANJ*, February 11, June 10, 1871, February 23, 1884, March 14, 1885.

38. *ANJ*, January 2, 23, February 6, 1886.

CHAPTER 3

1. AAG to Coxe, July 25, 1871; AG to Superintendent GRS, March 26, 1872; AG to Carroll, April 18, 1873; and AG to CG Dept. Texas, November 12, 1878, LS/RD, RG 94; AG's endorsement on Doubleday to AG, August 15, 1871, 1143-1871 LR/RD, RG 94.

2. Smither to Grierson, October 12, 1872, and Myrick to Grierson, May 25, 1871, Grierson Papers, ISHL.

3. AG to CO 9th Cav., September 15, 1873, LS/RD, RG 94. Enlistment papers and pension applications show that very few long-service soldiers, even the thirty-year men who began to retire in the 1890s, served continuously without taking some time out, especially between first and second enlistments, to sample civilian life again.

4. As three-year enlistments ended, the 25th Infantry discharged 705 men in six months, and its strength dropped to 400 in February 1870. That June, after 941 discharges, the 24th Infantry mustered 256 men. Regimental returns, 25th Inf., September 1869–February 1870, and 24th Inf., January–June 1870, RG 94. The depletion occurred later in the 24th, because it included men who had transferred from the 41st, the last of the black infantry regiments to complete its organization. Shortages like these were not so sharp or sudden in the regiments of white infantry, which had been receiving increments of recruits since the end of the Civil War rather than being raised all at once in 1866–67.

5. AG to Superintendent MRS, April 18, 1872, LS/RD, RG 94.

6. Quimby to AG, July 3, 1867, 33-Q-1870 LR/RD, RG 94; pension file of Zachariah Pope, IWWC11913, RG 15.

7. Rickey, *Forty Miles a Day*, 19; George Conrad Jr. interview in Rawick, *American Slave*, vol. 7, pt. 1:41; pension file of Joshua Johnson, SC179326, RG 15.

8. Medical rejection rates in years when the Surgeon General published statistics in his annual report varied from 32.5 percent in 1884 and 34.3 per-

cent in 1883 to 59 percent in 1896 and 59.1 percent in 1889. *SWAR* 1883, 629; *SWAR* 1884, 742, 744; *SWAR* 1890, 981; *SWAR* 1897, 637. In 1881 the War Department published a racial profile of causes for rejection. Of 18,297 rejected whites, "intemperance" was the grounds in 2,916 cases (15.9 percent) and syphilis in 509 (2.8 percent). Of 613 rejected blacks, 75 were intemperate (12.2 percent) and 43 syphilitic (7 percent). Whites' rate of rejection for "intemperance" was 30 percent greater than that of blacks, while blacks' rate of rejection for syphilis was 250 percent greater than that of whites. For both groups, "general unfitness" was the second most frequent medical cause for rejection: 2,588 whites (14.1 percent) and 52 blacks (8.5 percent). *SWAR* 1881, 62–63. Alcoholism statistic in *SWAR* 1886, 609.

In 1874, in order to reduce the size of the army and to screen out the most obvious potential deserters, the recruiting service instituted a waiting period between the initial visit to a recruiting office and the recruit's departure for one of the depots as well as a background investigation of sorts. Combing out impulsive applicants along with detectable minors, married men, convicted felons, and other undesirables reduced the rate of acceptance to between 20 and 30 percent in good economic times and well below that—as low as 13.5 percent—during national depressions, when recruiters could select from a larger pool of talent. *SWAR* 1876, 72; *SWAR* 1877, 44–47; *SWAR* 1881, 46; *SWAR* 1886, 81; *SWAR* 1887, 84; *SWAR* 1890, 56; *SWAR* 1895, 187.

9. Mackenzie to AG, August 1, 1870, 101-M-1870 LR/RD, RG 94; Hatch to AG, June 4, 1884, LS/9th Cav., RG 391.

10. *SWAR* 1881, 62; Woodward to Grierson, October 3, 1888, Grierson Papers.

11. Coffman, *Old Army*, 336; Rickey, *Forty Miles a Day*, 33–44.

12. *Harper's Weekly*, June 28, 1890.

13. Smither to Grierson, March 26, 1882, Grierson Papers. Enlistment papers of Augustus and Walter Dover; Daniel F., John, and John Kellum; George M., George W., and James H. Pumphrey; and Alfred and Anthony Saunders, RG 94.

14. The federal census of 1890 was the first to apply racial categories to occupational statistics. In that year, agriculture employed 56 percent of black workers and service (including waiters, cooks, and barbers) another 31 percent. There were only 40,000 black skilled workers—for example, blacksmiths, carpenters, and masons—in the country. Higgs, *Competition and Coercion*, 80.

15. CO to AG, April 9, 1877, LS/Concho, RG 393; CO to AAG Dept. Dakota, November 28 and December 31, 1882, and July 17, 1885, LS/Snelling, RG 393. Kusmer, *A Ghetto Takes Shape*, 61–63, offers a brief overview of the public education available to black children throughout the North. In Kentucky the only three cities that allowed black schools a proportionate share of funds were Lexington, Louisville, and Paducah; coincidentally, the army's favorite recruiting grounds in the state. Howard, *Black Liberation*, 172.

16. AG's endorsement on Dodge to AG, December 5, 1873, 29-1874 LR/RD, RG 94.

17. CO to AAG Dept. Dakota, November 15, 1883, LS/Snelling, RG 393.

18. Dawson to AG, June 8, 1875, 1342-1875 LR/RD, RG 94; AG to CG, October 23, 1886, 2627-1886 RLR/HQA, RG 108; Davidson to AAG Dept. Texas, May 22, 1874, LS/10th Cav., RG 391.

19. CO to AAG Dept. Arkansas, April 15, 1881, LS/Supply, RG 393; CO to AAG Dept. Dakota, January 17, 1882, LS/Hale, RG 393.

20. Grierson to AG, March 19, 1877, LS/Concho, RG 393; Richards to AAG Dept. Arizona, June 9, 1890, 2577-1890 RLR/Dept. Arizona, RG 393.

21. McChristian, *U.S. Army in the West*, 8, 37–39; endorsement on Davenport to AG, January 17, 1878, LS/RD, RG 94; *ANJ*, April 13, 1889; Sweet to Andrews, March 22, 1890, LS/"D" 25th Inf., RG 391.

22. AG's reports in *SWAR* 1879–90.

23. Andrews to AG, January 11, 1875, 219-1875 LR/RD, RG 94; Potter to AG, February 15, 1875, 585-1875 LR/RD, RG 94. The cause of this depletion was the expiration of the five-year enlistments of men who joined the regiments in 1870 to replace soldiers whose three-year enlistments expired that year. Since recruits usually arrived in parties of fifty men or more, who had all enlisted within a few months of each other, the simultaneous discharge of large numbers of men caused fluctuations in the strength of white regiments too, though seldom the severe depletion that occurred in the black regiments.

24. AG's endorsement on Ord to AG, August 13, 1875, 1801-1875 LR/RD, RG 94.

25. AAG to Superintendents GRS and MRS, November 27, 1877, LS/RD, RG 94.

26. Andrews to AG, November 25, 1878, and Sherman's endorsement, 3211-1878 LR/RD, RG 94; AG to CG Dept. Texas, December 11, 1878, LS/RD, RG 94; RTR/RD, RG 94.

27. AAG to Clous, November 29, 1880; and AG to Superintendent GRS, September 7, 1881, LS/RD, RG 94.

28. Bertaux, "Structural Economic Change," 137–46; Katzman, *Before the Ghetto*, 104–6, 124–26; Kusmer, *A Ghetto Takes Shape*, 66–75; Pleck, *Black Migration*, 128–32, 146–51.

29. Grierson to AG, August 22, 1876, LS/10th Cav., RG 391.

30. GO 88 AGO, August 22, 1876, published the "act to increase the cavalry force of the United States" recently passed by Congress; *SWAR* 1877, 30–33, shows the strength of the cavalry regiments after the law had been in effect for a year.

31. Woodward to Grierson, January 19, 1877, Grierson Papers; AG to Superintendent MRS, March 2, 1877, LS/RD, RG 94.

32. *Daily New Mexican*, January 10, September 17, 1877. Characterizing the few dozen Apaches who might be off their reservations at any one time as

"impossible odds" was typical of western editors, who did not want to see the Quartermaster Department's disbursements "dwindle down." For editorial opinion in Texas, see the *Waco Daily Examiner*, September 16, 1876, and the *San Antonio Daily Express*, May 26, 1877.

33. Muster rolls, "G" 25th Inf., April 30, 1880; and "B" 24th Inf., October 31, 1895, RG 94.

34. DB/"D" 25th Inf., 1885–97, RG 391, 118; Sweet to adj., August 6, 1891, LS/"D" 25th Inf., RG 391. Enlisted men's normal term for retirement was thirty years, but Civil War service counted double, and USCT veterans began retiring from the regular army in the early 1890s.

35. Smith's testimony in GCM transcript of Private Lewis Edwards, RR985, RG 153; Ball's testimony in GCM transcript of Private Richard Levill, RR1600, RG 153. Another sergeant who mentioned routine use of the telephone at Fort Snelling was Solomon Hare; see GCM transcript of Private William A. Royster, RR705, RG 153.

36. Sweet to adj., July 27, 1889, LS/"D" 25th Inf., RG 391.

37. Carpenter to AG, August 17, 1875, 1933-1875 LR/RD, RG 94; adj. to AG, January 13, 1890, LS/Custer, RG 393.

38. CO to AG, July 7, 1890, LS/Missoula, RG 393.

39. Norvell to AG, October 3, 1872, 1287-1872 LR/RD, RG 94; GCM transcript of Sergeant Daniel Turner, PP2492, RG 153.

40. Jones to Gaskill, April 27, 1870, with Gaskill to AG, May 27, 1870, 68-G-1870 LR/RD, RG 94.

41. AAG to Hatch, February 12, 1875, LS/RD, RG 94; adj. to AAG Dept. Dakota, July 1, 1890, LS/Custer, RG 393.

42. Foner, *United States Soldier*, 223.

43. *ANJ*, September 24, 1881; *SWAR* 1889, 9; McAnaney, "Desertion," 464. In 1881, with the black regiments representing 10 percent of the army's strength, their 74 desertions amounted to just over 3 percent of the year's total of 2,361. *SWAR* 1881, 72 and foldout. Their rate of desertion remained low throughout the decade; in 1889 it amounted to less than 2 percent of the army's total (51 of 2,835 desertions). *SWAR* 1889, 76, 83.

44. Quintard Taylor arrives at a figure of 12 percent by including the quarter-million black residents of eastern Texas. Taylor, *In Search of the Racial Frontier*, 104. Statistics are in the published census reports for 1870, 1:271, 273; 1880, 1:402; and 1890, 1:xcviii. The proportions of black residents to total population in these areas as reported in the 1890 census were: Arizona, 2.44 percent; Montana, 1.17; Nebraska, 0.85; New Mexico, 1.37; and Wyoming, 1.55.

45. "Annual Report of Desertions, 1889" enclosed in Grierson to AAG Mil. Div. Pacific, October 4, 1889, LS/Dept. Arizona, RG 393; CO to AAG Dept. Texas, July 2, 1883, LS/Davis, RG 393.

46. *SWAR* 1889, 8.

47. CO to AAG Dept. Texas, July 3, 1883, LS/Concho, RG 393; Rickey, *Forty Miles a Day*, 93–98.

48. Nolan to CO, June 10, 1882, RLR/Davis, RG 393; GCMO 39 Dept. Texas, July 22, 1874, RG 393; GCMO 28 Dept. Texas, September 7, 1882, RG 393; regimental returns, 10th Cav., October 1881–June 1882, RG 94.

49. GCM transcripts of Sergeant William Gibson and Privates Solomon Dickson, George Landers, and Nathan Smith, PP1245, and Private Robert L. Hopkins, PP1404, RG 153; regimental returns, 10th Cav., January 1869–May 1871, RG 94. Company C's 32 desertions out of the 10th Cavalry's 108 represents 350 percent of the average in a twelve-company regiment. First Sergeant John Franklin encouraged men to desert from Company D of the 25th Infantry, saying that "he would give twenty dollars to any man to go over the hill who didn't like the way he was doing." GCM transcript of Private William Lee, RR2541, RG 153; see also GCM transcripts of Privates Charles Lindsay and Luther Crocheron, RR2574, and Private Sheridan Demby, RR2575, RG 153.

50. *SWAR* 1880, 149; muster rolls, "L" 9th Cav., February 28, June 30, August 31, October 31, 1871; April 30, 1873; April 30, June 30, 1874, RG 94. During these years, Company L served at Fort Duncan, near the twin border towns of Eagle Pass and Piedras Negras; Fort McIntosh, near Laredo and Nuevo Laredo; and Ringgold Barracks, near Rio Grande City and Camargo.

51. Regimental returns for four years (10th Cav., 1874; 25th Inf., 1881; 9th Cav., 1888; and 24th Inf., 1896) show a total of 576 discharges, of which 69 were for disability and 48 were dishonorable.

52. Pension file of Henry Jenifer, SO1198312, RG 15.

53. CO to AG, September 12, 1892, and endorsement, September 29, 1892, LS/"D" 25th Inf., RG 391.

54. GCM transcript of Private Richard L. Dickerson, QQ3830, RG 153; GCMO 29 Dept. Missouri, April 10, 1883, RG 393. An account of Dickerson's trial and of Private Richard Kennedy's two years earlier (QQ2650, RG 153) is in Kenner, *Buffalo Soldiers and Officers*, 268–80. In 1867 Private William Monroe received a dishonorable discharge from the 10th Cavalry for fellating one of his comrades (OO2858, RG 153). A survey of GCMOs in the Department of Dakota, 1880–88; the Department of the Missouri, 1867–75 and 1881–88; and the Department of Texas, 1867–85, (all found in RG 393, by department) suggests that these were the only three cases in which homosexual conduct among black soldiers came to trial. Changes in the format of GCMOs in some departments, as well as the revised *Army Regulations* and the introduction of summary courts-martial in 1889, make proceedings difficult to follow further.

CHAPTER 4

1. One man who served in a white volunteer regiment before joining the black regulars was George Goldsby. When he joined the 21st Pennsylvania

Cavalry in 1864, the recruiting officer described his complexion as "dark." When he joined the regular army in 1867 and assigned to the 10th Cavalry, the recruiter described him as "fair." Pension file of George Goldsby, WC946600, RG 15; CMSR of George Goosby [*sic*], 21st Pennsylvania Cavalry; enlistment papers of George Goldsby, RG 94.

2. Although Kansas, Louisiana, and South Carolina had raised a few black regiments in 1862, a concerted Federal effort did not get under way until the spring of 1863. On the motives behind enlisting black soldiers, see Cornish, *Sable Arm*, 48–49, 93, 96–97; and Glatthaar, *Forged in Battle*, 9, 20–28. Glatthaar, 279–80, lists the names of eighty-eight black regimental officers, thirteen chaplains, and eight medical officers who served with the Union army.

3. On soldier's reasons for not reenlisting at once and officers' understanding of their motives, see the letters from 25th Infantry company commanders filed with Hinks to AG, February 1, 1870, 58-H-1870 LR/RD, RG 94.

4. Reynolds to AG, April 19, 1870, 113-1870 RLR/AGO, RG 94.

5. AG to Reynolds and Colonels of 24th and 25th Inf., May 16, 1870, typescript in SB/25th Inf., RG 391; Andrews to AG, November 25, 1878, 3211-1878 LR/RD, RG 94.

6. Foner, *Reconstruction*, 523, 549–53.

7. Utley, *Frontier Regulars*, 64, 353–54. During the Democratic ascendancy in Congress, the army disbursed an average of more than $2,500,000 a year in Texas. Smith, *U.S. Army in the Texas Frontier Economy*, 11.

8. *ANJ*, February 7, 1874.

9. Ord to AG, June 3, 1875, LS/Dept. Texas, RG 393; U.S. Congress, *Texas Frontier Troubles*, 35.

10. *ANJ*, March 11, 1876; *SWAR* 1875, 106.

11. *New York Times*, March 25, 1876.

12. *Congressional Record*, 44th Cong., 1st sess., 1876, vol. 4, pt. 4:3357.

13. Ibid., 3458, 3469.

14. AG to SW, May 18, 1876, LS/AGO, RG 94; QMG to AG, April 26, 1876, LS/QMG, RG 92.

15. Davies to Butler, December 7, 1876, 510-1877 LR/AGO, RG 94.

16. Butler's endorsement, January 20, 1877, and Sherman's endorsement, January 30, 1877, on 510-1877 LR/AGO, RG 94.

17. Butler to Cameron, February 15, 1877, 1011-1877 LR/AGO, filed with 510-1877 LR/AGO. It was Butler who coined the term "contraband" for slaves who fled to the Union lines in Virginia in 1861; who commanded the Union army in Louisiana in 1862 and helped organize some of the first black troops in Federal service; and who, again in Virginia, commanded the Army of the James when U.S. Colored Troops dug the Dutch Gap Canal near Richmond in 1864.

18. Sherman's endorsement, February 21, 1877, on 1011-1877 LR/AGO, filed with 510-1877 LR/AGO.

19. U.S. Congress, *Texas Border Troubles*, 20.

20. Ibid., 69–70.

21. Ibid., 103.

22. Ibid., 115–21.

23. Ibid., 125.

24. Ibid., 142.

25. *Congressional Record*, 45th Cong., 2d sess., 1878, vol. 7, pt. 3:2190, 2325.

26. Ibid., 2326–28, 2405, 2603.

27. *New York Times*, February 19, March 1, April 9, 1878; CO to Bragg, January 2, 1878, LS/McKavett, RG 393; *Congressional Record*, 45th Cong., 3d sess., 1878, vol. 8, pt. 1:148, 297.

28. *ANJ*, March 5, 1881, printed the Attorney General's opinion on the matter.

29. Hazen to Greene, May 8, 1884, printed in *ANJ*, June 21, 1884.

30. Webb to Lincoln, n.d. (probably late May 1884); and Lincoln to Hazen, June 4, 1884, printed in *ANJ*, June 21, 1884.

31. Hazen to Lincoln, July 23, 1884; and Lincoln to Hazen, September 12, 1884, printed in *ANR*, October 4, 1884.

32. *ANR*, June 27, October 10, 1885; *New York Times*, June 9, 1887.

33. *AR* 1889, 174–75.

34. The names of the thirty-seven men are in regimental returns, 9th Cav., October 1887; 10th Cav., November 1887–February 1888; 24th Inf., October–November 1887; and 25th Inf., September 1887–January 1888, RG 94. Enlistment papers of thirty-four of the men are in RG 94.

35. Leggett's and Kimball's endorsements, RLR/"B" 24th Inf., RG 391.

36. GO 38 AGO, March 20, 1873, RG 94; *ANJ*, August 30, 1879.

37. GO 89 AGO, August 7, 1884, RG 94; *ANJ*, February 21, 1885.

38. For Jeffers, see muster rolls, "H" 24th Inf., 1869–75, and "H" and FS&B, 9th Cav., 1875–79, RG 94; for Davis, see muster rolls, "M" 10th Cav., 1867–77, and FS&B, 9th Cav., 1877–79, RG 94; for Anderson, see muster rolls, "B" 9th Cav., 1866–85, RG 94. For all three men, see Register of Noncommissioned Officers, 1862–1904, RG 94.

39. Examples of black applicants are Sergeant Benjamin Arms, 24th Inf., May 9, 1889, and Sergeant Edward L. Baker, 10th Cav., March 3, 1891, both in LR/Dept. Arizona, RG 393; *ANR*, October 11, 1884; *SWAR* 1888, 703.

40. Endorsement by Maxon, September 26, 1879, Endorsements/10th Cav., RG 391; see also Finley to Hatch, February 12, 1886, LS/9th Cav., RG 391; AG to CO 25th Inf., July 26, 1884, LS/EB, 171:650, RG 94. The peacetime army rarely granted commissions to enlisted men until 1878, when Congress provided that enlisted men would have first chance—ahead of civilian political appointees—at vacancies in the officer corps after each year's West Point graduates received their assignments. Black soldiers seem not to have bothered to apply for a number of reasons: the likelihood of having their applications

rejected; the knowledge that white officers ostracized black West Point graduates; and the real possibility that, with only four regiments open to black officers, meeting former comrades who were still in the ranks might put an unbear-
able strain on an officer's authority. At any rate, none of the black regulars
received a commission until the four black "immune" regiments made lieutenancies available in 1898. Some later officered the two black regiments of
U.S. Volunteer Infantry in the Philippines, but no black enlisted man received
a regular commission until 1901. Foner, *United States Soldier*, 69–71, 137–38;
Fletcher, *Black Soldier*, 74.

41. *ANJ*, November 18, 1881. Many GCM transcripts attest to drunkenness
as a contributing factor in more serious crimes. The distinction seems to have
been the black regulars' reluctance to report sick with a hangover. When one
man of the 24th Infantry refused to believe that "as little as I did drink" could
"put me in the condition I was in," he fell asleep while weeding the company
garden, cursed the corporal in charge of the detail, and was sentenced to two
months' hard labor and a twenty-dollar fine. GCM transcript of Private Charles
W. Day, RR2602, RG 153.

42. Dolby to AG, May 6, 1890; and Beaty to SW, April 1890, both in 521-1890
LR/AGO, RG 94. Skilled men often remained privates so they could be
assigned as needed without dispersing a company's noncommissioned officers;
some skilled privates earned more than noncommissioned officers because of
the extra-duty pay that went with assignment outside their companies. Rickey,
Forty Miles a Day, 95.

43. Feaver, "Indian Soldiers," 109–18.

44. CG to SW, January 22, 1891, LS/HQA, RG 108.

45. During the early 1870s, with the 10th Cavalry constituting the entire garrison of Fort Sill and the other three regiments patrolling the Lower Rio
Grande and the trans-Pecos region of Texas, about 90 percent of the men
served in all-black garrisons. This changed abruptly when the 9th Cavalry
exchanged stations with the 8th and began sharing posts in New Mexico with
the 15th Infantry; the 8th Cavalry moved in with the 24th Infantry in Texas. By
1886, with the 10th Cavalry in Arizona, the 25th Infantry in Dakota, and the
9th Cavalry and 24th Infantry in Kansas and Indian Territory, more than 90
percent of the men lived in racially mixed garrisons. This had changed by 1896,
when the 24th Infantry occupied Fort Douglas—all companies together for the
first time, part of the army's policy of stationing infantry regiments at strategic
points on railroads—and the 10th Cavalry and 25th Infantry shared garrisons
in Montana. *ANJ*, December 16, 1871, June 10, 1876, October 16, 1886, October 17, 1896.

46. Armes, *Ups and Downs*, 230; Grierson to AAG, Dept. Missouri, June 19,
1867, Grierson Papers, ISHL. Grierson's letter contains a list of charges and
specifications against Armes. Captain George T. Robinson claimed that 10th
Cavalry officers at Fort Leavenworth suffered "petty acts of tyran[n]y and

persecution that have been an[n]oying in the extreme" and that the enlisted men were treated "*like Dogs*." Robinson to Grierson, June 25, 1867, Grierson Papers.

47. Roe, *Army Letters*, 65, 103–4. In 1878 the army attempted to standardize the names of its permanent posts; Camp Supply became Fort Supply, Ringgold Barracks became Fort Ringgold, and so on. GO 79 AGO, November 8, 1878, RG 94.

48. Pratt, *Battlefield and Classroom*, 29.

49. *ANJ*, February 6, 1869; PMH/Stanton, May 1877, RG 94.

50. According to the *St. Louis Post Dispatch*, an afternoon newspaper, the morning papers of January 4, 1888, had printed an overblown account of the previous night's events. For the morning papers' versions, see *ANR*, January 7, 1888.

51. *ANJ*, September 9, 1882. PMH/Griffin, September 1869; PMH/Wingate, August 1881; and PMH/Richardson, February 1874, RG 94.

52. *Cheyenne Weekly Leader*, August 29, 1889.

53. *ANJ*, May 23, 1885.

54. *ANR*, August 29, 1885.

CHAPTER 5

1. In 1844, 69 companies of dragoons and infantry manned 20 posts west of the Mississippi River, an average of 3.45 companies to a post; in 1856 there were 65 posts and 173 companies (average garrison, 2.66 companies); in 1868, 134 posts and 327 companies (average garrison, 2.44 companies); in 1880, 113 posts and 375 companies (average garrison, 3.32 companies); and in 1892, 62 posts and 287 companies (average garrison, 4.63 companies). In other words, it took the army about forty years to adjust to the territorial acquisitions of 1845–48. *SWAR* 1844, 132a, c; *SWAR* 1856, 241–47; *SWAR* 1868, 736–39, 744–47, 766–67; *SWAR* 1880, 10–16, 20–22; *SWAR* 1892, 80–84.

2. GO 101 AGO, May 30, 1865, RG 94; GO 62 Dept. Louisiana, October 23, 1865, RG 393; CO to AAG Dept. Gulf, January 10, 1867, LB/10th USCHA, RG 94.

3. The black regiments' distribution was the same as that of the cavalry and infantry force as a whole. In September 1867 seven of the eight white cavalry regiments and twenty of the thirty-seven white infantry regiments (apart from the Veteran Reserve Corps, made up of wounded veterans) were at western stations. *ANJ*, September 21, 1867.

4. After hearing of the disastrous fight at Fort Phil Kearny in December 1866, Sherman thought of sending the 10th and the 38th up the Bozeman Trail to Montana the next spring. "I will see if the two new colored regiments, now organizing in General Hancock's department, can be made available by April 1," he wrote to army headquarters. Sherman to Comstock, December 29, 1866, in U.S. Congress, *Indian Hostilities*, 28.

5. Pension index cards at the National Archives, which list the different military organizations in which an applicant served, show that it was common for men to change regiments, or from one company to another within a regiment, when they reenlisted. This suggests that enlisted men had more immediate concerns—the personalities of the company commander and first sergeant, the quality of the food, a better chance of promotion in a different company—than where their regiment served.

6. *ANJ*, February 23, 1889, on regiments' tenure in Texas; *ANJ*, June 17, 1876, for a complaining letter from an officer in the 10th Infantry.

7. *New York Times*, August 20, September 9, 1877; *SWAR* 1878, 81.

8. Andrews to AG, March 22, 1880, 2169-1880 LR/AGO, RG 94; *ANJ*, May 1, 1880.

9. *ANJ*, August 28, 1880; *SWAR* 1880, 110–11.

10. Stanley to AG, December 19, 1884, 6399-1884 LR/AGO, RG 94. On Grierson's real estate and ranching interests, see Leckie and Leckie, *Unlikely Warriors*, 280–82. Officers' widespread western investments prompted one of them to remark, "From time immemorial Army officers have always done a little money-making as they went along out on the plains." *ANJ*, May 24, 1884.

11. Andrews to AG, March 22, 1880, and Sherman's endorsement, April 22, 1880, 2169-1880 LR/AGO, RG 94.

12. U.S. Congress, *Report of the Joint Committee on Reconstruction*, 36–37; Hutton, *Phil Sheridan*, 202–27; Trelease, *White Terror*, 105–9; Richter, *Army in Texas*, 143–45, 148–52. In a recent study of black Texans during Reconstruction, each of six topical chapters (about emancipation, labor, education, religion, social life, and politics) contains a section about racial violence, eloquent testimony to its pervasiveness throughout the state. Smallwood, *Time of Hope*, 32–33, 60–63, 81–84, 106–8, 125–27, 134–36.

13. Regimental returns, 9th Cav., April 1867, and 41st Inf., June 1867, RG 94.

14. Troop stations in *ANJ*, June 1, 1872, June 11, 1873.

15. Sherman quoted in *ANJ*, February 7, 1874. The observation about race and climate that Sherman offered the congressmen was as vague as his chronology. The 41st Infantry had arrived in Texas in 1867; the 24th did not come into being until two years later. When generals wrote to each other, they gave logistical reasons—the cost of moving—why regiments stayed put for so long. Furthermore, military necessity trumped climatic theory: when Sherman needed troops in Wyoming and Montana in 1866, he thought first of the 10th Cavalry and 38th Infantry (see note 4 above). Fredrickson, *Black Image*, 137–45, describes nineteenth-century theories about the relation of climate and race.

16. Statistics in *SWAR* 1883, 624; *SWAR* 1884, 722, 738; *SWAR* 1885, 738; *SWAR* 1886, 616. Murray's emphasis on climatic rather than racial factors may have influenced his successor's decision to organize the statistical tables by geographical region rather than by race beginning in 1887. Eleven years later, when the army recruited "immunes" for tropical service in the Spanish-American

War, it restricted enlistments to the South. There were six white "immune" regiments and four black.

17. Meigs to Sherman, March 31, 1879, 1940-1879 LR/AGO, filed with 1269-1879 LR/AGO, RG 94; GCM transcript of Private Edward Mack, QQ2972, RG 153.

18. Conline to AG, October 7, 1889, 5083-1889 LR/AGO, RG 94; *ANJ,* March 3, 1888, November 30, 1889.

19. Mizner to AG, August 4, 1891, LS/10th Cav., RG 391.

20. Augur to AAG Mil. Div. Atlantic, March 17, 1879, 1758-1879 LR/AGO, RG 94. Chaplain Mullins agreed with Augur about the men's race consciousness: "They are possessed of the notion that the colored people of the whole country are more or less affected by their conduct in the army. . . . This is the bottom secret of their patient toil and surprising progress in the effort to get at least an elementary education." Mullins to AG, January 1, 1877, 5053-ACP-1874, RG 94.

21. Hancock's endorsement, March 24, 1879, and Sherman's endorsement, March 25, 1879, on 1758-1879 LR/AGO,.

22. *New York Age,* December 28, 1889; *ANJ,* December 21, 1889.

23. About Texas, see Sheridan to Throckmorton, October 16, 1866, Sheridan Papers, LC.

24. White troops' complaints included an officers' petition from the 6th Cavalry in Arizona (*ANR,* July 21, 1883), a statement by the 21st Infantry's colonel in the Department of the Columbia (*ANR,* August 4, October 13, 1883), and a letter from "One of the Old 23d Infantry," which had served "in Oregon, Washington Territory, Idaho, Arizona, Wyoming, Nebraska, Kansas, Indian Territory, Colorado, and . . . now in New Mexico and Texas" (*ANJ,* August 18, 1883).

25. *SWAR* 1867, 436–73; *SWAR* 1880, 53; *SWAR* 1893, 5, 94–99. One- and two-company garrisons in eastern Texas towns accounted for 26 of the army's 138 western posts in 1867.

26. *ANR,* August 13, 1889.

27. T-4-1873 and T-4-1876 LR/IG, RG 159.

28. *Outline Description of Posts* gives a brief verbal sketch and ground plan of each fort in the early 1870s; quotation from T8-1871 LR/IG, RG 159.

29. CO to AAG Dept. Missouri, September 12, 1881, LS/Supply, RG 393; PMH/Sisseton, April 1888, RG 94.

30. PMH/Thomas, February 1887, RG 94; diary entry for August 3, 1888, Leonard Wood Papers, LC; *Yankton Press and Dakotaian,* July 19, November 17, 1880, March 7, 1881.

31. 1303-1887 and 904-1888 LR/IG, RG 159.

32. Quotation in Rawick, *American Slave,* vol. 4, pt. 1:144.

33. Throughout the post–Civil War era, common laborers formed the largest occupational group among army recruits, black or white. The Adjutant General published annual figures in *SWAR* 1880, 44–45; *SWAR* 1881, 62–63;

and *SWAR* 1882, 60–63. On Union generals' use of U.S. Colored Troops as a labor force, see Cornish, *Sable Arm*, 242–47; and Glatthaar, *Forged in Battle*, 182–85.

34. Muster rolls, "F" and "M" 9th Cav., and "D" and "I" 41st Inf., April–August 1869, RG 94; Carpenter to Grierson, December 12, 1871, Grierson Papers, ISHL. See also M-13-1868, 1004-1883, and 887-1888 LR/IG, RG 159.

35. The shortage of skilled labor in the black regiments should have surprised no one, for few black men practiced those trades in a civilian world of mostly all-white labor unions. Gerber, *Black Ohio*, 73–80; Johnston, *Surviving Freedom*, 223; Katzman, *Before the Ghetto*, 124–26; Kusmer, *A Ghetto Takes Shape*, 67–69; Pleck, *Black Migration*, 131–32.

36. CO to AAG Dept. Arizona, May 19, 1889, LS/Apache, RG 393.

37. Butler to Hazen, March 27, 1867, RLR/38th Inf., RG 391; CO to AG, April 26, 1867, LS/38th Inf., RG 391; muster rolls, "B," "E," and "H" 39th Inf., June 30, 1868, RG 94; CO to AG, October 29, 1867; and Hinks to Caziare, February 11, 1868, LS/40th Inf., RG 391; Mackenzie to AAG, 5th Mil. Dist., June 16, 1867; and Mackenzie to Barden, July 20, 1867, LS/41st Inf., RG 391.

38. Quarterly Summary of Ordnance, 20:100–109, RG 156.

39. Davidson to AG, November 30, 1871, 4319-1871 LR/AGO, RG 94; AG to Davidson, December 20, 1871, LS/AGO, RG 94; Benet to CG Dept. Texas, June 29, 1872, 2032-1872 LR/Dept. Texas, RG 393.

40. Sherman's endorsement, December 17, 1873, on 4945 AGO 1873, LR/AGO, RG 94; Quarterly Summary of Ordnance, 22:71–82.

41. Circular letter, Dept. Texas, August 13, 1879, Carpenter Papers, Historical Society of Pennsylvania; 733-1882 LR/IG, RG 159; CO "C" 25th Inf. to AAG Dept. Dakota, August 6, 1885, RLR/Dept. Dakota, RG 393; Andrews to AG, July 15, 1886, 3492-1886 LR/AGO, filed with 530-1886 LR/AGO, RG 94; AG to CG Dept. Missouri, May 24, 1883, LS/AGO, RG 94; Phipps to CO, January 11, 1882, RLR/10th Cav., RG 391. In 1894, foreseeing no major campaigns, the army distributed the new Krag-Jorgensen rifles to regiments in the order of their rank in the previous years' target-shooting competition. AG to Chief of Ordnance, March 3, 1894, 3106 Document File, RG 94.

42. *ANJ*, June 22, 29, September 15, October 12, 1895, June 20, 1896, March 6, 1897.

43. *ANR*, August 29, 1896, September 25, October 2, 1897; Fletcher, "Black Bicycle Corps," 222, 226–27. An indication of the bicycle's popularity is the 1896 Independence Day "programme of sports" at Fort DuChesne, Utah, which listed seven races for 9th Cavalry cyclists. *ANJ*, July 18, 1896.

44. The 10th's regimental correspondence for 1867 contains no complaints or protests about inadequate mounts. When the Department of the Missouri's Chief Quartermaster sent 100 horses to Fort Gibson, where the 10th's Company D was organizing, the regimental adjutant told the company commander that "there should be enough to mount the Company well." Alvord to Walsh,

May 4, 1867, LS/10th Cav., RG 391. On hand-me-down horses in a white regiment, see King, *War Eagle*, 128–29; and Price, *Across the Continent*, 144–45.

45. SO 213 Dept. Texas, November 20, 1876, RG 393 (this item outlines the composition and procedures of a horse purchasing board that included the 10th Cavalry's Captain Louis H. Carpenter); RQM 9th Cav. to post adj. Riley, March 30, 1883, LR/Dept. Missouri, RG 393. Carpenter complained to Colonel Grierson in 1870 that since "our first mount in 1867 this regiment has received nothing but broken down horses and repaired equipment." Some companies of the 10th received their first horses at Fort Riley in central Kansas, and these may have included many of the 146 horses left behind by deserters from the 7th Cavalry that were there in 1867 as the 10th organized. These horses, although "second hand," would hardly have had a chance to break down. Leckie, *Buffalo Soldiers*, 51; Dobak, *Fort Riley and Its Neighbors*, 43.

46. *SWAR* 1889, 186.

47. QMG to SW, August 19, 1871, 6341-1871 LR/SW, RG 107.

48. CO Concho to AAG Dept. Texas, December 24, 1876, RLR/Dept. Texas, RG 393; Hatch to AAG Dist. New Mexico, September 3, 1879; and CG Dept. Missouri to AAG Dist. New Mexico, October 24, 1879, RLR/Dist. New Mexico, RG 393.

49. CO to AAG Dept. Missouri, March 18, 1882, LS/Riley, RG 393; *Hays Star Sentinel*, May 25, 1882.

50. 794-1884 and 980-1889 LR/IG, RG 159.

CHAPTER 6

1. Shafter to AAG 5th Mil. Dist. April 20, 1867, LS/41st Inf., RG 391.

2. *Congressional Globe*, 39th Cong., 1st sess., 1866, vol. 39, pt. 4:3332; Glatthaar, *Forged in Battle*, 180, 226–27; Stover, *Up from Handymen*, 2.

3. Coffman, *Old Army*, 179–80, 391–92; Stover, *Up from Handymen*, 3. Some scholars suggest that only between one-sixth and one-fourth of adult American slaves were professing Christians. Willis, "From the Dictates of Pride," 51.

4. *AR* 1881, 293. Among those supporting applicants for a chaplain's commission were Nathaniel P. Banks, former commander of Union troops in Louisiana and still a political power in Massachusetts, who wrote from the House of Representatives to endorse David E. Barr (4671-ACP-1872, RG 94); the editor of the *Louisville Journal* and General Philip H. Sheridan, who supported Elijah Guion (296-ACP-1872, RG 94); and Thomas A. Hendricks, a U.S. Senator from Indiana who supported John N. Schultz (2038-ACP-1871, RG 94). The monthly pay of a captain of infantry in 1866 was $127.50, or $1,530 a year (cavalry captains earned $1,650 a year and forage for their horses). In 1870 the infantry captain's pay increased to $150 a month, or $1,800 a year, with a longevity increase of 10 percent every five years. There it stayed until 1908, when Congress raised the pay of all captains to $2,400 a year. *OAR* 1866, 156–57; 1871, 221C; 1909, 580.

5. Jacobi to Johnson, August 27, 1866, 755-ACP-1874, RG 94.

6. 4671-ACP-1872 (Barr).

7. 296-ACP-1872 (Guion) and 1198-ACP-1880 (Weaver), RG 94.

8. 2038-ACP-1871 (Schultz).

9. Mullins to SW, December 1, 1874, in 5053-ACP-1874 (Mullins), RG 94.

10. 6474-ACP-1881 (Plummer), RG 94.

11. Adams to Lynch, August 27, 1892; Allensworth to Endicott, October 6, 1885; and Allensworth to Cleveland, April 1, 1885, all in 670-ACP-1886 (Allensworth), RG 94.

12. Steward to Wanamaker, May 25, 1891, and Wanamaker to SW, May 26, 1891, in 4634-ACP-1891 (Steward), RG 94. Wanamaker's department store was famous for hiring black sales clerks as well as white. "When Wanamaker heard a white woman complain [about black sales clerks], he was said to have answered that there were no 'niggers' in his place, only men and women of different colors." Lane, *Roots of Violence*, 37.

13. (Prioleau) 10315 Document file, RG 94; (Anderson) 53910 Document file.

14. CO to Mullins, May 3, 1881, LS/Randall, RG 393; Steward's reports for January, February, and March 1892 (4634-ACP-1891) show an average attendance of 148 out of 309 men in garrison. The comments on baseball and target practice are in his reports for April and June 1892. Sunday evening church attendance had averaged 37 in December 1893 and January 1894; in February and March, it was 68.

15. Barr to AG, January 3, 1872, 4671-ACP-1872, RG 94; Mullins to AG, July 12, 1875, 5053-ACP-1874, RG 94; Alexander, *Battles and Victories*, 261, 265.

16. Barr to AG, January 3, 1872, 4671-ACP-1872; Steward, monthly report, May 1895, 4634-ACP-1891; Prioleau, monthly report, June 1896, 10315 LR/AGO.

17. Barr to AG, January 2, 1871, 4671-ACP-1872; Plummer, monthly report, January 1892, 6474-ACP-1881; Steward, monthly report, February 1897, 4634-ACP-1891.

18. Barr to AG, January 2, 1871; CO to Hinton, March 23, 1882, LS/Randall, RG 393.

19. D-107-1875 LR/IG, RG 159; *ANJ*, July 7, 1888.

20. CO to AAG Dept. Dakota, April 20, 1890, LS/Missoula, RG 393; *Junction City Republican*, February 8, 1884; Alexander, *Battles and Victories*, 274.

21. Mullins to AG, July 12, 1875, 5053-ACP-1874. The diaries and letters of 10th Cavalry Lieutenant John Bigelow are full of rumor and scandal, some of it about the officers of Mullins' regiment. "I have heard that Capt. [David D.] Van Valzah wanting to go on a spree and not be called to account for it, obtained a leave of absence for 7 days during which he remained at the post having a good time." Bigelow to Father, November 11, 1878, Bigelow Papers, Union College.

22. Pierce to AG, October 1, December 1, 1883; and Hatch to AG, December 4, 1883, 1242-ACP-1880 (Pierce), RG 94.

23. Pierce to AG, February 1 (with Hatch's endorsement, February 6), April 5, 1884, 1242-ACP-1880.

24. Mullins to AG, July 12, September 3, 1875, May 2, 1877, 5053-ACP-1874, RG 94; Steward, monthly report, November 1892, 4634-ACP-1891, RG 94.

25. Steward's monthly reports, January 1893, June, August 1894, 4634-ACP-1891. Steward was the only chaplain who mentioned going hunting with the men. While on one hunting trip, he "attended the funeral of ex-Sergeant John White's wife who is settled on a ranch above Kalispel." Monthly report, August 1893, ibid.

26. Andrews's endorsement, August 15, 1872, on charges and specifications, 4671-ACP-1872; Merriam to Potter, October 12, 1875, 2038-ACP-1871; Stover, "Chaplain Henry V. Plummer," 36–44; Guion to AG, October 20, 1871; and Guion to Augur, July 14, 1874, 296-ACP-1872; memorandum, May 1, 1879, in 4167-ACP-1874 (Gonzalez), RG 94.

27. *Statutes at Large* 14 (1866): 336.

28. Quotation from ibid., sections 27 and 30.

29. Grover to AAG Dist. New Mexico, October 22, 1867, LS/38th Inf., RG 391; PMH/Davis, March 1869, RG 94; CO to AG, August 3, 1880, LS/Concho, RG 393; Mullins to AG, May 25, 1881, LR/FB, RG 94; CO to AG, April 26, 1882, LS/Riley, RG 393.

30. Coffman, *Old Army*, 362–65; Foner, *United States Soldier*, 24–28.

31. Corbin to AAG Dept. Missouri, July 27, 1867, in 1710-ACP-1876 (Corbin), RG 94.

32. Barr to AG, January 2, 1871, 4671-ACP-1872; Guion to adj., April 1, 1873, 296-ACP-1872, RG 94.

33. CO to AAG Dept. Dakota, January 4, 1882, LS/Randall, RG 393; CO to AAG Dept. Missouri, November 17, 1882, LS/Supply, RG 393; note dated January 31, 1880, RLR/Duncan, RG 393; Mullins to AG, April 6, 1882, 1135-1882 LR/RD, RG 94. Henry C. Taylor's enlistment papers show that he learned to sign his name some time between his first enlistment, at Nashville in 1867, and his second, at Fort Griffin in 1870.

34. Mullins to AG, December 31, 1875, 5053-ACP-1874, RG 94; Laverty to AG, September 29, 1877, 1596-ACP-1876, RG 94.

35. Mullins to AG, December 31, 1875, March 10, 1876, 5053-ACP-1874.

36. Barr to AG, January 2, 1871, January 2, 1872, 4671-ACP-1872; Mullins to AG, February 1, 1877, 1032-1877 LR/AGO, RG 94. The 10th Cavalry's Pvt. Mack McKinney must have been a star pupil. He could not sign his name when he enlisted in 1867 but three years later published a humorous poem about army clothing, "Ode to a Pair of Tight Breeches," in the *Army and Navy Journal.* Enlistment papers, RG 94; *ANJ*, February 5, 1870.

37. Andrews to adj., March 21, 1877, RLR/Davis, RG 393; CO to AG, December 7, 1878, LS/Davis, RG 393.

38. CO to AG, July 30, 1876, LS/Davis, RG 393; Order 148, September 28, 1877, OB/Davis, RG 393; Circular 1, November 20, 1877, SO/24th Inf., RG 391; Shafter to AG, November 30, 1878, LS/Duncan, RG 393. These orders did not apply to privates. There is no indication that Hatch and Grierson instituted compulsory schooling in their regiments.

39. GO 24 AGO, May 18, 1878 (RG 94),which published "Report of the Board on the Establishment of Schools at Military Posts and Garrisons."

40. "Proceedings of Board," in 9789-1877 LR/AGO, RG 94.

41. GO 24 AGO, May 18, 1878. That black soldiers' classrooms would be "equally well fitted up, and as comfortable" as those for whites seems about as likely as the rule for the children's school: "No favoritism was allowed towards children of officers."

42. CO to AAG Dept. Dakota, November 18, 1884, July 11, 1886, LS/Sisseton, RG 393; *ANJ*, September 13, 1884; Hatch to AG, November 3, 1882, 2943-1882 LR/RD, RG 94. A white enlisted man teaching in an all-black garrison would not be able to socialize with the officers.

43. Barber to AG, September 1, 1886, 5055-1886 LR/AGO, RG 94.

44. Plummer to AG, December 31, 1887, 6474-ACP-1881; 428-1890 LR/IG, RG 159.

45. Mullins to AG, February 1, 1879, 5053-ACP-1874, RG 94.

46. Ibid.; *SWAR* 1880, 295–96.

47. D-113-1875 LR/IG, RG 159; Mullins's statement to Retiring Board, July 7, 1886, 5053-ACP-1874; CO to adj., July 16, 1887, LS/"B" 24th Inf., RG 391. See also 1070-1886, 294-1890, and 428-1890 LR/IG.

48. *SWAR* 1882, 192; *ANR*, April 23, 1881.

49. *SWAR* 1882, 27, 192.

50. Plummer to AG, December 31, 1887, 6474-ACP-1881; GO 9 AGO, January 31, 1889, RG 94.

51. *AR* 1889, 31–32.

52. Plummer to AG, December 31, 1887, and elsewhere throughout 6474-ACP-1881; Allensworth to AG, October 29, 1888, 670-ACP-1886.

53. CO to AG, October 17, 1890, LS/Shaw, RG 393; Reports of Schools at Forts Grant and Bayard, November 1891–January 1892, LR/Dept. Arizona, Miscellaneous Letters, Box 119, RG 393; IG to Allensworth, March 31, 1891, 670-ACP-1886.

54. CO to AG, July 11, 1891, LS/Missoula, RG 393; *ANJ*, May 18, November 30, 1889; Circular 4 HQA, May 11, 1889, RG 108.

55. *SWAR* 1890, 95, 291; *ANJ*, November 22, 1890; Fletcher, *Black Soldier*, 104.

56. Many black civilians too were skeptical of "book learning." In the segregated South, to become educated was to stick one's neck out. Litwack, *Trouble in Mind*, 57–60.

CHAPTER 7

1. After 1871, a private beginning his first enlistment earned thirteen dollars a month, a just-promoted corporal received fifteen dollars, and a sergeant seventeen. Soldiers gained an added dollar a month for each reenlistment.

2. The ban on soldier-servants took effect in 1870, but "for the most part the army ignored the law." Coffman, *Old Army*, 306. CO to Henry, October 10, 1881, LS/Stanton, RG 393; CO to AAG Dept. Dakota, July 23, 1891, LS/Custer, RG 393.

3. Roe, *Army Letters*, 55. In 1881 the annual report of the Secretary of War listed the occupations and birthplaces of recruits by race. *SWAR* 1881, 62–63.

4. CO's endorsement, June 11, 1875, LS/Davis, RG 393.

5. PMH/Reno, November 1887, RG 94; Coffman, *Old Army*, 342.

6. GCM transcripts of Private William Perkins, QQ4107, and Private Henry Brown, QQ3914, RG 153; adj. to post surgeon, August 11, 1888, LS/Grant, RG 393.

7. Adj. to officers, June 29, 1890, LS/Robinson, RG 393; CO to AAG Dept. Arizona, January 9, 1891, LS/Grant, RG 393; GCM transcript of Private Charles L. Howell, QQ3725, RG 153.

8. CO to Commissioner of Agriculture, December 7, 1886, LS/"B" 24th Inf., RG 391; CO Meade to AAG Dept. Dakota, September 12, 1883, LR/Dept. Dakota, RG 393.

9. Hospital Corps applicants had to pass a test administered by the post surgeon, and results varied widely. For instance, four companies of the 25th Infantry at Fort Snelling provided five Hospital Corps privates; four companies at Fort Meade, two; and two companies at Fort Sisseton, four. Fort Leavenworth's post surgeon approved two Hospital Corps privates from one company of the 9th Cavalry stationed there, while Fort DuChesne's did not approve any from two companies of the 9th. Regimental returns, 9th Cav., 10th Cav., 24th Inf., and 25th Inf., September 1887–February 1888, RG 94.

10. PMH/Wallace, October 1868, RG 94. For statistics covering 1876–85, see *SWAR* 1886, 586; for 1885–94, see *SWAR* 1897, 580. The annual rate of hospital admissions for disease per 1,000 whites was 1,031.57 in 1885–94; for black solders it was 1,072.25. The number of discharges for disability per 1,000 was 21.74 for whites and 21.82 for blacks.

11. Wiley, *Life of Billy Yank*, 126, 133. PMH/Duncan, March 1873; PMH/Reno, July 1877; and PMH/Custer, June 1893, RG 94.

12. Testimony of Henry Adams in U.S. Congress, *Investigation of Causes of Migration of Negroes*, pt. 2:138; Bliss, *Autobiography*, 5:70, 165, Bliss Papers, USAMHI.

13. *Junction City Union*, August 3, 1867; *Leavenworth Conservative*, July 16, 1867; PMH/Harker, "Description of Post"; and PMH/Larned, "Locality and History of Post,", RG 94; regimental returns, July and August 1867, 10th Cav. and 38th Inf., RG 94.

14. *Valentine Republican,* June 21, 1889.

15. *ANR,* October 16, 1886. Enlistment papers, company muster rolls, and regimental returns contain details of Davis's and Ferguson's careers, including Ferguson's marital status.

16. *Cleveland Gazette,* April 23, 1887; muster rolls, "A" and "K" 24th Inf., April 30, 1887, RG 94; regular army enlistment papers, RG 94.

17. *Cleveland Gazette,* January 9, 1886; pension file of George Horton, IWWC10931, RG 15.

18. GCM transcript of Private Samuel Lundy, RR4200, RG 153. The atmosphere of a post guardhouse was usually more relaxed than that of a military prison. Sergeant Solomon Hare, a Civil War veteran in his sixth regular-army enlistment, lost his stripes for playing three-card monte with Lundy in the Fort Missoula guardhouse. GCM transcript of Sergeant Solomon Hare, RR4260, RG 153.

19. PMH/Sisseton, September 1887, RG 94. The post surgeon noted that Mrs. Williams was white; not the only interracial marriage in the historical record of the black regiments. Reports in LR/IG (RG 159) suggest that army children in the 1880s attended integrated schools at Forts Bayard (1023-1881), Meade (1198-1881), Supply (1039-1882) and Washakie (895-1887).

20. GCM transcript of Sergeant William Johnson, QQ740, RG 153.

21. *German-American Advocate,* July 19, 1884; *Chadron Democrat,* September 9, 1886.

22. *ANJ,* September 30, October 21, 1876, August 3, 1878, February 18, 1882; *Cleveland Gazette,* April 19, 1890.

23. Wilson to SW, October 16, 1871, 3507-1871 LR/AGO, RG 94.

24. *Junction City Union,* January 27, 1883.

25. Adj. to Council of Administration, April 30, 1878, LS/Concho, RG 393; CO to AG, May 9, 1890, LS/Missoula, RG 393.

26. PMH/McKinney, October 1889, RG 94; CO to AAG Platte, February 11, 1890, LS/Washakie, RG 393.

27. PMH/Reno, November 1887, RG 94.

28. Fusfeld and Bates, *Political Economy,* 13–18; testimony of Henry Adams in U.S. Congress, *Investigation of Causes of Migration of Negroes,* especially 176–77; T-14-1870 LR/IG, RG 159. White soldiers at Fort Richardson outnumbered those of the 24th Infantry 126 to 44. Troopers of the 6th Cavalry had a history of brawling with blacks that went back to 1865, but a fully armed, organized company of infantry would have been a formidable adversary. Camp to Taylor, October 17, 1865, C-1463-1865, LR/Dept. Washington, RG 393; Murtaugh to Tyler, May 22, 1867, M-42-1867, LR/5th Mil. Dist., Office of Civil Affairs, RG 393.

29. GCM transcript of Private William Robeson, RR1908, RG 153.

30. GCM transcript of First Sergeant Albert Ray, RR1128, RG 153; *Junction City Union,* October 3, 1885. Most soldiers, when they wrote to civilian newspapers,

treated army life in a light-hearted, humorous way, as did the 24th Infantry's Private Charles McCalley in the letters he sent from Fort Sill to the *Huntsville Gazette* between February 1882 and August 1884.

31. *Valentine Republican,* April 20, May 18, July 7, 1888, July 5, 1889; *Cleveland Gazette,* June 26, 1886; *Weekly Missoulian,* May 30, 1894; *ANJ,* May 29, June 19, 1897.

32. *Cleveland Gazette,* October 8, 1887.

33. *ANJ,* April 27, 1895, June 20, 1896, June 19, 1897, March 2, 1907. Reynolds J. Burt (West Point, 1896) was not the only colonel's son to start out in his father's regiment: George Andrews (West Point, 1876) of the 25th Infantry and Charles H. Grierson (West Point, 1879) of the 10th Cavalry were others.

34. QM Grant to AAG Dept. Arizona, March 19, 1888, RLR/Dept. Arizona, RG 393; CO to AAG Dept. Platte, December 1, 1889, LS/Washakie, RG 393.

35. *ANJ,* October 31, 1896. In that year's Independence Day festivities at Fort DuChesne, the versatile Morris had taken first place in the obstacle race and the wheelbarrow race. *ANJ,* July 18, 1896.

36. T-8-1871 LR/IG, RG 159; pension file of Benjamin Watkins, SC939875, RG 15; *ANJ,* December 28, 1889.

37. *New York Freeman,* October 16, 1886; *Huntsville Gazette,* March 1, 1884; pension file of Walker Anderson, IWSC13372, RG 15; Sweet to AG, October 11, 1895, LS/"D" 25th Inf., RG 391.

38. For typical reports, see *Huntsville Gazette,* July 14, 1883, and July 26, 1884. Quotation from *ANR,* July 14, 1888.

39. *Daily New Mexican,* May 28, 1877; *Ellis Headlight,* June 2, 1883; *German-American Advocate,* June 6, 1883; *Weekly Missoulian,* June 6, 1888, May 29, 1889, June 6, 1894; *Missoula Daily Gazette,* May 27, 1891, May 27, 1892; *Evening Missoulian,* May 27, 1893.

40. *ANR,* January 11, 1890, January 17, 1891.

41. *Cleveland Gazette,* January 9, 1886, April 23, 1887; *ANR,* January 29, 1887.

42. Charges and specifications, Dept. Arizona, 1890, RG 393; *ANR,* October 6, 1883; GCM transcript of Corporal Logan Goodpasture, PP3553, RG 153.

43. Steward's monthly report, December 1892, 4634-ACP-1891, RG 94; Prioleau's monthly report, November 1895, 10315 Document file, RG 94; Federal Writers' Project, *Army and Navy Union,* 15–32. The Regular Army and Navy Union, while changing its name several times, continued to welcome black participation. In 1919 a Union convention at Cincinnati "arranged a welcome for Negro veterans who had just returned from overseas duty," and photographs show black veterans and members of the Ladies' Auxiliary at gatherings in 1921 and 1927.

44. *Cleveland Gazette,* October 2, 1886; *ANJ,* September 21, 1878; *Leavenworth Advocate,* May 18, 1889. "Literary clubs" thrived throughout the army. Their main purpose was to collect dues from members for newspaper and magazine subscriptions.

45. *Cleveland Gazette*, November 7, 1885; *German-American Advocate*, July 19, 1884; *ANJ*, December 14, 1889.

46. Billings, *Report on Barracks*, 222.

47. PMH/Jackson and St. Philip, May 1870, RG 94; CO to QMG, May 7, 1879, LS/Davis, RG 94; PMH/DuChesne, "Description of Post"; and PMH/Duncan, May 1875, RG 94.

48. CO to Mullins, May 3, 1881, LS/Randall, RG 393; PMH/Gibson, 1872, 442:293, RG 94.

49. For soldier readership of black newspapers, see *Cleveland Gazette*, January 9, August 14, 1886; and *Huntsville Gazette*, May 6, 1882. For subscriptions at posts with black garrisons, see Grierson to QMG, August 1, 1879, LS/Concho, RG 393; CO to QMG, November 21, 1880, LS/Randall, RG 393; and CO to QMG, April 20, 1882, LS/Supply, RG 393.

50. *ANR*, November 15, 1890.

51. GCM transcript of Corporal Peter R. Roots, QQ3974, RG 153; *Montana Populist*, November 30, 1893.

52. AG to Hatch, May 21, 1874, LS/RD, RG 94; Smither to Grierson, October 2, 1872, Grierson Papers, ISHL.

53. Bliss to AG, May 4, 1876, 1074-1876 LR/RD, RG 94; adj. to Berge, March 26, 1886, LS/9th Cav., RG 391; Andrews to CG, July 11, 1890, 2910-1890 RLR/HQA, RG 108.

54. Adj. to Oechsle, May 5, 1886, LS/9th Cav., RG 391.

55. For a mention of 24th Infantry band concerts, see PMH/Duncan, August, September 1877, and January 1880, RG 94; *Weekly Missoulian*, June 27, 1894.

56. CO to Curtis, May 29, 1883; adj. to Perry, January 2, 1884; CO to Byron, May 22, 1886; CO to Dobbin, May 28, 1886, and May 26, 1887; and CO to Creigh, May 15, 1887, LS/Snelling, RG 393; Private Johnson's garrison court-martial, Post Orders 101, June 26, 1883, OB/Snelling, RG 393; CO to Muth, July 22, 1888, LS/Missoula, RG 393. The colonel of the 7th Infantry sent his band to Shattuck before the 25th Infantry arrived at Snelling, and the 3d Infantry band attended Shattuck's graduation ceremonies in 1888. CO to Curtis, June 3, 1881; and adj. to Dobbin, June 2, 1888, LS/Snelling, RG 393.

57. *ANR*, September 11, 1886, September 14, 1889.

CHAPTER 8

1. For surgeons' remarks, see PMH/Concho, November 1877; and PMH/McKinney, March 1890, RG 94. Quotation from Pierce to AG, December 1, 1883, 1242-ACP-1880, RG 94.

2. Article 99 of the Articles of War (renumbered 62 in 1881 and in later editions) contained the blanket charge "conduct to the prejudice of good order and military discipline," which was invoked to cover so many offenses. Barr to Gray, January 3, 1872, 4671-ACP-1872, RG 94.

3. Mullins to AG, July 12, December 31, 1875, August 31, 1876, 5053-ACP-1874, RG 94; Steward's monthly report, March 1896, 4634-ACP-1891, RG 94; Pierce to AG, August 1, October 1, December 1, 1883, February 1, 1884, 1242-ACP-1880, RG 94.

4. PMH/Duncan, June 1877, RG 94; Flipper, *Black Frontiersman*, 25–26; Sherman's endorsement on Butler to SW, February 15, 1877, 510-1877 LR/AGO, RG 94.

5. *ANR*, December 27, 1879, May 29, 1880.

6. PMH/Davis, November 1873, RG 94.

7. GCMO 6 Dept. Arizona, April 14, 1891, RG 393.

8. GCMO 17 Dept. Missouri, March 25, 1869, RG 393; Flipper, *Black Frontiersman*, 26.

9. Steelhammer to AAAG Dist. New Mexico, December 11, 1879, 2434-1879 LR/Dist. New Mexico, RG 393. Long-service Sergeant Solomon Hare lost his stripes for playing monte with Samuel Lundy, the prisoner who had eloped with another sergeant's daughter, in the Fort Missoula guardhouse. On the other hand, 24th Infantry Captain Alfred C. Markley did not regard a non-commissioned officer "running a bank" as gambling with privates in the same sense as playing poker or shooting craps. GCM transcripts of Sergeant Solomon Hare, RR4260, and Corporal Charles Stewart, SS95, RG 153.

10. Adj. to Post Trader, July 29, 1882, LS/Elliott; CO to CO "G" 10th Cav., January 29, 1890; and CO to Post Trader, January 30, 1890, LS/Grant, RG 393.

11. Mullins to AG, October 1, 1875, 5053-ACP-1874, RG 94.

12. *SWAR* 1883, 629; *SWAR* 1884, 738; *SWAR* 1886, 631; *SWAR* 1896, 548, 552. In 1885, recruiters rejected 23.58 whites and 6.05 blacks per 1,000 for alcoholism.

13. *Daily New Mexican*, August 17, 1875; Augur to AAG Dept. Missouri, September 28, 1874, LS/Dept. Texas, RG 393; PMH/Missoula, June 1891, RG 94.

14. Mullins to AG, March 10, 1876, 5053-ACP-1874, RG 94; PMH/Concho, November 1877, RG 94; PMH/McKinney, March 1890, RG 94.

15. GCM transcript of Private Charles W. Day, RR2602, RG 153.

16. Carpenter to adj., December 4, 1878, RLR/10th Cav., RG 391; FO 5, September 30, 1881, LO&RR/9th Cav., RG 391; CO to AAG 5th Mil. Dist., April 5, 1870, LS/McKavett, RG 393.

17. CO to adj., December —, 1889, LS/"D" 25th Inf., RG 391; Smither to Grierson, March 26, 1882, Grierson Papers, ISHL.

18. Schofield to AAG Dept. Texas, May 23, 1876, LS/Stockton, RG 393; Johnson to AG, March 6, 1876, 665-1876 LR/RD, RG 94.

19. *Valentine Republican*, May 10, 1889; *ANR*, March 24, 1883.

20. Barr to AG, January 2, 1871, 4671-ACP-1872, RG 94; CO to AAG Dept. Dakota, March 10, 1887, LS/Shaw, RG 393; Founded in 1865, the Freedman's Savings and Trust Company "actively sought deposits from the freedmen, while at the same time instructing them in the importance of thrift." Foner, *Recon-*

struction, 531. Unwise loans and investments caused the bank to fail, a year after the Panic of 1873.

21. *SWAR* 1882, xv; *SWAR* 1890, 291; LS/"B" 24th Inf. and LS/"D" 25th Inf., RG 391; muster rolls, "B" 24th Inf., December 31, 1895, and "D" 25th Inf., October 31, 1888, RG 94.

22. Mullins to AG, March 10, 1876, 5053-ACP-1874, RG 94.

23. CO to Post Trader, March 16, 1880, LS/Stanton, RG 393.

24. Adj. to McKay, June 11, 1868, LS/Duncan, RG 393; *ANJ,* April 29, 1869.

25. Adj. to Council of Administration, April 30, 1878, LS/Concho, RG 393.

26. Pension file of Benjamin C. Howard, IWW017324, RG 15; *ANR,* February 19, 1881; Mazzanovich, *Trailing Geronimo,* 180.

27. CO to AAG Dept. Texas, October 22, 1878, LS/Concho, RG 393; CO to AG, April 20, 1888, LS/Robinson, RG 393; Beck to Grierson, January 19, 1873, Grierson Papers.

28. Merritt to Taylor, January 6, 1874, LS/Concho, RG 393; PMH/DuChesne, 1886–90, 42, RG 94. The post surgeon at Fort DuChesne commented: "When white troops formed part of the garrison, there were a number of cases of alcoholism. In estimating the amount of intemperance . . . , it should be remembered that about five men were the subjects of repeated entries." Any discussion of deviant behavior among soldiers must take into account the presence in every company of a handful of habitual offenders.

29. CO to AAG Dept. Arizona, February 22, 1889, LS/San Carlos, RG 393; CO to AAG Dept. Arizona, February 29, 1889, LS/Grant, RG 393; CO Verde to AAG Dept. Arizona, March 3, 1889, LR/Dept. Arizona, RG 393. Captain Cooper of San Carlos was the same man who, as a lieutenant, had recruited for the 39th Infantry in Philadelphia more than twenty years earlier—a vivid instance of the slow pace of promotion.

30. Foner, *United States Soldier,* 92–94; AR 1889, 33.

31. *ANR,* February 8, 1890, May 30, 1891; CO to AAG Dept. Platte, January 28, 1891, LS/Washakie, RG 393.

32. 240-1890, 247-1891 LR/IG, RG 159.

33. CO to AAG Dept. Dakota, January 20, 1890, LS/Custer, RG 393; adj. to AAG Dept. Arizona, February 1, 1890, LS/Grant, RG 393.

34. *SWAR* 1896, 548; pension files of Hamilton Jackson, SO987536, and Samuel Bias, SC900635, RG 94.

35. GCM transcript of Musician George McKay, PP4037, RG 153. William Foster married Theodora Sanchez in Matamoras, Mexico, in 1872; pension file SC280812, RG 15. Mathew Grant married Catarina Vega in Silver City, New Mexico, in 1889; pension file W0662263, RG 15. The post surgeon at Fort Missoula complained that "the lowest class of white prostitutes pamper the passions of the *black* soldiers." PMH/Missoula, May 1891, RG 94.

36. PMH/Supply, December 1880, RG 94; PMH/Custer, January 1889, RG 94; PMH/McKinney, February 1889, RG 94.

37. PMH/Concho, November 1877, RG 94.

38. Pension file of Maxillary Wallace, SC775055, RG 15.

39. French to adj., January 14, 1878, LR/Davis, RG 393; Schubert, *Outpost of the Sioux Wars*, 62–63.

40. GCM transcript of Private William Maulsby, QQ539, RG 153.

41. PMH/McKavett, August 1870, RG 94; Nolan to adj., July 13, 1875, LR/Concho, RG 393.

42. GCM transcript of Sergeant Alexander Jones, RR737, RG 153; PMH/Grant, April 1889, RG 94; adj. to Holden, January 4, 1889, LS/Grant, RG 393.

43. PMH/Washakie, January 1889, RG 94.

44. Regimental return, 41st Inf., June 1869, RG 94; Gamble to AAG 5th Mil. Dist., September 20, 1869, LS/Concho, RG 393.

45. Hatch to AAG 5th Mil. Dist., February 21, 1870, LS/Davis, RG 393; PMH/Grant, April 1889, RG 94; PMH/DuChesne, 1886–90, RG 94, 816:41–42; PMH/Missoula, May 1891, RG 94.

46. CO to Board of Commissioners, September 30, 1887, March 26, 1888, LS/Meade, RG 393.

47. PMH/Duncan, May 1878, RG 94; CO to Andrus, July 12, 1880, LS/Randall, RG 393. Stories of a prostitute's suicide by drug overdose were common in nineteenth-century newspapers. Butler, *Daughters of Joy*, 67–68.

48. GCM transcript of Private Walter W. Boston, RR2706, RG 153; PMH/Shaw, March 1889, RG 94. Boston had been inside the house when Williams kicked in the door, and he hit Williams with the hammer. Attempting to establish the character of the house's occupants, the trial judge advocate asked a witness "what sort of a house" it was. "Frame house," the witness replied. Court-martial testimony suggests that most prostitution near army posts was carried on in small private residences rather than in more opulent (and highly capitalized) houses. A clientele that earned less than twenty dollars a month made it necessary to reduce overhead.

49. GCM transcripts of Private John Ewing, QQ559; Private Joseph Hale, QQ1851; and Sergeant Barney McDougal, RR1824, RG 153.

50. PMH/Grant, January 1888, RG 94; PMH/Brown, June 1874, RG 94; PMH/Concho, December 1879, RG 94.

51. Mullins to AG, May 2, 1877, 5053-ACP-1874, RG 94.

52. PMH/Robinson, December 1889, RG 94.

CHAPTER 9

1. CO to AAG Dept. Dakota, January 6, 1882, LS/Randall, RG 393. GCM transcripts of Recruits Edward Mack, QQ2972, and Robert Lincoln, QQ2973, RG 153. The court sentenced Mack to fifteen years' hard labor and Lincoln to ten, of which they served about thirty-eight months. GCMO 57 and 63 Dept. Dakota, April 1 and 6, 1885, RG 393.

2. A visiting inspector's report was typically a thick sheaf of handwritten manuscript that described a tour of several forts. The army also provided a printed form to be completed once a year by each post's commanding officer with statistics on the number of officers and men present and absent and the number and condition of animals, arms, buildings, and equipment, and a space for remarks.

3. Carleton to AAG Dept. Texas, June 27, 1870, T-21-1870 LR/IG, RG 159.

4. An examination of hundreds of company muster rolls for a thirty-year period shows that in stable, well-run companies, it was unusual for a corporal to get his stripes before the fourth year of his first enlistment and rare for a man in his first enlistment to rise as far as sergeant unless some special circumstance like literacy operated in his favor.

5. Curtis to AAG 5th Mil. Dist., n.d., T-14-1870 LR/IG, RG 159; diary entry, October 6, 1879, Bigelow Papers, USMA; Steelhammer to AAAG Dist. New Mexico, December 11, 1879, 2434-1879 LR/Dist. New Mexico, RG 393. During these years, members of the tiny black middle class complained that black domestic servants refused to work for them, while street toughs in Philadelphia boasted that they would not submit to arrest by the four black policemen the city hired in 1881. Gatewood, *Aristocrats of Color*, 196; Lane, *William Dorsey's Philadelphia*, 212. Many black people seem to have scorned anyone who put on airs of authority, in or out of uniform.

6. GO 7 AGO, February 1, 1866, RG 94.

7. GCMO 2 Dept. Texas, January 16, 1873, RG 393; *San Antonio Daily Herald*, November 12, 1868. These traditional, extralegal punishments expressed antebellum officers' low opinion of the men they led. Coffman, *Old Army*, 137–44, quotes a few remarks by army recruiters and examining surgeons.

8. Carleton to AAG Dept. Texas, March 6, 1871, T-8-1871 LR/IG, RG 159.

9. Hershler, *Soldier's Handbook*, 39; Barr to AG, January 2, 1871, 4671-ACP-1872, RG 94. There were four editions of *Army Regulations* in force during the post–Civil War years, each with a slightly different title. The 1861 edition underwent substantial revision in 1881, with expansion and renumbering of the Articles of War. The 1889 and 1895 editions incorporated further revisions.

10. The wording varied slightly in different editions. The phrase "as promptly as circumstances will permit" did not appear until 1889. Punishments were supposed to be "conformable to military law." When an army inspector found 25th Infantry soldiers in Captain Frank M. Coxe's company carrying logs and weighted knapsacks, he "advised the Captain to have none but legal punishments." The inspector mentioned "log drill" and "knapsack drill" in four other companies as well: in other words, half of the regiment's company commanders used extralegal punishments. Carleton to AAG Dept. Texas, June 27, 1870 T-21-1870 LR/IG.

11. Article 35 in the 1861 edition, Article 30 in 1881 and later editions.

12. Hershler, *Soldier's Handbook*, 27–39.

13. Article 38 (17 in 1881 and later editions) covered loss of horse, arms, or clothing. The articles covering striking a superior and mutiny were 7 and 9 (22 and 21 in 1881 and later). Paragraph 895 of *AR* 1861 listed the forms of legal punishment (896 in 1881, 1019 in 1889).

14. *SWAR* 1891, 324. Introduction of the summary court-martial in 1889 was intended to do away with extralegal company punishments but required officers and noncommissioned officers to prefer formal charges for minor disciplinary infractions.

15. In forty-five general court-martial decisions from the Department of the Missouri—fourteen from 1868 to 1871 involving the 10th Cavalry and 38th Infantry, thirty-one from 1880 to 1888 involving the 9th Cavalry and 24th Infantry—the department acting judge advocate lessened defendants' sentences or disapproved the court's proceedings four times during the earlier period (28.5 percent of cases) and nine (29 percent) during the 1880s. The most startling substitution was that of a twenty-dollar fine for a dishonorable discharge and one year's imprisonment. GCM transcript of Private Horace W. Ramsey, RR1715, RG 153. Changes in the army's judicial system in the 1890s and in the format of published GCMOs make comparable statistics for that decade hard to derive.

16. *AR* 1889, 224; SO 85 Snelling, May 25, 1883; and SO 90 Snelling, June 1, 1883, OB/Snelling, RG 393. Brigadier General Alfred H. Terry, commanding the Department of Dakota, had practiced law before the Civil War and took a keen interest in court-martial cases.

17. *AR* 1889, 224; GCM transcripts of Private George E. Freeman, PP3968, Private Horace W. Ramsey, RR1715, and Private George Wiles, RR1927, RG 153. In forty-five Department of the Missouri general court martial-cases (see note 14), seven defendants issued fifteen challenges (nine of them by Privates Ramsey and Wiles) of which the courts sustained all but two. That all but one of the challenges came during the 1880s may show the presence of a new generation of soldiers who knew how the system worked.

18. *AR* 1889, 224. A famous exception to the rule was Lieutenant John J. Pershing, who earned a law degree at the University of Nebraska before he joined the 10th Cavalry in 1895. Vandiver, *Black Jack*, 114–15, 124–26, 137.

19. Alvord to Grierson, September 19, 1867, Grierson Papers, ISHL; GCMO 5 Dept. Missouri, January 11, 1868, RG 393. Captain Vande Wiele had already punished Hampton by tying him up and had threatened to tie Gabbard when the two men left. Gabbard prejudiced his case somewhat by threatening to kill one of the sergeants. GCM transcripts of Privates Monroe Gabbard and Thornton Hampton, OO2858, RG 153.

20. GO 20 n.s. Dept. Missouri, November 11, 1867, RG 393. The department began a new series of general orders when General Philip H. Sheridan took command in September.

21. GO 9 n.s. Dept. Missouri, September 23, 1867; and GO 15 n.s. Dept. Missouri, October 22, 1867, RG 393. Deserters began to receive standard three-

year sentences in the mid-1870s, about the time the military prison at Fort Leavenworth opened.

22. Before construction of the U.S. Military Prison at Fort Leavenworth, the Department of the Missouri usually sent its worst offenders to the Missouri State Penitentiary at Jefferson City. Those from the Department of the Platte went to Iowa's penitentiary, and those from the Department of Dakota to Minnesota's. GO 4 n.s. Dept. Missouri, September 18, 1867; and GO 14 n.s. Dept. Missouri, October 21, 1867, RG 393.

23. GCMO 62 Dept. Texas, October 4, 1873, RG 393; *ANJ*, November 8, 1873; Bliss, *Autobiography*, 5:163–65, Bliss Papers, USAMHI.

24. Adj. to Carroll, August 4, 1879, LS/Stanton, RG 393; GCMO 39 Dept. Texas, July 22, 1874, RG 393. For examples of complaints, see Anonymous to AG, May 11, 1874, 2055-1874 LR/AGO, RG 94; "Old Soldiers" to CO, February —, 1879, Endorsements/10th Cav., RG 391.

25. "Sergeant of 24 Regiment of Infantry" to AG, June 21, 1871, 2372-1871 LR/AGO, RG 94.

26. "Justice O.K." to AG, January 1, 1872, 4554-1871 LR/AGO, RG 94.

27. The best study of the army's struggle to improve living conditions for enlisted men is Foner, *United States Soldier*.

28. "A Soldier at Fort Shaw" to SW, July 23, 1888, 3343-1888 LR/AGO, RG 94.

29. From 1866 to 1898, the average number of officers assigned to the Adjutant General's Department was eighteen; to the Inspector General, seven; and to the Judge Advocate General, seven. Heitman, *Historical Register*, 2:602–14. To perform the staff bureaus' functions in the army's geographical divisions and departments, about three dozen regimental officers had to be taken from their duties. Any special investigation also required the services of a regimental officer such as the 15th Infantry's Captain Charles Steelhammer, who interviewed Captain Ambrose E. Hooker and men of the 9th Cavalry's Company E in 1879.

The progress of Sullivant's letter from Sherman to the Secretary of War to the Congressional committee is recorded in 810-AGO-1877, RLR/AGO, RG 94; Endorsement Book 21:263, 287, Endorsements, RG 94; and 1460-1877, RLR/SW, RG 107. Legislative specialists at the National Archives have been unable to find Sullivant's letter. After a committee published its report, destruction of manuscript records was commonplace.

30. Steelhammer to AAAG Dist. New Mexico, December 11, 1879, 2434-1879 LR/Dist. New Mexico, RG 393. The 9th Cavalry's Colonel Hatch, who also commanded the District of New Mexico, was undoubtedly more interested in finding out what was wrong with his regiment than in awarding punishments. In any case, the understrength 9th could hardly afford a blanket dismissal of men from any of its companies.

31. These and other quotations are in Steelhammer to AAAG Dist. New Mexico, December 11, 1879.

32. *SWAR* 1880, 34; *SWAR* 1881, 73; *SWAR* 1882, 53; *SWAR* 1883, 81. The higher percentage in the cavalry comes from the two extraordinary years 1881 and 1882, when the 9th Cavalry had more men tried by general courts-martial than any other regiment in the army (roughly twice as many as in the 10th Cavalry). Brigadier General John Pope, commanding the Department of the Missouri, said in his 1881 report that the 9th Cavalry had "for several years been almost continuously in the field, the greater part of the time in harassing and wearisome pursuit of small bands of Indians," was "much run down in every way," and needed "not only to rest, but to re-establish discipline." *SWAR* 1881, 124.

33. Register of Charges and Specifications, Dept. Arizona, 1887 and 1890; Dept. Texas, 1872; and Dept. Dakota, 1884 and 1886–87, RG 393; LS/Stanton, 1877, RG 393, passim. Register of Charges and Specifications/Davis, RG 393, passim. When discussing garrison courts-martial, "cases" tried is a better term than "soldiers" because, while the charges in a general court-martial might be serious enough to result in a dishonorable discharge, making it a one-shot affair, the charges in garrison courts-martial—missing roll call, drunkenness, absence—were the kind that involved many repeat offenders. At some posts, one-third of the cases tried by garrison courts might involve recidivists.

34. *SWAR* 1880, 151–52; *ANR*, November 5, 1881; Register of Prisoners, U.S. Military Prison/Leavenworth, RG 393. In 1881 the 9th Cavalry led the army in the number of general courts-martial, with seventy-eight, as well as in the number of reversals, twenty-five.

35. Bliss, *Autobiography*, 5:48, Bliss Papers; CO McIntosh to AAG Dept. Texas, February 14, 1873, LR/Dept. Texas, RG 393.

36. King, *Campaigning with Crook*, 7; Roe, *Army Letters*, 77.

37. GCM of Private William Scott, PP5124, RG 153; CO to AAG 5th Mil. Dist., October 15, 1868, LS/Duncan, RG 393.

38. D-106-1875 LR/IG, RG 159; *Daily New Mexican*, June 8, 1876.

39. AAG Dept. Texas to CO Davis, July 3, 1877, No. 409, RLR/Davis, RG 393; SO 178 AGO, August 22, 1877, RG 94; regular army enlistment papers, RG 94; Register of Enlistments, RG 94. A career like Webber's was far more common among white soldiers, who had thirty-six regiments to which they might be assigned, than among the black regulars, who had only four, and therefore a far greater chance of being recognized.

40. *ANJ*, September 24, 1881.

41. GCM transcript of Musician Martin Peede, PP2809, RG 153. A letter from Colonel Andrews to department headquarters identified Annie Williams, the wife of Corporal John Williams, as white. Although civilian courts had a long record of dealing more severely with black rapists whose victims were white, there is little evidence of this in the records of military courts. CO to AAG Dept. Texas, November 21, 1872, LS/Davis, RG 393.

42. GCM transcript of Private William D. Manson, RR2884, RG 153.

43. Mullins to AG, May 2, 1877, 5053-ACP-1874, RG 94; GCM transcript of Private George Steele, QQ2041, RG 153.

44. GCM transcript of Corporal Charles Stewart, SS95, RG 153.

45. *German-American Advocate*, December 27, 1882; *Weekly Missoulian*, October 17, 1888.

46. CO to AAG Dept. Missouri, January 18, 1882, LS/Hays, RG 393; GCM transcript of Sergeant John Fields, QQ945, RG 153. The dead corporal was the man Captain Hooker had handcuffed to a wagon in New Mexico three years earlier.

47. The rate of death from homicide among white troops was 83 per 100,000; among black troops, 254. *SWAR* 1874, 232; PMH/Griffin, June 1875, RG 94; *Valentine Republican*, April 12, 1889. Black soldiers, of course, had had very real reasons in civilian life for going armed. A recent explanation is Lane, *Murder in America*, 117, 187–88.

48. GCMO 4 Dept. Arizona, February 7, 1890; and GCMO 5 Dept. Arizona, February 28, 1890, RG 393.

49. Pension file of John Anderson, WC542942, RG 15; PMH/Quitman, November 1873, RG 94; PMH/Davis, September 1878, RG 94.

50. GO 65 Davis, November 26, 1873, RG 393. Other orders banning weapons were GO 21 Quitman, July 19, 1868, cited in GO 253 5th Mil. Dist., December 18, 1869 RG 393; GO 59 Griffin, November 11, 1869, cited in GCMO 50 Dept. Texas, July 10, 1872, RG 393; and GO 36 McKavett, September 18, 1870, cited in GCMO 11 Dept. Texas, February 10, 1871, RG 393. Each of these citations means that personal weapons were involved in an encounter violent enough to warrant a general court-martial; the general court-martial order cited the post order that banned private weapons. GCM transcript of Private George W. Newman, RR2734, RG 153.

51. *ANR*, December 31, 1887, January 7, 1888; *Chadron Democrat*, March 1, 1888; Schubert, *Outpost of the Sioux Wars*, 84–87.

52. GCM transcript of Captain Phillip L. Lee, QQ736, RG 153.

53. CO to AAG Dept. Arizona, August 7, September 27, 1889; and CO to U.S. Attorney, September 17, 1889, LS/San Carlos, RG 393; muster roll, "E" 10th Cav., December 31, 1891, RG 94. Logan was a Civil War veteran serving his fifth regular-army enlistment at the time of Flemming's murder. Earlier that year, he had threatened another soldier with a revolver in a saloon near Fort Grant. GCMO 4 Dept. Arizona, February 14, 1889, RG 393.

54. Comparison of GCMOs in the Department of Texas, 1871–72, and the Department of the Missouri, 1882–83, shows that assault figured in 32 out of 212 GCMs of black soldiers (15 percent) and 15 out of 311 GCMs of white soldiers (4.8 percent). GCMs of unsuccessful deserters numbered 102 for whites (nearly one-third of their trials) and 25 for blacks. These figures derive from GCMOs issued during January, April, July, and either October or November of

each year. Relative troop strength during those years was three black regiments and three white in Texas, two black regiments and four white in the Department of the Missouri.

CHAPTER 10

1. Berlin et al., *Slaves No More*, 220, 225. Black soldiers' first widespread protest involved equal pay during the Civil War. Ibid., 214–15. On the other hand, the U.S. Colored Troops shared some concerns with white volunteers. After the Confederate surrender, white Union regiments en route to occupy Texas mutinied, while the 57th USCI, refusing an order to march from Arkansas to New Mexico, had to be disarmed. CO to AAAG, New Mexico Expedition, May 23, 24, 1866, LB/57th USCI, RG 94.

2. The "Organization Index to Pension Files of Veterans Who Served between 1861 and 1900" lists names of 1,193 veterans of the USCT (including one Connecticut and three Massachusetts regiments) who joined the regular army in 1866–68. The regimental books of eight USCT regiments that were still in service in the fall of 1866 list the names of 533 men who received early discharges in order to join the regulars; only 207 of these (38.8 per cent) also show up in the pension files index. This ratio suggests that the 1,193 USCT veterans who joined the regular army and later filed pension claims represented a total of about 3,000 who joined the new regular regiments during the first two years.

3. Company muster rolls, 40th Inf., 1866–67, RG 94; pension file of David Bentford, SO1177225, RG 15.

4. Coffman, *Old Army*, 197; Wiley, *Life of Billy Yank*, 200–201; GCM transcripts of First Sergeant Samuel Green and others, MM3244, and Private George Douglas, MM3067, RG 153. Douglas received ten years' hard labor for threatening to stab an officer with his bayonet.

5. In 1868 seven men of the 38th Infantry were tried for mutiny in New Mexico, but the incident was little more than a meeting to protest a dismissed officer's servant being turned out of the garrison; two sergeants in the company, both Civil War veterans from Nashville, were interested in the woman, who had followed the regiment from Tennessee, and one sergeant tried to secure the other's dismissal by court-martial. All seven men were defended by the lawyer and fledgling territorial politician Thomas Benton Catron. After Catron lost the first case, he secured the other men's release by destroying First Sergeant William Yeatman's credibility as a witness. GCM transcripts of Corporal Robert Davis, OO3148; Sergeant Thornton Reeves, OO3460; Sergeant Samuel Allen, Corporal James Francis, and Private John Holt, OO3527; and Privates Henry Watkins and George Stratton, OO3549, RG 153.

The 10th Cavalry had a mutiny trial in 1871 after Lieutenant Robert N. Price shot two of Company C's troopers: the first, he claimed, by accident; the second, "while in armed mutiny, justifiably." Privates David Adams, Luther Dandridge, and George Garnett—the former first sergeant whose tyrannical behavior had caused so many desertions (see chapter 3)—all received acquittals when defense witnesses discredited the testimony of one prosecution witness and raised the possibility that Lieutenant Price was drunk at the time of the shootings. Price's deposition in 2779-1871 LR/AGO, RG 94; GCM transcript of Privates David Adams, Luther Dandridge, and George Garnett, PP2540, RG 153.

6. About half of the seventy-eight men in Company E were USCT veterans. The regimental affiliations of twenty-seven of them are identifiable: thirteen had served in the 65th USCI; of the seven men tried for the San Pedro Springs mutiny, four were veterans—three of them from the 65th. Fourteen, when they joined the regulars, gave their occupation as "soldier."

Sergeant Harrison Bradford was one of the latter. The five-foot, ten-inch, "yellow" Kentuckian was not the five-foot, four-inch, "black" South Carolinian Harrison Bradford who served in the 104th USCI and is the only man by that name listed in the "Index to Compiled Military Service Records." The 9th Cavalry's Harrison Bradford may have been one of thousands of southern black people who changed their names during the years after Emancipation. In any case, he had three of the most important qualifications for appointment as a noncommissioned officer during the organization of the new black regiments: he was a veteran, taller than the average recruit, and light-skinned. When he enlisted in October 1866, he was able to sign his name, although with obvious effort.

GCM transcripts of the San Pedro Springs mutiny trials are OO2301, OO2488, and OO2523, RG 153. The information in the following account, unless otherwise cited, comes from these.

7. JAG to SW, July 16, 1867, in GCM transcript of Private Irving Charles, OO2301, RG 153.

8. Merritt to AAG Dist. Texas, April 11, 1867, M-991-CB-1863, RG 94. The 9th Cavalry moved its companies from Louisiana to Texas as rapidly as possible, and by the time the San Pedro Springs outbreak, Companies F, G, and Captain Purington's H had joined Merritt's command. By the end of April, ten companies of the regiment were in camp at San Antonio with Colonel Hatch, Merritt, the regimental quartermaster, and twelve company officers present. Regimental return, 9th Cavalry, April 1867, RG 94.

9. Merritt to AAG Dist. Texas, April 11, 1867, M-991-CB-1863.

10. GCMO 50 AGO, August 16, 1867, RG 94.

11. JAG to SW, October 2, 1867, in GCM transcript of Corporal Charles Wood [*sic*], OO2488, RG 153; GCMO 83 AGO, October 16, 1867, RG 94.

12. Fifteen of the twenty men tried for the mutiny were veterans, seven of whom had served in the 10th USCHA. All information about the New Iberia mutiny, unless otherwise noted, is taken from GCM transcripts OO2376, OO2388, OO2394, OO2490, OO2514 and OO2537, RG 153.

13. Warren's assignment to recruiting service is in regimental returns, 39th Inf., August 1867–January 1868, RG 94. Pertinent orders are GCMO 66 AGO, September 5, 1867; and GCMO 69 AGO, September 7, 1867, RG 94.

14. The army's overall desertion rate, always higher in the white regiments, dropped by nearly two-thirds, from 26 percent in 1867 to 9.5 percent two years later. Foner, *United States Soldier*, 223. *SWAR* 1867, 475, records a total of 574 desertions in the six black regiments. The 7th and 8th Cavalry between them had 1,028, equivalent to 43 percent of their authorized strength and just over 60 percent of their reported actual strength.

15. Quotations from JAG to SW, July 16, 1867, in OO2301; and OO3148, RG 153. On states recognizing the competence of black witnesses, see Foner, *Reconstruction*, 149–51, and Litwack, *Been in the Storm So Long*, 286–87, 522–24. Indiana courts did not admit black testimony until after the Civil War. Thornbrough, *Negro in Indiana*, 233–36.

CHAPTER 11

1. *Congressional Globe*, 39th Cong., 1st sess., 1866, vol. 39, pt. 4:3668.

2. *Dallas Herald*, August 8, 1868; *Daily New Mexican*, March 12, 1881; *Pueblo Chieftain*, April 18, 1879; *Kansas City Times*, January 17, 1882; *Helena Daily Herald*, June 12, 1888.

3. The 1870 census counted 7,739 black people in a western population, outside Texas, of 1,492,023. Texas had 252,634 black residents in a total population of 2,310,602, nearly all of them living north of the Nueces River and east of a line from San Antonio to Dallas. U.S. Bureau of the Census, *Compendium of the Ninth Census*, 92–97, 376, 388.

4. *Daily New Mexican*, May 20, 1881; *Kansas City Times*, January 11, 1882; *Kansas City Journal*, January 14, 1882; *Leavenworth Times*, January 15, 1882; *Junction City Union*, June 24, 1882. Whatever residents of Hays may have felt about black soldiers in the neighboring garrison, local businesses needed the soldiers as customers, and reports of violence would hurt the town's growth. Similarly, in some parts of the West, newspapers had to play down rumors of Indian wars that might discourage settlers while at the same time hinting at enough tension to justify a profitable military post nearby.

5. *Weekly Missoulian*, May 16, 23, 30, 1888, May 9, 1894.

6. Quoted in *ANJ*, October 7, 1882. See also *San Antonio Daily Express*, July 12, 1870 ("never did soldiers, black or white, behave themselves better."); *Cheyenne Weekly Leader*, August 29, 1889 ("splendidly mounted and excellently drilled"); and *Anaconda Standard*, quoted in *ANJ*, August 25, 1894 ("They are model soldiers when in garrison, and their conduct whenever they have been called into the field has been excellent.").

7. *Yankton Press and Dakotaian*, June 4, 28, 1880. Monthly report of Theophilus G. Steward, January 1895, 6034-ACP-1891, RG 94.

8. Men of the 9th Cavalry strung the first telephone line between Fort Riley and nearby Junction City. *Junction City Union*, April 14, May 5, 1883. A similar item about the 25th Infantry and Fort Snelling's telephone connections to St. Paul and Minneapolis appeared in the *St. Paul Pioneer Press*, December 27, 1882.

9. *ANJ*, October 14, 1871; *SWAR* 1880, 88.

10. Cardis to AG, August 2, 1877, and petition dated August 27, 1877, 7176-1877 LR/AGO, RG 94; adj. to Jenkins, November 6, 1878, LS/Davis, RG 393.

11. *San Antonio Daily Express*, August 17, 1872; CO to AAG Dept. Texas, May 13, 1873, LS/Stockton, RG 393; CO Ringgold to AAG Dept. Texas, May 21, 1873, LR/Dept. Texas, RG 393; muster rolls, "B," "C," "G," "H," and "L" 9th Cav., summer 1873–summer 1875, RG 94.

12. CO to AAG Dept. Texas, November 7, 1875, LS/Quitman, RG 393; CO to AAG Dist. Pecos, April 21, 1878, LS/Davis, RG 393.

13. *ANJ*, November 8, 1870; Leckie, *Buffalo Soldiers*, 186–90, 200–5; Schubert, "Suggs Affray."

14. Quoted in *ANJ*, August 25, 1894; *Weekly Missoulian*, May 30, 1894.

15. For "brunettes," see *Leavenworth Daily Conservative*, July 3, August 27, 1867; and *ANJ*, October 25, 1879. For "buffalo soldiers," see *The Nation*, October 30, 1873; Roe, *Army Letters*, 65; Remington, "Scout with the Buffalo Soldiers"; and *ANJ*, November 8, 1873, April 3, 1880, August 25, 1894. The term was coined long before the army began issuing buffalo overcoats for winter; both black and white troops at northern posts received buffalo overcoats beginning in the 1880s.

16. CO to AAG Dept. Texas, February 12, 1872, LS/Davis, RG 393; *Sturgis Weekly Union*, January 25, 1884.

17. *San Antonio Daily Express*, March 25, September 22, 1868.

18. *San Antonio Daily Herald*, June 11, 1870, May 3, 1872.

19. Quotation from Babcock to Grant, May 4, 1866, B-27½-1866 LR/HQA, RG 108.

20. *Daily New Mexican*, May 19, June 9, 1876, April 21, 1877. The 10th Cavalry's Lieutenant Henry E. Alvord believed that the best way to avoid Indian hostilities was "to keep their bellies constantly full." Alvord's and Grierson's opinions are in Smith, *View from Officers' Row*, 103–6.

21. *Daily New Mexican*, October 13, 1877; *Weekly New Mexican*, June 7, October 11, 25, 1879; *SWAR* 1880, 519; muster rolls, "A," "B," "C," and "G" 9th Cav., October 31, 1879, RG 94.

22. Utley, *Frontier Regulars*, 333–37.

23. *Weekly New Mexican*, October 25, November 1, 29, 1879.

24. *ANJ*, April 3, 1880; newspapers quoted in *ANR*, October 23, 1880.

25. *Leavenworth Daily Conservative*, July 3, 1867; *Junction City Union*, September 21, 1867.

26. "On the edge of the law" means that while towns in Kansas, for instance, did not license brothels, they received a steady income from fines paid by

proprietors and employees. When state prohibition came to Kansas, towns ceased to collect annual license fees from saloonkeepers, levying monthly fines instead. Illegal businesses continued to operate and municipal revenues never dried up. Colonel Hatch called these civilians "thieves and prostitutes" after Private Anderson Merriwether was murdered near Fort Davis in 1870 "by one of the scoundrels living in the neighborhood." Hatch to AAG Dept. Texas, October 18, 1870, LS/Davis, RG 393; muster roll, FS&B 9th Cav., October 31, 1870, RG 94. On peace officers and soldiers, see CO to CG Dept. Texas, February 8, 1881, TS/Concho, RG 393. For a report from an all-white garrison near Cheyenne, see *ANJ*, April 10, 1869.

27. *ANR*, January 21, 1888; *Valentine Republican*, April 5, 1889.

28. Augur to Sheridan, August 5, 1873, 3250-1873 LR/AGO, RG 94; San Antonio Daily Herald, August 5, 1873.

29. Augur to Sheridan, August 5, 1873, 3250-1873 LR/AGO.

30. *San Antonio Daily Herald*, August 10, 1873.

31. CO Concho to CG Dept. Texas, February 3, 1881, TS/Concho, RG 393. "In addition to the cold blooded murdering of soldiers which occurred lately, a great many others have been killed by citizens, and up to this time the murderers have invariably escaped punishment," Grierson telegraphed General Augur five days later. The 1869 killing of Private Boston Henry, mentioned in chapter 8, was one of the first.

32. CO to CG Dept. Texas, February 8, 1881, TS/Concho, RG 393.

33. This version of the handbill is taken from CO Concho to CG Dept. Texas, February 3, 1881, TS/Concho. The wording differs slightly from the version in *ANR*, February 19, 1881; and Leckie, *Buffalo Soldiers*, 235–36. According to muster roll, "F" 16th Inf., February 28, 1881, RG 94, Pindar was "shot and instantly killed . . . while preventing another soldier from being murdered."

34. Muster rolls, FS&B 10th Cav. and "B" 16th Inf., February 28, 1881, RG 94.

35. CO Concho to CG Dept. Texas, February 8, 1881, TS/Concho. By the time the grand jury met, many potential witnesses were in the field with their companies. Adj. to Foreman Grand Jury, April 14, 20, 1881, LS/Concho, RG 393.

36. Quotation in Buecker, "Confrontation at Sturgis," 243. The town took its name from Fort Meade's forerunner, Camp Sturgis, named after Colonel Samuel D. Sturgis's son, who was killed at the battle of the Little Bighorn.

37. "Proceedings of a Board of Officers," in 6443-1885 LR/AGO, RG 94. This file contains documents relating to the Sturgis case, among them a clipping from the *Deadwood Pioneer*, September 21, 1885, quoted.

38. Caulfield to Cleveland, September 27, 1885, 6443-1885 LR/AGO.

39. Terry to AG, November 10, 1885, 6443-1885 LR/AGO. For additional information, see *ANJ*, August 24, 1885; *ANR*, August 29, 1885; and *Yankton Press and Dakotaian*, October 1, 1885. When Terry claimed to "have had much experience with colored troops," he must have been referring to his Civil War command in North Carolina, which included nine regiments of U.S. Colored Troops.

The 25th Infantry was the first black regiment to serve in the Department of Dakota, which Terry had commanded during the late 1860s and again since 1873.

40. Schubert, "Suggs Affray," 60.

41. Guilfoyle to adj., June 18, 1892, and Bacon to AAG Dept. Platte, June 28, 1892, in 29763 Document File, RG 94.

42. Bacon to AAG Dept. Platte, June 28, 1892, ibid. Nowadays, it is hard to convey an idea of the gravity of the civilian's remark. One soldier's insulting another soldier's mother caused many general court-martial trials during this era, because the most frequent response was physical assault, and sometimes attempted murder.

43. Because Privates Abraham Champ, Emile Smith, and William H. Thompkins pleaded guilty, the court did not take their testimony, and the only enlisted men's views of the Suggs affair are in Champ's and Thompkins's statements to Major John M. Bacon (himself a former officer of the 9th), in Bacon to AAG Dept. Dakota, June 28, 1892, 29763 Document File. The trial records are in GCM transcripts, bundle SS919, RG 153.

44. Quotation in Buecker, "Confrontation at Sturgis," 254.

45. Dykstra, *Cattle Towns*, and Haywood, *Victorian West*, discuss the tiers of society in new western towns.

CHAPTER 12

1. Woodward to Grierson, October 10, 1866, Grierson Papers, ISHL. Nearly all of the officers in the new regiments, white and black, cavalry and infantry, came from the volunteer service. Woodward had served in Grierson's regiment, the 6th Illinois Cavalry.

2. Grant to Stanton, October 20, 1865; Grant to Schenck, December 18, 1865; and Grant to Wilson, January 12, 1866, Grant Papers, LC. The reorganization act of 1866 provided for an army of 54,641; a series of cuts reduced the army's strength to 27,472 by 1876. Heitman, *Historical Register*, 2:604, 613.

3. On the three "races," see Bartholow, *Manual of Instructions*, 203–4; and Higham, *Strangers in the Land*, 25–26.

4. See the exchange of letters quoted in chapter 4 in which Butler and Sherman called blacks "quiet, kindly, peaceful" and "docile, temperate, rugged." 510-1877 LR/AGO, RG 94. From the early 1870s on, articles by advocates of "scientific racism" appeared in the *Atlantic Monthly, Lippincott's, North American Review, Popular Science Monthly, Scientific American*, and other magazines that army officers often ordered for their post libraries. Haller, *Outcasts from Evolution*, 158–200.

5. Journal entry, December 15, 1877, quoted in Kinevan, *Frontier Cavalryman*, 57; journal entry, January 21, 1878, Bigelow Papers, Union College. Years later, during a winter campaign, Bigelow would write: "Very few of the men have

gloves and some have but one blanket. They feel the cold but are light hearted all the same, they are perfect children." John Bigelow to Mary Bigelow, December 9, 1885, Bigelow Papers, USMA.

6. Forsyth to AAG, Dept. Missouri, May 26, 1868, M-13-1868 LR/IG, RG 159.

7. *Congressional Record*, 44th Cong., 1st sess., 1876, vol. 4, pt. 4:3367.

8. Hughes to AAG Dept. Dakota, October 12, 1883, 5176-1883 LR/AGO, RG 94; Russell to AAG Dept. Missouri, May 30, 1884, 635-1884 LR/IG, RG 159.

9. *SWAR* 1880, 33; *ANJ*, March 19, 1881.

10. Schofield to AG, February 11, 1891; and AG to Henry, March 9, 1891, LS/HQA, RG 108; *ANJ*, May 2, 1891.

11. *ANR*, March 7, 1891; *Cleveland Gazette*, February 14, 1891.

12. Regimental returns, 9th Cav., October 1886, April 1893; and 10th Cav., May 1892, October 1894, RG 94. Post returns, Leavenworth, November 1881 et seq., RG 94. On the School of Application, see Coffman, *Old Army*, 274–76.

13. *New York Herald*, August 18, 1881, reprinted in *ANJ* and *ANR*, August 20, 1881. Johnson and Gaines were pretty typical 9th Cavalry troopers. Johnson was a thirty-five year-old Civil War veteran in his third regular-army enlistment who first joined the 9th at New Orleans in January 1867. He did not learn to sign his name until some time during his second enlistment. The twenty-four year-old Gaines, a native of Virginia, listed his occupation as waiter when he enlisted at Baltimore, just twenty months before being wounded. Enlistment papers and muster roll, "I" 9th Cav., August 31, 1881, RG 94.

14. The illustration *Captain Dodge's Colored Troopers to the Rescue* accompanied Edwin V. Sumner's article, "Besieged by the Utes," in the October 1891 issue of *The Century*.

15. *ANJ*, December 25, 1886.

16. Carlton to AAG Dept. Missouri, January 4, 1887, 6805-1886 LR/AGO, RG 94; *ANJ*, January 8, 29, March 26, 1887. On the army-wide fondness for meetings and resolutions, see Dobak, "Licit Amusements of Enlisted Men," 40–45.

17. *New York Herald*, April 11, 1873; Ord to AAG Mil. Div. Missouri, May 20, 1875, LS/Dept. Texas, RG 393.

18. 5738-1877 LR/AGO, RG 94, contains a clipping from the *New York Tribune*, September 8, 1877, quoting a letter from Lieutenant Charles L. Cooper, and a pamphlet, "A Brief Account of the Sufferings of a Detachment of United States Cavalry," by Assistant Surgeon Joseph H. T. King; muster roll, "A" 10th Cav., August 31, 1877, RG 94; Ord to AG, August 7, 1877, LS/Dept. Texas, RG 393; *San Antonio Daily Express*, August 5, 7, and 17, 1877; *ANJ*, September 15, 1877.

19. CO to AAG Dept. Texas, September 18, 30, 1877, LS/Concho, RG 393; GCMO 45 Dept. Texas, November 21, 1877, RG 393; muster roll, "A" 10th Cav., August 31, 1877, RG 94.

20. Burnett to Williams, June 20, 1896, 41940 Document File, RG 94.

21. Bigelow, "After Geronimo," 148; journal entry, January 18, 1878, in Bigelow Papers, USMA. Bigelow was not the only northern officer who had trouble with southern pronunciations. One 9th Cavalry trooper's name "became changed from Zeikel Gulley to Zeke Guddy by the people writing it so." Pension file of Zeke Guddy, SC506789, RG 15.

During the general court-martial of a 38th Infantry soldier in 1867, the defendant's civilian counsel, Thomas B. Catron, interrupted a prosecution witness to ask "that the examination be carried on by question and answer and not by a narrative form as it had commenced." The judge advocate responded that "Colored Men, . . . as a class, do not possess sufficient intelligence and self possession to prevent their becoming confused unless permitted to relate their knowledge of the case in their own way and in narrative form." Catron then "challenged the competency of the witness . . . because he had not sufficient intelligence to testify, he being a Colored Man," and the judge advocate protested that "he had merely stated his individual opinion, judging of Colored men generally, and . . . denied having said that the witnesses . . . did not possess sufficient intelligence to answer questions or to testify, on the contrary he believed these witnesses to be as intelligent as Colored Men usually are. . . . He referred to colored men as a class, and then only to their liability to *become confused*." GCM transcript of Corporal Robert Davis, OO3148, RG 153. The argument seems to foreshadow academic controversies in recent decades about "black" patterns of speech and thought.

22. Bigelow, "After Geronimo," 417–18. Bigelow's exasperation in 1885 did not keep him from being glad thirteen years later, when he was assigned a new company to command at the beginning of the Spanish-American War, to find that the first sergeant was William H. Givens, who had been a sergeant in 1877 when Bigelow joined the regiment from West Point. By 1898, Givens was nearing his thirtieth year of service, and Bigelow was pleased to find a familiar face in strange surroundings. Bigelow, *Reminiscences*, 9.

23. Bigelow, "Historical Sketch," 54–55, 62, RG 391. There is no date on this unpublished typescript, but Bigelow probably compiled it some time between the 10th Cavalry's return from Cuba in 1898 and his promotion to major in the 9th Cavalry in 1902. His informants' anonymity was a nineteenth-century literary convention, similar to the use of pen names in letters to the editor. See Whitford, "'Young Officer.'"

24. PMH/Concho, November 1869, July 1870, RG 94; Davis to IG, September 28, 1875, D-107-1875 LR/IG, RG 159.

25. CO to AAG Dept. Texas, June 2, 1871, LS/"D" 25th Inf., RG 391; PMH/Niobrara, February 1886, RG 94. "Nervousness," or "neurasthenia," was a nineteenth-century medical term. Haller, *American Medicine in Transition*, 9–10, 146. Private Reeder's condition was caused by "excessive use of chewing tobacco."

26. Bigelow, "After Geronimo," 228; Mullins quoted in *Congressional Record*, 44th Cong., 1st sess., 1876, vol. 4, pt. 4:3357; McConnell, *Five Years a*

Cavalryman, 212; Sherman's endorsement, February 6, 1877, 1011-1877 LR/AGO, RG 94.

27. "Record of Events," muster rolls, "B" 9th Cav., February 28, 1877, August 31, 1879; and "C" 9th Cav., August 31, 1872, RG 94.

28. Bentzoni to AG, January 11, 1874, 401-1874 LR/AGO, RG 94. Sergeant Joseph Luckadoe and Privates Joshua L. Newby, Benedict Thomas, and Henry Williams manned the mail station at Eagle Springs. Muster roll, "B" 25th Inf., December 31, 1873, RG 94. "The Col." was Captain Charles Bentzoni, Luckadoe's company commander, who had been colonel of the 56th USCI.

29. SO 218, December 1, 1882; SO 77, May 13, 1883; SO 46, April 6, 1884; SO 54, April 29, 1884; and SO 196, December 31, 1884, all in OB/Snelling, RG 393. The 25th was the only black regiment serving in the Department of Dakota at the time, so nearly all of the recruits conducted to their regiments by sergeants from Fort Snelling were white.

30. Schooley to CO, May 20, 1878, LS/Davis, RG 393; CO to Editor *ANJ,* July 2, 1887, LS/"B" 24th Inf., RG 391; *ANJ,* July 16, 1887.

31. For an outline of the origin and evolution of the Medal of Honor and Certificate of Merit, see Schubert, *Black Valor,* 1–8, 163–65. On changing criteria for awarding the Medal of Honor, see *Medal of Honor,* 13–15.

32. Johnson to AAG, Arizona, March 17, 1890, 5304-PRD-1890 (McBryar), RG 94; Morrow's endorsement, February 5, 1881, in 2426A-EB-1881 (Boyne), RG 94.

33. Schubert, *Black Valor,* 93–98. The Medal of Honor was for "distinguished bravery in action," the War Department eventually decided, while "Certificates of Merit should . . . be awarded for distinguished service, whether in action or otherwise, of a valuable character to the United States, as, for example, extraordinary exertion in the preservation of human life, or in the preservation of public property. . . . Simple heroism in battle . . . is fitly rewarded by a Medal of Honor, although such acts of heroism may not have resulted in any benefit to the United States." Circular 2 HQA, February 11, 1892.

34. Burnett to AG, August 21, 1890, 12608-PRD-1890 LR/AGO, RG 94; Burnett to AG, August 5, 1891, and Valois endorsement, November 15, 1891, 13292-PRD-1891 LR/AGO, RG 94. Of fourteen men who were serving in the black regiments when they won the Medal of Honor, seven—all of them in the 9th Cavalry—waited for nine years or longer before getting their medals. The longest waits were those of John Denny (1879–94) and Moses Williams (1881–96).

35. Burnett to Williams, June 20, 1896, 41940 Document File.

36. Taylor to adj., 9th Cav., April 10, 1894; Vincent endorsement, May 18, 1894; and Taylor endorsement, June 5, 1894, 5931 Document File.

37. GO 109 AGO, December 10, 1888; GO 18 AGO, February 24, 1891; and GO 100 AGO, December 17, 1891, RG 94. Quotations from Order 107, July 22, 1889, OB/Washakie, RG 393; and GO 59 AGO, November 10, 1894, RG 94.

38. Heitman, *Historical Register,* 2:435–48; *Medal of Honor,* 214–38. Men of the 7th Cavalry won twenty-four Medals of Honor in 1876 at the battle of the Little Bighorn, where all twelve companies were present. Later that year, men of the 5th Infantry, also operating with all its companies, won thirty medals in the regiment's fall campaign. In contrast, five companies of the 10th Cavalry and three of the 3d Infantry fought off a raid on the horse herd at Camp Supply in 1870; six companies of the 10th and five of other regiments took part in an expedition that included one "slight skirmish" in the fall of 1874; one company of the 9th Cavalry, along with thirteen from other regiments, occupied Crow Agency, Montana, in 1887; and eight companies of the 9th went to Pine Ridge Agency during the Ghost Dance disturbance in 1890. Leckie, *Buffalo Soldiers,* 53–54, 131, 252–58. Limiting the period to the years between 1870 and 1890 avoids a long discussion of the eighty-four medals awarded to members of the 8th Cavalry in Arizona during the late 1860s, including the extraordinary two-company action in the Chiricahua Mountains in October 1869, after which thirty-one of the fifty-four soldiers present received the medal. Bernard to Devin, October 22, 1869, 925-P-1869 LR/AGO, RG 94; *Medal of Honor,* 212–14; Schubert, *Black Valor,* 164. The army began to refuse wholesale recommendations for the Medal of Honor at least as early as 1874, when it turned down a request for thirty-five medals in a one-company action. Sheridan's endorsement, September 28, 1874, 2654-1874, LR/AGO. Although procedures for awarding the medal were certainly less stringent in the earlier years, the authors have seen no cases in which an enlisted man's account of an action did not require an officer's endorsement.

39. Assumptions like these were common outside the army, too. W. E. B. DuBois wrote in a sociological study at the end of the century: "Being few in number compared with the whites the . . . carelessness of a few . . . is easily imputed to all, and the reputation of the good, industrious and reliable suffer thereby. . . . The difficulties encountered by the Negro on account of sweeping conclusions made about him are manifold." *Philadelphia Negro,* 323, 339.

40. McKay, *Little Pills,* 44–45; Parker, *Old Army,* 93.

41. Bigelow, "Historical Sketch," 60–61.

42. *St. Louis Globe-Democrat,* August 4, 1889; Bigelow, "Historical Sketch," 66. Years earlier, Bigelow had chuckled when Captain John W. French asked a new officer, promoted into the 25th Infantry from a white regiment, "Well, Major, what sort of soldiers do these white men make, anyhow?" Kinevan, *Frontier Cavalryman,* 71.

43. *SWAR* 1889, 4–5, 8.

44. *ANJ,* November 30, 1889.

45. Black civilians faced the same problem. About the turn of the century, a black physician in Atlanta told a white audience that "living a sober, industrious, upright life, accumulating property and educating [their] children" was no guarantee of blacks' safety in the South. "When we aspire to be decent and

industrious we are told that we are bad examples," he said. Leon F. Litwack concludes: "Even as Southern whites reinforced white supremacy, circumscribing black political and civil rights and placing disabling limits on educational and economic opportunities, blacks were expected to play by the same rules whites followed to achieve success. That paradox defied resolution." *Trouble in Mind*, 318–19, 358.

CHAPTER 13

1. Years of wartime service in the volunteers counted double, which enabled several black Civil War veterans to retire from the regulars in the early 1890s. The 24th Infantry's Private Bassett Page seems to have been the first. *ANR*, February 6, 1892; Coffman, *Old Army*, 397–98; quotation from *SWAR* 1891, 10.

2. Quoted in Cooper, *Army and Civil Disorder*, 14. The Noble Order of the Knights of Labor was unusual in that it sought black members actively, beginning in 1885. Spero and Harris, *Black Worker*, 39–48.

3. Pension files of John A. Jackson, SC918662, and Jeremiah Harris, SC781663, RG 15; Schubert, *Outpost of the Sioux Wars*, 149–60. Addresses in the pension files of 418 black veterans included four in Junction City; four in San Angelo, Texas (Fort Concho); and four in Silver City, New Mexico (Fort Bayard).

4. Post returns, Sill, November 1871–October 1872, RG 94.

5. Ibid.; RPAH, Augustus G. Robinson and Almon F. Rockwell, January–October 1872, RG 92. Fifty-four of the quartermaster's new employees hired on just days after men with the same names received discharges at Fort Sill, and although the lists of civilian employees do not furnish ages, birthplaces, or physical descriptions (making it impossible to categorize the workers by race), the quartermaster's Wade Hampton and Zack Mosley—even Henry Johnson and William Smith—were undoubtedly the men of those names who had just left the 10th Cavalry.

6. RPAH, Almon F. Rockwell, January–March 1872, RG 92; regimental returns, 10th Cav., January–March 1872, RG 94.

7. SO 54 Sill, April 20, 1872; and SO 76 Sill, May 17, 1872, both in RPAH, Almon F. Rockwell, April–May 1872, RG 92; post returns, Sill, March–April 1872, RG 94.

8. Pension file of Wade Hampton, IWSC10802, RG 15; RPAH, Augustus G. Robinson, July–November 1872, RG 92.

9. James Martin interview in Rawick, *American Slave*, vol. 5, pt. 1:62–64; pension file of William H. Goldsborough, SC326506, RG 15.

10. A purely random sample of pension files might reveal a different settlement pattern. Since the original purpose of reading the pension files was to learn what the veterans had to say about their military service, the sample included only men who had served in the USCT as well as the regular army or

regulars who served more than one enlistment. Washington and Baltimore were the original recruiting ground for the 40th Infantry, as New Orleans was for the 39th Infantry and 9th Cavalry, which may explain these cities' predominance.

11. Pension files of William H. Green, SC603486; George Brummsick, SC314446; John A. Howard, IWSC7824; and Alexander Stepney, SC874522, RG 15.

12. French to adj., January 30, 1870, 58-H-1870 LR/RD, RG 94; pension files of Allen Downs, SC736179; David Lacey, SC476558; Henry Harrison, SC915398; James H. Massey, IWSC7982; and George Sperlin, C2580938, RG 15.

13. Pension files of David Dickerson, SC811464; William Garrett, IWSC6942; and George Thomas, SC421946, RG 15. Compare these quotations with those in Litwack, *Trouble in Mind*, 471–72. The pension act of March 3, 1917, is in *Statutes at Large* 39 (1917): 1199–1201.

14. Pension files of George Washington, SO1157875, and Cicero Starks, WC328558, RG 15. Taking a hero's name was common in the days after Emancipation. Enlistment papers from September 1866 to August 1867 show that twenty-four men named George Washington joined the black regiments, and only eighteen named John Smith. Three Andrew Jacksons enlisted at New Orleans, where Jackson's statue was the largest in the city. Every president— even Martin Van Buren—had a namesake among the black regulars. On the surnames of former slaves and the search for family members after the war, see Gutman, *Black Family*, 204–7, 230–56, 366–85; and Litwack, *Been in the Storm So Long*, 229–32, 247–51.

15. Pension files of George Bruce, SO1050594; William H. Gray, SC938829; John Fields, SC480915; Henry Johnson, IWSC13099; Robert Johnson, SC524986; and John Pettit, SC893138, RG 15. The 39th U.S. Infantry recruited in southern Louisiana; Company F of the 40th came entirely from Charleston, South Carolina. In 1869 the 40th moved to Louisiana and combined with the 39th to make the 25th Infantry. Stephen P. Peaker claimed to have served both in the "24th Pennsylvania" (24th USCI, organized at Philadelphia), and the "39th Louisiana." Peaker, SC229060, RG 15.

16. Pension file of Edward Somerville, SC896667, RG 15.

17. Coffman, *Old Army*, 155, 209; Foner, *United States Soldier*, 72; Rickey, *Forty Miles a Day*, 176. Forty-five of 418 black veterans' pension files showed residence in the Soldiers' Home or one of the National Military Homes.

18. Pension file of Henry Washington, SO1337020, RG 15.

19. Three of Washington's comrades were themselves residents of the Soldiers' Home. The others lived in Washington, D.C.; in nearby Waldorf, Maryland; and in Salt Lake City. Besides collecting affidavits from the Minneapolis doctor and Washington's two lodge brothers there, the Pension Bureau wrote to the doctors who had been post surgeons at Fort Reno and Fort Sisseton (both men were still in the army), but neither one could recall having treated Washington's rheumatism twenty years before.

20. Washington, a native of Baltimore, claimed to have been a servant with the 4th New Hampshire Infantry at Point Lookout, Maryland; to have gone north with the regiment when it mustered out in 1863; and to have enlisted as a draft substitute for a resident of Concord, New Hampshire, in 1864. In response to a query about the 4th New Hampshire's service, the Adjutant General's Office told the Bureau of Pensions that the regiment had served in the Carolinas until 1865. Just how Washington reached New England is a mystery. That the officer who signed him up for the 5th Massachusetts Cavalry—like the 54th and 55th Massachusetts Infantry, the regiment never received a Federal number—listed Concord, New Hampshire, as Washington's birthplace rather than his residence complicated the record further.

21. *Statutes at Large* 44 (1927): 1361–63.

22. *Winners of the West*, February 1924.

23. Ibid., June 1927, March, April, May, June 1929.

24. Pension Files of David Morgan, SC660226; George Brummsick, SC314446; and John Sims, SC847026, RG 15.

25. *Winners of the West*, October 1924, December 1926. John Ford's epic western *The Iron Horse* appeared in 1924, coincidentally the year *Winners of the West* began publishing.

26. Quotation from GO 89 AGO, August 7, 1884, RG 94. GO 38 AGO, March 20, 1873, announced the new rank of commissary sergeant; the army had had ordnance sergeants since 1832.

Bibliography

MANUSCRIPTS AND ARCHIVES

Freedmen and Southern History Project. University of Maryland, College Park.
Index card files and photocopied documents.

Historical Society of Pennsylvania. Philadelphia.
Louis H. Carpenter Papers.

Illinois State Historical Library. Springfield.
Benjamin H. Grierson Papers.

Library of Congress. Washington, D.C.
Henry C. Corbin Papers.
Ulysses S. Grant Papers.
Philip H. Sheridan Papers.
Edwin M. Stanton Papers.
Leonard Wood Papers.

Missouri Historical Society. St. Louis.
Powhatan H. Clarke Papers.

National Archives. Washington, D.C.
National Archives Microfilm Publication T289. "Organization List to Pension Files of Veterans Who Served between 1861 and 1900."
Record Group 15. Veterans' Administration. Bureau of Pensions. Pension Files.
Record Group 92. Quartermaster General's Office.
Letters Sent, 1871–83. E38.
Reports of Persons and Articles Hired. E238.
Record Group 94. Adjutant General's Office.
Letters Sent. E1.
Endorsements. E6.
Letters Received. E12.
Register of Letters Received. E14.
Document File. E25.
Orders and Circulars. E44.
Muster Rolls of Regular Army Organizations. E53.
Muster Rolls of Volunteer Organizations: Civil War. E57.

Returns of Military Posts. E63.

Returns of Military Organizations. E66.

Register of Enlistments. E89.

Enlistment Papers. E91.

Letter Books of Volunteer Organizations: Civil War. E112.

Appointment, Commission, and Personal Branch.
    Letters Received. E297.
    Register of Noncommissioned Officers. E329.

Enlisted Branch. Letters Sent. E406.

Fund Branch. Letters Received. E441.

Recruiting Division. Letters Sent. E467.

Letters Received. E471.

Register of Letters Received. E472.

Register of Trimonthly Reports. E483, E484.

Carded Records, Volunteer Organizations: Civil War. E519.

Medical Histories of Posts. E547. Forts Brown, Concho, Custer, Davis, DuChesne, Duncan, Gibson, Grant, Griffin, Harker, Jackson and St. Philip, Larned, McKavett, McKinney, Missoula, Niobrara, Quitman, Reno, Richardson, Robinson, Sisseton, Stanton, Supply, Thomas, Wallace, Washakie, and Wingate.

Record Group 105. Bureau of Refugees, Freedmen, and Abandoned Lands.
Office of the Commissioner. Letters Received. E15.

Louisiana. Lake Providence. Monthly Inspection Reports. E1662.

Record Group 107. Secretary of War. Letters Sent. E18.

Register of Letters Received. E17.

Record Group 108. Headquarters of the Army. Letters Sent. E2.

Registers of Letters Received. E21.

Letters Received. E22.

Record Group 153. Judge Advocate General's Office.
General Court-Martial Transcripts. E15.

Record Group 156. Chief of Ordnance's Office.
Quarterly Summary Statements of Ordnance . . . , 1862–67, 1870–71. E111.

Summary of Ordnance . . . , 1873–76. E112.

Record Group 159. Inspector General's Office.
Letters Received. E15.

Record Group 391. U.S. Regular Army Mobile Units.
9th Cavalry.
    Letters Sent. E903.
    Letters, Orders, and Reports Received. E911.
10th Cavalry.
    Letters Sent. E921.
    Endorsements. E925.

      Registers of Letters Received. E926.

      John E. Bigelow Jr. "Historical Sketch of the 10th Cavalry." E933.

   24th Infantry.

      Special Orders. E1758.

      Company B. Letters Sent. E1773.

      Company B. Registers of Letters Received. E1775.

   25th Infantry.

      Scrapbooks. E1805.

      Company D, Letters Sent. E1815.

      Company D, Descriptive Book. E1822.

   38th Infantry.

      Letters Sent. E1971.

      Registers of Letters Received. E1973.

      Descriptive Book. E1975.

   39th Infantry.

      Letters Sent. E1981.

      Letters Sent and Received by the Recruiting Officer. E1982.

      Registers of Letters Received. E1984.

   40th Infantry.

      Letters Sent. E1990.

      Company K, Descriptive Book. E1995.

   41st Infantry.

      Letters Sent. E1997.

Record Group 393. U.S. Army Continental Commands, 1821–1920.

   Part 1. Geographical Divisions and Departments.

      Department of Arizona.

         Letters Sent. E169.

         Registers of Letters Received. E180.

         Letters Received. E181.

         General Court-Martial Orders. E183.

         Registers of Charges and Specifications. E224.

      Department of Dakota.

         Registers of Letters Received. E1173.

         Letters Received. E1175.

         General Court-Martial Orders. E1190.

         Registers of Charges and Specifications. E1273.

      Department of the Missouri.

         Letters Received. E2601.

         General Orders. E2620.

         General Court-Martial Orders. E2629.

      Fifth Military District.

         General Orders. E4792.

         Office of Civil Affairs. Letters Received. E4835.

Department of Texas.
    Letters Sent. E4867.
    Registers of Letters Received. E4872.
    Letters Received. E4873.
    General Court-Martial Orders. E4885, E4891.
    Abstracts of Charges and Specifications. E4981.
Department and Defenses of Washington.
    Letters Received. E5382.
Part 3. Geographical Districts and Subdistricts.
District of New Mexico.
    Registers of Letters Received. E433.
    Letters Received. E434.
Part 5. Military Installations.
    Forts Apache, Concho, Custer, Davis, Duncan, Elliott, Grant,
        Hale, Hays, McKavett, Meade, Missoula, Randall, Riley, Robin-
        son, San Carlos, Shaw, Sisseton, Snelling, Stanton, Stockton,
        Supply, and Washakie. Letters Sent.
    Fort Concho. Telegrams Sent.
    Forts Davis, Duncan. Registers of Letters Received.
    Forts Concho, Davis. Letters Received.
    Forts Davis, Snelling, Washakie. Order Books.
    Fort Davis. Register of Charges and Specifications.
    Fort Leavenworth. U.S. Military Prison. Registers of Prisoners.
Union College. Schenectady, New York.
    John Bigelow Sr. Papers.
U.S. Army Military History Institute. Carlisle Barracks, Carlisle, Pennsylvania.
    Zenas R. Bliss Papers.
    Maus-Halstead Family Papers.
U.S. Military Academy. West Point, New York.
    John Bigelow Jr. Papers.

NEWSPAPERS AND PERIODICALS

Army and Navy Journal (New York)
Army and Navy Register (Washington)
Chadron (Nebraska) Democrat
Cheyenne Weekly Leader
Christian Recorder (Philadelphia)
Cleveland Gazette
Daily New Mexican (Santa Fe)
Dallas Herald
Ellis (Kansas) Headlight
Harper's Weekly

Hays (Kansas) German-American Advocate
Hays (Kansas) Star Sentinel
Helena (Montana) Daily Herald
Huntsville (Alabama) Gazette
Junction City (Kansas) Republican
Junction City (Kansas) Union
Kansas City (Missouri) Journal
Kansas City (Missouri) Times
Leavenworth (Kansas) Advocate
Leavenworth (Kansas) Daily Conservative
Leavenworth (Kansas) Times
Missoula (Montana) Daily Gazette
Missoula (Montana) Evening Missoulian
Missoula (Montana) Weekly Missoulian
Montana Populist (Missoula)
The Nation
New Orleans Tribune
New York Age
New York Freeman
New York Herald
New York Times
Pueblo (Colorado) Chieftain
St. Louis Globe Democrat
St. Louis Post Dispatch
St. Paul Pioneer Press
San Antonio Daily Express
San Antonio Daily Herald
Sturgis (South Dakota) Weekly Union
Valentine (Nebraska) Republican
Waco Daily Examiner
Weekly New Mexican (Santa Fe)
Winners of the West
Yankton Press and Dakotaian

BOOKS AND ARTICLES

Alexander, Charles. *Battles and Victories of Allen Allensworth.* Boston: Sherman, French, 1914.
Alexander, Roberta S. *North Carolina Faces the Freedmen: Race Relations during Presidential Reconstruction, 1865–67.* Durham, N.C.: Duke University Press, 1985.
Annual Reports of the Secretary of War. Washington, D.C.: GPO, 1866–98.
Armes, George A. *Ups and Downs of an Army Officer.* Washington, D.C.: privately printed, 1900.

Army Regulations. Washington, D.C.: GPO, 1861, 1881, 1889, 1895.

Bankole, Katherine. *Slavery and Medicine: Enslavement and Medical Practices in Antebellum Louisiana.* New York: Garland, 1998.

Bartholow, Roberts. *A Manual of Instructions for Enlisting and Discharging Soldiers.* Philadelphia: Lippincott, 1863.

Berlin, Ira. *Slaves without Masters: The Free Negro in the Antebellum South.* New York: Pantheon, 1974.

Berlin, Ira, et al. *Slaves No More: Three Essays on Emancipation and the Civil War.* New York: Cambridge University Press, 1992.

Bertaux, Nancy. "Structural Economic Change and Occupational Decline among Black Workers in Cincinnati." In *Race and the City: Work, Community, and Protest in Cincinnati, 1820–1970,* edited by Henry L. Taylor, 126–55. Urbana: University of Illinois Press, 1993.

Bigelow, John, Jr. "After Geronimo." *Outing* 8, no. 2 (May 1886): 147–56; 8, no. 4 (July 1886): 416–23; 9, no. 3 (December 1886): 223–33.

———. *Reminiscences of the Santiago Campaign.* New York: Harper, 1899.

Billings, John S. *A Report on Barracks and Hospitals, with Descriptions of Military Posts.* Washington, D.C.: GPO, 1870.

Billington, Monroe L. *New Mexico's Buffalo Soldiers.* Niwot: University Press of Colorado, 1991.

Blanton, DeAnne. "Cathay Williams: Black Woman Soldier, 1866–1868." *Minerva* 10, nos. 3, 4 (fall–winter 1992): 1–12.

Boatner, Mark M. III. *The Civil War Dictionary.* New York: David McKay, 1959.

Brechemin, Louis. "Promotion in the Line of the United States Army." *United Service Magazine* 6 (May 1882): 597–606.

Buecker, Thomas R. "Confrontation at Sturgis: An Episode in Civil-Military Race Relations, 1885." *South Dakota History* 14, no. 3 (fall 1984): 238–61.

Butler, Anne M. *Daughters of Joy, Sisters of Misery: Prostitution in the American West.* Urbana: University of Illinois Press, 1985.

Cashin, Herschel V., et al. *Under Fire with the Tenth U.S. Cavalry.* 1899. Reprint, New York: Arno Press, 1969.

Coffman, Edward M. *The Old Army: A Portrait of the American Army in Peacetime, 1784–1898.* New York: Oxford University Press, 1986.

Congressional Globe. 46 vols. Washington, D.C.: 1834–73.

Congressional Record.

Cooper, Jerry M. *The Army and Civil Disorder: Federal Military Intervention in Labor Disputes, 1877–1900.* Westport, Conn.: Greenwood, 1980.

Cornish, Dudley T. *The Sable Arm: Black Troops in the Union Army, 1861–1865.* 1956. Reprint, Lawrence: University Press of Kansas, 1987.

Dobak, William A. *Fort Riley and Its Neighbors: Military Money and Economic Growth, 1853–1895.* Norman: University of Oklahoma Press, 1998.

———. "Fort Riley's Black Soldiers and the Army's Changing Role in the West, 1867–1885." *Kansas History* 22, no. 3 (autumn 1999): 214–27.

————. "Licit Amusements of Enlisted Men in the Post–Civil War Army." *Montana: The Magazine of Western History* 45, no. 2 (spring 1995): 34–45.

DuBois, W. E. B. *The Philadelphia Negro: A Social Study.* 1899. Reprint, New York: Schocken Books, 1967.

Dykstra, Robert R. *The Cattle Towns.* New York: Alfred A. Knopf, 1968.

Feaver, Eric. "Indian Soldiers, 1891–95: An Experiment on the Closing Frontier." *Prologue* 7, no. 2 (summer 1975): 109–18.

Federal Writers Project. *The Army and Navy Union, U.S.A.: A History of the Union and Its Auxiliary.* [Flint, Mich.?]: Army and Navy Union, 1942.

First Class Annual of the Class of '86, United States Military Academy. Poughkeepsie, N.Y.: Haight and Dudley, 1887.

Fletcher, Marvin. "The Black Bicycle Corps." *Arizona and the West* 16, no. 3 (autumn 1974): 219–32.

————. *The Black Soldier and Officer in the United States Army, 1891–1917.* Columbia: University of Missouri Press, 1974.

Flipper, Henry O. *Black Frontiersman: The Memoirs of Henry O. Flipper, First Black Graduate of West Point.* Edited by Theodore D. Harris. Fort Worth: Texas Christian University Press, 1997.

Foner, Eric. *Reconstruction: America's Unfinished Revolution.* New York: Harper and Row, 1988.

Foner, Jack D. *The United States Soldier between Two Wars: Army Life and Reforms, 1865–1898.* New York: Humanities Press, 1970.

Fowler, Arlen L. *The Black Infantry in the West, 1869–1891.* Westport, Conn.: Greenwood, 1971.

Fredrickson, George M. *The Black Image in the White Mind: The Debate on Afro-American Character and Destiny, 1817–1914.* Hanover, N.H.: University Press of New England, 1987.

Fusfeld, Daniel R., and Timothy Bates. *The Political Economy of the Urban Ghetto.* Carbondale and Edwardsville: Southern Illinois University Press, 1984.

Gatewood, Willard D. *Aristocrats of Color: The Black Elite, 1880–1920.* Bloomington: Indiana University Press, 1990.

————. *Black Americans and the White Man's Burden, 1898–1903.* Urbana: University of Illinois Press, 1975.

————. *"Smoked Yankees" and the Struggle for Empire: Letters from Negro Soldiers, 1898–1902.* Urbana: University of Illinois Press, 1971.

Genovese, Eugene D. *Roll, Jordan, Roll: The World the Slaves Made.* New York: Pantheon, 1974.

Gerber, David A. *Black Ohio and the Color Line, 1860–1915.* Urbana: University of Illinois Press, 1976.

Glatthaar, Joseph T. *Forged in Battle: The Civil War Alliance of Black Soldiers and White Officers.* New York: Free Press, 1990.

Green, Constance M. *Washington: Village and Capital, 1800–1878.* Princeton, N.J.: Princeton University Press, 1962.

Gutman, Herbert G. *The Black Family in Slavery and Freedom, 1750–1925*. New York: Pantheon, 1976.

Hahn, Steven. *The Roots of Southern Populism: Yeoman Farmers and the Transformation of the Georgia Upcountry, 1850–1890*. New York: Oxford University Press, 1983.

Haller, John S., Jr. *American Medicine in Transition, 1840–1910*. Urbana: University of Illinois Press, 1981.

————. *Outcasts from Evolution: Scientific Attitudes of Racial Inferiority, 1859–1900*. Urbana: University of Illinois Press, 1971.

Hardwick, Kevin R. "'Your Old Father Abe Lincoln is Dead and Damned': Black Soldiers and the Memphis Race Riot of 1866." *Journal of Social History* 27, no. 1 (fall 1993): 109–28.

Haywood, C. Robert. *Victorian West: Class and Culture in Kansas Cattle Towns*. Lawrence: University Press of Kansas, 1991.

Hein, Otto L. *Memories of Long Ago*. New York: Putnam, 1925.

Heitman, Francis B. *Historical Register and Dictionary of the United States Army*. 2 vols. Washington, D.C.: GPO, 1903.

Hershler, N. *The Soldier's Handbook*. Washington, D.C.: GPO, 1884.

Higham, John. *Strangers in the Land: Patterns of American Nativism, 1860–1925*. New York: Atheneum, 1963.

Higginson, Thomas W. *Army Life in a Black Regiment*. 1890. Reprint, New York: Collier Books, 1962.

Higgs, Robert. *Competition and Coercion: Blacks in the American Economy, 1865–1914*. New York: Cambridge University Press, 1977.

Howard, Victor B. *Black Liberation in Kentucky: Emancipation and Freedom, 1862–1884*. Lexington: University Press of Kentucky, 1983.

Hutton, Paul A. *Phil Sheridan and His Army*. Lincoln: University of Nebraska Press, 1985.

Hyde, Sam C., Jr. *Pistols and Politics: The Dilemma of Democracy in Louisiana's Florida Parishes, 1810–1899*. Baton Rouge: Louisiana State University Press, 1996.

Johnston, Allan. *Surviving Freedom: The Black Community in Washington, D.C., 1860–1880*. New York: Garland, 1993.

Jordan, Winthrop D. *White over Black: American Attitudes toward the Negro, 1550–1812*. Chapel Hill: University of North Carolina Press, 1968.

Katzman, David M. *Before the Ghetto: Black Detroit in the Nineteenth Century*. Urbana: University of Illinois Press, 1973.

Kautz, August V. *Customs of Service for Non-Commissioned Officers and Soldiers*. Philadelphia: Lippincott, 1864.

Kenner, Charles L. *Buffalo Soldiers and Officers of the Ninth Cavalry, 1867–1898: Black and White Together*. Norman: University of Oklahoma Press, 1999.

Kinevan, Marcos. *Frontier Cavalryman: Lieutenant John Bigelow with the Buffalo Soldiers in Texas*. El Paso: Texas Western Press, 1998.

King, Charles. *Campaigning with Crook.* 1890. Reprint, Norman: University of Oklahoma Press, 1964.

King, James T. *War Eagle: A Life of General Eugene A. Carr.* Lincoln: University of Nebraska Press, 1963.

Kusmer, Kenneth L. *A Ghetto Takes Shape: Black Cleveland, 1870–1930.* Urbana: University of Illinois Press, 1976.

Lane, Roger. *Murder in America: A History.* Columbus: Ohio State University Press, 1997.

————. *Roots of Violence in Black Philadelphia, 1860–1900.* Cambridge: Harvard University Press, 1986.

————. *William Dorsey's Philadelphia and Ours: On the Past and Future of the Black City in America.* New York: Oxford University Press, 1991.

Leckie, William H. *The Buffalo Soldiers: A Narrative of the Negro Cavalry in the West.* Norman: University of Oklahoma Press, 1967.

Leckie, William H., and Shirley A. Leckie. *Unlikely Warriors: General Benjamin H. Grierson and His Family.* Norman: University of Oklahoma Press, 1984.

Litwack, Leon F. *Been in the Storm So Long: The Aftermath of Slavery.* New York: Alfred A. Knopf, 1979.

————. *North of Slavery: The Negro in the Free States, 1790–1860.* Chicago: University of Chicago Press, 1961.

————. *Trouble in Mind: Black Southerners in the Age of Jim Crow.* New York: Alfred A. Knopf, 1998.

McAnaney, William D. "Desertion in the United States Army." *Journal of the Military Service Institute* 10 (September 1889): 450–65.

McChristian, Douglas C. *The U.S. Army in the West, 1870–1880: Uniforms, Weapons, and Equipment.* Norman: University of Oklahoma Press, 1995.

McConnell, H. H. *Five Years a Cavalryman.* Norman: University of Oklahoma Press, 1996.

McDonald, Roderick A. *The Economy and Material Culture of Slaves: Goods and Chattels on the Sugar Plantations of Jamaica and Louisiana.* Baton Rouge: Louisiana State University Press, 1993.

McKay, Robert H. *Little Pills: An Army Story.* Pittsburg, Kans.: Pittsburg Headlight, 1918.

Marszalek, John F. *Sherman: A Soldier's Passion for Order.* New York: Free Press, 1993.

Mazzanovich, Anton. *Trailing Geronimo.* Hollywood, Calif.: privately printed, 1931.

The Medal of Honor of the United States Army. Washington, D.C.: GPO, 1948.

Official Army Register. Washington, D.C.: Adjutant General's Office, annually.

Outline Description of Posts in the Military Division of the Missouri. Chicago: Military Division of the Missouri, 1872.

Parker, James. *The Old Army: Memories, 1872–1918.* Philadelphia: Dorrance, 1929.

Pleck, Elizabeth H. *Black Migration and Poverty: Boston, 1865–1900.* New York: Academic Press, 1979.

Pratt, Richard H. *Battlefield and Classroom: Four Decades with the American Indian, 1867–1904.* Edited by Robert M. Utley. New Haven: Yale University Press, 1964.

Price, George F. *Across the Continent with the Fifth Cavalry.* New York: Van Nostrand, 1883.

Ransom, Roger L., and Richard Sutch. *One Kind of Freedom: The Economic Consequences of Emancipation.* New York: Cambridge University Press, 1977.

Rawick, George P., ed. *The American Slave: A Composite Autobiography.* 19 vols. Westport, Conn.: Greenwood, 1972.

Redkey, Edwin S. *A Grand Army of Black Men: Letters from African-American Soldiers in the Union Army, 1861–1865.* New York: Cambridge University Press, 1992.

Remington, Frederic. "A Scout with the Buffalo Soldiers." *The Century* 15, no. 6 (April 1889): 899–912.

Revised Statistics of the United States. Washington, D.C.: GPO, 1875.

Richter, William L. *The Army in Texas during Reconstruction, 1865–1870.* College Station: Texas A&M University Press, 1987.

Rickey, Don, Jr. *Forty Miles a Day on Beans and Hay: The Enlisted Soldier Fighting the Indian Wars.* Norman: University of Oklahoma Press, 1963.

Roe, Frances M. A. *Army Letters from an Officer's Wife, 1871–1888.* New York: D. Appleton, 1909.

Rousey, Dennis C. *Policing the Southern City: New Orleans, 1805–1889.* Baton Rouge: Louisiana State University Press, 1996.

Santmyer, Helen H. *Ohio Town: A Portrait of Xenia.* New York: Harper and Row, 1984.

Schubert, Frank N. *Black Valor: Buffalo Soldiers and the Medal of Honor, 1870–1898.* Wilmington, Del.: Scholarly Resources Books, 1997.

———. *Outpost of the Sioux Wars: A History of Fort Robinson.* Lincoln: University of Nebraska Press, 1993.

———. "The Suggs Affray: The Black Cavalry in the Johnson County War." *Western Historical Quarterly* 4, no. 1 (January 1973): 57–68.

Scott, Hugh L. *Some Memories of a Soldier.* New York: Century, 1928.

Seraile, William. *Voice of Dissent: Theophilus Gould Steward (1843–1924) and Black America.* New York: Carlson Publishing, 1991.

Smallwood, James W. *Time of Hope, Time of Despair: Black Texans during Reconstruction.* Port Washington, N.Y.: Kennikat Press, 1981.

Smith, Sherry L. *The View from Officers' Row: Army Perceptions of Western Indians.* Tucson: University of Arizona Press, 1990.

Smith, Thomas T. *The U.S. Army in the Texas Frontier Economy, 1845–1900.* College Station: Texas A&M University Press, 1999.

Spero, Sterling D., and Abram L. Harris. *The Black Worker: The Negro and the Labor Movement.* New York: Columbia University Press, 1931.

Statutes at Large of the United States of America.

Stiles, T. J. "Buffalo Soldiers." *Smithsonian* 29, no. 9 (December 1998): 82–94.

Stover, Earl F. "Chaplain Henry V. Plummer, His Ministry and His Court-Martial." *Nebraska History* 56, no. 1 (spring 1975): 20–50.

——. *Up from Handymen: The United States Army Chaplaincy, 1865–1920.* Washington, D.C.: Department of the Army, 1977.

Sumner, Edwin V. "Besieged by the Utes: The Massacre of 1879." *The Century* 20, no. 6 (October 1891): 837–47.

Taylor, Quintard. *In Search of the Racial Frontier: African Americans in the American West, 1528–1990.* New York: Norton, 1998.

Thornbrough, Emma L. *The Negro in Indiana before 1900.* Indianapolis: Indiana Historical Bureau, 1957.

Trelease, Allen W. *White Terror: The Ku Klux Klan Conspiracy and Southern Reconstruction.* Baton Rouge: Louisiana State University Press, 1995.

Tripler, Charles S. *Manual of the Medical Officer of the Army of the United States.* Washington, D.C.: GPO, 1866.

Tunnell, Ted. *Crucible of Reconstruction: War, Radicalism, and Race in Louisiana, 1862–1877.* Baton Rouge: Louisiana State University Press, 1984.

U.S. Bureau of the Census. *Compendium of the Ninth Census.* Washington, D.C.: GPO, 1872.

——. *Statistics of the Population of the United States.* Washington, D.C.: GPO, 1872.

U.S. Congress. *Indian Hostilities.* 40th Cong., 1st sess., 1867, S. Ex. Doc. 13. Serial 1308.

——. *Investigation of Causes of Migration of Negroes from Southern to Northern States.* 46th Cong., 2d sess., S. Rept. 693, part 2. Serial 1900

——. *Report of the Joint Committee on Reconstruction.* 39th Cong., 1st sess., 1866, H. Rept. 30. Serial 1273.

——. *Texas Border Troubles.* 45th Cong., 2d sess., 1878, H. Misc. Doc. 64. Serial 1820.

——. *Texas Frontier Troubles.* 44th Cong., 1st sess., 1876, H. Rept. 343. Serial 1709.

Utley, Robert M. *Frontier Regulars: The United States Army and the Indian, 1866–1891.* New York: Macmillan, 1973.

Vandiver, Frank E. *Black Jack: The Life and Times of John J. Pershing.* 2 vols. College Station: Texas A&M University Press, 1977.

Wayne, Michael. *The Reshaping of Plantation Society: The Natchez District, 1860–1880.* Baton Rouge: Louisiana State University Press, 1983.

Whitford, Kathryn. "'The Young Officer Who Rode beside Me': An Examination of Nineteenth-Century Naming Conventions." *American Studies* 23, no. 1 (spring 1982): 5–22.

Wiley, Bell I. *The Life of Billy Yank: The Common Soldier of the Union.* Indianapolis: Bobbs-Merrill, 1952.

Willis, John C. "From the Dictates of Pride to the Paths of Righteousness: Slave Honor and Christianity in Antebellum Virginia." In *The Edge of the South: Life in Nineteenth-Century Virginia.* Edited by Edward L. Ayers and John C. Willis, 37–55. Charlottesville: University Press of Virginia, 1991.

Woodward, William E. *Meet General Grant.* Garden City, N.Y.: Garden City Publishing, 1928.

Index of Personal Names

Different men of the same name are indicated by the numbers of their regiments and, when necessary, the year in which they were serving when mentioned in the text; page numbers in italics refer to illustrations.

Adair, George W., 178
Adams, David, 324–25n.5
Adams, Henry, 140
Allensworth, Allen, 116–18, 120, 123, 132–33
Alvord, Henry E., 327n.20
Anderson, Amos, 200
Anderson, John, 200
Anderson, Richard, 82–83
Anderson, Thomas M., 77
Anderson, William T., 117
Andrews, George, 314n.33
Andrews, George L., 33–34, 51, 53–55, 61, 94, 118, 120, 127, 129, 133, 179, 197, 228, 230, 322n.41
Armes, George A., 85
Arms, Benjamin, 302n.39
Augur, Christopher C., 99, 164, 236–37, 306n.20, 328n.28

Bacon, John M., 329
Badie, David, *59*
Bailey, Ephriam, 208, 210–11
Baily, John H., 58
Baker, Edward L., 66, 83, 302n.39
Baker, William, 270

Ball, John F., 60
Bambrick, Joseph, 222
Banks, Nathaniel P., 308n.4
Banning, Henry B., 70–72, 77, 248
Baqui, Rodolphe, 13, 290n.29
Barnes, Samuel, 60–61
Barr, David E., 115–16, 118–19, 122–23, 167, 308n.4
Batchelor, Joseph B., Jr., 41
Batties, Edward, 188
Baylor, Amanda, 87
Bell, Robert S., 240–41
Benteen, Frederick W., 30, 294n.10
Bentford, David, 204
Bentzoni, Charles, 180, 230, 332n.28
Bias, Samuel, 172
Bigelow, John, Jr., 182, 247, 255–58, 264–65, 309n.21, 329–30n.5, 331n.21, 333nn.41,42
Bird, Zedrick L., 141
Bishop, James, 213–14, 217, 222
Bivins, Horace W., 21, 133
Blaine, James G., 77
Blanchard, Brainerd P., 213, 217
Bliss, Zenas R., 33–35, 127, 161, 195, 200

General Index